WORKING LIFE OF WOMEN
IN THE
SEVENTEENTH CENTURY

Working Life of Women in the Seventeenth Century

ALICE CLARK

ROUTLEDGE & KEGAN PAUL
LONDON, BOSTON AND HENLEY

Originally published in 1919 by George Routledge & Sons, Ltd
This edition published in 1982
by Routledge & Kegan Paul Ltd
39 Store Street, London WC1E 7DD
9 Park Street, Boston, Mass. 02108, USA and
Broadway House, Newtown Road,
Henley-on-Thames, Oxon RG9 1EN
Printed in Great Britain by The Thetford Press, Norfolk

ISBN 0-7100-9045-5

CONTENTS

PREFACE   vii

INTRODUCTION   ix
BY MIRANDA CHAYTOR AND JANE LEWIS

BIBLIOGRAPHICAL NOTE   xli

I   INTRODUCTORY   1

II   CAPITALISTS   14

III   AGRICULTURE   42

IV   TEXTILES   93

V   CRAFTS AND TRADES   150

VI   PROFESSIONS   236

VII   CONCLUSION   290

      LIST OF AUTHORITIES   309

      LIST OF WAGE ASSESSMENTS   320

      INDEX   321

Errata

page x, line 9: *for* Clarks *read* Clark's
page x, line 27: *for* medical *read* medieval
page xvii, line 27: *for* middle-class women *read* middle-class woman
page xxviii, line 12: *for* or *read* of
page xl, line 3: *for* 'Household and Family' in *Past Time read* Household and Family in *Past Time*

PREFACE

THE investigation, whose conclusions are partly described in the following treatise, was undertaken with a view to discovering the actual circumstances of women's lives in the Seventeenth Century.

It is perhaps impossible to divest historical enquiry from all personal bias, but in this case the bias has simply consisted in a conviction that the conditions under which the obscure mass of women live and fulfil their duties as human beings, have a vital influence upon the destinies of the human race, and that a little knowledge of what these conditions have actually been in the past will be of more value to the sociologist than many volumes of carefully elaborated theory based on abstract ideas.

The theories with which I began this work of investigation as to the position occupied by women in a former social organisation have been abandoned, and have been replaced by others, which though still only held tentatively have at least the merit of resting solely on ascertained fact. If these theories should in turn have to be discarded when a deeper understanding of history becomes possible, yet the picture of human life presented in the following pages will not entirely lose its value.

The picture cannot pretend to be complete. The Seventeenth Century provides such a wealth of historical material that only a small fraction could be examined, and though the selection has been as representative as possible, much that is of the greatest importance from the point of view from which the enquiry has been made, is not yet available. Many records of Gilds, Companies, Quarter Sessions and Boroughs which must be studied *in extenso* before a just idea can be formed of women's position, have up to the present been published only in an abbreviated form, if at all.

Another difficulty has been the absence of knowledge regarding women's position in the years preceding the Seventeenth Century. This want has to some extent been supplied through the kindness of Miss Eileen Power, who has permitted me to use some of the material collected by her on this subject, but not yet published.

The Seventeenth Century itself forms a sort of watershed between two very widely differing eras in the history of Englishwomen—the Elizabethan and the Eighteenth Century. Thus characteristics of both can be studied in the women who move through its varied scenes, either in the pages of dramatists or as revealed by domestic papers or in more public records.

Only one aspect of their lives has been described in the present volume, namely their place in the economic organisation of society. This has its own special bearing on the industrial problems of modern times; but Life is a whole and cannot safely be separated into watertight departments.

The productive activity which is here described was not the work of women who were separated from the companionship of married life and the joys and responsibilities of motherhood. These aspects of their life have not been forgotten, and will, I hope, be dealt with in a later volume, along with the whole question of girls' education.

How inseparably intertwined are these different threads of life will be shown by the fact that apprenticeship and service are left to be dealt with in the later volume as links in the educational chain, although in many respects they were essential features of women's economic position.

The conception of the sociological importance of past economic conditions for women I owe to Olive Schreiner, whose epoch-making book "Women and Labour" first drew the attention of many workers in the emancipation of women to the difference between reality and the commonly received generalisations as to women's productive capacity. From my friend, Dr. K. A. Gerlach came the suggestion that I, myself, should attempt to supply further evidence along the lines so imaginatively outlined by Mrs. Schreiner. To Dr. Lilian Knowles I am indebted for the unwearied patience with which she has watched and directed my researches, and to Mrs. Bernard Shaw for the generous scholarship with which she assists those who wish to devote themselves to the investigation of women's historic past.

I should like here to express the deep sense of gratitude which I feel to those who have helped my work in these different ways, and to Mrs. George, whose understanding of Seventeenth Century conditions has rendered the material she collected for me particularly valuable. My thanks are also due to many other friends whose sympathy and interest have played a larger part than they know in the production of this book.

Mill Field,
Street, Somerset.

INTRODUCTION *
BY
MIRANDA CHAYTOR AND JANE LEWIS

Alice Clark was born in Street, Somerset in 1874, the fourth child and second daughter of William and Helen Clark. It was a privileged background with country walks, ponies, donkey-cart outings and a governess. Her father was the son of one of the original partners of C & J Clark, Shoemakers, and her mother was the daughter of the Liberal MP John Bright. Both families were Quakers. Helen Clark became actively involved in the suffrage movement despite Bright's disapproval. She is known to have reminded him that he had made but two parliamentary speeches on the subject, one in support and one against, and to have asked him which she was supposed to follow. After their marriage, William and Helen Clark kept up their association with the Liberal Party and the Society of Friends and continued to work for the suffrage movement and the campaign against the Contagious Diseases Acts. Their political involvement brought Alice into contact with committed and influential feminists such as Josephine Butler. The family as a whole continued in close contact with the feminist movement; Alice's sister Hilda was a close friend of Kathleen Courtney.

Both of Alice Clark's parents believed that their children should have equal educational and professional opportunities, and they hoped that one of their daughters would enter the family firm. The eldest, Esther, became a teacher, but Alice, having first taken a course in housewifery, started work at Clark's at the age of eighteen. Like her brothers, she served an 'apprenticeship', during which she learned all the women's processes in the factory[1] and was sent to serve in a shoe shop in Edinburgh to get the kind of insight into the needs of customers that her brothers gained as commercial travellers. She became supervisor of the machine room at Street, where most of the women and girls were employed, and in 1903, when the business was made into a private limited company, she was made one of the five original life directors. While her position as a businesswoman was unusual, Alice Clark's work at Street kept her well within the bounds of propriety, her principal involvement being with the female section of the labour force.

Throughout her life, Alice Clark had to fight against recurrent ill-health that probably dated back to a childhood infection with tuberculosis. In 1897, her career at Clarks was temporarily broken by a further period of serious illness, and in 1909 her life was again endangered. Her younger sister Hilda (who was a doctor) successfully supervised her treatment, but it was some years before she was strong enough to return to work. Towards the end of the First World War the experience of a friend drew her attention to Christian Science. Her friends believed it was here that she found the strength and insight that enabled her to come to terms both with her own ill-health and with the suffering and poverty she saw during the war.

In 1912, after a period of convalescence and travel abroad, she returned to England. It was a critical period in the struggle for women's suffrage and Alice joined the NUWSS and was appointed one of the honorary secretaries in charge of work in the constituencies. Her close connection with the suffragists perhaps encouraged her to apply for (and win) the Mrs G. B. Shaw Scholarship at the London School of Economics. Clark's predecessor was the medical historian Eileen Power. The award, open only to women, required them 'to perfect themselves in the methods of investigation and research'. They were then 'assisted under competent direction, to study their subjects at first hand, with a view to the preparation of short monographs'.[2] Clark was supervised by Lillian Knowles, whom she found both helpful and sympathetic to her interest in the history of seventeenth-century women.

The research and writing of *Working Life* was interrupted by the First World War. Alice immediately turned to supervising a toy-making work room set up by the suffragists to provide employment for women thrown out of work by the outbreak of war. Later she trained as a midwife, hoping to join her sister, Hilda, at the Quaker maternity hospital for French refugee women at Châlon. Ill-health stopped her going, but her training gave her first-hand experience of the home conditions endured by working-class women.[3] It was in part this which prompted her to set up a number of welfare schemes in the factory at Street on returning there briefly in 1917.[4]

After completing *Working Life* in 1918, Alice devoted herself to Quaker relief work. She first joined her sister Hilda in Vienna, but later took over the London office where she raised funds, organised personnel, bought cows in Holland, pigs in England and got together a collection of pedigree poultry for shipment. It was not until 1922 that she was able to return to Street to renew her work as a director of the firm and to take over the post of personnel manager. She also drew up the curriculum for the Day Continuation School started by Clark's; girls were offered art and craft work and boys classes in shoemaking. One of her last achievements was to advocate a non-contributory pension scheme for employees, which was put into effect in 1925. She died in 1934.[5]

Historical research and writing occupied only a few years of an exceptionally active and varied career. Nevertheless, Clark's meticulous scholarship was immediately recognised.[6] Her account of seventeenth-century women's working lives displays the grasp of detail she was reputed to show in her business activities; more important, it was informed by the compassion and conviction that determined her professional and political work as a whole. Many recurrent patterns in her life — her devotion and loyalty to family, work-place and neighbourhood, her employment in positions unusual for women but which observed the accepted bounds of the sexual division of labour — are reflected in her interpretation of the seventeenth century. She recognised the limits of women's lives but emphasised their courage, independence and con-scientiousness, qualities which marked her own austere and selfless career. Alice Clark brought to her research a powerful mind, a strong will and a breadth of experience and sympathetic understanding of the positions of women of all social classes which would be unusual today and probably unique at the time she wrote this book.

Working Life of Women is an impressive piece of research. Few writers since and virtually none before had taken such care over the empirical research necessary to determine the nature of women's position in society. Clark's detailed account of what wives and widows of all social classes actually did has not been surpassed. It is rather elements of her interpretation of the changing position of women which will strike the reader as strange and which need to be explained historically in terms of Clark's particular feminist perspective, as well as modified in the light of more recent developments in theory, methodology and research.

Clark describes the life and work of women from all socio-economic groups in both town and country. She uses traditional material, such as memoirs, letters and household account books, to document the activities of gentry women who managed vast households and supervised the administration of family estates. But she turns also to less accessible sources, for example, quarter sessions' petitions, court leet records and church wardens' and workhouse accounts, to uncover the reality of poorer women's working lives. She reconstructs the conditions of sweated labour in the silver-spinning sheds and over-crowded tenements of the towns, the meagre wages of the proto-industrial textile workers and the destitution of the labouring poor in the countryside. However oppressed, her women are more than passive victims of the brutalised conditions in which they lived, for their endurance and resourcefulness clearly emerge from her account of their destitution: she describes homeless women illegally erecting cottages on wasteland, East-Anglian spinsters driven to cheating by winding their yarn on shorter reels, a Cumbrian woman whose husband had left her forced to petition for a licence to sell shoes in the market; few mothers, Clark points out, ever abandoned their children, though they themselves were often deserted by men when their sexual desirability had faded and their strength been broken by childbearing, homelessness and the slow starvation induced by their efforts to feed their families at the cost of their own health and lives (pp. 74, 116, 203, 86). But while acknowledging the tenacity with which women struggled against poverty, Clark's main concern is to record the oppression and demoralisation of labouring women following the introduction of capitalism.

Working Life of Women is concerned with a question that went beyond the confines of the seventeenth century: how did industrialisation affect women's productivity and 'physical efficiency', their moral qualities and influence and, above all, their role as mothers? On all three counts Clark's conclusions were pessimistic. She believed her research to show that women had been more active in industry in the early seventeenth century than in the twentieth and that men had been more active in home life. Both sexes had thus led more balanced and richer lives in pre-industrial society and this had provided a better environment for the spiritual welfare of children.

Clark maintained that the pre-industrial, pre-capitalist economy was based on 'domestic industry' whereby goods were produced solely for home consumption, or 'family industry' in which the entire household unit shared the income obtained from the sale or exchange of its collective resources. Under this system, women were responsible for a wide range of activities: besides child care, cooking, washing and spinning, women in the countryside tended the orchard and garden, cared for domestic animals and poultry, sheared sheep, brewed beer, marketed dairy and other produce, kept the household accounts and worked in the fields, especially at harvest time. In the towns, women pursued their own trades such as millinery and mantua making. Wives were also, in Clark's view, virtual partners to their husbands in crafts and trades as various as brewing, printing, silk making and tanning. While carefully documenting women's varied work and experience, Clark stresses that wives of all social classes were equally involved in productive labour: she cites the case of Lady Gardiner 'almost melted with the double heat of the weather and her hotter employment, because the fruit is suddenly ripe and she is so busy preserving' (p.15) to show that even the gentry were expected to work with their hands. At the opposite end of the social scale, a poor husbandman's wife might have to supplement the income derived from his meagre holding by waged work, such as washing, shepherding, weeding or whipping dogs from the churchyard. Clark regards these occasional labouring jobs with the same approval that she accords the business speculations (in shipping or the salt and coal trades, for instance) of the wives of the land-owning classes; she presents seventeenth-century women's various activities as evidence of their vigour, competence and enterprise — qualities, which in her view, stemmed from their active and valued role in the pre-capitalist household and wider economy.

Clark argues that in the case of the prosperous family, capitalism destroyed domestic industry by bringing a huge increase in wealth, which made the production of goods for domestic consumption unnecessary. The capitalist system also involved the removal of the man's workplace from the home, which in turn destroyed the basis of family industry. Thus capitalism rendered the wives of prosperous men idle. At the other end of the socio-economic scale, the male labourer worked at his master's premises for wages and his wife was also often forced on to the wage labour market. Thus, family industry was subverted by the payment of individual wages.[7] Specialised training, which had been unnecessary when women worked within the family unit, now became essential, and women found that they could earn only extremely low wages without it. A mother's earnings just about made up for work lost by the father through sickness, but by no means enabled her to clothe herself and her children (p. 68). Thus women's productive capacity decreased under capitalism. Women wage earners' low standard of living also lowered their 'physical efficiency' and threatened the welfare of their surviving children (pp. 86, 118, 147). Both the exploitation of the woman wage earner and the narrow outlook of the wife of the rich man resulted in a deterioration in the moral influence exerted by women. Women were no longer respected as equal contributors to the family economy. Clark believed that women needed to fulfil both their productive and reproductive powers in order to live happy, full lives. This had been possible under the early seventeenth-century system of domestic and family industry, but capitalism, while 'producing wealth beyond the dreams of avarice, has hitherto robbed us of so large a part of the joy of creation' (p. 308).

Clark's interpretation is unique in the historiography of the period before the Second World War. Both Georgiana Hill, who published her history of women in 1896, and Ivy Pinchbeck, whose *Working Women and the Industrial Revolution, 1750-1850* appeared in 1930, arrived at virtually the opposite conclusion to Clark. Hill believed that industrialisation 'had lifted the middle-class woman out of the purely domestic sphere by lessening her household duties, and so leaving her free for other occupations'.[8] Pinchbeck was also convinced that the industrial revolution represented an advance for women, although her emphasis was a little different. The factory system removed industry from the home thus rendering it a pleasanter place and, by eventually providing the male breadwinner with a family wage, it enabled married women to devote themselves to home and children. In addition, industrial capitalism opened up a much greater variety of jobs to single women, affording them new opportunities, independence and status.[9]

It is, then, important to investigate the roots of Clark's differing analysis. *Working Life of Women* reads as a very detailed and lively description of the work women did and the material conditions of their lives; at the same time, its careful and generous documentation is contained within a strong explanatory framework. It is clear from her introductory and concluding chapters (where her ideological perspective is stated most explicitly) that Clark's research was heavily indebted to the early twentieth-century feminist concern with the possible balance between motherhood, domestic labour and work outside the home. Here, two influences were of special importance. In her Preface, Clark acknowledges the inspiration provided by Olive Schreiner, whose *Woman and Labour* (1911) first drew her attention to the 'difference between reality and the commonly received generalisation as to women's productive capacity' (Preface). The ideas of the Fabian Women's Group, whose members included Mrs George Bernard Shaw (who provided the money for Clark's research) were also influential. The Group stressed the economic basis of women's subjection and in a 1914 Fabian Tract entitled *The Economic Foundations of the Women's Movement*, Mabel Atkinson analysed the historical aspects of women's work in terms very similar to Clark's.

Clark developed Olive Schreiner's idea that women in pre-industrial society were more productive than in industrial society. Schreiner claimed that 'modern civilization' had robbed woman of her[10]

> ancient domain of productive and social labour. . . . Our spinning wheels are all broken . . . and we dare no longer say, proudly as of old, that we and we alone clothe our peoples. Our hoes and our grindstones passed from us long ago, when ploughman and miller took our place, but for a time we kept fast possession of the kneading trough and the brewing vat [brewing was examined in detail by Clark]. Today, steam often shapes our bread, the loaves are set down at our very door.

She estimated that if the decline in women's productive labour was taken together with the decrease in family size, then fully three-quarters of women's traditional tasks had disappeared.

The parallels between Clark's analysis of women's position in the seventeenth century and that of Mabel Atkinson in her 1914 Fabian Tract, are even more striking. Atkinson stressed the economically productive role of women in the pre-industrial economy. Usually, women worked within the family to produce use values rather than exchange values, although they also worked for profit. Clark did not use the terms use and exchange values, but the idea is clearly present in her discussion of domestic and family industry. Clark followed Atkinson's argument that marriage was a partnership as well as a relation of affection. Atkinson also believed that capitalism was responsible for destroying this situation and that it affected rich and poor differently. Here we find the idea that is so central to Clark's analysis, that industrialisation resulted in the idleness of wives of the aristocracy and gentry and the exploitation of working-class women.[11]

Schreiner was concerned above all with what she called the 'parasitism' of middle-class women. She demanded: 'Give us labour and the training which fits us for labour! We demand this not for ourselves alone but for the race!' In her view, women's 'deep and overmastering need for motherhood'[12] had to be accompanied by productive labour to ensure individual fulfilment and a healthy race, a proposition accepted by Clark, although the strong awareness of female sexuality which permeates Schreiner is absent from Clark. According to Schreiner, 'sex parasitism' represented a threat to civilisation and she cited the examples of the fate of Ancient Greece and Rome. Parasitic mothers could only expect to rear 'softened sons'. The parasitic woman, dependent on the sex function for her support, was to Schreiner but one step away from the prostitute, who brought disease and death.[13]

Both Schreiner and Atkinson faced the problem of resolving the conflict between work and motherhood faced by women in industrial society. Schreiner's claim (on behalf of the middle-class women) that women needed to be both mothers and workers led to an uneasy tension regarding the two roles. Schreiner's justification for taking 'all labour for our province' was that it would lead to a fuller and racially better motherhood.[14] In Atkinson's view, there was no doubt but that the exploitation of working-class women's labour under capitalism had led to racial deterioration and she was more cautious than Schreiner in her consideration of the position of the idle, middle-class woman. Mixing marriage and work was certainly possible, but to mix motherhood and work was not so easy; the child's welfare had to take precedence.[15]

Ideas regarding the place of motherhood in women's lives and the status that should be accorded it were of central importance in the early twentieth century and served to differentiate the various strands of feminist thought. It is important to locate Clark's analysis in the context of the feminist debate on the conflicting demands of motherhood and work. Her enthusiasm for the position of women in pre-industrial society can only be understood in the light of her agreement with Schreiner as to the proper balance between productive and reproductive labour and her shared concern with the Fabian Women's Group as to the inappropriate nature of much of women's work under capitalism.

Early twentieth-century feminists had to work out where they stood on the issue of motherhood and work outside the home because of the pressure being exerted on women to stay at home and devote themselves to childbearing and child-rearing. Middle-class women were encouraged by eugenicists in particular to have more children, because statistics showed the middle-class birth rate to be falling faster than that of the working class. Working-class women were encouraged above all to become better mothers. Medical officers of health believed that the high working-class infant mortality rate could only be reduced if mothers stopped going out to work and attended the new 'schools for mothers' or infant consultation centres to learn proper methods of infant care.[16] Mabel Atkinson became very involved in the infant welfare movement during the First World War[17] and the importance of efficient motherhood to an imperial race was stressed by government committees, philanthropists and politicians from all points on the political spectrum.[18]

By virtue of her association with Karl Pearson, who occupied the Galton Chair of Eugenics at University College, Schreiner was aware of the nationalist and imperialist arguments for raising the status of motherhood. But in *Woman and Labour*, she also stressed the need for greater recognition of motherhood as a means to personal dignity. Because she believed that women needed to be productive workers as well as mothers for self-fulfilment, Schreiner appealed to women who accepted the importance of motherhood, but who still desired an independent career. Vera Brittain believed her to have been the most influential feminist theorist in Edwardian Britain.[19] In a sense, Schreiner occupied the middle ground between the egalitarian and maternal feminists. Representative of the former, Cicely Hamilton believed that women should lay claim to a 'fair field and no favour', competing on equal terms with men and remaining celibate if necessary.[20] This school of thought was not in favour of protective legislation for women workers, a position which infuriated Fabian and trade-union women, who desired to stop what they saw as the exploitation of working-class female wage earners. Beatrice Webb described the egalitarian feminists as 'a batch of excellent ladies (eager for the Rights of Women to work at all hours of day and night with the minimum space and sanitation)'.[21]

The Fabian Women's Group considered the question of wage-earning mothers very carefully and concluded that motherhood in and of itself was adequate labour. Women should not be forced through poverty to do two jobs in and outside the home.[22] Labour Party Women agreed that the best activity beyond the home for mothers was not waged work, but a church, chapel or cooperative meeting, or a sewing party.[23] However, the Fabian Women's Group did agree with Schreiner that all individuals, male and female, needed to have the economic independence brought by wages. They therefore decided that the status of motherhood should be raised by paying the mother a pension. Such a scheme was outlined in a Fabian Tract of 1910[24] and was also part of Mabel Atkinson's argument in 1914. Mothers' pensions would enable each mother to remain at home and retain economic independence.

The main point of difference between Schreiner and the Fabian Women's Group was the nature of work suitable for mothers. Schreiner had no desire to return to the pre-industrial patterns of domestic production. Rather, she called for women to have access to all the new forms of labour available under capitalism. She used John Stuart Mill's argument, first put forward in his essay *On the Subjection of Women* (1869), which suggested that it was impossible to predict what women would be good at because of their social conditioning. Because Schreiner was writing to justify the right of middle-class women to work, she did not consider the relative compatability of various occupations with mother-hood. She used the example of working-class women's work only to refute the arguments of those who would confine middle-class women to the home. She argues that in private life, the lofty male theorist did not say to his domestic servant: 'Divine child bearer! Potential mother of the race! Why should you clean my boots or bring up my tea, while I lie in bed?'[25] Mabel Atkinson agreed that eugenist demands for women to remain totally dependent on their husbands during the child-bearing years and for primacy to be given to the patriarchal ideal in the name of the good of the race must be resisted. But she, and the rest of the Fabian Women's Group, agreed that the most suitable form of labour for mothers lay within the home.[26]

Alice Clark began her work familiar with these ideas and her analysis is derived from them. Her initial assumption that women need active productive and reproductive lives comes from Schreiner. But Clark believed that motherhood was morally superior to any other calling and that any work done by mothers outside the home had to be suitable. In this respect the seventeenth-century woman's contribution to the family economy, directly through domestic production, or indirectly through assistance to the husband, was surely ideal. There is a sense of regret in *Working Life of Women* at the passing of such a system. If Clark had written about women's work in the nineteenth and twentieth centuries, it is likely that she would have followed the analysis of Atkinson more closely than that of Schreiner. It is doubtful however that she would have agreed with Pinchbeck that the loss of women's independent economic status under capitalism posed no problem: 'while from the individualist standpoint [a clear reference to the ideas of the Fabian Women's Group] this might appear to be a retrogressive tendency, yet among the working classes, it was not always a sound economic proposition for the married woman to be a wage earner'.[27] Pinchbeck put the welfare of mothers before economic independence. It is likely that Clark would have followed the Fabian Women's Group in their attempt to find a formula that would ensure both.

These tensions and concerns, as well as her own working life, provide the framework for Clark's research. In the following sections we look more closely at some of the principal themes in *Working Life of Women*: motherhood, capitalism, household and family relations and the sexual division of labour — issues that are important not just to Clark herself but to all social and feminist historians. Sixty years on, interests and emphases have changed and it is unavoidable that our approach and interpretation of these themes often differs from Clark's own. Our greater concern with sexuality, inheritance and the inter-generational reproduction of family relations (and relative neglect of local government, guild regulations and the organisation of the professions) reflects the changed priorities of feminist historians. Where we have disagreed with Clark's analysis we have said so directly, for her work deserves serious critical attention, not a condescending distance which commends it for unknowingly anticipating the concerns of a later generation.

We have therefore tried to look closely at the concepts and assumptions that underlie Clark's argument, which inform it and explain its omissions. This has not been easy, for although her views are stated explicitly, her analysis is rarely fully developed. Her use of images, allusions and turns of phrase is suggestive, but Clark's work ideally deserves a full-length study which would place it in a wider historiographical, intellectual and political context as well as relate it to her own life and immediate environment.

Motherhood

Working Life of Women was researched and written because Alice Clark believed that the experience of working mothers deserved historical study. She may have accepted women's primary responsibility for domestic work and childcare as 'natural' and desirable, but the diverse conditions under which children were born and raised suggested that motherhood could not be reduced to women's a-historical capacity to bear and breast-feed babies. Even 'sexual and maternal instincts', she insisted, 'are subject to modification' (p.1) and must be understood in the context of the specific familial and social structures in which they were lived.

It is therefore surprising that the ideology and experience of mothering, though a central theme in *Working Life*, are never discussed directly. Even Clark's own attitudes are difficult to decipher, but her account reflects the values of her Non-Conformist middle-class background. Her unsympathetic portrayal of the bourgeois society wife as 'over-sexed' and 'devoted to a life of pleasure' (p.284) conveys a strong distaste for frivolity, idleness and perhaps female sexuality in its more power-seeking form. Conversely, emotional and physical strength, austerity and all-round competence — qualities admired in the social environment in which she was born and brought up — are associated with 'good motherhood' in seventeenth-century England. The 'muscular and well-nourished' husbandmen's wives, 'able to bear healthy children and to suckle them', who lived frugally but secure 'in the respect and love of their families and in the sense of duties worthily fulfilled' (pp.58-9), clearly represented Clark's ideal. But there is little about birth, breast-feeding, wet nursing, family love or duty in *Working Life of Women*. Clark wrote that she felt it 'almost degrading' to consider 'the spiritual creation of the home and the physical creation of the child' (p.4) as an integral part of women's work.

Present-day historians may regret her reluctance to weigh such achievements of 'creative power . . . in the balance with productions that are bought and sold in the market', but her diffidence is understandable: her idealisation of motherhood and emphasis on physical and emotional 'efficiency' must have been, at least partly, shaped by her own single, childless and exceptionally hard-working life; certainly her preoccupations reflected the political tensions of the period in which she wrote. But it is possible also to identify less immediate concerns and currents. Clark's scathing and passionate attack on the male control of medicine and midwifery (though informed by her own professional training and experience) can be read as a protest against long-standing sexual and moral stereotypes. The identification of men with reason and responsibility and women with 'instinctive emotions, frailty, frivolity and excessive sensibility', originated with the Enlightenment 'discovery' of science, and was used to justify women's original exclusion from the schools of anatomy. The persistence of some of these assumptions is reflected both in Clark's distaste for feminine fragility and incompetence, and in her attempt to discredit spurious biologism by an appeal to earlier values and practices. She insisted on women's intelligence, their capacity for systematic study and need for access to scientific knowledge and research (see especially pp.202, 269). Her account of healers, midwives and mothers in the seventeenth century emphasises their knowledge, common sense and responsibility. 'In rural England', she maintained, 'it was customary when travail began, to send for all the neighbours who were responsible women, . . . because it was important to spread the understanding of midwifery as widely as possible' (p.269). The sense of calm and reason conveyed by this passage scarcely accords with the carefully-guarded supernatural and symbolic skills of many country midwives. Significantly, Clark does not mention the use of herbs, spells, charms or witchcraft to determine the moment of conception and the sex of the foetus, procure abortions, ease labour pains and ensure a safe delivery. The magical powers and practices that surrounded childbirth are underplayed, and she records, but does not comment on, the midwife's reputation for superstition, drunkenness, blasphemy and bawdiness. The stress on respectability, 'womanly resourcefulness', and a healthy knowledge of 'the structure and functions of her own body' (pp.282, 284) reveals much about Clark's own concerns but little of those of the midwives and mothers she describes.

Nevertheless, *Working Life*'s overall emphasis on women's skills, energy and competence is accurate and perceptive. Social historians today might attempt a more closely-focused analysis of both the ideology of motherhood and the ways in which the rhetoric of the period was reproduced in the perceptions and experience of individual women. But recent research would support Clark's treatment of the wives of yeomen and husbandmen, not as 'mothers', but as mistresses of households filled with step-children, orphaned kin, servants and apprentices. Mothering was not the prerogative of married women in a society where high adult mortality and frequent remarriage meant that many children were raised in the households of neighbours and kin: babies were cared for by their grandmothers, father's new wife, her widowed aunt, an older step-sister, a cousin or maid servant, as often as by their natural mothers.[28] Seventeenth-century women valued their reputation for chastity, health and hard work, their integrity as housewives and traders; the qualities today associated with 'mothering' — tenderness, self-sacrifice, caring — seem significantly absent as a source of honour or shame. The insults recorded in defamation cases brought before the church courts suggest that a woman's sense of her sexual and social identity was closely bound up with the requirement for chastity and marital fidelity. 'Whore' was the commonest term of abuse, often combined with references to disreputable origins or to veneral disease. Both the implication that her faults were inherited from her parents and the emphasis on a disease which could impair her ability to bear healthy children suggest that it was as a child-breeder not a child-rearer that a woman's reputation was at stake. There are occasional accusations of theft or the use of false weights and measures, but no reproaches for neglect of or cruelty to children.[29]

There may not have been a clearly discernible ideology of motherhood in the seventeenth century, but women still bore and raised children under material and cultural conditions which varied across class and time. Clark's lack of sympathy for the 'decadence' of upper-class mothers at the end of the century is understandable but her very schematic treatment of the moral effects of increasing wealth obscures the cluster of conflicting precepts and practices which shaped their lives. The use of wet nurses, for example, was encouraged by husbands who resented the baby's 'tossing and tumbling', 'bawls and cries'; they may have resented still more their wives' lack of interest in their sexual attentions and the loss of 'their pretty breasts, firm nipples, round and smooth'.[30] The new emphasis on the breast (which replaced the womb as the focus of attention in the medical literature) reflected changed sexual and social pressures: breasts were increasingly seen as the source of both sexual attractiveness and moral and physical worth; they symbolised the emotional tie between husband and wife and the nurturing bond between mother and child, evidence of a growing concern with familial love and sensibility.[31] Propaganda against wet nurses (whose milk was believed to be both morally and physically contaminating) intensified towards the end of the century.

The effects of these competing ideologies are hard to measure. Even the feelings of literate, élite women — more exposed to changed fashions and moralities and able to confide their reactions to diaries and letters — are virtually unknown. The meaning of motherhood for husbandmen's wives, labouring women and the wet nurses themselves is still more obscure. *Working Life* reveals the exhaustion, anxiety and despair of many mothers, but we learn little about attitudes to pregnancy and parenthood in a society where children were valued (and loved) but infant mortality was high and deaths in childbirth and perhaps abortion were common. We need to explore the conflicting discourses of womanhood, sexuality, marriage and motherhood (noting the absence of ideologies as well as their presence) not just as revealed in medical and household manuals, sermons, religious language and imagery, but in the actual experience of seventeenth-century working women.

Capitalism

On first reading *Working Life*, we are left with the impression that it is above all an account of the transition to capitalism and an indictment of its consequences for women. The argument seems clear and insistent for the capitalist mode of production is specifically identified as 'the means by which the revolution in women's economic position was effected' (pp.295-6). The seventeenth century, which saw the widespread destruction of family and domestic industry, is depicted as the critical period in which productive and familial relations were transformed.

But a closer reading reveals ambiguities and qualifications. Women's emotional and material oppression is not consistently or wholly attributed to capitalism: their exclusion from the professions is presented as an autonomous development and their sweated labour in the textile industries suggests 'obscure actions and reactions between capitalism and the position of women, worthy of more careful investigation' (p.98); Clark hinted at deeper causes and tendencies which were 'merely hastened by the economic cataclysm' (p.13) and pointed to women's longstanding, perhaps universal reputation as spinners and weavers. She recognised the interdependence of pre-existing divisions of labour and new forms of class exploitation which reinforced and transformed them. But the specific relationship between capitalist production and women's subordination in the seventeenth century is never fully articulated.

The role of capitalism in Clark's analysis seems then both central and elusive. Few of the developments usually associated with the early-modern period are discussed in her account of changing forms and relations of production. *Working Life of Women* specifies the accumulation of wealth and the destruction of the self-sufficient domestic economy, but there is no mention of inflation, enclosures, land ownership and tenure, changed attitudes to wealth and poverty, banking, international finance, war, overseas trade or the discovery of the New World. Instead, frequent references to 'modern life', the effects of the 'industrial revolution' and the spread of 'the capitalist organisation of industry' suggest that Clark was more concerned with the consequences of nineteenth-century industrial capitalism than with changes that took place in the early-modern period.

Why then did she choose to investigate the seventeenth

century? Her choice of period seems strange in view of her apparent indifference to the processes involved in the transition to capitalism. We might expect her to have turned rather to the Middle Ages or to the industrial revolution, for her account is structured by the sharp contrast she drew between the material and emotional poverty of modern women's lives and the skills and respect she believed they commanded in feudal England.

This polarisation of capitalist and pre-capitalist society is one striking feature of Clark's interpretation; another is her concern with conditions of life, moral values and personal qualities rather than with abstract historical models or syntheses. In both she is drawing on a long tradition of social, aesthetic and political criticism that runs through the thought of Cobbett, Carlyle, Ruskin, Pugin, William Morris and can be found in the writings of Tawney. Common to them all (despite their very different political positions) is the belief that change is located in production and moral and cultural values, and progress achieved through the reclamation of an earlier heritage. The past/present opposition (most conspicuous in Carlyle) which Clark takes up, does not, for her, imply a rejection of contemporary industrial society but provides the basis for its critique.

Much of the rhetoric of this tradition and of early twentieth-century socialism appears in *Working Life* where references to 'competitive individualism' and the 'mechanical state' are juxtaposed to the ideal of the 'Commonwealth' and the organic 'wholeness' of pre-capitalist society (see especially her concluding chapter). Nevertheless there are differences and unresolved ambiguities in Clark's position. Despite allusions to 'the spiritual poverty' of modern life where the cash nexus formed the basis of all human relations, she did not share that disenchantment with the 'acquisitive society' which fuelled Tawney's work on early modern capitalism and led the Webbs (founders of the London School of Economics) to advocate collectivist solutions and the eventual establishment of a socialist cooperative commonwealth. Clark's position was both original and feminist, for her objection was not to the capitalist system as such but to women's oppression within it. She retained the past/present paradigm but transformed it into a model of women's subordination. Her oppositions are based not simply on the capitalist/pre-capitalist dichotomy, but on the polarised notions of masculinity and femininity created in the nineteenth century: she counterposed the workshop and the boudoir, productive energy and decadence, skill and incompetence, freedom and 'charming' or 'abject' dependence. The heritage Clark sought to reclaim was the values and conditions of life which nineteenth-century capitalist ideology had destroyed by its relegation or bourgeois women to the private and ornamental sphere.

Clark's own life defied the suffocating domesticity then imposed on many middle-class daughters. Her career as a paternalist businesswoman no doubt aroused her admiration for the seventeenth-century women capitalists who exemplified for her the energy and independence that had been appropriated by the male-dominated business world. She describes the early phase of capitalist expansion with enthusiasm: women's contribution to the commercialisation of agriculture in England and development of merchant capitalism in Holland is applauded; their accumulation of wealth and land is not condemned as ruthless profit seeking, nor is it connected with the destitution of the wives of the labouring poor described in the following chapter; rather, women's capitalist ventures are celebrated as evidence of more equal relations between husband and wife, and of a 'comradeship' which was 'stimulating and inspiring to both' (p.41). Hard work, self-help, business acumen, thrift and energy, which Clark recognised in seventeenth-century women, were precisely the values on which *male-dominated* industrial capitalism was founded.

Clark's perspective was feminist and personal, owing more to her own working experience and political environment than to existing discourses in social and economic history.[32] Her unusual emphasis and interpretation (despite its ambivalence towards capitalism) enriches rather than flaws her account, for her deep convictions lend a tension to her description, without ever distorting the reality of women's working lives.

Nevertheless, recent research, informed by different theoretical perspectives, would suggest a more complex and varied pattern than Clark's explanatory framework allows. In both town and countryside women's roles, status, opportunities and survival depended upon the economy in which they lived. Agrarian capitalism did not develop evenly; the course it took and the rate of change depended on local conditions: on soil types, population structure, inheritance customs, transport facilities and the availability of markets. Women's roles, experience and status varied considerably. Wood-pasture, dairying areas or market-garden, suburban parishes, dependent on traditionally female activities — butter and cheese making, vegetable growing, the marketing of produce — afforded women a more central role in production than in the corn-growing counties of central England or the sheep-raising areas of the north. Certainly, in parts of Wiltshire and Somerset, intensive cheese production for the expanding capitalist market made many households not just richer but unusually dependent on women's traditional work. Their status, however, did not improve with prosperity: male dominance was publicly reaffirmed by the use of skimmington rituals[33] — the collective humiliation of those husbands whose private authority seemed threatened by their wives' increasing control over the means of production.

Conversely, poor migrant or unsettled groups may have allowed women a limited independence. Woodland and forest people were dependent on men's seasonal labour elsewhere and on subsistence activities which were not rigidly sex or age specific. Women and children could successfully keep pigs, gather firewood, peel bark for the tanning industry, strip osiers and weave baskets. Similarly, in coastal villages fishermen's wives left in charge of the small-holding for much of the year, must have commanded a variety of unusual skills and perhaps enjoyed a correspondingly greater autonomy.

Women's lives also varied from town to town where their experience was shaped by class, demographic determinants and family structure as well as the extent of capitalist expansion. Gregory King observed that 'the Richer ye parish, ye more Females, by reason ye Daurs remain more at home, and there are more Maid servants'.[34] His comments suggest the two-fold process by which male power and prosperity were consolidated: through the marriage of wealthy women and the exploitation of the labour of their poorer sisters. An expanding town with a buoyant economy attracted ambitious immigrants, who were drawn as much by the dowries of the daughters of already established tradesmen as by the opportunities for work and profit. Marriage was the means by which newcomers were assimilated into the trades and structures of government; continuity was provided through family connections. But not all daughters had dowries. The eldest might marry well, into a trading family as prosperous as her father's, but the maid servants King observed were usually her less fortunate younger sisters. Clark's somewhat idealised account of the family business, centred on the naturalness of the husband-wife partnership, the equality between them and the complementarity of their roles, overlooks the exploitation of other household members — the younger sons and daughters, the maid servants without dowries or prospects whose exclusion and drudgery ensured the comfort of the prosperous few.

Emergent capitalism exploited poor women, but it also provided the destitute with a minimal chance of survival. Expanding towns and proto-industrial economies attracted not just the ambitious but the disinherited poor from the countryside. The coal industry in the Tyne valley employed women both as colliers and transport workers, who carried the coal from the pit head to wharf and loaded it on to barges for shipment to London and beyond. Some were killed in mining accidents and they often lived in considerable poverty, but their conditions were not necessarily worse than in the poor and over-populated hills of Northumberland and Scotland from which they migrated.[35] Even where women were excluded from waged labour, many urban and proto-industrial areas offered a range of part-time, subsistence activities: laundering, ale house keeping, street vending, stealing, prostitution and the peddling of thread, ribbons and food, could all keep women alive when they were too old or ill for other work, abandoned or widowed with young children to care for. 'The fishwives, oysterwomen and others that do crye thinges up and downe the streets' (p.220) were able to ply their trade freely in the densely-populated capital where there was a constant demand for their wares. In small market towns, however, women hawkers were continually harassed by the authorities. The shop keepers in Reading — a town where economic opportunities were more limited and competition more threatening — complained of the burden imposed by poor widows and orphans, who were not only maintained at the expense of the parish, but whose small-scale peddling undercut the trade of the more established families (p.204).

Relations within families and between them formed the limits of women's working lives. Their place in the wider economy depended on familial circumstances, their productivity and talents on the domestic conditions which fostered or precluded them. The wife of a yeoman or successful printer or baker had a more respected role in production than the apprentice or maid servant she housed and supervised; but her status, expertise and authority were not the inevitable reward of age and experience. Perhaps 15 per cent of women never married at all, and the working lives of most wives and widows were far from skilled, valued or independent. Coal miners, field workers, silk spinners, old 'smoke sellers'[36] or manure gatherers, had often spent months or years as servants in the households of yeoman and traders; but without property expectations or prestige, they could never have married into the family that employed them, become the expert and respected mistress of the farmhouse or workshop. Clark saw domestic service as a desirable arrangement that freed mothers from drudgery and taught young women the skills they would need in married life. She regarded the household as a natural unit where the division of tasks reflected genuine physiologically-based differences between the sexes and generations. It is a reasonable view for only women could suckle babies, the very old or ill were not capable of heavy manual work, children might help with weeding or planting but they only gradually acquired the strength and skill for more demanding tasks. Nevertheless, Clark's emphasis on the naturalness of the domestic economy overlooks the social and economic inequalities between household members — the fundamental divisions between masters and servants, children with property expectations and marriage prospects and those with none — which lay alongside the sharing, cooperation and mutual respect. She does not examine how propertied women were recruited into established farms and businesses, and the propertyless servant used but excluded from long-term access to resources and power; how land and goods were transmitted from one generation to the next by marriage alliances and strict inheritance rules. Precisely because these practical arrangements took on the language of genealogy, kinship and affinity (son/heir, daughter/heiress, widow/doweress), they appear natural and inevitable and their basis in social and economic relations outside the family unit is concealed.[37]

Working Life is a passionate and painstaking account of the precarious position of poor, disinherited, migrant women from childhood to old age. Clark records their ever-changing roles and tasks. She recognises their exploitation but does not connect it with the survival of the prosperous households she admired. She observed the 'strange . . . cruelty and callousness' (p.89) with which church wardens and magistrates drove pregnant, homeless women from the parish, pulled down their cottages and evicted them and their children from barns and churches. Expecting greater chivalry and compassion, she considered that 'the *strangest* feature of the situation was the fact that the magistrates who were trying to exterminate wage-earners were often themselves capitalists creating the demand' (p.91, our italics).

Clark's confusion sprang from her concept of seventeenth-century society as a loose federation of semi-autonomous peasant farms and family trades and workshops. She stressed women's productivity, enterprise and energy and, in her enthusiasm for the day-to-day reality of domestic duties, over-looked the long-term processes by which prosperity and exploitation were reproduced. Clark acknowledged that 'economic forces constantly recruited wage-earners from the class above them' (p.90) but does not specify the nature of these forces (the accumulation of land and enclosure of wastes and commons on which poor families once grazed their cows and goats), nor assign any responsibility to the emergent capitalist class. Their quality of life is set apart from the eventual decadence of the bourgeoisie and the misery and oppression of the poor. Seventeenth-century capitalism is invoked not as a system of social and economic relations but as a disembodied power, 'a blind force' imposed from above and uniform in its consequences (pp.300, 308). *Working Life* celebrates the productivity and moral and human values of the early capitalist household as women's rightful heritage, to be rediscovered and reclaimed.

Sex, labour and the separation of spheres

The sexual division of labour is a political as well as an economic phenomenon. Tasks, roles and rewards are rarely haphazardly allocated between women and men; more often they reflect and perpetuate a system of hierarchy prestige and exploitation. We need to discover not only what work women did but how their activities were represented, valued and controlled.

Clark's account of the seventeenth-century household stresses the complementarity of men and women's activities, the 'naturalness' of a society where there was no rigid separa-tion between home and work, and where a woman's place in the wider economy flowed inevitably from the skills she acquired in the domestic sphere. Wives who bore children and clothed and fed their families, were 'natural' midwives, bakers, weavers and brewers. The 'lively understanding of human nature', 'quick perception and social tact' which enabled women to take over the workshop or retailing side of the business were gained through long experience in the care and supervision of children, apprentices and servants. Clark's emphasis on women's competence and energy is a welcome one. Nevertheless, her notion of natural and innate qualities (she refers to 'the services which nature fitted them to perform' and suspects 'some physiological inability on the part of men to spin a fine, even thread at the requisite speed' (pp.286, 93)), would be questioned by many feminists today. Such skills and abilities were socially produced *through* women's relegation to the domestic sphere; they do not themselves explain the sexual division of labour, and the allocation of areas of responsibility and power. Many activities were interchangeable between the sexes, but we need also to consider the existence and significance of taboos — on ploughing in some areas and on food preparation during menstruation (when women could not pickle beef or salt bacon).[38] There was a separation of public and domestic spheres which reflected and reproduced deeper divisions between women and men.

Yeomen and husbandmen worked the land, reared livestock, repaired hedges, ditches and tools. They also monopolised judicial and administrative offices within the parish or manor. Their activities took them outside the household, to the fields, pastures and woods beyond the village, and although some tasks were shared between fathers and sons, masters and labourers, men worked in relative isolation, shepherding, ploughing or mowing their separate plots of land. Harvesting was exceptional in demanding the collective labour of the whole household. Women's work centred on the domestic sphere, the house and its immediate surroundings, and their activities were possibly more collaborative than men's. Domestic labour and childcare were necessarily collective enterprises involving grandmothers, wives, older children and servants. Marketing, water fetching and firewood gathering brought women into contact with neighbours and kin from nearby households, while spinning circles provided the opportunity for more prolonged gossip.

This division of tasks and of the social and physical space of the rural community parallels the divisions of influence and authority between women and men. Husbands controlled the land and its produce; wives organised consumption and distribution at the level of the individual household. Within the domestic sphere women had undisputed power: they controlled children, servants and animals, not just in their own homes but throughout the village or hamlet in which they lived. Female friendships, work and kin ties cut across the barriers of the separate domestic units. Women helped to maintain the flow of mutual services, support and goodwill that created bonds between households and kin within the village community: dowries (in cash or animals) could be lent out, carts and cooking pots borrowed, adolescent children 'loaned' to a neighbouring household that needed their labour and was better able to support them. There were also more disruptive sources of power: women could break up friendships or betrothals, could hide things (food, clothes, information) or withhold them (sex, work, approval); perhaps most important was their capacity to edit and distort gossip to manipulate and undermine male authority.

The two spheres were separate and interdependent but the relationship between them was unequal: women's areas of influence and responsibility were subordinate to and controlled by men's. The limits of the domestic world of food, shelter, clothing, babies and sex were defined outside — in the ale house where decisions were taken informally and in the meetings of the church vestry and manorial court where they were officially confirmed and effected. The boundaries of women's lives were set locally and nationally by institutionalised sources of power from which they were excluded: guilds, manor courts, the church and law in different ways regulated social, sexual and marital behaviour and determined rights to shelter, maintenance, poor relief and work. *Working Life of Women* is an account of the consequences of men's control over women's productive and reproductive lives. Clark vividly describes the starvation, homelessness, ill health and loneliness of women exploited by back-breaking field work or long hours in the spinning sheds; she also examines the way men monopolised the more rewarding and lucrative trades and professions. We could include too the active persecution of unsanctioned beliefs and activities: sporadic outbreaks of witch hunting were only an extreme manifestation of the continual repression of specifically female sources of power and protest — healing, cursing, prophesying, mocking and scolding.

There is plenty of evidence of sexual violence and direct legal repression in the seventeenth century, but coercion could take more subtle forms. Women depended on men and marriage, not just for economic security or survival, but for social acceptability, self respect and prestige. We need to examine the processes by which this dependence was created and upheld, ideologically and in material relations. An analysis of inheritance customs may reflect sexual asymmetry through the unequal distribution of real sources of wealth and power (the farmhouse itself, the land it stood on, the dairies, livestock and crops sown or stacked in the barns). In some areas, sons inherited all the major resources while daughters marrying into another household merely took domestic animals or butter churns, spinning wheels, bedding and tableware as their dowries. Customs varied considerably, but it is important to uncover not just formal legal rights to land, shelter, goods or guild privileges, but also the conditions under which they were granted or withheld. A widow or daughter might inherit the farm, its land and the oxen and ploughs needed to cultivate it, but this did not necessarily afford her independence or control. Prosperous women of child-bearing age were rarely allowed to remain single for long; their land, shops or livestock attracted men, not as subordinate labourers but as potential husbands and masters.

To work the farm or business effectively, a woman needed the goodwill of neighbours and kin. Very high rates of remarriage suggest that support for single women, who were independent and thus deemed 'insubordinate', could be withheld in a number of ways. Sara Weston, a feltmaker's widow, was left with a small child and her husband's house, goods and his two apprentices. One of them, 'she being left in good estate for livelyhood,...became a suitor unto her in the way of marriage'. Once in control of her property, he 'often beat and abused her, sold and consumed what her former husband left her, threatened to kill her and her child (and) turned them out of doors, refusing to afford them any means of subsistence'. Because Sara Weston was heard to have threatened to poison him, no one in the neighbourhood would take her in 'nor suffer her to work for the livelyhood of her and her child' (pp.190-1). Domestic violence was common enough, but there were other pressures, less obvious in the sources and less easy to particularise. Unmarried women with no adult sons to support them didn't always have access to labour, information, credit or tools: they needed to known when an ox should be sold, where a plough could be borrowed, whether a neighbour's son was available to help with the harvest. A widow could be ostracised and forced to remarry if her friends and kin both envied her wealth and resented her independence. Still harder to live with was the constant suspicion of sexual misconduct. Women were viewed as unruly, insubordinate and sexually demanding; widows, whose sexual needs and desires had been awoken, were considered the most voracious of all. Unlike men's, a widow's property rights were often made conditional on sexual abstinence. Female promiscuity threatened the established order, disrupting inheritance claims and the whole system of rights, obligations and hierarchies by which household relations were reproduced from one generation to the next.

This sort of analysis is far removed from Clark's largely descriptive, non-explanatory account of women's work and experience. It also presents serious difficulties: an approach that simply *explains* oppression, leaves women trapped, uncomplaining and colluding, in a tidy system that denies the possibilty of resistance. Certainly we need to uncover the material basis of gender subordination, and the attempt to do so is an important component of feminist history. Nevertheless, a wholly materialist analysis cannot measure the effects of the absence of economic choices or opportunities, the impact of a climate of opinion. It obliterates the ways women acquired, felt and expressed their individual needs, grudges, scorn, resentment and hopes.

Clark describes wives, widows and daughters struggling, often successfully, with their hard but essential work. She emphasises the skill, energy and ingenuity of peddlers, printers, glovers, sheep shearers and field workers, who were not just peasants, artisans or labourers, but wives and mothers as well. Present-day historians, concerned with the interaction of family relations and wider socio-economic structures, class oppression and gender subordination, may disagree with points in her interpretation. They are, none the less, in Alice Clark's debt for her sensitive and generously documented account of the lived experience of seventeenth-century women.

References

* The division of labour in this piece reflects our respective interests; thus Jane Lewis is primarily responsible for the first part of the Introduction and Miranda Chaytor for the second.

1 B. Drake, *Women in Trade Unions* (1920), pp.143-6, explains the sexual division of labour in shoemaking in more detail.
2 LSE *Calendar*, 1912-13.
3 M. Llewelyn Davies (ed.), *Maternity: Letters from Working Women* (1978) gives an excellent idea of the conditions experienced by members of the Women's Cooperative Guild at about the same time that Clark trained as a midwife.
4 Gail Braybon, *Woman Workers in the First World War* (1980), treats the often controversial issue of welfare supervision during the War in more detail.
5 Biographical material on Alice Clark was obtained from a memorial privately printed by her sister, Margaret Clark Gillett and generously made available by Mr Neil MacDonald and Mr James Boswell, archivists at the Clark's factory; the obituary in *The Friend*, 25 May 1934, p.460; *The Times*, Obituary: Helen Clark, 17 January 1927; and Alice Clark to Kathleen Courtney, LSE, Courtney College, vol. 14, f.44, 13 September 1919 and vol. 15, f.100, 12 March 1928.
6 Reviews appeared in *The Times Literary Supplement*, 4 December 1919, p.707 and the *Athenaeum*, 2 January 1920, p.9.

7 Clark actually refers to the substitution of 'individual wages' for a 'family wage', by which she really means a 'family economy'. Today the family wage has come to mean the ability of the (male) breadwinner to support a family. See Hilary Land, 'The Family Wage', *Feminist Review*, 6 (1980), for the evolution of this concept.

8 Georgiana Hill, *Women in English Life from Medieval to Modern Times* (1896), p. xi.

9 Ivy Pinchbeck, *Women Workers and the Industrial Revolution, 1750-1850* (1930), pp.4, 307.

10 Olive Schreiner, *Women and Labour*, 1st edn, 1911 (1978), p. 50.

11 Mabel Atkinson, 'The Economic Foundations of the Women's Movement', Fabian Tract, no. 175 (1914).

12 Schreiner, op. cit., p.67.

13 Ibid., pp.104-9.

14 Ibid., p.127.

15 Atkinson, op. cit., p.18.

16 See Jane Lewis, *The Politics of Motherhood* (1980), for a fuller discussion of these themes.

17 Mabel Palmer, *Life Saving in Wartime: a Campaign Handbook* (1916).

18 See for example: PP, 'Report of the Inter-Departmental Committee on Physical Deterioration', vol. 1, 1904, Cd 2178, 32, 1, pp.57 and 62-3; Mrs Helen Bosanquet, *The Economics of Women's Work and Wages* (1907), p.10; and Sidney Webb, 'The Decline in the Birth Rate', Fabian Tract no. 131 (1907).

19 For the influences upon and the impact of Olive Schreiner, see Ruth First and Ann Scott, *Olive Schreiner* (1980).

20 Cicely Hamilton, *Marriage as a Trade* (1909).

21 B. Webb, 'The Lords and the Sweating System', *Nineteenth Century*, 210 (1890).

22 Mrs G. B. Shaw (ed.), *Summary of Eight Papers and Discussions upon the Disabilities of Mothers as Workers* (1910).

23 Mrs J. R. MacDonald *et al.*, *Wage Earning Mothers* (1907), p.16. For an introduction to the work of the Fabian Women's Group, see Sally Alexander's Introduction to M. S. Pember Reeves's *Round About a Pound a Week* (1979).

24 H. D. Harben, 'The Endowment of Motherhood', Fabian Tract no. 149 (1910).

25 Schreiner, op. cit., p.201.

26 Atkinson, op. cit., p.23. An example of the eugenist argument referred to by Atkinson may be found in Arabella Kenealy, *Feminism and Sex Extinction* (1920), which was written to counter Schreiner's argument.

27 Pinchbeck, op. cit., p.312.

28 This view of the seventeenth-century household is explored in greater detail in Miranda Chaytor, 'Household and Kinship', *History Workshop Journal*, 10 (1980); it would, however, be disputed by many

historians (in particular those associated with the Cambridge Group for the Study of Population and Social Structure). See Peter Laslett and Richard Wall (eds), 'Household and Family', in *Past Time* (1972).

29 The discussion of insults is based on an analysis of the consistory court deposition books for Durham and Northumberland in the sixteenth and seventeenth centuries.

30 Lawrence Stone, *The Family, Sex and Marriage in England 1500-1800* (1977), pp. 426-7.

31 For a thoughtful and complex discussion of this see L. J. Jordanova, 'Natural Facts: a Historical Perspective on Science and Sexuality', in C. MacCormack and M. Strathern (eds), *Nature, Culture and Gender* (1980).

32 A significant omission in Clark's account is any reference to R. H. Tawney's *The Agrarian Problem in the Sixteenth Century* (1912).

33 We are grateful to David Underdown for information about skimming-tons in the west country. Unfortunately too little is still known about these rituals. Clearly they were fairly elaborate, involving traditional forms of role reversal and humiliation (transvestism, being paraded through the village seated backwards on a donkey, beating with the skimming ladle, etc.). But without more intensive research it is difficult to ascertain their significance. (We need to know precisely when and where they occurred, whether the woman was accused of sexual infidelity as well as general insubordination, which kin and neighbours participated, and how particular roles in the ritual were allocated.)

34 Manuscript Notebook (1695-1700) in *The Earliest Classics: John Graunt and Gregory King* (1973), p.59). We are very grateful to Mary Prior for this reference and for access to her unpublished paper, 'Women and Trade in Oxford', on which we have drawn heavily. Her research also shows a greater number of independent women traders in Oxford in the second part of the seventeenth century (when the economy was stagnant) than in the early period of economic prosperity. See also Rebecca Scott, 'Women in the Stuart Economy', M.Phil. thesis, LSE, 1973, p.85, which suggests a similar pattern in York.

35 Information on women's work on the coal industry is taken from J. U. Nef, *The Rise of the British Coal Industry* (1932) and from the parish records of Ryton, a community in the Tyne valley.

36 Parish registers of Newcastle-upon-Tyne record the burial of old women who sold tobacco in the city streets.

37 See Olivia Harris, 'Households as Natural Units', in Kate Young, Carol Wolkowitz and Roslyn McCullagh (eds), *Of Marriage and the Market* (1981).

38 Keith Thomas, *Religion and the Decline of Magic* (1971), p.649.

BIBLIOGRAPHICAL NOTE

Since the first publication of Clark's research, our understanding of the conditions of seventeenth-century women's
lives has broadened. The growth of the 'new social history',
with its focus on radical popular beliefs, the socially marginal
and deviant, sexuality and sentiment, has uncovered aspects
of early modern culture that may have seemed distasteful or
merely bizarre to Clark. There are no thieves, fortune tellers,
vagrants or prostitutes in her account; nor, more surprisingly, does she mention the revolutionary and millenarian
beliefs of the Civil War sects. Witchcraft accusations are
tentatively linked to women's traditional healing skills, and
Clark rightly emphasises the importance of gossip; but
historians today might more confidently treat cursing, curing
and the manipulation of information and rumour (all forms of
control over the physical and social environment) as an integral part of women's work. In addition, many of the issues
central to Clark's analysis have been the subject of recent
research and debate: studies of the transition to capitalism,
family and household relations, population structure,
agriculture and property holding, have proliferated. More
recently, a new generation of feminist historians has begun to
develop a more complex analysis of the nature of women's
subordination and the processes by which it was maintained
or resisted.

Not surprisingly, many of Clark's statements can now be
questioned and qualified. Her chronology in particular has
been criticised both for its internal contradictions and in the
light of new information and models: some of the changes she
located in the seventeenth century have been variously
ascribed to the 1530s, the 1720s, traced back to the fourteenth

century or seen as incomplete by the nineteenth; others have been more specifically identified with the 1620s or 1680s. As we have felt it inappropriate (and beyond our competence) to indicate every gap in Clark's knowledge and every point which is disputed by recent research, we have included a guide to some of the works we have found most useful, where our debt has not been specifically acknowledged in the footnotes. Inevitably our response to *Working Life* has been influenced by current research and discussion as well as by our different political perspective and fields of interest. But our respect for Clark's work has been enhanced rather than undermined by the uncertainty which still surrounds her analysis of women's working lives.

References

The transition to capitalism: Immanuel Wallerstein, *The Modern World System: Capitalist Agriculture and the Origins of the European World Economy in the Sixteenth Century* (1974). Robert Brenner, 'The Origins of Capitalist Development: a Critique of Neo-Smithian Marxism', *New Left Review*, 104 (1978) and 'Agrarian Class Structure and Economic Development in Pre-Industrial Europe', *Past and Present*, 70 (1976); see also the ensuing symposium in nos 78, 79 and 80 (1978).

Motherhood and parent/child relations: Philippe Ariès, *Centuries of Childhood* (1962). Jacques Donzelot, *The Policing of Families* (1980). Anna Davin, 'Imperialism and Motherhood', *History Workshop Journal*, 5 (1978).

Household and family relations: Hans Medick, 'The Proto-Industrial Family Economy: The Structural Function of Household and Family during the Transition from Peasant Society to Industrial Capitalism', *Social History*, 3 (1976). Jane Humphries, 'Protective Legislation, the Capitalist State and Working-Class Men', *Feminist Review*, 7 (1981). Sally Alexander, Anna Davin and Eve Hostettler, 'Labouring Women', *History Workshop Journal*, 8 (1979). Hans Medick and David Sabean, 'Family and Kinship: Material Interest and Emotion', *Peasant Studies*, 8:2 (1979).

Agriculture and inheritance: Margaret Spufford, *Contrasting Communities* (1974). Jack Goody, Joan Thirsk and E. P. Thompson (eds), *Family and Inheritance: Rural Society in Western Europe, 1200-1800* (1976). Joan Thirsk (ed.), *The Agrarian History of England and Wales 1500-1640* (1967).

The sexual division of labour: Kate Young, 'A Methodological Approach to Analysing the Effects of Capitalist Agriculture on Women's Roles and their Position within the Community', *Women in Rural Development: Critical Issues*, International Labour Office, Geneva (1980). Christopher Middleton, 'The Sexual Division of Labour in Feudal England', *New Left Review*, 113-14 (1979).

Natalie Zemon Davis, 'Women's History in Transition', *Feminist Studies*, 3 (1976), includes a discussion of Alice Clark's work.

CHAPTER I

INTRODUCTORY

Effect of environment on Women's development. Possible reaction on men's development—Importance of seventeenth century in historic development of English women—Influence of economic position—Division of Women's productive powers into Domestic, Industrial, and Professional—Three systems of Industrial Organisation—Domestic Industry—Family Industry—Capitalistic Industry or Industrialism—Definition of these terms—Historic sequence. Effect of Industrial Revolution on Women—in capitalistic class—in agriculture—in textile industries—in crafts and other trades. Transference of productive industry from married women to unmarried women—with consequent increase of economic independence for the latter and its loss for the former. Similar evolution in professions shows this was not due wholly to effect of capitalism.

HITHERTO the historian has paid little attention to the circumstances of women's lives, for women have been regarded as a static factor in social developments, a factor which, remaining itself essentially the same, might be expected to exercise a constant and unvarying influence on Society.

This assumption has however no basis in fact, for the most superficial consideration will show how profoundly women can be changed by their environment. Not only do the women of the same race exhibit great differences from time to time in regard to the complex social instincts and virtues, but even their more elemental sexual and maternal instincts are subject to modification. While in extreme cases the sexual impulses are liable to perversion, it sometimes happens that the maternal instinct disappears altogether, and women neglect or, like a tigress in captivity, may even destroy their young.

These variations deserve the most careful examination, for, owing to the indissoluble bond uniting the sexes, and the emotional power which women exert over men, the character of men's development is determined in some sort by the development which is achieved by women. In a society where women are highly developed men's characters are insensibly modified by association with them, and in a society where women are secluded and immature, men lack that stimulus which can only be supplied by the other sex.

It may be true, as Goethe said, that the eternal feminine leadeth us onwards, but whether this be upwards or downwards depends upon the characters of individual women.

Owing to the subtle reactions which exist between men and women and between the individual and the social organism in which he or she lives, accurate and detailed knowledge of the historic circumstances of human life becomes essential for the sciences of Sociology and Psychology. The investigation, of which the results are described in the following chapters, was undertaken with the object of discovering these circumstances as regards women in a limited field and during a short period.

The economic field has been chosen because, though woman no more than man lives by bread alone, yet without bread assuredly she cannot live at all, and without an abundant supply of it she cannot worthily perform her maternal and spiritual functions. These latter are therefore dependent upon the source of her food supply. The economic position has a further attraction to the student because it rests upon facts which can be elucidated with some degree of certainty. When these have once been made clear the way will have been prepared for the consideration of other aspects of women's lives.

The period under review, namely the seventeenth century, forms an important crisis in the historic development of Englishwomen. The gulf which separates the women of the Restoration period from those of the Elizabethan era can be perceived by the most casual reader of contemporary drama. To the objection that the heroines of Shakespeare on the one hand and of Congreve and Wycherley on the other are creations of the imagination, it must be replied that the dramatic poet can only present life as he knows it. It was part of Shakespeare's good fortune to live in a period so rich and vivid in its social life as was the reign of Elizabeth ; and the objective character of his portraits can be proved by the study of contemporary letters and domestic papers. Similarly the characters of the Restoration ladies described in the diary of Samuel Pepys and by other writers, confirm the picture of Society drawn by Congreve.

So profound a change occurring in the character of women indicates the seventeenth century as a period of special interest for social investigation, and consequently the economic position has been approached less from its direct effect upon the production of wealth than from its influence upon women's development. The mechanical aspect has in fact only been touched incidentally ; an attempt being rather made to discover how far the extent of women's productive capacity and the conditions under which it was exercised affected their maternal functions and reacted upon their social influence both within and beyond the limits of the family.

Generalisations are of little service for this purpose. Spinoza has said that the objects of God's knowledge are not universals but particulars, and it is in harmony with this idea that the following chapters consist chiefly of the record of small details in individual lives which indicate the actual relation of women to business and production, whether on a large scale or a small. The pictures given are widely representative, including not only the women of the upper classes, but still more important, those of the " common people," the husbandmen and tradesmen who formed the backbone of the English people, and also those of the tragic class of wage earners, who, though comparatively few in numbers, already constituted a serious problem in the seventeenth century.

In the course of the investigation, comparison is frequently made with the economic position of medi-æval women on the one hand, and with women's position under modern industrial conditions, on the other. It must be admitted, however, that compar-isons with the middle ages rest chiefly on conjecture.

Owing to the greater complexity of a woman's life her productive capacity must be classified on different lines from those which are generally followed in dealing with the economic life of men.

For the purposes of this essay, the highest, most intense forms to which women's productive energy is directed have been excluded ; that is to say, the spiritual creaton of the home and the physical creation of the child. Though essentially productive, such achievements of creative power transcend the limi-tations of economics and one instinctvely feels that there would be something almost degrading in any attempt to weigh them in the balance with productions that are bought and sold in the market or even with professional services. Nevertheless it must never be forgotten that the productive energy which is described in the ensuing chapters was in no sense alternative to the exercise of these higher forms of creative power but was employed simultaneously with them. It may be suspected that the influences of home life were stronger in the social life of the seventeenth century than they are in modern England, and certainly the birth-rate was much higher in every class of the community except perhaps the very poorest.

But, leaving these two forms of creative power aside, there remains another special factor complicating women's economic position, namely, the extent of her production for domestic purposes—as opposed to industrial and professional purposes. The domestic category includes all goods and services, either material or spiritual, which are produced solely for the benefit of the family, while the industrial and professional are those which are produced either for sale or exchange.

In modern life the majority of Englishwomen devote the greater part of their lives to domestic occupations, while men are freed from domestic occupations of any sort, being generally engaged in industrial or professional pursuits and spending their leisure over public services or personal pleasure and amusement.

Under modern conditions the ordinary domestic occupations of Englishwomen consist in tending babies and young children, either as mothers or servants, in preparing household meals, and in keeping the house clean, while laundry work, preserving fruit, and the making of children's clothes are still often included in the domestic category. In the seventeenth century it embraced a much wider range of production ; for brewing, dairy-work, the care of poultry and pigs, the production of vegetables and fruit, spinning flax and wool, nursing and doctoring, all formed part of domestic industry. Therefore the part which women played in industrial and professional life was in addition to a much greater productive activity in the domestic sphere than is required of them under modern conditions.

On the other hand it may be urged that, if women were upon the whole more actively engaged in industrial work during the seventeenth century than they were in the first decade of the twentieth century, men were much more occupied with domestic affairs then than they are now. Men in all classes gave time and care to the education of their children, and the young unmarried men who generally occupied positions as apprentices and servants were partly employed over domestic work. Therefore, though now it is taken for granted that domestic work will be done by women, a considerable proportion of it in former days fell to the share of men.

These circumstances have led to a different use of terms in this essay from that which has generally been adopted ; a difference rendered necessary from the fact that other writers on industrial evolution have considered it only from the man's point of view, whereas this investigation is concerned primarily with its effect upon the position of women.

To facilitate the enquiry, organisation for production is divided into three types :
(a) Domestic Industry.
(b) Family Industry.
(c) Capitalistic Industry, or Industrialism.

No hard-and-fast line exists in practice between these three systems, which merge imperceptibly into one another. In the seventeenth century all three existed side by side, often obtaining at the same time in the same industries, but the underlying principles are quite distinct and may be defined as follows :

(a) *Domestic Industry* is the form of production in which the goods produced are for the exclusive use of the family and are not therefore subject to an exchange or money value.

(b) *Family Industry* is the form in which the family becomes the unit for the production of goods to be sold or exchanged.

The family consisted of father, mother, children, household servants and apprentices ; the apprentices and servants being children and young people of both sexes who earned their keep and in the latter case a nominal wage, but who did not expect to remain permanently as wage-earners, hoping on the contrary in due course to marry and set up in business on their own account. The profits of family industry belonged to the family and not to individual members of it. During his lifetime they were vested in the father who was regarded as the head of the family ; he was expected to provide from them marriage portions for his children as they reached maturity, and on his death the mother succeeded to his position as head of the family, his right of bestowal by will being strictly limited by custom and public opinion.

Two features are the main characteristics of Family Industry in its perfect form ;—first, the unity of capital and labour, for the family, whether that of a farmer or tradesman, owned stock and tools and themselves contributed the labour : second, the situation of the workshop within the precincts of the home.

These two conditions were rarely completely fulfilled in the seventeenth century, for the richer farmers and tradesmen often employed permanent wage-earners in addition to the members of their family, and in other cases craftsmen no longer owned their stock, but made goods to the order of the capitalist who supplied them with the necessary material. Nevertheless, the character of Family Industry was retained as long as father, mother, and children worked together, and the money earned was regarded as belonging to the family, not to the individual members of it.

From the point of view of the economic position of women a system can be classed as family industry while the father works at home, but when he leaves home to work on the capitalist's premises the last vestige of family industry disappears and industrialism takes its place.

(c) *Capitalistic Industry*, or *Industrialism*, is the system by which production is controlled by the owners of capital, and the labourers or producers, men, women and children receive individual wages.[1]

---

[1] The term " individual wages " is used here to denote wages paid either to men or women as individuals, and regarded as belonging to the individual person, while " family wages " are those which cover the services of the whole family and belong to the family as a whole. This definition differs from the common use of the terms, but is necessary for the explanation of some important points. In ordinary conversation " individual wages " indicate those which maintain an individual only, while " family wages " are those upon which a family lives. This does not imply a real

Domestic and family industry existed side by side during the middle ages ; for example, brewing, baking, spinning, cheese and butter making were conducted both as domestic arts and for industrial purposes. Both were gradually supplanted by capitalistic industry, the germ of which was apparently introduced about the thirteenth century, and gradually developed strength for a more rapid advance in the seventeenth century.

While the development of capitalistic industry will always be one of the most interesting subjects for the student of political economy, its effect upon the position and capacity of women becomes of paramount importance to the sociologist.

This effect must be considered from three standpoints :—

(1) Does the capitalistic organisation of industry increase or diminish women's productive capacity ?

(2) Does it make them more or less successful in their special function of motherhood ?

(3) Does it strengthen or weaken their influence over morals and their position in the general organisation of human society ?

These three questions were not asked by the men who were actors in the Industrial Revolution, and apparently their importance has hitherto escaped the notice of those who have written chapters of its history.

Mankind, lulled by its faith in the " eternal feminine " has reposed in the belief that women remain the same, however completely their environment may alter, and having once named a place " the home " thinks it makes no difference whether it consists of a workshop or a boudoir. But the effect of the

difference in the wages, as the same amount of money can be used to support one individual in comfort or a family in penury. In modern times the law recognises a theoretic obligation on the part of a man to support his children, but has no power to divert his wages to that purpose. His wages are in fact recognised as his individual property. The position of the family was very different in the seventeenth century.

Industrial Revolution on home life, and through that upon the development and characters of women and upon their productive capacity, deeply concerns the sociologist, for the increased productive capacity of mankind may be dearly bought by the disintegration of social organisation and a lowering of women's capacity for motherhood.

The succeeding chapters will show how the spread of capitalism affected the productive capacity of women :—

(1) In the capitalist class where the energy and hardiness of Elizabethan ladies gave way before the idleness and pleasure which characterised the Restoration period.

(2) In agriculture, where the wives of the richer yeomen were withdrawing from farm work and where there already existed a considerable number of labourers dependent entirely on wages, whose wives having no gardens or pastures were unable to supply the families' food according to old custom. The wages of such women were too irregular and too low to maintain them and their children in a state of efficiency, and through semi-starvation their productive powers and their capacity for motherhood were greatly reduced.

(3) In the Textile Trades where the demand for thread and yarn which could only be produced by women and children was expanding. The convenience of spinning as an employment for odd minutes and the mechanical character of its movements which made no great tax on eye or brain, rendered it the most adaptable of all domestic arts to the necessities of the mother. Spinning became the chief resource for the married women who were losing their hold on other industries, but its return in money value was too low to render them independent of other means of support. There is little evidence to suggest that women shared in the capitalistic enterprises of the clothiers during

this period, and they had lost their earlier position as monopolists of the silk trade.

(4) In other crafts and trades where a tendency can be traced for women to withdraw from business as this developed on capitalistic lines. The history of the gilds shows a progressive weakening of their positions in these associations, though the corporations of the seventeenth century still regarded the wife as her husband's partner. In these corporations the effect of capitalism on the industrial position of the wage-earner's wife becomes visible.

Under family industry the wife of every master craftsman became free of his gild and could share his work. But as the crafts became capitalised many journeymen never qualified as masters, remaining in the outer courts of the companies all their lives, and actually forming separate organisations to protect their interests against their masters and to secure a privileged position for themselves by restricting the number of apprentices. As the journeymen worked on their masters' premises it naturally followed that their wives were not associated with them in their work, and that apprenticeship became the only entrance to their trade.

Though no written rules existed confining apprenticeship to the male sex, girls were seldom if ever admitted as apprentices in the gild trades, and therefore women were excluded from the ranks of journeymen. As the journeyman's wife could not work at her husband's trade, she must, if need be, find employment for herself as an individual. In some cases the journeyman's organisations were powerful enough to keep wages on a level which sufficed for the maintenance of their families ; then the wife became completely dependent on her husband, sinking to the position of his unpaid domestic servant.

In the Retail and Provision Trades which in some respects were peculiarly favourable for women, they experienced many difficulties owing to the restrictive rules of companies and corporations ; but where a man was engaged in this class of business, his wife shared his labours, and on his death generally retained the direction of the business as his widow.

The history of brewing is one of the most curious examples of the effect of capitalism on women's position in industry, for as the term " brewster " shows, originally it was a woman's trade but with the development of Capitalism it passed completely from the hands of women to those of men.

The tendency of capitalism to lessen the relative productive capacity of women might be overlooked if our understanding of the process was limited to the changes which had actually taken place by the end of the seventeenth century. No doubt the majority of the population at that time was still living under conditions governed by the traditions and habits formed during the period of Family and Domestic Industry. But the contrast which the life described in the following chapters presents to the life of women under modern conditions will be evident even to readers who have not closely followed the later historical developments of Capitalism.

In estimating the influence of economic changes on the position of women it must be remembered that Capitalism has not merely replaced Family Industry but has been equally destructive of Domestic Industry.

One unexpected effect has been the reversal of the parts which married and unmarried women play in productive enterprise. In the earlier stages of economic evolution that which we now call domestic work, *viz.*, cooking, cleaning, mending, tending of children, etc., was performed by unmarried girls under the direction of the housewife, who was thus enabled to take an important position in the family industry. Under modern conditions this domestic work falls upon the mothers, who remain at home while the unmarried girls go out to take their place in industrial or professional life. The young girls in modern life have secured a position of economic independence, while the mothers remain in a state of dependence and subordination—an order of things which would have greatly astonished our ancestors.

In the seventeenth century the idea is seldom encountered that a man supports his wife ; husband and wife were then mutually dependent and together supported their children. At the back of people's minds an instinctive feeling prevailed that the father furnished rent, shelter, and protection while the mother provided food ; an instinct surviving from a remote past when the villein owed to his lord the labour of three or four days per week throughout the year in addition to the boon work at harvest or any other time when labour was most wanted for his own crops ; surely then it was largely the labour of the mother and the children which won the family's food from the yard-land.

The reality of the change which has been effected in the position of wife and mother is shown by a letter to *The Gentleman's Magazine* in 1834 criticising proposed alterations in the Poor Law. The writer defends the system then in use of giving allowances from the rates to labourers according to the number of their children. He says that the people who animadvert on the allowance system " never observe the cause from which it proceeds. There are, we will say, twenty able single labourers in a parish ; twenty equally able married, with large families. One class wants 12s. a week, one 20s. The farmer, who has his choice of course takes the single." The allowance system equalises the position of married and single. Formerly this inequality did not exist " *because it was of no importance to the farmer whether he employed the single or married labourer, inasmuch as the labourer's wife and family could provide for themselves.* They are now dependent on the man's labour, or nearly so ; except in particular cases, as when women go out to wash, to nurse, or take in needlework, and so on.   The machinery and manufactures have destroyed cottage labour—spinning, the only resource formerly of the female poor, who thus were earning their bread at home, while their fathers and husbands were earning theirs abroad. . . .   In agricultural parishes the men, the labourers, are not too numerous or more than are wanted ; but the families hang as a dead weight upon the rates for want of employment.   The girls are now not brought up to *spin*—none of them know the art. They all handle when required, the hoe, and their business is weeding. Our partial remedy for this great and growing evil is allotments of land, which are to afford the occupation that the distaff formerly did ; and so the wife and daughters can be cultivating small portions of ground and raising po-tatoes and esculents, etc., the while the labourer is at his work."[1]

These far reaching changes coincided with the triumph of capitalistic organisation but they may not have been a necessary consequence of that triumph. They may have arisen from some deep-lying cause, some tendency in human evolution which was merely hastened by the economic cataclysm.

The fact that the evolution of women's position in the professions followed a course closely resembling that which was taking place in industry suggests the existence of an ultimate cause influencing the direction in each case.

---

[1] *Gentleman's Magazine*, 1834, Vol. I., p. 531. *A Letter to Lord Althorp on the Poor Laws*, by Equitas.

Chapter II

CAPITALISTS

Term includes aristocracy and *nouveau-riche*. Tendency of these two classes to approximate in manners—Activity of aristocratic women with affairs of household, estate and nation—Zeal for patents and monopolies—Money lenders—Shipping trade—Contractors—Joan Dant—Dorothy Petty—Association of wives in husbands' businesses—Decrease of women's business activity in upper classes—Contrast of Dutch women—Growing idleness of gentlewomen.

PERHAPS it is impossible to say what exactly constitutes a capitalist, and no attempt will be made to define the term, which is used here to include the aristocracy who had long been accustomed to the control of wealth, and also those families whose wealth had been newly acquired through trade or commerce. The second group conforms more nearly to the ideas generally understood by the term capitalist; but in English society the two groups are closely related.

The first group naturally represents the older traditional relation of women to affairs in the upper classes, while the second responded more quickly to the new spirit which was being manifested in English life. No rigid line of demarcation existed between them, because while the younger sons of the gentry engaged in trade, the daughters of wealthy tradesmen were eagerly sought as brides by an impoverished aristocracy. Therefore the manners and customs of the two groups gradually approximated to each other.

At the beginning of the seventeenth century it was usual for the women of the aristocracy to be very busy with affairs—affairs which concerned their household, their estates and even the Government.

Thus Lady Barrymore writes she is " a cuntry lady living in Ireland and convercing with none but masons and carpendors, for I am now finishing a house, so that if my govenour [Sir Edmund Verney] please to build a new house, that may be well seated and have a good prospect, I will give him my best advice gratis."[1]

Lady Gardiner's husband apologises for her not writing personally to Sir Ralph Verney, she " being almost melted with the double heat of the weather and her hotter employment, because the fruit is suddenly ripe and she is so busy preserving."[2] Their household consisted of thirty persons.

Among the nobility the management of the estate was often left for months in the wife's care while the husband was detained at Court for business or pleasure. It was during her husband's absence that Brilliana, Lady Harley defended Brampton Castle from an attack by the Royalist forces who laid siege to it for six weeks, when her defence became famous for its determination and success. Her difficulties in estate management are described in letters to her son :

" You know how your fathers biusnes is neglected ; and alas ! it is not speaking will sarue turne, wheare theare is not abilltise to doo other ways ; thearefore I could wisch, that your father had one of more vnderstanding to intrust, to looke to, if his rents are not payed, and I thinke it will be so. I could desire, if your father thought well of it, that Mr. Tomas Moore weare intrusted with it ; he knows your fathers estate, and is an honnest man, and not giuen to great expences, and thearefore I thinke he would goo the most frugally way. I knowe it would be some charges to haue him and his wife in the howes ; but I thinke it would quite the chargess. I should be loth to haue a stranger, nowe your father is away."[3]

---

[1] Verney Family, *Memoirs during the Civil War*, Vol. I., p. 210.

[2] Ibid, Vol. I., p. 12.

[3] Harley, *Letters of Brilliana, the Lady*, pp. 146-7, 1641.

" I loos the comfort of your fathers company, and am in but littell safety, but that my trust is in God ; and what is doun to your fathers estate pleases him not, so that I wisch meselfe, with all my hart, at Loundoun, and then your father might be a wittnes of what is spent; but if your father thinke it beest for me to be in the cuntry, I am every well pleased with what he shall thinke best."[1]

One gathers from these letters that in spite of her devotion and ability and his constant absence Sir E. Harley never gave his wife full control of the estate, and was always more ready to censure than to praise her arrangements ; but other men who were immersed in public matters thankfully placed the whole burthen of family affairs in the capable hands of their wives.

Lady Murray wrote of her father, Sir George Baillie, " He had no ambition but to be free of debt ; yet so great trust and confidence did he put in my mother, and so absolutely free of all jealousy and suspicion, that he left the management of his affairs entirely to her, without scarce asking a question about them ; except sometimes would say to her, ' Is my debt paid yet ? ' though often did she apply to him for direction and advice ; since he knew enough of the law for the management of his own affairs, when he would take the time or trouble or to prevent his being imposed upon by others."[2]

Mrs. Alice Thornton wrote of her mother :
" Nor was she awanting to make a fare greater improvement [than her dowery of £2000] of my father's estate through her wise and prudential government of his family, and by her care was a meanes to give opportunity of increasing his patrimony."[3]

---

[1] Harley, *Letters of Brilliana, The Lady*, p. 167, 1642.

[2] Murray (Lady), *Memoirs of Lady Grisell Baillie*, p. 13.

[3] Thornton (Mrs. Alice), *Autobiography*, p. 101, (Surtees' Society Vol. lxii.)

In addition to the Household Accounts those of the whole of Judge Fell's estate at Swarthmore, Lancashire, were kept by his daughter Sarah. The following entries show that the family affairs included a farm, a forge, mines, some interest in shipping and something of the nature of a Bank.

July 11, 1676, is entered : " To m^o Rec^d. of Tho : Greaves wife wch. I am to returne to London fo^r her, & is to bee p^d, to her sonn J^{no}. ffellp Walt^r. miers in London, 001. 00. 00.

Jan., 14, 1676-7, by money lent Willm Wilson our forge Clarke till hee gett money in for Ireon sold 10. 0. 0.

Aug. ye 9° 1677 by m^o in expence at adgarley when wee went to chuse oare to send father 000. 00. 04."

Other payments are entered for horses to " lead oare."[1] &c., &c.

In addition to those of her family Sarah Fell kept the accounts for the local " Monthly Meeting " of the Society of Friends, making the payments on its behalf to various poor Friends.

One of the sisters after her marriage embarked upon speculations in salt ; of her, another sister, Margaret Rous, writes to their mother : " She kept me in the dark and had not you wrote me them few words about her I had not known she had been so bad. But I had a fear before how she would prove if I should meddle of her, and since I know her mind wrote to her, being she was so wickedly bent and resolved in her mind, I would not meddle of her but leave her to her husbands relations, and her salt concerns, since which I have heard nothing from her. But I understand by others she is still in the salt business. I know not what it will benefit her but she spends her time about it. I have left her at present."[2]

---

[1] Fell (Sarah), *Household Account Book*.

[2] Crosfield (H. G.), *Life of Margaret Fox, of Swarthmore Hall*, p. 232, 1699.

A granddaughter of Oliver Cromwell, the wife of Thos. Bendish, was also interested in the salt business, having property in salt works at Yarmouth in the management of which she was actively concerned. It was said of her that " Her courage and presence of mind were remarkable in one of her sex, . . . she would sometimes, after a hard day of drudgery go to the assembly at Yarmouth, and appear one of the most brilliant there."[1]

Initiative and enterprise were shown by Lady Falkland during her husband's term of office in Ireland whither she accompanied him.

" The desire of the benefit and commodity of that nation set her upon a great design : it was to bring up the use of all trades in that country, which is fain to be beholden to others for the smallest commodities ; to this end she procured some of each kind to come from those other places where those trades are exercised, as several sorts of linen and woollen weavers, dyers, all sorts of spinners and knitters, hatters, lace-makers, and many other trades at the very beginning."

After a description of her methods for instruction in these arts the biographer continues : " She brought it to that pass that they there made broad-cloth so fine . . . that her Lord being Deputy wore it. Yet it came to nothing ; which she imputed to a judgment of God on her, because the overseers made all those poor children go to church ; . . . . and that therefore her business did not succeed. But others thought it rather that she was better at contriving than executing, and that too many things were undertaken at the very first ; and that she was fain (having little choice) to employ either those that had little skill in the matters they dealt in, or less honesty ; and so she was extremely cozened . . . but chiefly the ill order she took for paying money in this . . . having the

---

[1] Costello, *Eminent Englishwomen*, Vol. III, p. 55.

worst memory in such things in the world . . .
and never keeping any account of what she did, she
was most subject to pay the same things often (as
she hath had it confessed to her by some that they have
in a small matter made her pay them the same thing
five times in five days)."[1]

Lady Falkland received small sympathy from her
husband in her dealings with affairs—and though her
methods may have been exasperating, their unfortunate
differences were not wholly due to her temperament.
He had married her for her fortune and when this
was settled on their son and not placed in his control,
his disappointment was so great that his affections
were alienated from her.

Of her efforts to further his interests Lord Falkland
wrote to Lord Conway :

" My very good Lord,

By all my wife's letters I understand my obligations to your Lordship to be very many ; and she
takes upon her to have received so manifold and noble
demonstrations of your favour to herself, that she
begins to conceive herself some able body in court,
by your countenance to do me courtesies, if she had the
wit as she hath the will. She makes it appear she hath
done me some good offices in removing some infusions
which my great adversary here (Loftus) hath made
unto you . . . it was high time ; for many evil
consequences of the contrary have befallen me since
that infusion was first made, which I fear will not be
removed in haste ; and must thank her much for
her careful pains in it, though it was but an act of duty
in her to see me righted when she knew me wronged
. . and beseech your Lordship still to continue that
favour to us both ; —to her, as well in giving her
good counsel as good countenance within a new world
and court, at such a distance from her husband a poor

---

[1] *Falkland, (The Lady), Her Life*, pp. 18-20.

weak woman stands in the greatest need of to dispatch her suits," . . . etc., etc.

"Dublyn Castle this 26th of July, 1625."[1]

Later he continues in the same strain :

" . . . I am glad your Lordship doth approve my wife's good affection to her husband, which was a point I never doubted, but for her abilities in agency of affairs, as I was never taken with opinion of them, so I was never desirous to employ them if she had them, for I conceive women to be no fit solicitors of state affairs for though it sometimes happen that they have good wits, it then commonly falls out that they have over-busy natures withal. For my part I should take much more comfort to hear that she were quietly retired to her mother's in the country, than that she had obtained a great suit in the court."[2]

The sentiments expressed by Lord Falkland were not characteristic of his time, when husbands were generally thankful to avail themselves of their wives' services in such matters.

While Sir Ralph Verney was exiled in France, he proposed that his wife should return to England to attend to some urgent business. His friend, Dr. Denton replied to the suggestion :

" . . . not to touch upon inconveniences of y^r comminge, women were never soe usefull as now, and though y^u should be my agent and sollicitour of all the men I knowe (and therefore much more to be preferred in y^r own cause) yett I am confident if y^u were here, y^u would doe as our sages doe, instruct y^r wife, and leave her to act it wth committees, their sexe entitles them to many priviledges and we find the comfort of them more now than ever."[3]

---

[1] *Falkland (The Lady), Her Life*, pp. 131-132.

[2] *Ibid*, pp. 132-3.

[3] *Verney Family*, Vol. II., p. 240, 646.

There are innumerable accounts in contemporary letters and papers of the brave and often successful efforts of women to stem the flood of misfortune which threatened ruin to their families.

Katharine Lady Bland treated with Captain Hotham in 1642 on behalf of Lord Savile " and agreed with him for the preservation of my lords estate and protection of his person for £1,000," £320 of which had already been taken "from Lord Savile's trunk at Kirkstall Abbey . . . and the Captain . . . promised to procure a protection from the parliament . . . . for his lordships person and estate."[1]

Lady Mary Heveningham, through her efforts restored the estate to the family after her husband had been convicted of high treason at the Restoration.[2]

Of Mrs. Muriel Lyttelton the daughter of Lord Chancellor Bromley, it was said that she " may be called the second founder of the family, as she begged the estate of King James when it was forfeited and lived a pattern of a good wife, affectionate widow, and careful parent for thirty years, with the utmost prudence and economy at Hagley to retrieve the estate and pay off the debts ; the education of her children in virtue and the protestant religion being her principal employ. Her husband, Mr. John Lyttelton, a zealous papist, was condemned, and his estates forfeited, for being concern'd in Essex's plot."[3]

Charles Parker confessed, " Certainly I had starved had I not left all to my wife to manage, who gets something by living there and haunting some of her kindred and what wayes I know not but I am sure

---

[1] *Calendar State Papers, Domestic*, April 8, 1646.

[2] *Hunter (Joseph), History and Topography of Ketteringham*, p, 46.

[3] Nash, *Hist. and Antiq. of Worcester*, Vol. I,, p. 492.   It appears by depositions in the Court of Chancery that she paid off £25,000 which was charged upon the estate, and only sold lands to the value of £8,854, *Ibid*, p. 496.

such as noe way entangle me in conscience or loyalty nor hinder me from serving the King."[1]

Lady Fanshawe said her husband " thought it conveniente to send me into England again, ... there to try what sums I could raise, both for his subsistence abroad and mine at home. . . . I . . . . embarked myself in a hoy for Dover, with Mrs. Waller, and my sister Margaret Harrison and my little girl Nan, ... I had . . . . . the good fortune as I then thought it, to sell £300 a year to him that is now Judge Archer in Essex, for which he gave me £4,000 which at that time I thought a vast sum ; . . . . five hundred pounds I carried to my husband, the rest I left in my father's agent's hands to be returned as we needed it."[2]

The Marquis of Ormonde wrote : " I have written 2 seuerall ways of late to my wife about our domestick affaires, which are in great disorder betweext the want of meanes to keepe my sonnes abroad and the danger of leaueing them at home. . . . I thank you for your continued care of my children. I haue written twice to my wife to the effect you speake of. I pray God shee be able to put it in execution either way."[3]

This letter does not breathe that spirit of confidence in the wife's ability which was shown in some of the others and it happened sometimes that the wife was either overwhelmed by procedure beyond her understanding, or at least sought for special consideration on the plea of her sex's weakness and ignorance.

Sarah, wife of Henry Burton, gives an account of Burton's trial in the Star Chamber, his sentence and punishment (fine, pillory, imprisonment for life) and his subsequent transportation to Guernsey, " where

---

[1] *Nicholas Papers*, Vol. I., p. 97. Charles Parker to Lord Hatton.

[2] *Fanshawe (Lady)*, *Memoirs of*, pp. 80-81.

[3] *Nicholas Papers*, Vol. III., pp. 274-6. Marquis of Ormonde to Sir Ed. Nicholas, 1656.

he now is but by what order your petitioner knoweth not and is kept in strict durance of exile and imprisonment, and utterly denied the society of your petitioner contrary to the liberties and privileges of this kingdome . . . debarred of the accesse of friends, the use of pen, inck and paper and other means to make knowne his just complaintes," and she petitions the House of Commons " to take her distressed condition into your serious consideracion and because your peticioner is a woman not knowing how to prosecute nor manage so great and weighty busines" begs that Burton may be sent over to prosecute his just complaint.[1]

Similarly, Bastwick's wife pleads that he is so closely imprisoned in the Isle of Scilly " that your petitioner is not permitted to have any access unto him, so that for this 3 yeares and upward hir husband hath been exiled from hir, and she in all this time could not obtayne leave, although she hath earnestly sued for it, neither to live with him nor so much as to see him, and whereas your peticioner hath many smale children depending uppon hir for there mauntenance, and she of hir selfe being every way unable to provide for them, she being thus separated from her deare and loving husband and hir tender babes from there carefull father (they are in) great straights want and miserie," and she begs that her husband may be sent to England," your Petitioner being a woman no way able to follow nor manage so great and weighty a cause . . ."[2]

The above efforts were all made in defence of family estates, but at this time women were also concerned with the affairs of the nation, in which they took an active part.

Mrs. Hutchinson describes how " When the Parliament sat again, the colonel [Hutchinson] sent up his

---

[1] *State Papers, Domestic*, cccclxxi. 36, Nov. 7, 1640.

[2] *S.P.D.*, cccclxxi. 37, 1640.

wife to solicit his business in the house, that the Lord Lexington's bill might not pass the lower house . . she notwithstanding many other discouragements waited upon the business every day, when her adversaries as diligently solicited against her " a friend told her how " the laste statemen's wives came and offered them all the information they had gathered from their husbands, and how she could not but know more than any of them ; and if yet she would impart anything that might show her gratitude, she might redeem her family from ruin, . . . but she discerned his drift and scorned to become an informer, and made him believe she was ignorant, though she could have enlightened him in the very thing he sought for ; which they are now never likely to know much of, it being locked up in the grave."[1]

Herbert Morley wrote to Sir William Campion in 1645 :

" I could impart more, but letters are subject to miscarriage, therefore I reserve myself to a more fit opportunity. . . . If a conference might be had, I conceive it would be most for the satisfaction of us both, to prevent of any possible hazard of your person. If you please to let your lady meet me at Watford . . . or come hither, I will procure her a pass."[2]

Sir William replied : " For any business you have to impart to me, I have that confidence in you, by reason of our former acquaintance, that I should not make any scruple to send my wife to the places mentioned ; but the truth is, she is at present soe neare her time for lying downe, for she expects to be brought to bed within less than fourteen days, that she is altogether unfit to take soe long a journey. . . ."[3]

---

[1] *Life of Colonel Hutchinson*, by his Wife, pp. 334-336.

[2] *Sussex Arch. Coll.*, Vol. x., p. 5. To Sir William Campion from Herbert Morley, July 23rd, 1645.

[3] *Ibid*, Vol. x., p. 6.

A book might be wholly filled with a story of the part taken by women in the political and religious struggles of this period. They were also active among the crowd who perpetually beseiged the Court for grants of wardships and monopolies or patents.

Ann Wallwyn writes to Salisbury soliciting the wardship of the son of James Tomkins who is likely to die.[1] The petition of Dame Anne Wigmore, widow of Sir Richard Wigmore, states that she has found out a suit which will rectify many abuses, bring in a yearly revenue to the Crown and give satisfaction to the Petitioner for the great losses of herself and her husband. Details follow for a scheme for a corporation of carriers and others.[2]

Dorothy Selkane reminds Salisbury that a patent has been promised her for the digging of coals upon a royal manor. The men who manage the business for her are content to undertake all charges for the discovery of the coal and to compensate the tenants of the manor according to impartial arbitrators. She begs Salisbury that as she has been promised a patent the matter may be brought to a final conclusion that she may not be forced to trouble him further "having alredie bestowed a yeres solicitinge therein."[3] In 1610 the same lady writes again:—" I have bene at gte toyle and charges this yere and a halfe past as also have bene put to extraordinarie sollicitacion manie and sundry waies for the Dispatching of my suite . . ." and begs that the grant may pass without delay.[4]

A grant was made in 1614 to Anne, Roger and James Wright of a licence to keep a tennis court at St. Edmund's Bury, co. Suffolk, for life.[5] Bessy

---

[1] *C.S.P.D.* lxvii, 129, 1611.

[2] *C.S.P.D.* clxii, 8. March 2, 1630.

[3] *S.P.D.*, xlviii. 119. 22nd October. 1609.

[4] *S.P.D.* liii, 131, April 1610.

[5] *C.S.P.D.* lxxvii, 5 April 5, 1614.

Welling, servant to the late Prince Henry, petitioned for the erecting of an office for enrolling the Apprentices of Westminster, etc. As this was not granted, she therefore begs for a lease of some concealed lands [manors for which no rent has been paid for a hundred years] for sixty-one years. The Petitioner hopes to recover them for the King at her own charges.[1] Lady Roxburgh craves a licence to assay all gold and silver wire "finished at the bar" before it is worked, showing that it is no infringement on the Earl of Holland's grant which is for assaying and sealing gold and silver after it is made. This, it is pointed out, will be a means for His Majesty to pay off the debt he owes to Lady Roxburgh which otherwise must be paid some other way.[2]

A petition from Katharine Elliot "wett nurse to the Duke of Yorke" shows that there is a moor waste or common in Somersetshire called West Sedge Moor which appears to be the King's but has been appropriated and encroached upon by bordering commoners. She begs for a grant of it for sixty years ; as an inducement the Petitioner offers to recover it at her own costs and charges and to pay a rent of one shilling per acre, the King never previously having received benefit therefrom.[3] The reference by Windebank notes that the king is willing to gratify the Petitioner. Another petition was received from this same lady declaring that "Divers persons being of no corporation prefers the trade of buying and selling silk stockings and silk waistcoats as well knit as woven uttering the Spanish or baser sort of silk at as dear rates as the first Naples and also frequently vending the woven for the knit, though in price and goodness there is almost half in half difference." She prays a grant for thirty-

---

[1] *S.P.D.* cxi, 121, 1619.

[2] *S.P.D.* clxxx, 66, 1624.

[2] *S.P.D.* cccxxiii, 109, 18th June, 1637.

one years for the selling of silk stockings, half stockings and waistcoats, to distinguish the woven from the knit receiving from the salesmen a shilling for every waistcoat, sixpence per pair of silk stockings and fourpence for every half pair.[1]

Elizabeth, Viscountess Savage, points out that Freemen of the city enter into bond on their admittance with two sureties of a hundred marks to the Chamberlain of London not to exercise any trade other than that of the Company they were admitted into. Of late years persons having used other trades and contrived not to have their bonds forfeited, and the penalty belonging to His Majesty, she begs a grant of such penalties to be recovered at her instance and charge.[2]

The petition of Margaret Cary, relict of Thomas Cary Esquire, one of the Grooms of the Chamber to the King on the behalf of herself and her daughters, begs for a grant to compound with offenders by engrossering and transporting of wool, wool fells, fuller's earth, lead, leather, corn and grain, she to receive a Privy Seal for two fourth-parts of the fines and compositions. Her reasons for desiring this grant are that her husband's expense in prosecuting like cases has reaped no benefit of his grant of seven-eighths of forfeited bonds for the like offences. She urges the usefulness of the scheme and the existence of similar grants.[3]

Mistress Dorothy Seymour petitions for a grant of the fines imposed on those who export raw hides contrary to the Proclamation and thereby make coaches, boots, etc., dearer. The reference to the Petition states : " It is His Majesty's gratious pleasure that the petitioner cause impoundr. to be given to the Attorney General touching the offences above mencioned . · . and as proffyt shall arise to His

---

[1] *S.P.D.* cccxxiii , 7. *Bk. of Petitioners*, Car. I.

[2] *S.P.D.* cccciii., 65, Dec. 6th, 1635.

[3] *S.P.D.* cccvi., 27, 1635.

Majesty . . . he will give her such part as shall fully satisfy her pains and good endeavours."[1]

The projecting of patents and monopolies was the favourite pursuit of fashionable people of both sexes. Ben Johnson satirises the Projectress in the person of Lady Tailebush, of whom the Projector, Meercraft says :

> . . . . . . " She and I now
> Are on a Project, for the fact, and venting
> Of a new kind of fucus (paint for Ladies)
> To serve the Kingdom ; wherein she herself
> Hath travel'd specially, by the way of service
> Unto her sex, and hopes to get the monopoly,
> As the Reward of her Invention."[2]

When Eitherside assures her mistress

> " I do hear
> You ha' cause madam, your suit goes on "

Lady Tailebush replies :

> " Yes faith, there's life in't now. It is referr'd
> If we once see it under the seals, wench, then,
> Have with 'em, for the great caroch, six horses
> And the two coachmen, with my Ambler bare,
> And my three women ; we will live i' faith,
> The examples o' the Town, and govern it.
> I'll lead the fashion still." . . . . . . [3]

From the women who begged for monopolies which if granted must have involved much worry and labour if they were to be made profitable, we pass naturally to women who actually owned and managed businesses requiring a considerable amount of capital. They not infrequently acted as pawn-brokers and money-lenders. Thus, complaint is made that Elizabeth Pennell had stolen " two glazier's vices with the screws and appurtenances " and pawned them to

---

[1] *S.P.D.* cccxlvi, 2, Feb. 1st, 1637.

[2] Jonson, (Ben.) *The Devil is an A ss*, Act III, Scene iv.

[3] (*Ibid*), Act IV., Scene ii.

one Ellianor Troughton, wife of Samuel Troughton broker.[1]

Richard Braithwaite tells the following story of a " Useresse " as though this occupation were perfectly usual for women. " Wee reade in a booke entituled the *Gift of Feare*, how a Religious Divine comming to a certaine Vseresse to advise her of the state of her soule, and instruct her in the way to salvation at such time as she lay languishing in her bed of affliction ; told her how there were three things by her to be necessarily performed, if ever she hoped to be saved : She must become *contrite* in heart . . . *confesse* her sins . . . . make *restitution* according to her meanes whereto shee thus replyed, *Two of those first I will doe willingly : but to doe the last, I shall hold it a difficulty ; for should I make restitution, what would remaine to raise my children their portion ?* To which the Divine answered ; *Without these three you cannot be saved. Yea but,* quoth shee, *Doe our Learned Men and Scriptures say so ? Yes, surely* said the Divine. *And I will try,* (quoth shee) *whether they say true or no, for I will restore nothing.* And so resolving, fearefully dyed . . . for preferring the care of her posterity, before the honour of her Maker."[2]

The names of women often occur in connection with the shipping trade and with contracts. Some were engaged in business with their husbands as in the case of a fine remitted to Thomas Price and Collet his wife for shipping 200 dozen of old shoes, with intention to transport them beyond the seas contrary to a Statute (5th year Edward VI) on account of their poverty.[3] Others were widows like Anne Hodsall whose husband, a London merchant, traded for many

---

[1] *Middlesex Co. Rec. Sess. Books*, p. 18, 1690.

[2] Braithwaite, (Richd.), *The English Gentleman*, p. 300, 1641.

[3] Overall *Remembrancia, Analytical Index to*, p. 519, 1582.

years to the Canary Islands, the greatest part of his estate being there. He could not recover it in his lifetime owing to the war with Spain and therefore his wife was left in great distress with four children. Her estate in the Canary Islands is likely to be confiscated, there being no means of recovering it thence except by importing wines, and it would be necessary to take pipe-staves over there to make casks to bring back the wines. She begs the council therefore " in commiseration of her distressed estate to grant a licence to her and her assignes to lade one ship here with woollen commodities for Ireland, To lade Pipe staves in Ireland (notwithstanding the prohibition) and to send the same to the Canary Islands."[1]

Joseph Holroyd employed a woman as his shipping agent ; in a letter dated 1706 he writes re certain goods for Holland : that these " I presume must be marked as usual and forward to Madam Brown at Hull. . ." and he informs Madam Hannah Browne, that " By orders of Mr. John Whittle I have sent you one packe and have 2 packes more to send as und[r]. You are to follow Mr. Whittle's directions in shipping."[2]

In 1630 Margrett Greeneway, widow of Thos. Greeneway, baker, begged leave to finish carrying out a contract made by her husband notwithstanding the present restraint on the bringing of corn to London. The contract was to supply the East India Company with biscuit. Margrett Greeneway petitions to bring five hundred quarters of wheat to London—some are already bought and she asks for leave to buy the rest. The petition was granted.[3]

A Petition of " Emanuell Fynche, Wm. Lewis Merchantes and Anne Webber Widow on the behalfe

---

[1] *Council Register*, 8th August, 1628.

[2] Holroyd, Joseph (Cloth Factor) and Saml. Hill (clothier), *Letter Bks. of*, pp. 18-25.

[3] *C.R.*, 3rd December, 163c.

of themselves and others owners of the shipp called the *Benediction* was presented to the Privy Council stating that the ship had been seized and detained by the French and kept at Dieppe where it was deteriorating. They asked to be allowed to sell her there.[1] The name of another woman ship-owner occurs in a case at Grimsby brought against Christopher Claton who " In the behalfe of his Mother An Alford, wid.,hath bought one wessell of Raffe of one Laurence Lamkey of Odwell in the kingdome of Norway, upon w[ch] private bargane there appeares a breach of the priviledges of this Corporation."[2]

In 1636 upon the Petition of Susanna Angell " widowe, and Eliz. her daughter (an orphan) of the cittie of London humbly praying that they might by their Lordshipps warrant bee permitted to land 14 barrels of powder now arrived as also 38 barrells which is daily expected in the *Fortune* they paying custome and to sell the same within the kingdome or otherwise to give leave to transport it back againe into Holland from whence it came " the Officers of the customs were ordered to permit the Petitioners to export the powder.[3]

Women's names appear also in lists of contractors to the Army and Navy. Elizabeth Bennett and Thomas Berry contracted with the Commissioners to supply one hundred suits of apparel for the soldiers at Plymouth.[4]

Cuthbert Farlowe, Elizabeth Harper Widowe, Edward Sheldon and John Davis," poore Tradesmen of London " petition " to be paid the £180 yet unpaid of their accounts for furnishing the seamen for Rochelle with clothes and shoes " att the rates of ready money."[5]

---

[1] *S.P.D.* ccxxxvi., 45, 12th, April, 1633.

[2] *Hist. MSS. Com.*, 14 Rep., VIII., p. 284, 1655.

[3] *S.P.D.* ccxcii., 24. March 23, 1636/7., *Proceedings of Gunpowder Commissioners.*

[4] *S.P.D.* xx., 62, Feb. 9th, 1626.

[5] *S.P.D.* cxcvii., 64, July, 1631.

A warrant was issued " to pay to Alice Bearden £100 for certain cutworks furnished to the Queen for her own wearing."[1]

Edward Prince brought a case in the Star Chamber, v. Thomas Woodward, Ellenor Woodward, and Georg. Helliar defendants being Ironmongers for supposed selling of iron at false weights to undersell plaintiff. " Defendants respectively prove that they ever bought and sold by one sort of weight."[2]

For her tenancy of the Spy-law Paper Mill, Foulis " receaved from M^{rs}. lithgow by W^{m}. Douglas Hands 85 lib. for ye 1704 monie rent. She owes me 3 rim of paper for that yeir, besydes 4 rim she owes me for former yeirs."[3]

Joan Dant was one of the few women " capitalists " whose personal story is known in any detail. Her husband was a working weaver, living in New Paternoster Row, Spital Fields. On his death she became a pedlar, carrying an assortment of mercery, hosiery, and haberdashery on her back from house to house in the vicinity of London. Her conduct as a member of the Society of Friends was consistent and her manners agreeable, so that her periodic visits to the houses of Friends were welcomed and she was frequently entertained as a guest at their tables. After some years, her expenses being small and her diligence great, she had saved sufficient capital to engage in a more wholesale trade, debts due from her correspondents at Paris and Brussels appearing in her executor's accounts. In spite of her success in trade Joan Dant continued to live in her old frugal manner, and when she applied to a Friend for assistance in making her will, he was astonished to find her worth rather more than £9,000. He advised her to obtain the assistance

---

[1] *S.P.D.*, clix., 27th Jan. 1630.

[2] *S.P.D.*, dxxxi., 138, 1630.

[3] Foulis, Sir John, *Account Book*, 5th Jan., 1705.

of other Friends more experienced in such matters. On their enquiring how she wished to dispose of her property, she replied, " I got it by the rich and I mean to leave it to the poor."

Joan Dant died in 1715 at the age of eighty-four. In a letter to her executors she wrote, " It is the Lord that creates true industry in his people, and that blesseth their endeavours in obtaining things necessary and convenient for them, which are to be used in moderation by all his flock and family everywhere. . . And I, having been one that has taken pains to live, and have through the blessing of God, with honesty and industrious care, improved my little in the world to a pretty good degree ; find my heart open in that charity which comes from the Lord, in which the true disposal of all things ought to be, to do something for the poor,—the fatherless and the widows in the Church of Christ, according to the utmost of my ability."[1]

Another venture initiated and carried on by a woman, was an Insurance Office established by Dorothy Petty. An account of it written in 1710 states that :— " The said *Dorothy* (who is the Daughter of a Divine of the Church of *England*, now deceas'd) did Set up an *Insurance Office* on *Births*, *Marriages*, *and Services*, in order thereby to serve the Publick, and get an honest Livelyhood for herself. . . . . The said *Dorothy* had such Success in her Undertaking, that more Claims were paid, and more Stamps us'd for Policies and Certificates in her Office than in all other the like Offices in *London* besides ; which good Fortune was chiefly owing to the Fairness and Justice of her Proceedings in the said Business : for all the Money paid into the Office was Entered in one Book, and all the Money paid out upon Claims was set down in another Book, and all People had Liberty to peruse

---

[1] *British Friend*, II., p. 113.

both, so that there could not possibly be the least Fraud in the Management thereof."[1]

In 1622 the names of Mary Hall, 450 coals, Barbara Riddell, 450 coals, Barbara Milburne, 60 coals, are included without comment among the brothers of the fellowship of Hostmen (coal owners) of Newcastle who have coals to rent.[2] The name of Barbara Milburne, widow, is given in the Subsidy Roll for 1621 as owning land.[3] That these women were equal to the management of their collieries is suggested by the fact that when in 1623 Christopher Mitford left besides property which he bequeathed direct to his nephews and nieces, five salt-pans and collieries to his sister Jane Legard he appointed her his executrix,[4] which he would hardly have done unless he had believed her equal to the management of a complicated business.

The frequency with which widows conducted capitalistic enterprises may be taken as evidence of the extent to which wives were associated with their husbands in business. The wife's part is sometimes shown in prosecutions, as in a case which was brought in the Star Chamber against Thomas Hellyard, Elizabeth his wife and John Goodenough and Hugh Nicholes for oppression in the country under a patent to Hellyard for digging saltpetre . . . "in pursuance of his direction leave and authority. . . Nicholes Powell, Defendants servant, and the said Hellyard's wife, did sell divers quantities of salt petre. More particularly the said Hellyard's wife did sell to Parker 400lbs. at Haden Wells, 300 or 400 lbs. at Salisbury and 300 or 400 lbs. at Winchester at £9 the hundred." Hellyard was sentenced to a fine of £1,000, pillory, whipping and imprisonment.

---

[1] *Case of Dorothy Petty*, 1710.

[2] *Newcastle and Gateshead, History of*, Vol. III., p. 242.

[3] *Ibid*, p. 237.

[4] *Ibid*, p. 252.

" As touching the other defendant Elizabeth Hellyard the courte was fully satisfyed with sufficient matter whereupon to ground a sentence against the defendant Eliz. but shee being a wyfe and subject to obey her husband theyr Lord ships did forbeare to sentence her."[1]

Three men, " artificers in glass making," beg that Lady Mansell may either be compelled to allow them such wages as they formerly received, or to discharge them from her service, her reduction of wages disabling them from maintaining their families, and driving many of them away.[2] Lady Mansell submits a financial statement and account of the rival glass-makers' attempts to ruin her husband's business, one of whom " hath in open audience vowed to spend 1000li, to ruine your petitioners husband joyninge with the Scottish pattentie taking the advantage of your petitioners husbands absence, thinckinge your petitioner a weake woman unable to followe the busines and determininge the utter ruine of your petitioner and her husband have inticed three of her workemen for windowe glasse, which shee had longe kepte att a weeklie chardge to her great prejudice to supplie the worke yf there should be anie necessitie in the Kingdome," etc., etc.," she begs justice upon the rivals, " your petitioner havinge noe other meanes nowe in his absence (neither hath he when he shall returne) but onelie this busines wherein he hath engaged his whole estate."[3]

Able business women might be found in every class of English society throughout the seventeenth century, but their contact with affairs became less habitual as the century wore away, and expressions of surprise occur at the prowess shown by Dutch women in

---

[1] *S.P.D.*, cclx., 21, 1634.

[2] *S.P.D.*, cxlviii., 52, 1623,

[3] *S.P.D.*; dxxi., 147. Addenda Charles I., 1625.

business. "At *Ostend*, *Newport*, and *Dunkirk*, where, and when, the *Holland* pinks come in, there daily the Merchants, that be but Women (but not such Women as the Fishwives of *Billingsgate* ; for these *Netherland* Women do lade many Waggons with fresh Fish daily, some for *Bruges*, and some for *Brussels*, etc., etc.) I have seen these Women-merchants I say, have their Aprons full of nothing but *English Jacobuses*, to make all their Payment of."[1]

Sir J. Child mentions "the Education of their Children as well Daughters as Sons ; all which, be they of never so great quality or estate, they always take care to bring up to write perfect good Hands, and to have the full knowledge and use of Arithmetick and Merchant Accounts," as one of the advantages which the Dutch possess over the English ; "the well understanding and practise whereof doth strangely infuse into most that are the owners of that Quality, of either Sex, not only an Ability for Commerce of all kinds, but a strong aptitude, love and delight in it ; and in regard the women are as knowing therein as the Men, it doth incourage their Husbands to hold on in their Trades to their dying days, knowing the capacity of their Wives to get in their Estates, and carry on their Trades after their Deaths : Whereas if a Merchant in England arrive at any considerable Estate, he commonly with-draws his Estate from Trade, before he comes near the confines of Old Age ; reckoning that if God should call him out of the World while the main of his Estate is engaged abroad in Trade, he must lose one third of it, through the un-experience and unaptness of his Wife to such Affairs, and so it usually falls out. Besides it hath been ob-served in the nature of Arithmetick, that like other parts of the Mathematicks, it doth not only improve the Rational Faculties, but inclines those that are expert

---

[1] *England's Way*, 1614. *Harleian Misc.*, Vol. III., p. 383.

in it to Thriftiness and good Husbandry, and prevents both Husbands and Wives in some measure from running out of their estates."[1]

This account is confirmed by Howell who writes of the Dutch in 1622 that they are " well versed in all sorts of languages . . . Nor are the Men only expert therein but the Women and Maids also in their common Hostries ; & in Holland the Wives are so well versed in Bargaining, Cyphering & Writing, that in the Absence of their Husbands in long sea voyages they beat the Trade at home & their Words will pass in equal Credit. These Women are wonderfully sober, tho' their Husbands make commonly their Bargains in Drink, & then are they more cautelous."[2]

This unnatural reversing of the positions of men and women was censured by the Spaniard Vives who wrote " In Hollande, women do exercise marchandise and the men do geue themselues to quafting, the which customes and maners I alowe not, for thei agre not with nature, ye which hath geuen unto man a noble, a high & a diligent minde to be busye and occupied abroade, to gayne & to bring home to their wiues & families to rule them and their children, ... and to ye woman nature hath geuen a feareful, a couetous & an humble mind to be subject unto man, & to kepe y^t he doeth gayne."[3]

The contrast which had arisen between Dutch and English customs in this respect was also noticed by Wycherley, one of whose characters, Monsieur Paris, a Francophile fop, describes his tour in Holland in the following terms : " I did visit, you must know, one of de Principal of de State General . . . and did find his Excellence weighing Sope, jarnie ha, ha, ha, weighing sope, ma foy, for he was a wholesale Chandeleer ; and

---

[1] Child, Sir J., *A New Discourse of Trade*, pp. 4-5. 1694,

[2] Howell, (Jas.), *Familiar Letters*, p. 103,

[3] Vives, *Office and Duties of a Husband*, trans. by Thos. Paynell.

his Lady was taking de Tale of Chandels wid her own witer Hands, ma foy ; and de young Lady, his Excellence Daughter, stringing Harring, jarnie . . . his Son, (for he had but one) was making the Tour of France, etc. in a Coach and six."[1]

The picture is obviously intended to throw ridicule on the neighbouring state, of whose navy and commercial progress England stood at that time in considerable fear.

How rapidly the active, hardy life of the Elizabethan gentlewoman was being transformed into the idleness and dependence which has characterised the lady of a later age may be judged by Mary Astell's comment on " Ladies of Quality." She says, " They are placed in a condition which makes that which is everyone's chief business to be their only employ. They have nothing to do but to glorify God and to benefit their neighbours."[2] After a study of the Restoration Drama it may be doubted whether the ladies of that period wished to employ their leisure over these praiseworthy objects. But had they the will, ignorance of life and inexperience in affairs are qualifications which perhaps would not have increased the effectiveness of their efforts in either direction.

The proof of the change which was taking place in the scope of upper class women's interests does not rest only upon individual examples such as those which have been quoted, though these instances have been selected for the most part on account of their representative character.

It is quite clear that the occupation of ladies with their husband's affairs was accepted as a matter of course throughout the earlier part of the century, and it is only after the Restoration that a change of fashion in this respect becomes evident. Pepys, whose milieu was

---

[1] Wycherley, *The Gentleman Dancing Master*, p. 21.

[2] Astell, (Mary), *A Serious Proposal*, p. 145, 1694.

typical of the new social order, after a call upon Mr. Bland, commented with surprised pleasure on Mrs. Bland's interest in her husband's affairs. "Then to eat a dish of anchovies," he says "and drink wine and syder and very merry, but above all things, pleased to hear Mrs. Bland talk like a merchant in her husband's business very well, and it seems she do understand it and perform a great deal."[1] The capacity of a woman to understand her husband's business seldom aroused comment earlier in the century, and would have passed unnoticed even by many of Pepys' contemporaries who lived in a different set. Further evidence of women's business capacity is found in the fact that men generally expected their wives would prove equal to the administration of their estates after their death, and thus the wife was habitually appointed executrix often even the sole executrix of wills. This custom was certainly declining in the latter part of the century. The winding up of a complicated estate and still more the prosecution of an extensive business, could not have been successfully undertaken by persons who hitherto had led lives of idleness, unacquainted with the direction of affairs.

That men did not at this time regard marriage as necessarily involving the assumption of a serious economic burden, but on the contrary, often considered it to be a step which was likely to strengthen them in life's battles, is also significant. This attitude was partly due to the provision of a dot by fathers of brides, but there were other ways in which the wife contributed to the support of her household. Thus in a wedding sermon woman is likened to a merchant's ship, for "She bringeth her food from far" . . . not meaning she is to be chosen for her dowry, "for the worst wives may have the best portions, . . . a good wife tho' she bring nothing in with her, yet,

---

[1] Pepys, (Sam.) *Diary*, Vol. II., p. 113, Dec. 31, 1662.

thro' her Wisdom and Diligence great things come in by her ; she brings in with her hands, for, *She putteth her hands to the wheel.* . . . . If she be too high to stain her Hands with bodily Labour, yet she bringeth in with her Eye, for, *She overseeth the Ways of her Household*, . . . and eateth not the Bread of *Idleness.*" She provides the necessities of life. " If she will have Bread, she must not always buy it, but she must sow it, and reap it and grind it, . . . She must knead it, and make it into bread. Or if she will have Cloth, she must not always run to the Shop or to the score but she begins at the seed, she carrieth her seed to the Ground, she gathereth Flax, of her Flax she spinneth a Thread, of her Thread she weaveth Cloth, and so she comes by her coat."[1]

The woman here described was the mistress of a large household, who found scope for her productive energy within the limits of domestic industry, but it has been shown that the married woman often went farther than this, and engaged in trade either as her husband's assistant or even on her own account.

The effect of such work on the development of women's characters was very great, for any sort of productive, that is to say, creative work, provides a discipline and stimulus to growth essentially different from any which can be acquired in a life devoted to spending money and the cultivation of ornamental qualities.

The effect on social relations was also marked, for their work implied an association of men and women through a wide range of human interests and a consequent development of society along organic rather than mechanical lines. The relation between husband and wife which obtained most usually among the upper classes in England at the opening of the seventeenth century, appears indeed to have been that of partner-

---

[1] Wilkinson, (Robert), *Conjugal Duty*, pp. 13-17.

ship; the chief responsibility for the care of children and the management and provisioning of her household resting on the wife's shoulders, while in business matters she was her husband's lieutenant. The wife was subject to her husband, her life was generally an arduous one, but she was by no means regarded as his servant. A comradeship existed between them which was stimulating and inspiring to both. The ladies of the Elizabethan period possessed courage, initiative, resourcefulness and wit in a high degree. Society expected them to play a great part in the national life and they rose to the occasion; perhaps it was partly the comradeship with their husbands in the struggle for existence which developed in them qualities which had otherwise atrophied.

Certainly the more circumscribed lives of the Restoration ladies show a marked contrast in this respect, for they appear but shadows of the vigorous personalities of their grandmothers. Prominent amongst the many influences which conspired together to produce so rapid a decline in the physique, efficiency and morale of upper class women, must be reckoned the spread of the capitalistic organisation of industry, which by the rapid growth of wealth made possible the idleness of growing numbers of women. Simultaneously the gradual perfecting by men of their separate organisations for trade purposes rendered them independent of the services of their wives and families for the prosecution of their undertakings. Though the stern hand of economic necessity was thus withdrawn from the control of women's development in the upper classes, it was still potent in determining their destiny amongst the " common people," whose circumstances will be examined in detail in the following chapters.

Chapter III

AGRICULTURE

Agriculture England's leading Industry—Has provided the most vigorous stock of
English race—Division into three classes :—

(A) *Farmers*. Portraits of Farmers' Wives—Fitzherbert's " Prologue for
the Wyves Occupacyon." Size of household—The Wife who " doth not take
the pains and charge upon her." Financial aptitude—Market—Occupation
of gentlewomen with Dairy and Poultry—Expectation of the wife's ability
to work and do service.

(B) *Husbandmen*. Economy of their Small Holding—The more they
worked for wages the greater their poverty—Strenuous but healthy life of the
women—Extent to which they worked for wages—Character of work—Best's
account of Yorkshire Farms—other descriptions. Spinning—The wife's
industry no less constant when not working for wages, but more profitable to
her family, whom she clothed and fed by domestic industry.

(C) *Wage-earners*. Maximum rates of wages fixed at Assizes represent
generally those actually paid. Common labourers' wage, winter and summer
—Women's wages seasonal—Not expected when married to work week in, week
out. Cost of living—Cost of labourers' diet—Pensions and Allowances—Poor
Relief—Cost of clothes and rent—Joint wages of father and mother insufficient
to rear three children—Recognised insolvency of Labourers' Family—Disputes
concerning labourers' settlements. Farmers' need for more labourers—
Demoralisation—Demand for sureties by the Parish. Infant mortality—Life
history of labourers' wife—Explanation for magistrates' action in fixing
maximum wages below subsistence level—Proportion of wage-earning families.

ALTHOUGH the woollen trade loomed very large
upon the political horizon because it was a chief
source of revenue to the Crown and because rapidly
acquired wealth gave an influence to clothiers and
wool merchants out of proportion to their numbers,
agriculture was still England's chief industry in
the seventeenth century.

The town population has had a tendency to wear out
and must be recruited from rural districts. The
village communities which still persisted at this period
in England, provided a vigorous stock, from which the
men whose initiative, energy and courage have made
England famous during the last two centuries were
largely descended. Not only were the farming fam-

ilies prolific in numbers but they maintained a high standard of mental and moral virtue. It must be supposed therefore that the conditions in which they lived were upon the whole favourable to the development of their women-folk, but investigation will show that this was not the case for all members alike of the agricultural community, who may be roughly divided into three classes :

(a) Farmers. (b) Husbandmen. (c) Wage-earners.

(a) *Farmers* held sufficient land for the complete maintenance of the family. Their household often included hired servants and their methods on the larger farms were becoming capitalistic.

(b) *Husbandmen* were possessed of holdings insufficient for the complete maintenance of the family and their income was therefore supplemented by working for wages.

(c) *Wage-earners* had no land, not even a garden, and depended therefore completely on wages for the maintenance of their families.

In addition to the above, for whom agriculture was their chief business, the families of the gentry, professional men and tradesmen who lived in the country and smaller towns, generally grew sufficient dairy and garden produce for domestic consumption.

The above classification is arbitrary, for no hard and fast division existed. Farmers merged imperceptibly into husbandmen, and husbandmen into wage earners and yet there was a wide gulf separating their positions. As will be shown, it was the women of the first two classes who bore and reared the children who were destined to be the makers of England, while few children of the wage-earning class reached maturity.

A. *Farmers.*

However important the women who were the mothers of the race may appear to modern eyes, their history was unnoticed by their contemporaries and no analysis was made of their development. The existence of vigorous, able matrons was accepted as a matter of course. They embodied the seventeenth century idea of the " eternal feminine " and no one suspected that they might change with a changing environment. They themselves were too busy, too much absorbed in the lives of others, to keep journals and they were not sufficiently important to have their memoirs written by other people.

Perhaps their most authentic portraits may be found in the writings of the Quakers, who were largely drawn from this class of the community. They depict women with an exalted devotion, supporting their families and strengthening their husbands through the storms of persecution and amidst the exacting claims of religion.

John Banks wrote from Carlisle Prison in 1648 to his wife, " No greater Joy and Comfort I have in this world . . . than to know that thou and all thine are well both in Body and Mind . . . though I could be glad to see thee here, but do not straiten thyself in any wise, for I am truly content to bear it, if it were much more, considering thy Concerns in this Season of the Year, being Harvest time and the Journey so long."[1] After her death he writes, " We Lived Comfortably together many Years, and she was a Careful Industrious Woman in bringing up of her Children in good order, as did become the Truth, in Speech, Behaviour and Habit ; a Meet-Help and a good Support to me, upon the account of my Travels, always ready and willing to fit me with Necessaries, . . . and was never known to murmur, tho' I was often Concerned, to leave her with a weak Family, . . . She was well beloved amongst good Friends and of her Neighbours, as witness the several hundreds that were at her Burial. . . . our Separation by Death,

---

[1] Banks (John), *Journal*, p. 101, 1684.

was the greatest Trial that ever I met with, above any-thing here below. Now if any shall ask, Why I have writ so many Letters at large to be Printed . . . how can any think that I should do less than I have done, to use all Endeavours what in me lay, to Streng-then and Encourage my Dear Wife, whom I so often, and for so many Years was made to leave as aforesaid, having pretty much concerns to look after."[1]

Of another Quaker, Mary Batt, her father writes in her testimony that she was " Married to *Phillip Tyler* of *Waldon* in the County of *Somerset* before she attained the age of twenty years. . . . The Lord blessed her with Four Children, whereof two dyed in their Infancy, and two yet remain alive : at the Burial of her Husband, for being present, she had two Cows valued at Nine Pounds taken from her, which, with many other Tryals during her Widowhood, she bore with much Patience, . . . After she had remained a Widow about four Years, the Lord drew the affection of *James Taylor* . . . to seek her to be his Wife, and there being an answer in her, the Lord joyned them together. To her Husband her Love and Subjection was suitable to that Relation, being greatly delighted in his Company, and a Meet-Help, a faithful Yoak-fellow, . . . and in his Absence, not only carefully discharging the duty as her Place as a Wife, but diligent to supply his Place in those affairs that more immediately concerned him."[2] And her husband adds in his testimony, " My outward Affairs falling all under her charge (I, being absent, a Prisoner for my Testimony against Tythes) she did manage the same in such care and patience until the time she was grown big with Child, and as she thought near the time of her Travail (a condition much to be born with and pittyed) she then desired so much Liberty as to have my Company home

---

[1] Banks, (John), *Journal*, pp. 129-30.
[2] Batt (Mary), *Testimony of the Life and Death of*, pp. 1-3, 1683.

two Weeks, and went herself to request it, which small matter she could not obtain, but was denied ; and as I understood by her, it might be one of the greatest occasions of her grief which ever happened unto her, yet in much Meekness and true Patience she stooped down, and quietly took up this her last Cross also, and is gone with it and all the rest, out of the reach of all her Enemies, . . . Three Nights and Two Days before her Death, I was admitted to come to her, though I may say (with grief) too late, yet it was to her great joy to see me once more whom she so dearly loved ; and would not willingly suffer me any more to depart out of her sight until she had finished her days, . . . Her Sufferings (in the condition she was in) although I was a Prisoner, were far greater then mine, for the whole time that she became my Wife, which was some Weeks above Three Years, notwithstanding there was never yet man, woman, nor child, could justly say, she had given them any offence . . . yet must . . . unreasonable men cleanse our Fields of Cattle, rummage our House of Goods, and make such havock as that my Dear Wife had not wherewithal to dress or set Food before me and her Children.[1]

The duties of a Farmer's wife were described a hundred years earlier by Fitzherbert in the " Boke of Husbandrie." He begins the " Prologue for the wyves occupacyon," thus, " Now thou husbande that hast done thy diligence and laboure that longeth to a husband to get thy liuing, thy wyues, thy children, and thy seruauntes, yet is there other thynges to be doen that nedes must be done, or els thou shalt not thryue. For there is an olde common saying, that seldom doth ye husbande thriue without leue of his wyf. By thys saying it shuld seem that ther be other occupaciõs and labours that be most cõvenient

---

[1] Batt (Mary), *Testimony to Life and Death of*, pp. 5-7, 1683.

for the wyfes to do, and how be it that I haue not the experience of all their occupacyions and workes as I haue of husbandry, yet a lytel wil I speake what they ought to do though I tel thẽ not how they should do and excersyse their labour and occupacions.

A lesson for the wyfe . . . alway be doyng of some good workes that the deuil may fynde the alway occupied, for as in a standyng water are engendred wormes, right so in an idel body are engendered ydel thoughtes. Here maie thou see y^t of idelnes commeth damnatiõ, & of good workes and labour commeth saluacion. Now thou art at thy libertie to chose whither waye thou wilte, wherein is great diversite. And he is an unhappye man or woman that god hath given both wit & reason and putteth him in choise & he to chose the worst part. Nowe thou wife I trust to shewe unto the diuers occupacions, workes and labours that thou shalt not nede to be ydel no tyme of ye yere. What thinges the wife is bounde of right to do. Firste and principally the wyfe is bound of right to loue her husband aboue father and mother and al other men . . .

What workes a wyfe should do in generall. First in the mornyng when thou art wakéd and purpose to rise, lift up thy hãd & blis the & make a signe of the holy crosse . . . and remembre thy maker and thou shalte spede muche the better, & when thou art up and readye, then firste swepe thy house; dresse up thy dyscheborde, & set al thynges in good order within thy house, milke ye kie, socle thy calues, sile up thy milke, take up thy children & aray thẽ, & provide for thy husbandes breakefaste, diner, souper, & for thy children & seruauntes, & take thy parte wyth them. And to ordeyne corne & malt to the myll, to bake and brue withall whẽ nede is. And mete it to the myll and fro the myll, & se that thou haue thy mesure agayne besides the tole or elles the mylner dealeth not truly wyth the, or els thy corne is not drye as it should be, thou must make butter and chese when thou may, serue thy swine both mornyng and eueninge, and giue thy polen meate in the mornynge, and when tyme of yeare cometh thou must take hede how thy henne, duckes, and geese do ley, and to gather up their egges and when they waxe broudy to set them there as no beastes, swyne, nor other vermyne hurte them, and thou must know that all hole foted foule wil syt a moneth and al clouen foted foule wyl syt but three wekes except a peyhen and suche other great foules as craynes, bustardes, and suche other. And when they haue brought forth theyr birdes to se that they be well kepte from the gleyd, crowes, fully martes and other vermyn, and in the begynyng of March, of a lytle before is time for a wife to make her garden and to get as manye good sedes and herbes as she can, and specyally such as be good for the pot and for to eate & as ofte as nede shall require it muste be weded, for els the wede wyll ouer grow the herbes, and also in Marche is time to sowe flaxe and hempe, for I haue heard olde huswyues say, that better is Marche hurdes then Apryll flaxe, the reason appereth, but howe it shoulde be sowen, weded, pulled, repealed, watred, washen, dried, beten, braked, tawed, hecheled, spon, wounden, wrapped, & ouen. It nedeth not for me to shewe for they be wyse ynough, and thereof may they make shetes, bord clothes, towels, shertes, smockes, and suche other necessaryes, and therfore lette thy dystaffe be alwaye redy for a pastyme, that thou be not ydell. And undoubted a woman cannot get her livinge honestly with spinning on the dystaffe, but it stoppeth a gap and must nedes be had. The bolles of flaxe whan they be rypled of, muste be rediled from the wedes and made dry with the sunne to get out the seedes. How be it one maner of linsede called lokensede wyll not open by the sunne, and therefore when they be drye they must be sore bruien and broken the wyues know how, & then wynowed and kept dry til peretime cum againe. Thy femell hempe must be pulled fro the chucle hĕpe for this beareth no sede & thou muste doe by it as thou didest by the flaxe. The chucle hempe doth beare seed & thou must beware that birdes eate it not as it groweth, the hempe thereof is not so good as the femel hĕpe, but yet it wil do good seruice. It may fortune sometime y^t thou shalte haue so many thinges to do that thou shalte not wel know where is best to begyn. Thẽ take hede whiche thinge should be the greatest losse if it were not done & in what space it would be done, and then thinke what is the greatest loss & there begin. . . . It is cõvenient for a husbande to haue shepe of his owne for many causes, and then may his wife have part of the wooll to make her husbande and her selfe sum clothes. And at the least waye she may haue ye lockes of the shepe therwith to make clothes or blankets, and couerlets, or both. And if she haue no wol of her owne she maye take woll to spynne of cloth makers, and by that meanes she may have a conuenient liuing, and many tymes to do other workes. It is a wiues occupacion to winow al maner of cornes, to make malte wash and wring, to make hey, to shere corne, and in time of nede to helpe her husbande to fyll the mucke wayne or donge carte, dryve the plough, to lode hey, corne & such other. Also to go or ride to the market to sell butter, chese, mylke, egges, chekens, kapons, hennes, pygges, gees, and al maner of corne. And also to bye al maner of necessary thinges belonging to a houshold, and to make a true rekening & accompt to her husband what she hath receyued and what she hathe payed. And yf the husband go to the market to bye or sell as they ofte do, he then to shew his wife in lyke maner. For if one of them should use to disceiue the other, he disceyveth him selfe, and he is not lyke to thryve, & therfore they must be true ether to other.[1]

---

[1] Fitzherbert (Sir Anth.), *Boke of Husbandrye.*

Fitzherbert's description of the wife's occupation probably remained true in many districts during the seventeenth century. The dairy, poultry, garden and orchard were then regarded as peculiarly the domain of the mistress, but upon the larger farms she did not herself undertake the household drudgery. Her duty was to organise and train her servants, both men and women.

The wages assessments of the period give some idea of the size of farmers' households, fixing wages for the woman servant taking charge of maulting in great farms, every other maulster, the best mayde servant that can brewe, bake and dresse meate, the second mayd servant, the youngest mayd servant, a woman being skilful in ordering a house, dayry mayd, laundry mayd, and also for the men-servants living in the house, the bailiff of husbandry, the chief hinde, and the common man servant, the shepherd, and the carter.

That some women already aspired to a life of leisure is shown in an assessment for the East Riding of Yorkshire, which provides a special rate of wages for the woman servant " that taketh charge of brewing, baking, kitching, milk house or malting, that is hired with a gentleman or rich yeoman, whose wife doth not take the pains and charge upon her."[1]

In addition to the management of the dairy, etc., the farmer's wife often undertook the financial side of the business. Thus Josselin notes in his Diary : " This day was good wife Day with mee ; I perceive she is resolved to give mee my price for my farme of Mallories, and I intend to lett it goe." A few days later he enters " This day I surrendered Mallories and the appurtenances to Day of Halsted and his daughter."[2]

---

[1] Rogers (J. E. Thorold), *Hist. Agric. and Prices*, Vol. VI., pp. 686-9, assess. for Yorks, East Riding, Ap. 26, 1593.

[2] Josselin (R), *Diary*, p. 86, April 9th, and 30th, 1650.

The farmer's wife attended market with great regularity, where she became thoroughly expert in the art of buying and selling. The journey to market often involved a long ride on horseback, not always free from adventure as is shown by information given to the Justices by Maud, wife of Thomas Collar of Woolavington, who stated that as she was returning home by herself from Bridgwater market on or about 7th July, Adrian Towes of Marke, overtook her and calling her ugly toad demanded her name ; he then knocked her down and demanded her purse, to which, hiding her purse, she replied that she had bestowed all her money in the market. He then said, ' I think you are a Quaker,' & she denied it, he compelled her to kneel down on her bare knees and swear by the Lord's blood that she was not, which to save her life she did. Another woman then came up and rebuked the said Towes, whereupon he struck her down ' atwhart ' her saddle into one of her panniers.[1]

Market was doubtless the occasion of much gossip, but it may also have been the opportunity for a wide interchange of views and opinions on subjects important to the well-being of the community. While market was frequented by all the women of the neighbourhood it must certainly have favoured the formation of a feminine public opinion on current events, which prevented individual women from relying exclusively upon their husbands for information and advice.

The names of married women constantly appear in money transactions, their receipt being valid for debts due to their husbands. Thus Sarah Fell enters in her Household Book, " Pd. Bridget Pind[r] in full of her Husband's bills as appeares £3. 17s. 6d."[2] by m[o] p[d] Anthony Towers wife in p[t] fo[r] manne[r] wee are to

---

[1] *Somerset Quarter Sessions Records*, Vol. III, pp. 370-1,1659.

[2] *Fell (Sarah) Household Accounts*, p, 317, 1676.

have of he^r 1.00^1 to m^o Rec^d. of Myles Gouth wife
fo^r ploughing for her 1.04 "^{2}

Arithmetic was not considered a necessary item
in the education of girls, though as the following
incident shows, women habitually acted in financial
matters.

Samuel Bownas had been sent to gaol for tithe, but
the Parson could not rest and let him out, when he
went to Bristol on business and spent two weeks
visiting meetings in Wiltshire. After his return, while
away from home a distant relation called and
asked his wife to lend him ten pounds as he was
going to a fair. She not thinking of tithe which was
much more, lent it and he gave her a note, which
action was approved by her husband on his return ;
but the relation returned again in Samuel Bownas's
absence to repay, and tore the note as soon as he received it, giving her a quittance for the tithe instead.
She was indignant, saying it would destroy her
husband's confidence in her. The relation assured her
that he would declare her innocence, but he could
not· have persuaded her husband, for "he would
have started so many questions that I could not possibly
have affected it any other way than by ploughing
with his heifer."^{3}

Women's names frequently occur in presentments
at Quarter Sessions for infringements of bye laws.
The Salford Portmote "p' sent Isabell the wyef of
Edmunde Howorthe for that she kept her swyne
unlawfull, and did trespas to the corn of the said
Raphe Byrom."^{4}

Katharine Davie was presented " for not paving
before her doore." Mrs. Elizabeth Parkhurst for

---

^{1} *Fell (Sarah), Household Accounts*, p. 339, 1676.

^{2} *Ibid*, p. 386, 1677.

^{3} *Bownas (Samuel), Life*, pp. 116-17.

^{4} *Salford Portmote Records*, Vol. I, p. 3, 1597.

" layinge a dunghill anenst her barne and not makinge the street cleane." Isabell Dawson and Edmund Cowper for the like and Mrs. Byrom and some men "for letting swyne go unringed and trespassinge into his neighbors corne & rescowinge them when they have beene sent to the fould."[1] " Charles Gregorie's wife complained that shee is distrained for 3s. for an amerciament for hoggs goeing in the Streete where-upon, upon her tendring of 3s. xijd is restored with her flaggon."[2] The owner of the pig appears very often to be a married woman. At Carlisle in 1619 : ,' We amarye the wief of John Barwicke for keping of swine troughes in the hye streyt contrary the paine and therefore in amercyment according to the orders of this cyttie, xiid."[3]

Such women may often not have been farmers in the full sense of the word, but merely kept a few pigs to supplement the family income. Even the gentry were not too proud to sell farm and garden produce not needed for family consumption, and are alluded to as " . . . our Country Squires, who sell Calves and Runts, and their Wives perhaps Cheese and Apples."[4]

Many gentlewomen were proficient in dairy manage-ment. Richard Braithwaite writes of his wife :

> " Oft have I seen her from her Dayrey come
> Attended by her maids, and hasting home
> To entertain some Guests of Quality
> Shee would assume a state so modestly
> Sance affectation, as she struck the eye
> With admiration of the stander-by."

The whole management of the milch cows belonged to the wife, not only among farming people but also

---

[1] *Salford Portmote Records*, Vol. II., pp. 6-7, 1633.

[2] Guilding. *Reading Records*, Vol. IV., p. 512, 1653.

[3] Ferguson, *Municipal Records of Carlisle*, p. 278.

[4] Howell, *Familiar Letters*, p. 290, 1644.

among the gentry. The proceeds were regarded as
her pin-money, and her husband generally handed over
to her all receipts on this account, Sir John Foulis
for example entering in his account book : " June 30
1693. To my wife ye pryce of ye gaird kowes
Hyde, £4 0 0."[1]

Sometimes when the husband devoted himself to
good fellowship, the farm depended almost entirely
on his wife ; this was the case with Adam Eyre, a
retired Captain, who enters in his Dyurnall,
Feb. 10, 1647, " This morning Godfrey Bright
bought my horse of my wife, and gave her £5, and
promised to give her 20s. more, which I had all but
20s. and shee is to take in the corne sale £4." *May* 18,
1647, " I came home with Raph Wordsworth of the
Water hall who came to buy a bull on my wife, who
was gone into Holmefrith."[2]

The business capacity of married women was even
more valuable in families where the father wished to
devote his talents to science, politics, or religion, unencumbered by anxiety for his children's maintenance.
It is said in Peter Heylin's Life that " Being deprived
of Ecclesiastical preferments, he must think of some
honest way for a livelihood. Yet notwithstanding he
followed his studies, in which was his chief delight. . .
. . In which.pleasing study while he spent his time, his
good wife, a discreet and active lady, looked both after
her Housewifery within doors, and the Husbandry
without ; thereby freeing him from that care and
trouble, which otherwise would have hindered his
laborious Pen from going through so great a work in
that short time. And yet he had several divertise-
ments by company, which continually resorted to his
house ; for having (God be thanked) his temporal
Estate cleared from Sequestration, by his Composition

---

[1] Foulis (Sir John, of Ravelston), *Acct. Bk*, p. 158.

[2] Eyre, (Capt. Adam), *A Dyurnall*, p. 16, p. 36.

with the Commissioners at *Goldsmith's Hall*, and this Estate which he Farmed besides, he was able to keep a good House, and relieve his poor brethren."[1]

Gregory King's father was a student of mathematics, " and practised surveying of land, and dyalling, as a profession ; but with more attention to *good-fellow-ship*, than mathematical studies generally allow : and, the care of the family devolved of course on the mother, who, if she had been less obscure, had emulated the-most eminent of the Roman matrons."[2]

Adam Martindale's wife was equally successful. He writes " about Michaelmas, 1662, I removed my family from the Vicarage to a little house at Camp-greene, . . . where we dwelt above three years and half . . . I was three score pounds in debt, . . . but (God be praised) while I staid there I paid off all that debt and bestowed £40 upon mareling part of my ground in Tatton. . . . If any aske how this could be without a Miracle, he may thus be satisfied. I had sent me . . . £41 . . . and the £10 my wife wrangled out of my successor, together with a table, formes and ceiling, sold him for about £4 more."[3] Later on he adds " My family finding themselves straitened for roome, and my wife being willing to keep a little stock of kine, as she had done formerly, and some inconvenience falling out (as is usual) by two families under a roofe, removed to a new house not completely furnished."[4]

That in the agricultural community women were generally supposed to be, from a business point of view, a help and not a hindrance to their husbands— that in fact the wife was not " kept " by him but helped him to support the family is shown by terms proposed

---

[1] *Heylin*, (*Peter*), pp. 18-19.

[2] King (Gregory), *Natural and Political Observations, etc.*

[3] *Martindale*, (*Adam*,) *Life*, p. 172.

[4] *Ibid*, p. 190.

for colonists in Virginia by the Merchant Taylors who offer "one hundred acres for every man's person that hath a trade, or a body able to endure day labour as much for his wief, as much for his child, that are of yeres to doe service to the Colony."[1]

B. *Husbandmen.*

Husbandmen were probably the most numerous class in the village community. Possessed of a small holding at a fixed customary rent and with rights of grazing on the common, they could maintain a position of independence.

Statute 31 Eliz., forbidding the erection of cottages without four acres of land attached, was framed with the intention of protecting the husbandman against the encroachments of capitalists, for a family which could grow its own supply of food on four acres of land would be largely independent of the farmer, as the father could earn the money for the rent, etc., by working only at harvest when wages were highest. As however this seasonal labour was not sufficient for the farmers' demands, such independence was not wholly to their mind, and they complained of the idleness of husbandmen who would not work for the wages offered. Thus it was said that " In all or most towns, where the fields lie open there is a new brood of upstart intruders or inmates . . . loiterers who will not work unless they may have such excessive wages as they themselves desire."[2] " There is with us now rather a scarcity than a superfluity of servants, their wages being advanced to such an extraordinary height, that they are likely ere long to be masters and their masters servants, many poor husbandmen being forced to pay near as much to their servants for wages as to their landlords for rent."[3]

---

[1] Clode, (C.M.) *Merchant Taylors*, Vol. I., p. 323.

[2] Pseudonismus, *Considerations concerning Common Fields and Enclosures*, 1654.

[3] Pseudonismus, *A Vindication of the Considerations concerning Common Fields and Enclosures*, 1656.

The holdings of the husbandmen varied fom seven acres or more to half an acre or even less of garden ground, in which as potatoes[1] were not yet grown in England the crop consisted of wheat, barley, rye, oats, or peas. Very likely there was a patch of hemp or flax and an apple-tree or two, a cherry tree and some elder-berries in the hedge, with a hive or two of bees in a warm corner. Common rights made it possible to keep sheep and pigs and poultry, and the possession of a cow definitely lifted the family above the poverty line.

Dorothy Osborne describing her own day to her lover, gives an idyllic picture of the maidens tending cows on the common : " The heat of the day is spent in reading or working, and about six or seven o'clock I walk out into a common that lies hard by the house, where a great many young wenches keep sheep and cows, and sit in the shade singing of ballads. I go to them and compare their voices and beauties to some ancient shepherdesses that I have read of, and find a vast difference there ; but trust me, I think these are as innocent as those could be. I talk to them and find they want nothing to make them the happiest people in the world but the knowledge that they are so. Most commonly, when we are in the midst of our discourse, one looks about her, and spies her cows going into the corn, and then away they all run as if they had wings at their heels. I, that am not so nimble, stay behind, and when I see them driving home their cattle, I think 'tis time for me to retire too."[2]

Husbandmen have been defined as a class who could not subsist entirely upon their holdings, but must to some extent work for wages. Their need for wages varied according to the size of their holding and according to the rent. For copy-holders the rent

---

[1] Potatoes were already in use in Ireland, but are scarcely referred to during this period by English writers.

[2] *Osborne (Dorothy), Letters,* pp. 103,4. 1652-1654.

was usually nominal,[1] but in other cases the husbandman was often forced to pay what was virtually a rack rent. Few other money payments were necessary and if the holding was large enough to produce sufficient food, the family had little cause to fear want.

Randall Taylor wrote complacently in 1689 that in comparison with the French peasants, " Our *English* husbandmen are both better fed and taught, and the poorest people here have so much of brown Bread, and the Gospel, that by the Calculations of our *Bills* of *Mortality* it appears, that for so many years past but One of Four Thousand is starved."[2]

The woman of the husbandman class was muscular and well nourished. Probably she had passed her girlhood in service on a farm, where hard work, largely in the open air, had sharpened her appetite for the abundant diet which characterised the English farmer's housekeeping. After marriage, much of her work was still out of doors, cultivating her garden and tending pigs or cows, while her husband did his day's work on neighbouring farms. Frugal and to the last degree laborious were her days, but food was still sufficient and her strength enabled her to bear healthy children and to suckle them. It was exactly this class of woman that the gentry chose as wet nurses for their babies. Their lives would seem incredibly

---

[1] 30s. Susanna Suffolke a young maid holds a customary cottage, . . . and renteth per annum 2d.
£28 Eliz. Filoll (widdow) holdeth one customary tenement. Rent per annum 26s. 8d.
£2 Mary Stanes holdeth one customary cottage (late of Robert Stanes) and renteth per annum 7d.
£12 Margaret Dowe (widdow) holdeth one customary tenement (her eldest son the next heir) rent 7s. 8d.
Among freeholders. Johan Mathew (widow) holdeth one free tenement and one croft of land thereto belonging . . . containing three acres and a half and renteth 3d.
(Stones, Jolley. 1628. From a List of Copyholders in West & S. Haningfield, Essex.)

[2] Taylor. (Randall), *Discourse of the Growth of England, etc.*, p. 96, 1689.

hard to the modern suburban woman, but they had their reward in the respect and love of their families and in the sense of duties worthily fulfilled.

The more prosperous husbandmen often added to their households an apprentice child, but in other cases the holdings were too small to occupy even the family's whole time.

At harvest in any case all the population of the village turned out to work ; men, women, and children, not only those belonging to the class of husbandmen, but the tradesmen as well, did their bit in a work so urgent ; for in those days each district depended on its own supply of corn, there being scarcely any means of transport.

Except during the harvest, wages were so low that a man who had a holding of his own was little tempted to work for them, though he might undertake some special and better-paid occupation, such as that of a shepherd. Pepys, describing a visit to Epsom, writes : " We found a shepherd and his little boy reading, far from any houses or sight of people, the Bible to him, I find he had been a servant in my Cozen Pepys's house . . . the most like one of the old patriarchs that ever I saw in my life . . . he values his dog mightily, . . . about eighteen score sheep in his flock, he hath four shillings a week the year round for keeping of them."[1]

Probably this picturesque shepherd belonged to the class of husbandmen, for the wages paid are higher than those of a household servant. Four shillings a week comes to £10. 8. o by the year, whereas a Wiltshire wages assessment for 1685 provided that a servant who was a chief shepherd looking after 1,500 sheep or more was not to receive more than £5 by the year.[2] On the other hand, four shillings a week would not

---

[1] Pepys, Vol. IV, p. 428. 14 July, 1667.

[2] Hist. MSS. Miss. Com. Var. Coll., Vol. I. .p. 170.

maintain completely the shepherd, his boy and a dog, not to speak of a wife and other children. Thus, while the shepherd tended his sheep, we may imagine his wife and children were cultivating their allotment.

The wages for the harvest work of women as well as men, were fixed by the Quarter Sessions.[1] References to their work may be found in account books and diaries. Thus Dame Nicholson notes : " *Aug.* 13, 1690, I began to sher ye barin croft about 11 o'clock, ther was Gordi Bar and his wife—also Miler's son James and his sister Margit also a wife called Nieton—they sher 17 threv and 7 chivis."[2]

Best gives a detailed account of the division of work between men and women on a Yorkshire farm : " Wee have allwayes one man, or else one of the ablest of the women, to abide on the mowe, besides those that goe with the waines.[3] The best sort of men-shearers have usually 8d. a day and are to meate themselves ; the best sorte of women shearers have (most commonly) 6d. a day.[4] It is usuall in some places (wheare the furres of the landes are deepe worne with raines)

---

[1] A comparison of the assessments which have been preserved, in the different counties shows that men's earnings varied in the hay harvest from :—

    4d. and meat and drink, or 8d. without, to
    8d. „   „ „ „ „ 1s. 4d. „
and in the corn harvest from :—

    5d. and meat and drink, or 10d. without, to
    1s. „   „ „ „ „ 2s. „
Women's wages varied in the hay harvest from :—

    1d. and meat and drink, or 4d. without, to
    6d. „   „ „ „ „ 1s. „
and in the corn harvest from :—

    2d. and meat and drink, or 6d. without, to
    6d. „   „ „ „ „ 1s. „

The variations in these wages correspond with the price of corn in different parts of England and must not be regarded as necessarily representing differences in the real value of wages.

[2] Society of Antiquarians of Scotland, vol. xxxix, p. 125. *Dame Margaret Nicholson's Account Book.*

[3] Best, *Rural Economy*, p. 36.

[4] *Ibid*, p. 42.

to imploy women, with wain-rakes, to gather the corne
out of the said hollow furres after that the sweath-
rakes have done.[1]   .   . We use meanes allwayes to gett
eyther 18 or else 24 pease pullers, which wee sette
allwayes sixe on a lande, viz., a woman and a man, a
woman and a man, a woman or boy and a man, etc.,
the weakest couple in the fore furre.   .   . it is usuall
in most places after they gette all pease pulled, or the
last graine downe, to invite all the worke-folkes and
wives (that helped them that harvest) to supper, and
then have they puddinges, bacon, or boyled beefe,
flesh or apple pyes, and then creame brought in platters,
and every one a spoone ; then after all they have
hotte cakes and ale ; some will cutte theire cake
and putte into the creame and this feaste is called the
creame-potte or creame-kitte . . . wee send
allwayes, the daye before wee leade, [pease] two of our
boys, or a boy and one of our mayds with each of them a
shorte mowe forke to turn them."[2]

For thatching, Best continues : " Wee usually provide
two women for helpes in this kinde, viz, one to drawe
thacke, and the other to serve the thatcher ; she that
draweth thacke hath 3d. a day, and shee that serveth
the thatcher 4d. a day, because shee also is to temper
the morter, and to carry it up to the toppe of the
howse . . . Shee that draweth thatch shoulde
always have dry wheate strawe . . . whearewith
to make her bandes for her bottles. She that serveth
will usually carry up 4 bottles at a time, and sometimes but 3 if the thatch bee longe and very wette."[3]

---

[1] Best, *Rural Economy*, p. 59.

[2] *Ibid*, pp. 93-4.

[3] *Ibid*, pp. 138-9. " The thatchers," Best says, " have in most places 6d. a day
& theire meate in Summer time, . . . yett we neaver use to give them above 4d . . .
. . because their dyett is not as in other places ; for they are to have three meale
a day, *viz*. theire breakfaste att eight of the clocke, . . . theire dinner about twelve and
theire supper about seaven or after when they leave worke ; and att each meale.
fower services, viz. butter, milke, cheese, and either egges, pyes, or bacon, and sometimes porridge insteade of milke : if they meate themselves they have usually 10d.
a day."

" Spreaders of mucke and molehills are (for the most parte) women, boyes and girles, the bigger and abler sorte of which have usually 3d. a day, and the lesser sorte of them 2d. a day."[1] " Men that pull pease have 8d. women 6d. a day."[2]

A picture of hay-harvesting in the West of England given by Celia Fiennes suggests that in other parts of England to which she was accustomed, the labour, especially that of women, was not quite so heavy. All over Devon and Cornwall she says, hay is carried on the horses' backs and the people " are forced to support it wth their hands, so to a horse they have two people, and the women leads and supports them, as well as ye men and goe through thick and thinn. . . . I wondred at their Labour in this kind, for the men and the women themselves toiled Like their horses."[3]

There was hardly any kind of agricultural work from which women were excluded. Everenden " payed 1s. 2d. to the wife of Geo. Baker for shearing 28 sheep."[4] In Norfolk the wages for a " woman clipper of sheepe " were assessed at 6d. per day with meat and drink, 1s. without, while a man clipper was paid 7d. and 14d. It is noteworthy that only 4d. per day was allowed in the same assessment for the diet of " women and such impotent persons that weed corn and other such like Laborers " and 2d. per day for their wages.[5] Pepys on his visit to Stonehenge " gave the shepherd-woman, for leading our horses, 4d.,"[6] while Foulis enters, " Jan. 25, 1699 to tonie to give ye women at

---

[1] Best, *Rural Economy*, p. 140.

[2] *Ibid*, p. 142.

[3] Fiennes (Celia), *Through England on a Side-saddle*, p. 225.

[4] Suss. Arch. Coll. Vol. IV., p. 24. *Everendon Account Book*

[5] Tingye (J. C.) *Eng. Hist. Rev*, Vol. XIII., pp. 525-6.

[6] Pepys, Vol. V., p. 302. (11th June, 1668).

restalrig for making good wailings of strae, 4s. (Scots money)."[1]

But the wives of husbandmen were not confined to agricultural work as is shown by many payments entered to them in account books :[2] Thus the church wardens at Strood, in Kent, paid the widow Cable for washing the surplices 1s.[3] ; and at Barnsley they gave " To Ricard Hodgaris wife for whipping dogs " (out of the Church) 2s.[4] while " Eustace Lowson of Salton (a carrier of lettres and a verie forward, wicked woman in that folly) and Isabell her daughter are included in a Yorkshire list of recusants.[5]

No doubt the mother with young children brought them with her to the harvest field, where they played as safely through the long summer day as if they and she had been at home. But at other times she chose work which did not separate her from her children, spinning being her unfailing resource. It is difficult living in the age of machinery to imagine the labour which clothing a family by hand-spinning involved, though the hand-spun thread was durable and fashions did not change.

In spite of the large demand the price paid was very low, but when not obliged to spin for sale,

[1] Foulis (Sir John) *Acct. Bk.*, p. 246.

[2] " Aug. 7th. 1701 to my wife, to a Bleicher wife at bonaley for bleitching 1. 3. 4." (Scots)

" Jan. 28th, 1703 to my good douchter jennie to give tibbie tomsome for her attendance on my wife the time of her sickness 5.16.0 (Scots). (*Foulis (Sir John*) *Acct. Bk. p.* 295, 314.)

" Sep. 11th, 1676, pd. her (Mary Taylor) more for bakeing four days. Mothers Acct. 8d. (*Fell, (Sarah) Household Accts.* p. 309.)

" Pd. Widow Lewis for gathering herbs two daies 6d. (Sussex, Arch. Coll. xlviii. p. 120. *Extracts from the Household Account Book of Herstmonceux Castle.*)

Paid to goodwife Stopinge for 2 bundles of Rushes at Whitsuntide for the Church, iiijd. (*Churchwarden's Account Book, Strood*, p. 95, 1612.

[3] *Churchwarden's Account Book, Strood*, p. 197. 1666.

[4] Cox (J. C.) *Churchwarden's Accts.*, p. 309.

[5] *Yorks. North Riding, Q. S. Rec.*, Vol. I,, p. 62, Jan. 8. 1606-7.

time was well spent in spinning for the family. The flax or hemp grown on the allotment, was stored up for shirts and house-linen. If the husband-man had no sheep, the children gathered scraps of wool from the brambles on the common, and thus the only money cost of the stuff worn by the husbandman's household was the price paid to the weaver.

The more prosperous the family, the less the mother went outside to work, but this did not mean, as under modern conditions, that her share in the productive life of the country was less. Her productive energy remained as great, but was directed into channels from which her family gained the whole profit. In her humble way she fed and clothed them, like the wise woman described by Solomon.

The more she was obliged to work for wages, the poorer was her family.

C. *Wage-earners.*

In some respects it is less difficult to visualise the lives of women in the wage-earning class than in the class of farmers and husbandmen. The narrowness of their circumstances and the fact that their desti-tution brought them continually under the notice of the magistrates at Quarter Sessions have preserved data in greater completeness from which to reconstruct the picture. Had this information been wanting such a reconstruction would have demanded no vivid imagination, because the results of the semi-starvation of mothers and small children are very similar whether it takes place in the seventeenth or the twentieth century; the circumstances of the wives of casual labourers and men who are out of work and " unemployable " in modern England may be taken as representing those of almost the whole wage-earning class in the seventeenth century.

The most important factors governing the lives of wage-earning women admit of no dispute. First among these was their income, for wage-earners have already been defined as the class of persons depending wholly upon wages for the support of their families.

Throughout the greater part of the seventeenth century the rate of wages was not left to be adjusted by the laws of supply and demand, but was regulated for each locality by the magistrates at Quarter Sessions. Assessments fixing the maximum rates were published annually and were supposed to vary according to the price of corn. Certainly they did vary from district to district according to the price of corn in that district, but they were not often changed from year to year.

Prosecutions of persons for offering and receiving wages in excess of the maximum rates frequently occurred in the North Riding of Yorkshire, but it is extremely rare to find a presentment for this in other Quarter Sessions. The Assessments were generally accepted as publishing a rate that public opinion considered fair towards master and man, and outside Yorkshire steps were seldom taken to prevent masters from paying more to valued servants. That upon the whole the Assessments represent the rate ordinarily paid can be shown by a comparison with entries in contemporary account-books.

The Assessments deal largely with the wages of unmarried farm servants and with special wages for the seasons of harvest, intended for the occasional labour of husbandmen, but in addition there are generally rates quoted by the day for the common labourer in the summer and winter months. Even when meat and drink is supplied, the day-rates for these common labourers are higher than the wages paid to servants living in the house and are evidently intended for married men with families.

In one Assessment different rates are expressly given for the married and unmarried who are doing the same work,[1] a married miller receiving with his meat and drink, 4d. a day which after deducting holidays would amount to £5 0 0 by the year, while the unmarried miller has only 46s. 8d. and a pair of boots.

Assessments generally show a similar difference between the day-wages of a common labourer and the wages of the best man-servant living in the house, and it may therefore be assumed that day labourers were generally married persons.

Day rates were only quoted for women on seasonal jobs, such as harvest and weeding. It was not expected that married women would work all the year round for wages, and almost all single women were employed as servants.

The average wage of the common agricultural labourer as assessed at Quarter Sessions was 3½d. per day in winter, and 4½d. per day in summer, in addition to his meat and drink. Actual wages paid confirm

---

[1] " A shoemaker servant of the best sorte being married, to have without m-ate and drinke for every dosin of shoes   xxijd.
ditto unmarried to have by the yeare with meat and drink and withowte a leverye
                                                                                                                        liijs.
Millers and drivers of horses beinge batchelors then with meate and drinke and without a liverye and a payre of boots   xlvis viijd.
Millers and drivers of horses beinge married men shall not take more by the daye then with meate and drinke   ivd. and without viijd.
a man servant of the best sorte shall not have more by the yeare then with a levereye   xls. and without xlvjs viiid.
the same, of the thirde sorte has only with a leverye
                                                                          xxvjs viiid. and without xxxiijs iiijd.
while any sort of labourer, from the Annunciation of our Ladye until Michellmas has with meat and drink by the day   ivd. and without viijd.
From Michellmas to the Annunciation   iiijd. and wıthout vijd.
The best sorte of women servants shall not have more by the yeare than with a liverye   xxjs. and without xxvjs viiid.
while " a woman reaping of corne " shall not have " more by the daye then vd with meat and drink."

(*Hertfordshire Assessment*, 1591).

Every man-servant serving with any person as a Comber of Wooll to have by the yeare 40s.

Every such servant being a single man and working by ye pound to have by ye pound 1d.

Every such servant being a marryed man and having served as an apprentice thereto according to the statute to have by ye pound 2d.

(*Assessment for Suffolk*, 1630).

the truth of these figures, though it is not always clear whether the payments include meat and drink.[1]

If we accept the Assessments as representing the actual wages earned by the ordinary labourer we can estimate with approximate accuracy the total income of a labourer's family, for we have defined the wage earner as a person who depended wholly upon wages and excluded from this class families who possessed gardens. Taking a figure considerably higher then the one at which the Assessment averages work out, namely 5d. per day instead of 4d. per day, to be the actual earnings of a labouring man in addition to his meat and drink, and doubling that figure for the three months which include the hay and corn harvests, his average weekly earnings will amount to 3s. 2d.

---

[1] Paid to a shovele man for 2 days to shovell in the cart rakes, 2s. (*Hertford Co. Rec.*, Vol. I, p. 233, 1672.) 2½ days' work of a labourer, 2s. 6d. (*ibid*, p. 130, 1659).

For one daies work for one labourer, 1s. (*Stro.d Churchwarden's Acc.* p. 182, 1662.)

Pd. to James Smith for one days' work thatching about Widow Barber's house, she being in great distress by reason she could not lie down in her bed and could get no help to do the same. 1s. 2d. (*Cratford Parish Papers*, p. 152, 1622.) Thatchers were paid more than ordinary labourers, being generally assessed at the same rate as a carpenter, or a mower in the harvest.

July 15, 1676. Tho. Scott for workeinge hay 2 dayes, 4d.

Tho. Greaves younger for workeinge hay 2 dayes, 4d.

May 5, 1678, Will Braithwt for threshing 6 dayes 1.00

April 27, 1676, by mᵒ. pᵈ. him for thatching 2 days at Petties Tenemt, 8d.

August 2. 1676. pd. Margt Dodgson for workinge at hay & other worke 5 weekes 03.06.

pd. Mary Ashbrner for workinge at hay & other worke 4 weekes & 3 dayes, 03. 0.0.

Sept 4. pᵈ. Will Nicholson wife for weedinge in yᵉ garden & pullinge hempe 12 dayes 01. 0. 0.

Oct. 2. pᵈ. Issa. Atkinson for her daughtr Swingleinge 6 dayes 01. 0. 0.

May. 7, 1677. pᵈ.Will Ashbrner for his daughter harrowing here 2 weekes 01. 0. 0. (*Fell (Sarah), House Acct.*)

Labourers' wages 4d. per day.

(*Hist. MSS. Comm. Var. Coll.* Vol. IV. 133, 1686. Sir Jno. Earl's Inventory of goods.

Weeks' work common labourer, 3s. Thos. West, 1 week's haying 2s. (*Sussex Arch. Coll.*, Vol. IV, p. 24, *Everendon Acc. Book*, 1618.)

Paid for a labourer 3 dayes to hoult the alees and carrying away the weedes, 1s. 6d. (*Cromwell Family, Bills and Receipts*, Vol. II, p. 233, 1635.)

Jan. 26. 1649. Payd. to John Wainwright for 5 days worke 1s. 8d. [Yorkshire]. (*Eyre (Capt. Adam) Dyurnall*, p. 117.)

Thos. Hutton, xiiij days work ijs. iiijd, his wyfe xij dayes iiijs. Thos. Hutton xiij dayes at hay vid, his wyfe 4 dayes xvjd. Leonell Bell, xiij dayes about hay, vjs. vjd. Tho. Bullman the lyke. iiijs. iiijd, Thos. Hutton 4 dayes at mowing corne, xvjd. *Howard Household Book*, p. 40-41).

Except in exeptional circumstances his wife's earnings would not amount to more than 1s. a week and her meat and drink. The more young children there were, the less often could the wife work for wages, and when not doing so her food as well as the chidren's must be paid for out of the family income.

In a family with three small children it is unlikely that the mother's earnings were more than what would balance days lost by the father for holidays or illness, and the cost of his food on Sundays, but allowing for a small margin we may assume that 3s. 6d. was the weekly income of a labourer's family, and that this sum must provide rent and clothing for the whole family and food for the mother and children.

A careful investigation of the cost of living is necessary before we can test whether this amount was adequate for the family's maintenance.

There is no reason to suppose that a diet inferior to present standards could maintain efficiency in the seventeenth century. On the contrary, the English race at that time attributed their alleged superiority over other nations to a higher standard of living.[1]

---

[1] The dietary in charitable institutions gives an idea of what was considered bare necessity.

(*Children's Diet in Christ Church Hospital*, 1704.)

For breakfast, Bread and Beer. For dinner, Sunday, Tuesday, and Thursday, boiled beef and pottage. Monday, milk pottage, Wednesday, furmity. Friday old pease & pottage. Saturday water gruel. For supper bread and cheese or butter for those that cannot eat cheese. Sunday supper, legs of mutton. Wednesday and Friday, pudding pies.

(*Stow, London*, Book I, p. 182.)

Diet for Workhouse, Bishopsgate Street, London.

They have Breakfasts, dinners, and suppers every day in the week. For each mea 4 oz. bread, 1½ oz. cheese, 1 oz. butter, 1 pint of beer. Breakfast, four days, bread and cheese or butter and beer. Mondays a pint of Pease Pottage, with Bread and Beer. Tuesdays a Plumb Pudding Pye 9 oz. and beer. Wednesdays a pint of Furmity. On Friday a pint of Barley Broth and bread. On Saturdays, a plain Flower Sewet Dumpling with Beer. Their supper always the same, 4 oz. bread, 1½ of cheese or 1 oz. of butter, and beer sufficient. (Stow, *London*, Book I, p. 199).

Lady Grisell Baillie gives her servant's diet :

Sunday they have boild beef and broth made in the great pot, and always the broth made to serve two days. Monday, broth made on Sunday, and a Herring. Tuesday, broth and beef. Wednesday, broth and two eggs each. Thursday, broth and beef. Friday, Broth and herring. Saturday, broth without meat, and cheese, or a pudden

A comparison between the purchasing power of money in the seventeenth and twentieth centuries is unsatisfactory for our purpose, because the relative values of goods have changed so enormously. Thus, though rent, furniture and clothes were much cheaper in the seventeenth century, there was less difference in the price of food. Sixpence per day is often given in Assessments as the cost of a labourer's meat and drink and this is not much below the amount spent per head on these items in wage-earners' families during the first decade of the twentieth century.

One fact alone is almost sufficient to prove the inadequacy of a labourer's wage for the maintenance of his family. His money wages seldom exceeded the estimated cost of his own meat and drink as supplied by the farmer, and yet these wages were to supply all the necessaries of life for his whole family. Some idea of the bare cost of living in a humble household may be gained by the rates fixed for pensions and by allowances made for Poor Relief. From these it appears that four shillings to five shillings a week was considered necessary for an adult's maintenance.

The Cromwell family paid four shillings weekly " to the widd. Bottom for her bord."[1] Pensions for maimed soldiers and widows were fixed at four shillings per week " or else work to be provided which will make their income up to 4s. per week. Sick and wounded soldiers under cure for their wounds to have 4s. 8d per week."[2]

---

or blood-pudens, or a hagish, or what is most convenient. Breakfast and super, ha an oat loaf or a proportion of broun bread, but better set down the loaf, and see non is taken or wasted, and a muchkin of beer or milk whenever there is any. At dinner a mutchkin of beer for each. *Baillie (Lady Grisell). Household Book* pp. 277-8. 1743.

[1] *Cromwell Family, Bills and Receipts*, Vol. II., p. 233, 1635.

[2] *Acts and Ordinances of the Interregnum*, II., p. 556. (For Maimed Soldiers and Widows of Scotland and Ireland, Sept 30, 1651.

The Justices in the North Riding of Yorkshire drew up a scale of reasonable prices for billeted soldiers by which each trooper was to pay for his own meat for each night—6d ; dragoon, 4½d ; foot soldier, 4d.[1]

" Edward Malin, blacksmith, now fourscore and three past and his wife fourscore, wanting a quarter " very poor and unable " to gett anything whereby to live," complained to the Hertfordshire Quarter Sessions that they receive only 1s. 6d. a week between them ; " others have eighteen pence apiece single persons " and desire that an order be made for them to have 3s. together which is but the allowance made to other persons.[2]

In cases of Poor Relief where payments were generally intended to be supplementary to other sources of income, the grants to widows towards the maintenance of their children were often absurdly small ; In Yorkshire, Parish officers were ordered to " provide convenient habitation for a poor woman as they shall think fit and pay her 4d. weekly for the maintenance of herself and child."[3] In another case to pay a very poor widow 6d. weekly for the maintenance of herself and her three children.[4] The allowance of 12d. weekly to a woman and her small children was reduced to 6d., " because the said woman is of able body, and other of her children are able to work."[5] On the other hand when an orphan child was given to strangers to bring up, amounts varying from 1s. to 5s. per week were paid for its maintenance.[6]

---

[1] *Yorks. North Riding,* Q. S. Rec., Vol. VII., p. 106, 1690.

[2] *Hertfordshire, Co. Rec.,* Vol. I., p. 258, 1675.

[3] *Yorks. N.R. Q.S. Rec.,* Vol. VI., p. 242, 1675.

[4] *Ibid,* p. 217, 1674.

[5] *Ibid,* p. 260, 1674

[6] Joane Weekes . . . " hadd a maide childe placed to her to bee kept & brought upp, the mother of which Childe was executed at the Assizes, six pounds per ann, proporconed toward the keepinge of the said childe . . . besides she

Thus the amount paid by the Justices for maintaining one pauper child sometimes exceeded the total earnings of a labourer and his wife. Other pauper children were maintained in institutions. The girls at a particularly successful Industrial School in Bristol were given an excellent and abundant diet

---

desireth some allowance extraordinary for bringinge the said Childe to bee fitt to gett her livinge." (*Somerset, Q.S. Rec.*, Vol. III, p. 28-9, 1647).

In 1663 a woman who was committed to the Castle of Yorke for felony and afterwards executed, was while there delivered of a male child, which was left in the gaol, and as it was not known where the woman was last an inhabitant the child could not be sent to the place of her settlement, Sir Tho. Gower was desired by Justices of Assize to take a course for present maintenance of the child. He caused it to be put unto the wife of John Boswell to be nursed and provided for with other necessaries. John Boswell and his wife have maintained the child ever since and have hitherto received no manner of allowance for the same. Ordered that the several Ridings shall pay their proportions to the maintenance past and present, after the rate of £5 per annum. (*Yorks. N.R. Q.S.Rec.*, Vol. VI, pp. 102-3, 1666.)

Marmaduke Vye was only to have £4 a year for keeping the child born in the gaol of Ivelchester whose mother was hanged for cutting of purses. (*Somerset Q.S. Rec.*, Vol. I, p. 101., 1613.)

Item payd to the said widowe Elkyns for Dyett and keeping of a poore child leafte upon the chardge of the parish at 11d. the weecke from the 14th of August, 1599, till this secound of Sept., 1601, every Saturday, being two yeres and three weeckes, videlicet 107 weeckes in toto v^li vij^s. (*Ch. Accs., St. Michael's in Bedwendine, Worcester*, p. 147.)

Itm pd. to Batrome's wife of Linstead for keeping of Wright's child 52 weeks £3. os. 8d. (Cratfield *Parish Papers*, p. 129, 1602.)

Pd to Geo. Cole to take and bring up Eliz. Wright, the daughter of Ann Wright according to his bond, £4. os. od. More towards her apparell 5s. (*Ibid*, p. 137. 1609.)

Item paide Chart's Child's keeping by the week £4. 11s. 8d. Item for apparrell £1. 18s. 2d. Item paid to the surgeon for her. 3s. 6d. (*Suss. Arch. Coll.*, Vol. xx., p. 101, *Acct. Bk of Cowden.* 1627.)

for apparrelling Wm. Uridge and for his keeping this yeare £5. 12s. 9d. (*Ibid*, p. 103, 1632.)

For the keep of William Kemsing 14 weeks £1. 2s.8d and 23 weeks at 2s per week, £2. 6s. od. and for apparrelling of him; and for his indentures; and for money given with him to put him out apprentice; and expended in placing him out £11. 17s. 9d. (*Ibid*, p. 107, 1650.)

John Mercies wief for keeping Buckles child, weekly,	1s. 6d.
John Albaes wief for keeping Partickes child	1s. 4d.

(*S.P.D.* cccxlvii, 67, 1. Feb, 1637. Answer of Churchwardens to Articles given by J.P's for St. Albans).

George Arnold and Jas. Michell late overseers of the poore of the parishe of Othery . . . had committed a poore child to the custody, keepinge and maintenance of . . . Robert Harris promising him xijd. weekly. (*Somerset, Q.S. Rec.*, Vol. III, p. 1, 1646.) Order for Thos. Scott, a poor, lame, impotent child, to be placed with Joanna Brandon; She to be paid 5s. a week for his maintenance. (*Middlesex Co. Rec.*, p. 180, *Sess. Book*, 1698).

at a cost of 1s. 4d. per head per week.[1] At Stepney, the poor were maintained at 2s. 10d or 3s. per week, including all incidental expenses, firing and lodging. At Strood in Kent, 2s. was paid for children boarded out in poor families, while the inmates of the workhouse at Hanstope, Bucks, were supposed not to cost the parish more than 1s. 6d. a week per head.[2] At Reading it was agreed " that Clayton's wief shall have xiiiid. a weeke for every poore childe in the hospitall accomptinge each childe's worke in parte of payment.[3]

These and many other similar figures show that a child must have cost from 1s. to 1s. 6d. a week for food alone, the amount varying according to age. Above seven years of age, children began to contribute towards their own support, but they were not completely self-supporting before the age of thirteen or fourteen.

According to the wages assessments, a woman's diet was reckoned at a lower figure than a man's, but whenever they are engaged on heavy work such as reaping corn or shearing sheep, 6d. or 8d. a day is allowed for their " meate and drinke." On other work, such as weeding or spinning, where only 2d. a day is reckoned for wages, their food also is only estimated as costing 2d. to 4d. As in such cases they are classed with " other impotent persons " it must not be supposed that 2d. or 3d. represents the cost of the food needed by a young active woman ; it may even have been prolonged semi-starvation that had reduced the woman to the level of impotency. Unfortunately, there is often a wide difference between the cost of what a woman actually eats and what is necessary to

---

[1] Cary, *Acc. Proceedings of the Corporation of Bristol.* 1700. "Their diets were made up of such provisions as were very wholesome, viz. Beef, Pease, Potatoes, Broath, Pease-porridge, Milk-porridge, Bread and Cheese, good Beer, Cabage, Carrots, Turnips, etc. it stood us (with soap to wash) in about sixteen pence per week for each of the one hundred girls."

[2] *Account Workhouses,* 1725, p. 13, p. 37, p. 79.

[3] Guilding, *Reading,* Vol. II., p. 273, Jan. 16, 1625-6.

maintain her in efficiency. Probably the woman who was doing ordinary work while pregnant or suckling a baby may have needed as much food as the woman who was reaping corn ; but in the wage-earner's family she certainly did not get it ; thus when a writer[1] alleges that a man's diet costs 5d. a day and a woman's 1s. 6d per week, his statement may be correct as to fact, though the babies have perished for want of nourishment and the mother has been reduced to invalidism.

Another writer gives 2s. as being sufficient to " keep a poor man or woman (with good husbandry) one whole week."[2] Certainly 2s. is the very lowest figure that can have sufficed to keep up the mother's strength. The bare cost of food for a mother and three children must have amounted to at least 5s. 6d. per week, but there were other necessaries to be provided from the scanty wages. The poorest family required some clothes, and though these may have been given by charitable persons, rent remained to be paid. Building was cheap. In Scotland, the " new house " with windows glazed with " ches losens " only cost £4 12s. 3d. to build, while a " cothouse " built for Liddas " the merchant " cost only £1 0 0 ;[3] other cots were built for 4s., 11s. 1d, 5s. and 14s. 4d. These Scottish dwellings were mud hovels, but in England the labourers' dwellings were not much better.

Celia Fiennes describes the houses at the Land's End as being " poor Cottages, Like Barns to Look on, much Like those in Scotland, but to doe my own country its right ye Inside of their Little Cottages are Clean and plaister'd and such as you might Comfortably Eat and drink in, and for curiosity sake I dranck there and met with very good bottled ale."[4]

[1] Dunning, R. *Plain and Easie Method*, p. 5, 1686.
[2] *Trade of England*, p. 10, 1681.
[3] Baillie (Lady Grisel), *House Book*, Introd. lxiv.
[4] Fiennes (Celia), *Through England on a Side-saddle*, p. 224.

In some places the labourers made themselves habitations on the waste, but this was strictly against the law, such houses being only allowed for the impotent poor.

Many fines are entered in Quarter Sessions Records for building houses without the necessary quantity of land. By 39 Eliz. churchwardens and overseers were ordered, for the relief of the impotent poor, to build convenient houses at the charges of the Parish, but only with the consent of the Lord of the Manor. 43 Eliz. added that such buildings were not at any time after to be used for other inhabitants but only for the impotent poor, placed there by churchwardens and overseers.

The housing problem was so acute that many orders were made by the justices sanctioning or ordering the erection of these cottages. " Rob. Thompson of Brompton and Eliz. Thompson of Aymonderby widow, stand indicted for building a cottage in Aymonderby against the statute, etc., upon a piece of ground, parcell of the Rectorie of Appleton-on-the-street, and in which the said Eliz. doth dwell by the permission of John Heslerton, fermour of the said Rectorie, and that the same was so erected for the habitation of the said Eliz[th]. being a poore old woman and otherwise destitute of harbour and succour . . ordered that the said cottage shall continue . . for the space of twelve yeares, if the said Eliz[th]. live so long, or that the said Heslerton's lease do so long endure."[1]   In another case, Nicholas Russell, the wife of Thomas Waterton, and Robert Arundell, were presented for erecting cottages upon the Lord's waste . . . at the suit of parishioners these cottages are allowed by Mr. Coningsby, lord of the manor.[2]

It was often necessary to compel unwilling over-

---

[1] *Yorks. N.R. Q.S. Rec.*, Vol. I., p. 29. 1605-6.

Hertfordshire Co. Rec., Vol. I., p. 63, 1639,-41.

seers to build cottages for the impotent poor, and for widows. " A woman with three children prays leave for the erection of a cottage in East Bedwyn, she having no habitation, but depending upon alms ; from lying in the street she was conveyed into the church where she remained some small time, but was then ejected by the parish." The overseers are ordered to provide for her.[1]

The overseers at Shipley were ordered to build a house on the waste there for Archelaus Braylsford, to contain " two chambers floored fit for lodgings " or in default 5s. a week. At the following sessions his house was further ordered to be " a convenient habitation 12 feet high upon the side walls soe as to make 2 convenient chambers."[2]

The housing problem however could not be settled by orders instructing the overseers to build cottages

---

[1] *Hist., MSS. Com. Var. Coll.*, Vol. I, p. 113, *Wilts. Q.S.Rec.* 1646.

[2] Cox. *Derbyshire Annals*, Vol. II, p. 176, 1693.
The following cases are representative of an immense number of petitions from widows and the impotent poor :

1608. Margaret Johns having dwelt in Naunton Beauchamp for 55 years has now no house or room but dwells in a barn, she desires to have house room and will not charge the parish so long as she is able to work.

1620. Eleanor Williams charged with keeping of young child is now unprovided with house room for herself and her poor child, her husband having left the soile where they lately dwelled and is gone to some place to her unknown. She is willing " to relieve her child by her painful labour but wanteth a place for abode " prays to be provided with house room.
(Bund, J. W. Willis, *Worcestershire Co. Records*, Vol. I., pp. 116-7, 337).

1621. Overseers of Uggliebarbie to provide a suitable dwelling for 2 women (sisters) if they refuse them a warrant, etc. (*Yorks. North Riding Q.S. Recs.*, Vol. III., p. 118.)

1672. Parish Officers of Scruton to provide a convenient habitation for Mary Hutchinson and to set her on work, and provide for her, etc., until she shall recover the possession of certain lands in Scruton. (*Ibid*, Vol. VI., p. 175).

1684. Mary Marchant . . . livinge in good estimation And repute for many years together ; being very Carefull to maintaine herself And family for being prejudice to ye sd. Towne ; ye petitioners husbande beinge abroad and driven Away ; and returninge not backe Againe to her leaveinge ye petitioner with a little girle ; being In want was put into a little cottage by & with ye consent of ye sd. Towne ; ye sd. Owner of ye sd. Tenement comeinge when ye petitioner was gon forth to worke leavinge her little girle in ye sd. house ; ye sd. Owner get a locke And Key upp on ye door, where as your petitioner cannot Injoy her habitation wth peace and quietness ; soe yt your petitioner is likely to starve for want of A habitation and child, etc.
(Cox. J. C., *Derbyshire Annals*, Vol. II., pp. 175-6, *Q.S. Recs.*, 1684).

for the impotent poor alone. Petitions were received as often from able-bodied labourers and for them the law forbade the erection of a cottage without four acres of land attached. The magistrates had no power to compel the provision of the land and thus they were faced with the alternatives of breaking the law and sanctioning the erection of a landless cottage on the waste or else leaving the labourer's family to lie under hedges. The following petitions illustrate the way in which this situation was faced :

George Grinham, Norton-under-Hambton, " in ye behalfe of himselfe, his poore wife and famelye " begged for permission " for my building y^{er}, of a little poor house for ye comfort of my selfe, my poore wife and children betwixt those other 2 poore houses erected on the glebe . . . being a towne borne childe y^{er} myselfe."[1]

Another from William Dench, " a very poor man and having a wife and seven children all born at Longdon," who was destitute of any habitation, states that he was given by William Parsons of Longdon, yeoman, in charity, " a little sheep-cote which sheep cote petitioner, with the consent of the church-wardens and overseers converted to a dwelling. After-wards he having no licence from Quarter Sessions, nor under the hands of the Lord of the Manor so to do, and the sheepcote being on the yeoman's freehold and not on the waste or common, contrary to Acts 43 Eliz. c. 2 and 31 Eliz. c. 7 he was indicted upon the Statute against cottages and sued to an outlawry. He prays the benefit of the King's pardon and for licence in open session for continuance of his habitation." [2]

Eliz. Shepperd of Windley alleged she " was in possession of a Certayne cottage situate in Chevin, which was pulled downe and taken away by the

---

[1] *Somerset, Q.S. Rec.*, Vol. I., p. 41, 1609.

[2] *Hist. MSS. Com. Var. Coll.*, Vol. I., p. 296, *Worcestershire, Q.S. Rec.*, 1617.

Inhabitants of Dooeffield, shee left without habitation and hath soe Continued Twelve months at the least, shee being borne in Windley, and hath two small children" prayed the inhabitants should find her a homestead—the case was adjourned because the overseers raised a technical objection ; that Eliz. Shepherd was married, & a woman's petition could only proceed from a spinster or widow—meanwhile another child was born, and at the Michaelmas Sessions a joint petition was presented by Ralph Shepherd and Eliz. his wife, with the result that " the overseers are to find him habitation or show cause."[1]

Joseph Lange of Queene Camell " being an honest poore laborer and havinge a wife and 2 smale Children " prayed that he " might haue libertie to erect a Cottage uppon a wast ground " . . . This was assented to " for the habitacon of himselfe for his wife and afterwards the same shall be converted to the use of such other poore people etc."

Order that Robert Morris of Overstowey, husbandman, a very poor man having a wife and children, and no place of habitation " soe that hee is like to fall into greate misery for want thereof " may erect and build him a cottage on some part of the " wast " of the manor of Overstowey . . . (subject to the approbation of the Lord of the said Manor)."[2]

The predicament of married labourers is shown again in the following report to the Hertfordshire Quarterly Sessions : " John Hawkins hath erected a cottage on the waste of my mannour of Benington, in consideration of the great charge of his wife and children that the said Hawkins is to provide for, I do hereby grant and give leave to him to continue the said cottage during his life and good behaviour."[3]

---

[1] Cox, J. C. *Derbyshire Annals*, Vol. II., pp. 173-4, 1649.

[2] *Somerset Q.S. Rec.*, Vol. III., pp. 29, 58.

[3] *Hertford Co. Rec.*, Vol. I., p. 100, 1652.

Labourers naturally were unwilling to hire cottages
while there was a possibility of inducing the justices to
provide one on the waste rent free. The churchwardens of Great Wymondley forwarded a certificate
stating " that the poor people of the said parish that are
old and not able to work are all provided for and none
of the poor people of the said parish have been driven
to wander into other unions to beg or ask relief, for this
thirty years last past. This Nathaniel Thrussel,
which now complains, is a lusty young man, able to
work and always brought up to husbandry, his wife,
a young woman, always brought up to work, and know
both how to perform their work they are hired to
do, and have at present but one child, but did not care
to pay rent for a hired house when he had one nor
endeavour to hire a house for himself when he wants."[1]

The scarcity of cottages resulted in extortionate
rents for those that existed ; Best noted that in his
district " Mary Goodale and Richard Miller have a
cottage betwixt them ; Mary Goodale hath two roomes,
and the orchard and payeth 6s. per annum ; and
Richard Miller, hayth one roomestead and payeth 4s.
per annum. . . . They usually lette their cottages
hereaboutes, for 10s. a piece, although they have not
soe much as a yard, or any backe side belonging to
them."[2]

The rents paid elsewhere are shown in the returns
made in 1635 by the Justices of the Peace for the
Hundreds of Blofield and Walsham in Norfolk concerning cottages and inmates :

Thos. Waters hath 3 inmates :

  Wm. Wyley pays £1. per annum
  Anthony Smith ,, £1. per annum
  Roger Goat ,, 12s. per annum

" which are all poore labourers and have wifes and

---

[1] *Hertford Co. Rec.*, Vol. I., p. 370, 1687.

[2] Best, *Rural Econ.*, p. 125.

severall children and if they be put out cannot be provided in this towne and by reason of their charge and poverty are not likely to be taken elsewhere."

" Wm. Browne hath 2 inmates :

Edmund Pitt	14s. per annum
Wm. Jostling	14s. per annum

that are very poor and impotent and take colleccion.

Wm. Reynoldes hath 2 inmates :

Anthony Durrant	£1 16s. per annum
Wm. Yurely	16s. per annum

both are very poore labourers and have wifes and small children. Jas. Candle owner of a cottage [has] Robert Fenn, 13s. a poore man. Anne Linckhorne 1 inmate Philip Blunt that pay £1. 17. 0 that is a poore man and hath wife and children."[1]

Thus it appears that while a labourer who obtained a cottage on the waste lived rent free, twenty or thirty shillings might be demanded from those who were less fortunate.

Whatever money was extorted for rent meant so much less food for the mother and children, for it has been shown that the family income was insufficient for food alone, and left no margin for rent or clothes.

The relation of wages to the cost of living is seldom alluded to by contemporary writers, but a pamphlet published in 1706 says of a labourer's family, " a poor Man and his Wife may have 4 or 5 children, 2 of them able to work, and 3 not able, and the Father and Mother not able to maintain themselves and Families in Meat, Drink, Cloaths and House Rent under 10s. a week."[2]

A similar statement is made by Sir Matthew Hale, who adds " and so much they might probably get if employed." [3] But no evidence has been found from

---

[1] *S.P.D.*, cccx., 104. 1635. Returns made by Justices of the Peace.

[2] Haynes, (John.), *Present State of Clothing*, p. 5. 1706.

[3] Hale, (Sir Matt). *Discourse touching Provision for the Poor*, p. 6, 1683

which we can imagine that an agricultural labourer's family could possibly earn as much as 10s. a week in the seventeenth century. Our lower estimate is confirmed by a report made by the Justices of the Peace for the half hundred of Hitching concerning the poor in their district ; "when they have worke the wages geven them is soe small that it hardlye sufficeth to buy the poore man and his familye breed, for they pay 6s. for one bushell of mycelyn grayne and receive but 8d. for their days work. It is not possible to procure mayntenance for all these poore people and their famylyes by almes nor yet by taxes."[1]

The insolvency of the wage-earning class is recognized by Gregory King in his calculations of the income and expense of the several Families of England, for the year 1680. All other classes, including artisans and handicrafts show a balance of income over expenditure but the families of seamen, labourers and soldiers show an actual yearly deficit.[2]

A still more convincing proof of the universal destitution of wage earners is shown in the efforts made by churchwardens and overseers in every county throughout England to prevent the settlement within the borders of their parish of families which depended solely on wages.

Their objection is not based generally upon the ground that the labourer or his wife were infirm, or idle, or vicious ; they merely state that the family is likely to become chargeable to the parish. Each parish was responsible for the maintenance of its own

---

[1] *S.P.D.* ccclxxxv., 43. Mar. 8, 1638.

[2] King (Gregory). *Nat. and Political Observations*, pp. 48-9.

NO. OF FAMILIES.	PERSONS.	YEARLY INCOME PER HEAD.	EXPENSE PER HEAD.	LOSS PER HEAD
50,000 Common Seamen	150,000	£7.	£7. 10s.	10s.
364,000 Labouring people & outservants	1,275,000	£4. 10s.	£4. 12s.	2s.
400,000 Cottagers & Paupers	1,300,000	£2.	£2. 5s.	5s.
35,000 Common soldiers	70,000	£7.	£7. 10s.	10s.

poor, and thus though farmers might be needing more labourers, the parish would not tolerate the settlement of families which could not be self-supporting.

The disputes which arose concerning these settlements contain many pitiful stories.

" Anthony addams " tells the justices that he was born in Stockton and bred up in the same Parish, most of his time in service and has " taken great pains for my living all my time since I was able and of late I fortuned to marry with an honest young woman, and my parishioners not willing I should· bring her in the parish, saying we should breed a charge amongst them. Then I took a house in Bewdley and there my wife doth yet dwell and I myself do work in Stockton . . . and send or bring my wife the best relief I am able, and now the parish of Bewdley will not suffer her to dwell there for doubt of further charge. . . . I most humbly crave your good aid and help in this my distress or else my poor wife and child are like to perish without the doors : . . . that by your good help and order to the parish of Stockton I may have a house there to bring my wife & child unto that I may help them the best I can."[1]

Another petition was brought by Josias Stone of Kilmington . . . " shewinge that he hath binn an Inhabitant and yet is in Kilmington aforesaid and hath there continued to and fro these five yeares past and hath donn service for the said parishe and hath lately married a wife in the said parish intendinge there to liue and reside yet since his marriage is by the said parishe debarred of any abidinge for him and his said wife there in any howse or lodginge for his mony."[2]

Another dispute occurred over the case of Zachary Wannell and his wife who came lately from Wilton " into the towne of Taunton where they haue been

---

[1] *Hist. MSS. Com. Var. Coll.*, Vol. I., p. 298, *Worcestershire Q.S. Rec.*, 1618.

[2] *Somerset, Q.S. Rec.*, Vol. III., p. 15, 1647.

denyed a residence and they ly upp and downe in barnes and hay lofts, the said Wannell's wife being great with child; the said Wannell and his wife to be forthwith set to Wilton and there to continue until the next General Sessions. The being of the said Wannell and his wife at Wilton not to be interpreted as a settlement of them there."[1]

There were endless examples of these conflicts often attended as in the above case with great cruelty.[2]

---

[1] *Somerset Q.S. Rec.*, Vol. III., p. 246, 1654.

[2] One Humfrey Naysh, a poore man hath ben remayning and dwellinge within the pish of Newton St. Lowe by the space of five years or thereabouts and now being maryed and like to haue charge of children, the pishioners Do endeuor to put the said Naishe out of their pish by setting of amcents and paynes in their Courts on such as shall give him house-roome, or suffer him to liue in their houses which he doth or offereth to rent for his money which the court conceiveth to be vnjust and not accordinge to lawe." Overseers ordered to provide him a house for his money. *Ibid.*, Vol. II, p. 19, 1626.)

The petition of the "overseer of the poore of the parishe of East Quantoxhead . . . that one Richard Kamplyn late of Kilve with his wife and three small children are late come as Inmates into the Parish of East Quantoxhead which may hereafter become very burdensome and chargeable to the said parish if tymley prevention bee not taken therein." *Ibid.*, Vol. III, p. 9, 1646.

"John Tankens, his wife and three children . . . had lived twoe yeares in Chewstoake undisturbed and from thence came to Chew Magna and there took part of a Cottage for their habitation for one yeare . . . whereof the parishe of Chew Magna taking notice found themselves aggrieved thereatt, and brought the same in question both before the next Justice of the peace of Chew Magna and att the Leete or Lawday, and yett neither the said Tankens, his wife or children, had beene actually chardgeable to the said parishe of Chew Magna. This Court in that respect thinketh not fitt to disturbe the said Tankens, his wife or children duringe the said terme, but doth leave them to thend of the same terme to bee settled accordinge by lawe they ought. And because the parishioners of Chew Magna haue been for the most parte of the tyme since the said Tankens, his wife and Children came to Chew Magna complayninge against them, This court doth declare that the beinge of them att Chew Magna aforesaid duringe the said terme shall not bee interpreted to bee a settlement there. (*Ibid.*, Vol. III, pp. 94-5, 1649).

"Pet. of Richard Cookesley of Ashbrettle shewing that he is married in the said parish and the said parish endeavour to haue him removed from thence although hee is no way chargeable, this court doth see noe cause but that the said Cookesley may remaine att Ashbrittle aforesaid; provided that his being there shall not be interpretted to bee a settlement of him there." (*Ibid.*, Vol. III., p. 248, 1654).

James Hurde a poor labourer stated that for these two years last past he had dwelt in the parish of Westernemore "In a house wch he hired for his monie" and had taken great pains to maintain himself, his wife and two children, wherewith he never yet charged the said parish nor hopeth ever to do. And yet the parishioners and church-wardens there, do "indeavour" and threaten to turn him out of the parish unless he will put in sufficient sureties not to charge the said parish which he cannot by reason he is but a poor labourer; he humbly requests that he may quietly inhabit in the said parish so long as he doth not charge the same, otherwise he and his family are like to perish. (*Ibid.*, Vol. I, p. 94, 1612.)

The Justices were shocked at the consequent demoralization and generally supported the demands of the labourers as regards their settlement and housing. One writes to the clerk of the Peace : " I have sent you enclosed the recognizance of William Worster and William Smith, of Bovindon, for contempt of an order of sessions . . . in the behalfe of one, John Yorke, formerly a vagrant, but now parishionir of Bovingdon. Yet I believe the rest of the inhabitants will doe their utmost to gett him thence though they force him to turn vagrant againe. Yorke will be with you to prove that he was in the parish halfe-a-year or more before they gave him any disturbance, and that not privately, for he worked for severall substantiall men and was at church, and paid rent."[1]

But the Justices never suspected that the rate of wages which they themselves had fixed below subsistence level was at the root of the settlement difficulty. The overseers believed that all the troubles might be solved if only young people would not marry imprudently, and they petitioned the Justices begging that overseers of parishes might not be compelled to provide houses for such young persons " as will marry before they have provided themselves with a settling."[2]

While the overseers were seeking to exclude all wage earners from the parish, individual farmers, perchance the overseers themselves wanted more labourers. To meet this difficulty, the overseers discovered an ingenious device. Before granting a settlement, they required the labourer to find sureties to save the parish harmless from his becoming chargeable to it. Obviously a labourer could not himself find sureties, but the farmer who wished to employ him was in a position to do so, and thus the responsibility for the wage-earner's family would be laid upon the person who profited

---

[1] *Hertford Co. Rec.*, Vol. I., p. 321. 1681. Letter from Francis Leigh to Clerk of Peace.

[2] *Hist. MSS. Com, Var. Coll.* Vol. I., p. 322 *Worcestershire Q. S. Rec.*, 1661.

by his services. Petitions against this demand for sureties came before the Quarter Sessions. One from Robert Vawter stated that he was " a poore Day labourer about a quarter of a yere sithence came into the said parish of Clutton, and there marryed with a poore Almesmans Daughter, now liveing with her said father in the Almeshouse of Clutton aforesaid, and would there settle himselfe with his said wife." He was ordered to find sureties or to go to gaol.[1]

It was reported at Salford " Whereas Rich. Hudson is come lately into the towne with his wife and ffoure children to Remaine that the Burrow-reeve and Constables of this towne shall give notice unto Henry Wrigley, Esq., upon whose land he still remaynes that hee remove him and his wife and children out of this Towne within this moneth unlesse hee give sufficient security upon the paine of ffive pounds."[2]

Similar orders were made re Nathan Cauliffe, his wife and three children, Robert Billingham with wife and two children, Peter ffarrant and his wife, & Roger Marland and wife. Later the record continues, " and yet the said parties are not removed " order was therefore made " that this order shalbee put in execution."[3] Another step in the proceedings is recorded in the entry, " Whereas James Moores, George Moores and Adam Warmeingham stand bound unto Henry Wrigling Esq. in £20 for the secureinge the Towne from any poverty or disability which should or might befall unto the said James, his wife, children, or family or any of them. And whereas it appeares that the said James Moores hath been Chargeable whereby the said bond is become forfeit yet this Jury doth give the said George Moores and Adam Warmeingham this

[1] *Somerset Q.S. Rec.*, Vol. II., p. 292, 1637-8.

[2] *Salford Portmote Records*, Vol. II., p. 144, 1655.

[3] *Ibid.*, p. 151, 1656.

libtie that the said James shall remove out of this towne before the next Court Leet."[1]

Fines were exacted from thóse who harboured unfortunate strangers without having first given security for them, and no exception was made on the score of relationship. James Meeke of Myddleton was presented " for keeping of his daughter Ellen Meeke, having a husband dwelling in another place, and having two children borne forth of the parishe."[2]

Rules made at Steeple Ashton by the Churchwardens declare : " There hath much povertie happened unto this p'ish by receiving of strangers to inhabit there and not first securing them ag'st such contingencies and avoyding the like occasions in tyme to come, It is ordered by this vestrie that ev'ry p'son or p'sons whatsoev'r w'ch shall lett or sett any houseinge or dwellinge to any stranger and shall not first give good securite for defending and saving harmeless the said inhabitants from the future charge as may happen by such stranger comeing to inhabite w'thin the said p'ish and if any p'son shall doe to the contrary Its agreed that such p'son soe receiving such stranger shal be rated to the poor to 20s. monethlie over and above his monethlie tax."[3]

The penalties at Reading were higher. " At this daye Wm. Porter, th'elder was questioned for harboringe a straunger woman, and a childe, vizt, the wief of John Taplyn ; he worketh at Mr. Ed. Blagrave's in Early : Confesseth. The woman saith she hath byn there ever syns Michaellmas last, and payed rent to goodman Porter, xxs a yeare ; her kinsman Faringdon did take the house for them. Wm. Porter was required to paye xs a weeke according to the orders and was willed to ridd his tenant with all speed upon

---

[1] *Salford Portmote Rec.*, Vol. II., p. 150.

[2] *Yorks. N.R. Q.S. Rec.*, Vol. I., p. 170, 1609.

[3] *Wilts. Notes and Queries*, Vol. VII., p. 281, 1664.   *Churchwarden's Acct. Book. Steeple Ashton.*

payne of xs a weeke and to provide suretyes to discharge
the towne of the childe."[1]

The starvation and misery described in Quarter
Sessions Records were not exceptional calamities, but
represent the ordinary life of women in the wage
earning class. The lives of men were drab and
monotonous, lacking pleasure and consumed by
unending toil, but they did not often suffer hunger.
The labourer while employed was well fed, for the
farmer did not grudge him food, though he did not
wish to feed his family. There was seldom want of
employment for agricultural labourers, and when
their homes sank into depths of wretchedness and the
wife's attractiveness was lost through slow starvation,
the men could depart and begin life anew elsewhere.

The full misery of the labourer's lot was only felt
by the women ; if unencumbered they could have
returned, like the men, to the comfortable conditions
of service, but the cases of mothers who deserted their
children are rare.

The hardships suffered by the women of the wage-
earning class proved fatal to their children. Gregory
King estimated that there were on an average only 3½
persons, including father and mother in a labourer's
family though he gives 4.8 as the average number of
children for each family in villages and hamlets.[2]
Another writer gives 3 persons as the average
number for a labourer's family.[3] The cases of disputed
settlements which are brought before Quarter Sessions
confirm the substantial truth of these estimates. It
is remarkable that where the father is living seldom
more than two or three children are mentioned, often
only one, though in cases of widows where the poverty
is recent and caused as it were by the accidental effect of

---

[1] Guilding, *Reading Records*, Vol. II., p. 181, 1624.

[2] King (Gregory) *Natural and Political Observations and Conclusions*, p. 44,
pp. 48-9.

[3] *Grasier's Complaint*, p. 60.

the husband's premature death, there are often five to ten children. In Nottingham, of seventeen families, who had recently come to the town and been taken in as tenants, and which the Council wanted to eject for fear of overcrowding, only one had four children, one three, and the rest only two or one child apiece.[1]

In fact, however large the birth rate may have been, and this we have no means of ascertaining, few children in the wage-earning class were reared. Of those who reached maturity many were crippled in mind or body, forming a large class of unemployables destined to be a burthen instead of strength to the community.

This appalling loss and suffering was not due to the excessive work of married women but to their under-feeding and bad housing. Probably the women of the wage-earning class actually accomplished less work than the women of the husbandman class ; but the latter worked under better conditions and were well nourished, with the result that their sons and daughters have been the backbone of the English nation.

The sacrifice of the wage-earners' children was caused by the mother's starvation ; vainly she gave her own food to the children for then she was unable to suckle the baby and grew too feeble for her former work. Probably she had herself been the daughter of a husbandman and was inured to labour from child hood. " Sent abroad into service and hardship when but 10 years old " as Oliver Heywood wrote of a faithful servant, she met the chances which decide a servant's life. The work on farms was rough, but generally healthy. At first the child herded the pigs or the geese and followed the harrow and as she grew older the poultry yard and the cows divided her attention with the housework. Sometimes she was brutally treated and often received little training in

---

[1] *Nottingham, Records of the Borough of*, Vol. IV., pp. 312-5. 1613.

her work, but generosity in meat and drink has always been characteristic of the English farmer, and during the hungry years of adolescence the average girl who was a servant in husbandry was amply nourished. Then came marriage. The more provident waited long in the hope of securing independence, and one of those desirable cottages with four acres of land, but to some the prospect seemed endless and at last they married hoping something would turn up ; or perhaps they were carried away by natural impulses and married young without any thought for the future. Such folly was the despair of Churchwardens and Overseers, yet the folly need not seem so surprising when we consider that delay brought the young people no assurance of improvement in their position. Church and State alike taught that it was the duty of men and women to marry and bring forth children, and if for a large class the organisation of Society made it impossible for them to rear their children, who is to blame for the fate of those children, their parents or the community ?

After one of these imprudent marriages the husband sometimes continued to work on a farm as a servant, visiting his wife and children on Sundays and holidays. By this means he, at least, was well fed and well housed. The woman with a baby to care for and feed, could not leave her home every day to work and must share the children's food. In consequence she soon began to practise starvation. Her settlement was disputed, and therefore her dwelling was precarious. Nominally she was transferred on marriage to the parish where her husband was bound as servant for the term of one year, but the parish objected to the settlement of a married man lest his children became a burden on them.

No one doubted that it was somebody's duty to care for the poor, but arrangements for relief were strictly parochial and the fear of incurring unlimited future responsibilities led English parishioners to strange lengths of cruelty and callousness. The fact that a woman was soon to have a baby, instead of appealing to their chivalry, seemed to them the best reason for turning her out of her house and driving her from the village, even when a hedge was her only refuge.

The once lusty young woman who had formerly done a hard day's work with the men at harvesting was broken by this life. It is said of an army that it fights upon its stomach. These women faced the grim battle of life, laden with the heavy burden of child-bearing, seldom knowing what it meant to have enough to eat. Is it surprising that courage often failed and they sank into the spiritless, dismal ranks of miserable beings met in the pages of Quarter Sessions Records, who are constantly being forwarded from one parish to another.

Such women, enfeebled in mind and body, could not hope to earn more than the twopence a day and their food which is assessed as the maximum rate for women workers in the hay harvest. On the contrary, judging from the account books of the period, they often received only one penny a day for their labour. Significant of their feebleness is the Norfolk assessment which reads, " Women and such impotent persons that weed corne, or other such like Labourers 2d with meate and drinke, 6d without."[1] Such wages may have sufficed for the infirm and old, but they meant starvation for the woman with a young family depending on her for food. And what chance of health and virtue existed for the children of these enfeebled starving women ?

On the death or desertion of her husband the labouring woman became wholly dependent on the Parish for support.

---

[1] *Eng. Hist. Rev.*, Vol. xiii., p. 522.

The conduct of the magistrates in fixing maximum wages at a rate which they knew to be below subsistence level seems inexplicable ; is in fact inexplicable until it is understood that these wages were never intended to be sufficient for the support of a family. Statute 31 Eliz. and others, show that the whole influence of the Government and administration was directed to prevent the creation of a class of wage-earners. It was an essential feature of Tudor policy to foster the Yeomanry, from whose ranks were recruited the defenders of the realm. Husbandmen were recognised as " the body and stay " of the kingdom.[1] They made the best infantry when bred " not in a servile or indigent fashion, but in some free and plentiful manner."[2] If the depopulation of the country-side went on unchecked, there would come to pass " a mere sollitude and vtter desolation to the whole Realme, furnished only with shepe and shepherdes instead of good men ; wheareby it might be a prey to oure enymies that first would sett vppon it."[3]

Probably the consideration of whether a family could be fed by a labourer's wage, seldom entered the Justices' heads. They wished the family to win its food from a croft and regarded the wages as merely supplementary. The Justices would like to have exterminated wage-earners, who were an undesirable class in the community, and they might have succeeded as the conditions imposed upon the women made the rearing of children almost impossible, had not economic forces constantly recruited the ranks of wage-earners from the class above them.

The demands of capital however for labour already exceeded the supply available from the ranks of husbandmen, and could only be met by the establish-

---

[1] Lipson, *Economic Hist. of England*, p. 153.

[2] Bacon, *Works*, Vol. VI., p. 95.

[3] Lamond (Eliz.) *Discourse of the Common weal*, 1581.

ment of a class of persons depending wholly on wages. The strangest feature of the situation was the fact that the magistrates who were trying to exterminate wage-earners were often themselves capitalists creating the demand.

'The actual proportion of wage-earners in the seventeenth century can only be guessed at. The statement of a contemporary[1] that Labourers and Cottagers numbered 2,000,000 persons, out of a population of only 5,000,000 must be regarded as an exaggeration ; in any case their distribution was uneven.

Complaints are not infrequently brought before Quarter Sessions from parishes which say they are burdened with so great a charge of poor that they cannot support it ; to other parishes the Justices are sometimes driven to issue orders on the lines of a warrant commanding " the Churchwardens of the townes of Screwton and Aynderby to be more diligent in relieving their poore, that the court be not troubled with any further claymours therein."[2]

On the other hand there were many districts where the wage earner was hardly known and the authorities, like the Tithing men of Fisherton Delamere could report that they " have (thanks to the Almighty God theirfor) no popish recusants ; no occasion to levy twelvepence, for none for bear to repair to divine service; no inns or alehouses licensed or unlicensed, no drunken person, no unlawful weights or measures, no neglect of hues and cries, no roads out of repair, no wandering rogues or idle persons, and no inmates of whom they desire information."[3]   Or the Constable of Tredington who declared that " the poor are weekly relieved, felons none known. Recusants one Bridget Lyne, the

---

[1] *Grasier's Complaint*, p. 60.

[2] *Yorks. N.R. Q.S. Rec.*, Vol. I., p. 22-3, 1605.

[3] *Hist. MSS. Com.Var. Coll.*,Vol. I., p, 93. *Wilts Q.S. Rec.*, 1621. A similar detailed return was made from the Hundred of Wilton in 1691. Many often return ' omnia bene ' and the like in brief.

wife of Thos. Lyne. Tobacco none planted. Vagrants Mary How, an Irish woman and her sister were taken and punished according to the Statute and sent away by pass with a guide towards Ireland in the County of Cork."[1] or as in another report " We have no bakers or alehouses within our parish. We cannot find by our searches at night or other time that any rogues or vagabonds are harboured saving Mr. Edward Hall who lodged a poor woman and her daughter. We do not suffer any vagrants which we see begging in our parish but we give them punishment according as we ought."[2]

A review of the whole position of women in Agriculture at this time, shows the existence of Family Industry at its best, and of Capitalism at its worst. The smaller farmers and more prosperous husbandmen led a life of industry and independence in which every capacity of the women, mental, moral and physical had scope for development and in which they could secure the most favourable conditions for their children —while among capitalistic farmers a tendency can already be perceived for the women to withdraw from the management of business and devote themselves to pleasure. At the other end of the scale Capitalism fed the man whom it needed for the production of wealth but made no provision for his children; and the married woman, handicapped by her family ties, when she lost the economic position which enabled her through Family Industry to support herself and her children, became virtually a pauper.

---

[1] Bund (J. W. Willis) *Worcestershire Co. Rec.*, Vol. I., p. 564, 1634.

[2] *Ibid*, Vol. I, p. 571, 1634.

Chapter IV.

TEXTILES.

(A) *Introductory.* Historical importance in women's economic development —Predominance of women's labour—Significance in development of Industrialism—Low wages.

(B) *Woollen Trade.* Historical importance—Proportions of men and women employed—Early experiments in factory system abandoned—Declining employment of women in management and control—Women Weavers—Burling— Spinning—Organization of spinning industry—Women who bought wool and sold yarn made more profit than those who worked for wages—Methods of spinning—Class of women who span for wages—Rates of wages—Disputes between spinsters and employers—Demoralisation of seasons of depression— Association of men and women in trade disputes.

(C) *Linen.* Chiefly a domestic industry—Introduction of Capitalism—Increased demand caused by printing linens—Attempt to establish a company— Part taken by women—weaving—bleaching—spinning—Wages below subsistence level—Encouragement of spinning by local authorities to lessen poor relief—Firmin.

(D) *Silk. Gold and Silver.* Silk formerly a monopoly of gentlewomen—In seventeenth century virtually one of the pauper trades. Gold and Silver furnished employment to the poorest class of women—Factory system already in use.

(E) *Conclusion.*

FROM the general economic standpoint, the textile industries rank second in importance to agriculture during the seventeenth century, but in the history of women's economic development they hold a position which is quite unique. If the food supply of the country depended largely on the work of women in agriculture, their labour was absolutely indispensable to the textile industries, for in all ages and in all countries spinning has been a monopoly of women. This monopoly is so nearly universal that we may suspect some physiological inability on the part of men to spin a fine even thread at the requisite speed, and spinning forms the greater part of the labour in the production of hand-made textile fabrics.

It requires some effort of the imagination in this mechanical age to realize the incessant industry which the duty of clothing her own family imposed on every woman, to say nothing of the yarn required for the famous Woollen Trade. The service rendered by women in spinning for the community was compared by contemporaries to the service rendered by the men who ploughed. " Like men that would lay no hand to the plough, and women that would set no hand to the wheele, deserving the censure of wise Solomon, Hee that would not labour should not eat."[1]

Textile industries fall into three groups : Woollen, Linen, and Miscellaneous, comprising silk, etc. Cotton is seldom mentioned although imported at this time in small quantities for mixture with linen.

The predominance of women's labour in the textile trades makes their history specially significant in tracing the evolution of women's industrial position under the influences of capitalism ; for the woollen trade was one of the first fields in which capitalistic organization achieved conspicuous success.

The importance of the woollen trade as a source of revenue to the Crown drew to it so much attention that many details have been preserved concerning its development ; showing with a greater distinctness than in other and more obscure trades, the steps by which Capitalistic Organization ousted Family Industry and the Domestic Arts. It is surely not altogether accidental that Industrialism developed so remarkably in two trades where the labour of women predominated —in the woollen trade which in the seventeenth century was already organized on capitalistic lines, and, one hundred years later, in the cotton trade.

Some characteristic features of modern Industrialism were absent from the woollen trade in the seventeenth century. The work of men and women alike was carried

---

[1] *Declaration of the Estate of Clothing*, p. 2, 1613.

on chiefly at home, and thus the employment of married
women and children was unimpeded ; nor are there any
signs of industrial jealousy between men and women,
who on the contrary, stand by each other during this
period in all trade disputes. Nevertheless, the position
of the woman wage-earner in the textile trades was
extraordinarily bad, and this in spite of the fact that
the demand for her labour appears nearly always to
have exceeded the supply. The evidence contained in
the following chapter shows that the wages paid to
women in the seventeenth century for spinning linen
were insufficient, and those paid for spinning wool,
barely sufficient, for their individual maintenance, and
yet out of them women were expected to support, or
partly support, their children.

Possibly the persistence of such low wages throughout
the country was due in a measure to the convenience
of spinning as a tertiary occupation for married
women. She who was employed by day in the inter-
vals of household duties with her husband's business
or her dairy and garden, could spin through the long
winter evenings when the light was too bad for other
work. The mechanical character of the movements,
and the small demand they make on eye or thought,
renders spinning wonderfully adapted to women whose
serious attention is engrossed by the care or training
of their children. A comparison of spinster's wages
with those of agricultural labourers, which were also
below subsistence level, will show however that such
an explanation does not altogether meet the cse.

The fact is that far from underselling the spinsters[1]
who were wholly dependent on wages for their living,
it seems probable that the women who only span for
sale after the needs of their own households had been
supplied, received the highest rates of pay, just as the
husbandman, who only worked occasionally for wages,

---

[1] Spinster in the seventeenth century is used in its technical sense and refers
equally to women who are married, unmarried or widows.

was paid better than the labourer who worked for them all the year round, and whose family depended exclusively on him. Disorganization and lack of bargaining power, coupled with traditions founded upon an earlier social organization, were responsible for the low wages of the spinsters. The agricultural labourer was crippled in his individual efforts for a decent wage because society persisted in regarding him as a household servant. The spinster was handicapped because in a society which began to assert the individual's right to freedom, she had from her infancy been trained to subjection.

It must however be remembered that though a large part of the ensuing chapter is concerned with spinsters and their wages, much, perhaps most, of the thread spun never came into the market, but was produced for domestic consumption. Thus we find all three forms of industrial organisation existing simultaneously in these trades—Domestic Industry, Family Industry, and Capitalistic Industry.

Domestic Industry lingered especially in the Linen Trade until machinery made the spinning wheel obsolete, and Family Industry was still extensively practised in the seventeenth century; but Capitalistic Industry, already established in the Woollen Trade, was making rapid inroads on the other branches of the Textile Trades.

Although Capitalism undermined the position of considerable economic independence enjoyed by married women and widows in the tradesman and farming classes, possibly its intoduction may have improved the position of unmarried women, and others who were already dependent on wages; but such improvements belong to a later date. Their only indication in the seventeenth century is the clearly proved fact that wages for spinning were higher in the more thoroughly capitalistic woollen trade, than in the linen trade. Further evidence is a suggestion by Defoe that wages for spinning in the woollen trade were doubled, or even trebled, in the first decade of the eighteenth century, but no sign of this advance can be detected in our period.

(B.) *Woollen Trade*.

The interest of the Government and of all those who studied financial and economic questions, was focussed upon the Woollen Trade, owing to the fact that it formed one of the chief sources of revenue for the Crown. At the close of the seventeenth century woollen goods formed a third of the English exports.[1]

Historically the Woollen Trade has a further importance, due to the part which it played in the development of capitalism. The manufacture of woollen materials had existed in the remote past as a family industry, and even in the twentieth century this method still survives in the remoter parts of the British Isles ; but the manufacture of cloth for Foreign trade was from its beginning organized on Capitalistic lines, and the copious records which have been preserved of its development, illustrate the history of Capitalism itself.

It was estimated that about one million men, women and children were exclusively employed in the clothing trade,—" all have their dependence solely and wholly upon the said *Manufacture*, without intermixing themselves in the labours of *Hedging*, *Ditching*, *Quicksetting*, and others the works belonging to Husbandry."[2]

In 1612 eight thousand persons, men, women and

---

[1] Davenant (Inspector-General of Exports and Imports). *An account of the trade between Greate Britain, France, Holland, Spain, Portugal, Italy, Africa, Newfoundland etc., with the importations and exportations of all Commodities, particularly of the Woollen Manufactures, delivered in his reports made to the Commissioners for Publick Accounts.* 1715, p. 71. Our general exports for the year 1699 are valued at £6, 788,166, 17s. 6¼d. Whereof the Woollen Manufacture for the same year are valued at £2,932,292, 17s. 6¼d.

[2] *Proverb Crossed*, p. 8, 1677. See also *Case of the Woollen Manufacturers of Great Britain* which states that they are " the subsistance of more than a Million of Poor of both sexes, who are employed therein."

children were said to be employed in the clothing trade in Tiverton alone.[1] While giving 933,966 hands as the number properly employed in woollen manufacture, another writer says that women and children (girls and boys) were employed in the proportion of about eight to one man.[2]

Such figures must be taken with reserve, for the proportions of men and women employed varied according to the quality of the stuff woven, and pamphleteers of the seventeenth century handled figures with little regard to scientific accuracy.[3] But the uncertainty only refers to the exact proportion ; there can be no doubt that the Woollen Trade depended chiefly upon women and children for its labour supply.

For the student of social organization it is noteworthy that in the two textile trades through which capitalism made in England its most striking advances —the woollen trade, and in later years, the cotton trade, the labour of women predominated,—a fact which suggests obscure actions and reactions between capitalism and the economic position of women, worthy of more careful investigation than they have as yet received.

The woollen trade passed through a period of rapid progress and development in the sixteenth century. It was then that the Clothiers of Wiltshire and Somerset acquired wealth and fame, building as a memorial for posterity the Tudor houses and churches which

---

[1] Dunsford. *Hist. Tiverton*, p. 408.

[2] *Short Essay upon Trade*, p. 18, 1741.

[3] The following estimates were made by different writers : out of 1187 persons supposed to be employed for one week in making up 1200 lbs. weight of wool, 900 are given as spinners. (*Weavers True Case*, p. 42, 1714.)

One pack of short wool finds employment for 63 persons for one week, viz : 28 men and boys : 35 women and girls who are only expected to do the carding and spinning.

A similar pack made into stockings would provide work for 82 men and 102 spinners and if made up for the Spanish trade, a pack of wool would employ 52 men and 250 women.

(Haynes (John) *Great Britain's Glory*, p. 6, p. 8. 1715.)

still adorn these counties. Leland, writing of a typical clothier and his successful enterprises and ambitions, describes at Malmesbury, Wiltshire " a litle chirch joining to the South side of the *Transeptum* of thabby chirch, . . . Wevers hath now lomes in this litle chirch, but it stondith . . . the hole logginges of thabbay be now longging to one Stumpe, an exceding riche clothiar that boute them of the king. This Stumpes sunne hath maried Sir Edward Baynton's doughter. This Stumpe was the chef causer and contributer to have thabbay chirch made a paroch chirch. At this present tyme every corner of the vaste houses of office that belongid to thabbay be fulle of lumbes to weve clooth yn, and this Stumpe entendith to make a stret or 2 for clothier in the bak vacant ground of the abbay that is withyn the toune waulles."[1]

There must have been a marked tendency at this time to bring the wage-earners of the woollen industry under factory control, for a description which is given of John Winchcombe's household says that

> " Within one room being large and long
> There stood two hundred Looms full strong,
> Two hundred men the truth is so
> Wrought in these looms all in a row,
> By evry one a pretty boy
> Sate making quills with mickle joy.
> And in another place hard by,
> An hundred women merrily,
> Were carding hard with joyful cheer
> Who singing sate with voices clear.
> And in a chamber close beside,
> Two hundred maidens did abide,
> In petticoats of Stammell red,
> And milk-white kerchers on their head."[2]

These experiments were discontinued, partly because they were discountenanced by the Government, which considered the factory system rendered the wage-earners too dependent on the clothiers ; and also because the collection of large numbers of workpeople under one

---

[1] Leland (John) *Itinerary*, 1535-1543 ; Part II, pp. 131-2.

[2] Lipson, *Econ. Hist. of England*, p. 420.

roof provided them with the opportunity for combination and insubordination.[1] Moreover the factory system was not really advantageous to the manufacturer before the introduction of power, because he could pay lower wages to the women who worked at home than to those who left their families in order to work on his premises. Thus the practice was dropped. In 1603 the Wiltshire Quarter Sessions published regulations to the effect that " Noe Clotheman shall keepe above one lombe in his house, neither any weaver that hath a ploughland shall keepe more than one lombe in his house. Noe person or persons shall keepe any lombe or lombs goeinge in any other house or houses beside their owne, or mayntayne any to doe the same."[2]

Few references occur to the wives of successful clothiers or wool-merchants who were actively interested in their husband's business, though no doubt their help was often enlisted in the smaller or more struggling concerns. Thus the names of three widows are given in a list of eleven persons who were using handicrafts at Maidstone. " The better sorte of these we take to bee but of meane ability and most of them poore but by theire trade the poore both of the towne and country adjoyning are ymploied to spynnyng."[3]

A pamphlet published in 1692 describes how in former days " the Clothier that made the cloth, sold it to the merchant, and heard the faults of his own cloth ; and forc'd sometimes not only to promise amendment himself, but to go home and tell *Joan*, to have the Wool better pick'd, and the Yarn better spun."[4]

A certain Rachel Thiery applied for a monopoly

---

[1] See *Weavers' Act*, 1555.

[2] *Hist. MSS. Com. Var. Coll.*, Vol. I., p. 75, *Wilts. Q.S. Rec.*, 1603.

[3] *S.P.D.*, cxxix, 45, Ap. 10, 1622, *Return of the Mayor.*

[4] *Clothier's Complaint, etc.*, p. 7, 1692.

in Southampton for the pressing of serges, and having heard that the suit had been referred by the Queen to Sir J. Cæsar, the Mayor and Aldermen wrote, July 2, 1599, to let him know how inconvenient the granting of the suit would be to the town of Southampton.

I. Those strangers who have presses already would be ruined.

II. Many of their men servants (English and strangers) bred up to the trade would be idle.

III. "The woeman verie poore and beggarlie, altogether unable to performe it in workmanshipp or otherwise. . . . Againe she is verie idle, a prattling gossipp, unfitt to undertake a matter of so great a charge, her husband a poore man being departed from her and comorant in Rochell these 11 yeres at least. She is verie untrustie and approoved to have engaged mens clothes which in times past have been putt to her for pressinge. Verie insufficient to answer of herself men's goodes and unable to procure anie good Caution to render the owners there goodes againe, havinge not so much as a howse to putt her head in, insomuch as (marvellinge under what coullour she doth seeke to attaine to a matter of such weight) we . . . should hold them worsse than madd that would hazzard or comitt there goodes into her handes. And to conclude she is generallie held amongest us an unfitt woeman to dwell in a well governed Commonwealth."[1]

An incident showing the wife as virtual manager of her husband's business is described in a letter from Thomas Cocks of Crowle to Sir Robert Berkely, Kt., in 1633. He writes complaining of a certain Careless who obtained a licence to sell ale "because he was a surgeon and had many patients come to him for help, and found it a great inconvenience for them to go to remote places for their diet and drink, and in that

---

[1] Lansdowne, 161, fo. 127, 2nd July, 1599.

respect obtained a licence with a limitation to sell ale
to none but his patients. . . but now of late
especially he far exceeds his bounds. . . . A poor
fellow who professed himself an extraordinary carder
and spinner . . . was of late set a work by my
wife to card and spin coarse wool for blankets and when
he had gotten some money for his work to Careless
he goes." Having got drunk there and coming back in
the early hours of the morning he made such a noise
in the churchyard " being near my chamber I woke
my wife who called up all my men to go into the
churchyard and see what the matter was."[1]

That Mrs. Cocks should engage and direct her husband's workpeople would not be surprising to seventeenth century minds, for women did so naturally in
family industry; but when capitalized, business tended
to drift away beyond the wife's sphere, and thus even
then it was unusual to find women connected with
the clothing trade, except as wage-earners.

Of the processes involved in making cloth, weaving
was generally done by men, while the spinning, which
was equally essential to its production, was exclusively
done by women and children.

In earlier days weaving had certainly been to some
extent a woman's trade. " Webster " which is the
feminine form of the old term " Webber " is used in
old documents, and in these women are also specifically
named as following this trade ; thus on the Suffolk Poll
Tax Roll are entered the names of

> " John Wros, shepherd.
> Agneta his wife, webster.
> Margery, his daughter, webster.
> Thomas his servant and
> Beatrice his servant."

It appears also that there were women among the
weavers who came from abroad to establish the cloth
making in England, for a Statute in 1271 provides that

" all workers of woollen cloths, male and female, as well of Flanders as of other lands, may safely come into our realm there to make cloths . . . upon the understanding that those who shall so come and make such cloths, shall be quit of toll and tallage, and of payment of other customs for their work until the end of five years."[1]

Later however, women were excluded from cloth weaving on the ground that their strength was insufficient to work the wide and heavy looms in use ; thus orders were issued for Norwich Worsted Weavers in 1511 forbidding women and maids to weave worsteds because " thei bee nott of sufficient powre to werke the said worsteddes as thei owte to be wrovght."[2]

Complaint was made in Bristol in 1461 that weavers " puttyn, occupien, and hiren ther wyfes, doughters, and maidens, some to weve in ther owne lombes and some to hire them to wirche with othour persons of the said crafte by the which many and divers of the king's liege people, likely men to do the king service in his wars and in defence of this his land, and sufficiently learned in the said craft, goeth vagrant and unoccupied, and may not have their labour to their living."[3]

At Kingston upon-Hull, the weavers Composition in 1490, ordained that " ther shall no woman worke in any warke concernyng this occupacon wtin the towne of Hull, uppon payn of xls. to be devyded in forme by fore reherced."[4]

A prohibition of this character could not resist the force of public opinion which upheld the woman's claim to continue in her husband's trade. Widow's rights are sustained in the Weaver's Ordinances

---

[1] Riley. *Chronicles of London*, p. 142.

[2] Tingye, *Norwich Records*, Vol. II., p, 378.

[3] *Little Red Book of Bristol*, Vol. II., p. 127.

[4] Lambert, 2000 *years of Gild Life*, p. 6.

formulated by 25 Charles II. which declare that " it shall be lawfull for the Widow of any Weaver (who at the time of his death was a free Burgesse of the said Town, and a free Brother of the said Company) to use and occupy the said trade by herselfe, her Apprentices and Servants, so long as shee continues a Widow and observeth such Orders as are or shalbe made to be used amongst the Company of Weavers within this Town of Kingston upon Hull.[1]

Even when virtually excluded from the weaving of " cloaths " women continued to be habitually employed in the weaving of other materials. A petition was presented on their behalf against an invention which threatened a number with unemployment : " Also wee most humbly desire your worship that you would have in remembrance that same develishe invention which was invented by strangers and brought into this land by them, which hath beene the utter over-throwe of many poore people which heretofore have lived very well by their handy laboure which nowe are forced to goe a begginge and wilbe the utter Destruccion of the trade of weaving if some speedy course be not taken therein. Wee meane those looms with 12, 15, 20, 18, 20, 24, shuttles which make tape, ribbon, stript garteringe and the like, which heretofore was made by poore aged woemen and children, but none nowe to be seene."[2]

The Rules of the Society of Weavers of the " Stuffs called Kiddirminster Stuffes" required that care should be taken to have apprentices " bound according to ye Lawes of ye Realme . . . for which they shall be allowed 2s. 6d and not above, to be payd by him or her that shall procure the same Apprentice to be bound as aforesayd."[3]

---

[1] Lambert, 2000 *Years of Gild Life*, p. 210.

[2] *S.P.D.*, cxxi, 155, 1621.

[3] Burton, J. R., *Hist. of Kidderminster.*, *p.* 175, *Borough Ordinances*, 1650.

John Grove w as bound about the year 1655 to " the said George and Mary to bee taught and instructed in the trade of a serge-weaver," and a lamentable account is given of the inordinate manner in which the said Mary did beat him.[1]

It is impossible from the scanty information available to arrive at a final conclusion concerning the position of women weavers. Clearly an attempt had been made to exclude them from the more highly skilled branches of the trade, but it is also evident that this had not been successful in depriving widows of their rights in this respect. Nor does the absence of information concerning women weavers prove that they were rarely employed in such work. The division of work between women and men was a question which aroused little interest at this time and therefore references to the part taken by women are accidental. They may have been extensively engaged in weaving for they are mentioned as still numerous among the hand-loom weavers of the nineteenth century.[2] Another process in the manufacture of cloth which gave employment to women was " Burling." The minister and Mayor of Westbury presented a petition to the Wiltshire Quarter Sessions in 1657 on behalf of certain poor

---

[1] *Somerset Q.S. Rec.*, Vol. III., pp. 268-9. 1655.

[2] *Report of the Commissioners on the condition of the Handloom Weavers*, 1841. x p. 323, *Mr. Chapman's report*.

" The young weaver just out of his apprenticeship is perhaps as well able to earn as he will be at any future period setting aside the domestic comforts incidental to the married state, his pecuniary condition is in the first instance improved by uniting himself with a woman capable of earning perhaps nearly as much as himself, and performing for him various offices involving an actual pecuniary saving. A married man with an income, the result of the earnings of himself and wife of 20s. will enjoy more substantial comfort in every way than he alone would enjoy with an income of 15s. a week. This alone is an inducement to early marriage. In obedience to this primary inducement the weaver almost invariably marries soon after he is out of his apprenticeship. But the improvement of comfort which marriage brings is of short duration ; . . About the tenth year the labour of the eldest child becomes available. . . . Many men have depended on their wives & their children to support themselves by their own earnings, independent of his wages. The wives and children consequently took to the loom, or sought work in the factories ; and now that there is little or no work in the district, the evil is felt, and the husband is obliged to maintain them out of his wages."

people who had obtained their living by the " Burling of broad medley clothes," thrée of whose daughters had now been indicted by certain persons desirous to appropriate the said employment to themselves ; they show " that the said employment of Burling hath not been known to be practised among us as any prentice trade, neither hath any been apprentice to it as to such, but clothiers have ever putt theyr clothes to Burling to any who would undertake the same, as they doe theyr woolles to spinning. Also that the said imployment of Burling is a common good to this poore town and parish, conducing to the reliefe of many poore families therein and the setting of many poore children on work. And if the said imployment of Burling should be appropriated by any particular persons to themselves it would redound much to the hurt of clothing, and to the undoing of many poore families there whoe have theyre cheife mainteynance therefrom."[1]

It was not however the uncertain part they played in the processes of weaving, burling or carding, which constituted the importance of the woollen trade in regard to women's industrial position. Their employment in these directions was insignificant compared with the unceasing and never satisfied demand which the production of yarn made upon their labour. It is impossible to give any estimate of the quantity of wool spun for domestic purposes. That this was considerable is shown by a recommendation from the Commission appointed to enquire into the decay of the Cloth Trade in 1622, who advise " that huswyves may not make cloth to sell agayne, but for the provision of themselves and their famylie that the clothiers and Drapers be not dis-coraged."[2]

The housewife span both wool and flax for domestic

[1] *Hist. MSS. Com. Var. Coll.*, Vol. I., p. 135, *Wilts. Q.S. Rec.*, 1657.

[2] *Report of Commission of Decay of Clothing Trade*, 1622, Stowe, 554, fo. 48b.

use, but this aspect of her industry will be considered more fully in connection with the linen trade, attention here being concentrated on the condition of the spinsters in the woollen trade. Their organization varied widely in different parts of the country. Sometimes the spinster bought the wool, span it, and then sold the yarn, thus securing all the profit of the transaction for herself. In other cases she was supplied with the wool by the clothier, or a " market spinner " and only received piece wages for her labour. The system in vogue was partly decided by the custom of the locality, but there was everywhere a tendency to substitute the latter for the former method.

Statute I. Edward VI. chap. 6 recites that " the greatest and almost the whole number of the poor inhabitants of the county of Norfolk and the city of Norwich be, and have been heretofore for a great time maintained and gotten their living, by spinning of the wool growing in the said county of Norfolk, upon the rock [distaff] into yarn, and by all the said time have used to have their access to common markets within the said county and city, to buy their wools, there to be spun as is aforesaid, of certain persons called retailers of the said wool by eight penny worth and twelve penny worth at one time, or thereabouts, and selling the same again in yarn, and have not used to buy, ne can buy the said wools of the breeders of the said wools by such small parcels, as well as for that the said breeders of the said wools will not sell their said wools by such small parcels, as also for that the most part of the said poor persons dwell far off from the said breeders of the said wools."[1]

During a scarcity of wool the Corporation at Norwich compelled the butchers to offer their wool fells exclusively to the spinsters during the morning hours

---

[1] James (John) *Hist. of Worsted*, p. 98.

until the next sheep-shearing season, so that the tawers and others might not be able to outbid them. [1]

It is suggested that nearly half the yarn used in the great clothing counties at the beginning of the seventeenth century was produced in this way: "Yarn is weekly broughte into the market by a great number of poor people that will not spin to the clothier for small wages, but have stock enough to set themselves on work, and do weekly buy their wool in the market by very small parcels according to their use, and weekly return it in yarn and make good profit, having the benefit both of their labour and of their merchandize and live exceeding well. . . . So many that it is supposed that more than half the cloth of Wilts., Gloucester and Somersetshire is made by means of these yarnmakers and poor clothiers that depend wholly on the wool chapman which serves them weekly for wools either for money or credit." [2]

Apparently this custom by which the spinsters retained in their own hands the merchandize of their goods still prevailed in some counties at the beginning of the following century, for it is said in a pamphlet which was published in 1741 "that poor People, chiefly Day Labourers, ... whilst they are employed abroad themselves, get forty or fifty Pounds of Wool at a Time, to employ their Wives and Children at home in Carding and Spinning, of which when they have 10 or 20 pounds ready for the Clothier, they go to Market with it and there sell it, and so return home as fast as they can. . . the common way the poor women in *Hampshire, Wiltshire*, and *Dorsetshire*, and I believe in other counties, have of getting to Market (especially in the Winter-time) is, by the Help of some Farmers' Waggons, which carry them and their yarn; and as soon as the Farmers have set down their

---

[1] Tingye. *Norwich*, Vol II. xcvii, 1532.

[2] *S.P.D.* lxxx., 13., Jan. 1615. *General Conditions of Wool and Cloth Trade,*

corn in the Market, and baited their Horses, they return home. . . . During the Time the waggons stop, the poor Women carry their Yarn to the Clothiers for whom they work ; then they get the few Things they want, and return to the Inn to be carried home again. . . . Many of them ten or twelve miles . . . there will be in Market time 3 or 400 poor People (chiefly Women) who will sell their Goods in about an Hour."[1]

According to this writer other women worked for the " rich clothier " who " makes his whole year's provision of wool beforehand . . . in the winter time has it spun by his own spinsters . . . at the lowest rate for wages," or they worked for the " market spinner " or middleman who supplied them with wool mixed in the right proportions and sold their yarn to the clothiers. In either case the return for their labour was less than that secured by the spinsters who had sufficient capital to buy their wool and sell the yarn in the dearest market. When the Staplers tried to secure a monopoly for selling wool, the Growers of wool, or Chapmen petitioned in self-defence explaining " that the clothier's poor are all servants working for small wages that doth but keepe them alive, whereas the number of people required to work up the same amount of wool in the new Drapery is much larger. Moreover, all sorts of these people are masters in their trade and work for themselves, they buy and sell their materials that they work upon, so that by their merchandize and honest labour they live very well. These are served of their wools weekly by the wool-buyer."[2]

Opinion was divided as to whether the spinster found it more advantageous to work direct for the Clothier or for the Market Spinner. A proposal in

---

[1] *Remarks upon Mr. Webber's scheme*, pp. 21-2, 1741.

[2] *S.P.D.*, lxxx., 15-16., Jan, 1615.

1693 to put down the middle man, was advised against by the Justices of Assize for Wiltshire, on the ground that it was " likely to cause great reduction of wages and employment to the spinners and the poor, and a loss to the growers of wool, and no advantage in the quality of the yarn."

The Justices say in their report : " We finde the markett spinner who setts many spinners on worke spinnes not the falce yarn, but the poorer sorte of people (who spinne theyr wool in theyr owne howses) for if the markett spinners who spinne greate quantitys and sell it in the markett should make bad yarne, they should thereby disable themselves to maynetayne theyre creditt and livelyhood. And that the more spinners there are, the more cloth will be made and the better vent for Woolls (which is the staple commodity of the kingdome) and more poor will be set on worke. The markett spinners (as is conceived) are as well to be regulated by the lawe, for any falcity in mixing of theyr woolles as the Clothier is, who is a great markett spinner himselfe and doth both make and sell as falce yarne as any market spinner . . . We finde the markett spinner gives better wages than the Clothier, not for that reason the Clothier gives for the falcity of the yarne, but rather in that the markett spinners vent much of their yarne to those that make the dyed and dressed clothes who give greater prizes than the white men do."[1]

The fine yarn used by the Clothiers required considerable skill in spinning, and the demand for it was so great in years of expansion that large sums of money were paid to persons able to teach the mysteries of the craft in a new district. Thus the Earl of Salisbury made an agreement in 1608 with Walter Morrell that he should instruct fifty persons of the parish of Hatfield, chosen by the Earl of Salisbury, in

[1] *S.P.D.*,ccxliii., 23, July 23, 1633.

the art of clothing, weaving, etc. He will provide work for all these persons to avoid idleness and for the teaching of skill and knowledge in clothing will pay for the work at the current rates, except those who are apprentices. The Earl of Salisbury on his part will allow Walter Morrell a house rent free and will pay him £100 per annum "for instructing the fifty persons, to be employed in:—the buying of wool, sorting it, picking it, dying it, combing it, both white and mingle colour worsted, weaving and warping and quilling both worsted of all sorts, dressing both woollen and stuffes, spinning woollen (wofe and warpe), spinning all sortes of Kersey both high wheel and low wheel, knitting both woollen and worsted."[1]

A similar agreement is recorded in 1661-2 between the Bailiffs and Burgesses of Aldeburgh and " Edmund Buxton of Stowmarket, for his coming to set up his trade of spinning wool in the town and to employ the poor therein, paying him £50—for 5 years and £12—for expense of removing, with a house rent free and the freedom of the town."[2]

The finest thread was produced on the distaff, but this was a slow process, and for commoner work spinning wheels were in habitual use —

> " There are, to speed their labor, who prefer
> ·' Wheels double spol'd, which yield to either hand
> " A sev'ral line ; and many, yet adhere
> " To th' ancient distaff, at the bosom fix'd,
> " Casting the whirling spindle as they walk."[3]

The demands made on spinning by this ever expanding trade were supplied from three sources : (1) the wives of farmers and other well to do people, (b) the wives of husbandmen and (c) women who depended wholly

---

[1] *S.P.D.*, xxxviii., 72, 73, Dec. 1608..

[2] *Hist. MSS. Com. Var. Coll.*, Vol. IV., p. 311.

[3] Dyer John., *The Fleece*, 1757.

on spinning for their living, and who are therefore called here spinsters. The first care of the farmers' wives was to provide woollen stuffs for the use of their families, but a certain proportion of their yarn found its way to the market. The clothiers at Salisbury who made the better grades of cloth were said to " buy their yarn of the finer kinds that come to the market at from 17d the lb. to 2s. 4d, made all of the finer sortes of our owne Welshire wool, and is spun by farmers' wives and other of the better sorte of people within their owne houses, of whose names wee keep due Register and do write down with what cardes they promise us their several bundles of yarne are carded, and do find such people just in what they.tell us, or can otherwise controule them when wee see the proofe of our cloth in the mill, . . . and also some very few farmers' wives who maie peradventure spinne sometimes a little of those sortes in their own houses and sell the same in the markett and is verie current without mixture of false wooll grease, etc."[1]

Probably a larger supply of yarn came from the families of husbandmen where wife and children devoted themselves to spinning through the long winter evenings. Children became proficient in the art at an early age, and could often spin a good thread when seven or eight years old. This subsidiary employment was not sufficient to supply the demand for yarn, and in the clothing counties numbers of women were withdrawn from agricultural occupations to depend wholly upon their earnings as spinsters.

The demand made by the woollen trade on the labour of children is shown by a report from the Justices of the Peace of the Boulton Division of the Hundred of Salford, . . . "for apprentices there hath beene few found since our last certificate by reason of the greate tradeing of fustians and woollen cloth

---

[1] *S.P.D.*, cclxvii., 17, May 2, 1634. Certificate from Anthony Wither, Commissioner or reformation of clothing.

within the said division, by reason whereof the inhabitants have continuall employment for their children in spinning and other necessary labour about the same."[1]

Those who gave out the wool and collected the yarn were called market spinners, but the qualifying term " market " is sometimes omitted, and when men are referred to as spinners it may be assumed that they are organising the work of the spinsters, and not engaged themselves in the process of spinning.[2] Though the demand for yarn generally exceeded the supply, wages for spinning remained low throughout the seventeenth century. A writer in the first half of the eighteenth century who urges the establishment of a nursery of spinners on the estate of an Irish landlord admits that their labour is " of all labour on wools the most sparingly paid for."[3]

Wages for spinning are mentioned in only three of the extant Quarter Sessions' Assessments, and it is not specified whether the material is wool or flax :

1654. Devon. 6d. per week with meat and drink, or 1s. 4d. without them.

1688. Bucks. Spinners shall not have by the day more than 4d. without meat and drink.

1714. Devon. 1s. per week with meat and drink, 2s. 6d. without them.

These rates are confirmed by entries in account

---

[1] *S.P.D.*, ccclxiv., 122, July, 1637.

[2] *Somerset Q.S. Rec.*, Vol. III., p. 56, 1648. *Complaint . . . by . . . Thos Chambers, Randall Carde, Dorothy Palmer, Stephen Hodges and Wm. Hurman, persons ymployed by Henry Denmeade servant to Mr. Thos. Cooke, Clothier for the spinning of certen wool and convertinge it into yarne and twistinge it thereof for the benefitt of the said Mr. Cooke that theire wages for the same spinninge and twistinge had been deteyned from them by the said Mr Cooke . . . it is ordered that the said Mr. C. doe forthwith pay to the said Thos. Chambers the some of ffowerteene shillings to the said Randall Carde the some of nyne shillings and fower pence, to the said Dorothy Palmer the some of eighteen shillings and one penny to the said Stephen Hodges the some of nyne shillings and four pence and to the said Wm. Hurman the some of nyne shillings.*

[3] *Scheme to prevent the running of Irish wools to France*, p. 19.

books,[1] but it was more usual to pay by the piece. Though it is always more difficult to discover the possible earnings per day of women who are working by a piece rate in their own homes, it so happens that several of the writers who discuss labour questions in the woollen trade specially state that their estimates of the wages of spinners are based on full time. John Haynes quoted figures in 1715 which work out at nearly 1s. 6d. per week for the spinners of wool into stuffs for the Spanish Trade, and about 2s. 11d. for stockings,[2] another pamphlet gives 24s. as the wages of 9 spinsters for a week,[3] while in 1763 the author of the "Golden Fleece" quotes 2s. 3d. a week for Spanish wools.[4] Another pamphlet says that the wages in the fine woollen trade "being chiefly women and children, may amount, one with another to £6 per annum."[5] A petition from the weavers, undated, but evidently presented during a season of bad trade, declares that "there are not less than a Million of poor unhappy objects, *women and children only*, who . . . are employed in Spinning Yarn for the Woollen Manufacturers ; Thousands of these have now no work at all, and all of them have suffered an Abatement of Wages ; so that now a Poor Woman, perhaps a Mother of many Children, must work very hard to gain Three Pence or Three Pence Farthing per Day."[6]

---

[1] (*Howard Household Book*, p. 63, 1613.) "Widow Grame for spinning ij stone and 5ˡ of wooll vjs. To the wench that brought it iijd. To Ellen for winding yarn iij weekes xviijd.

(Fell, Sarah; *Household Accounts*, Nov. 28, 1677, p. 439.) Pd. Agnes Holme of Hawxhead forᵗ spininge woole here 7 weeks 02.04

[2] Haynes, *Great Britain's Glory*, pp. 8, 9.

[3] *Weavers' True Case*, p. 43, 1719.

[4] James, John, *Hist of the Worsted Manufacture*, p. 239.

[5] *Further considerations for encouraging the Woollen Manufactures.*

[6] *Second Humble Address from the Poor Weavers.*

Though these wages provided no margin for the support of children, or other dependants, it was possible for a woman who could spin the better quality yarns to maintain herself in independence.

John Evelyn describes " a maiden of primitive life, the daughter of a poore labouring man, who had sustain'd her parents (some time since dead) by her labour, and has for many years refus'd marriage, or to receive any assistance from the parish, besides ye little hermitage my lady gives her rent free : she lives on fourepence a day, which she gets by spinning ; says she abounds and can give almes to others, living in greate humility and content, without any apparent affectation or singularity ; she is continualy working, praying, or reading, gives a good account of her knowledge in religion, visites the sick ; is not in the least given to talke ; very modest, of a simple not unseemly behaviour, of a comely countenance, clad very plaine, but cleane and tight. In sum she appeares a saint of an extraordinary sort, in so religious a life as is seldom met with in villages now-a-daies."[1]

It is probable that the wages for spinning were advanced soon after this date, for Defoe writes in 1728 that " the rate for spinning, weaving and all other Manufactory-work, I mean in Wool, is so risen, that the Poor all over *England* can now earn or gain near twice as much in a Day, and in some Places, more than twice as much as they could get for the same work two or three Years ago . . . the poor Women now get 12d. to 15d. a Day for spinning, the men more in proportion, and are full of work."[2] " The Wenches . . . . wont go to service at 12d. or 18d. a week while they can get 7s. to 8s. a Week at spinning ; the Men won't drudge at the Plow and Cart &c., and perhaps get £6 a year . . . . when they can sit

---

[1] Evelyn (John) *Diary*, Vol. III., p. 7, 1685

[2] Defoe, *Behaviour*, p. 83.

still and dry within Doors, and get 9s. or 10s. a Week at Wool-combing or at Carding.[1] "Would the poor Maid-Servants who choose rather to spin, while they can gain 9s. per Week by their Labour than go to Service at 12d. a week to the Farmers Houses as before; I say would they sit close to their work, live near and close, as labouring and poor People ought to do, and by their Frugality lay up six or seven shillings per Week, none could object or blame them for their Choice."[2] Defoe's statement as to the high rate of wages for spinning is supported by an account of the workhouse at Colchester where the children's "Work is Carding & Spinning Wool for the Bay-makers; some of them will earn 6d. or 7d. a Day."[3] But there is no sign of these higher wages in the seventeenth century.

Continual recriminations took place between clothiers and spinsters, who accused one another of dishonesty in their dealings. A petition of the Worsted Weavers of Norwich and Norfolk, and the Bayes and Sayes makers of Essex and Suffolk, to the Council proposes: "That no spinster shall winde or reele theire yarne upon shorter reeles (nor fewer thriddes) than have bene accustomed, nor ymbessell away their masters' goodes to be punished by the next Justices of the Peace."[4]

And again in 1622 the Justices of the Peace of Essex inform the Council: "Moreover wee understand that the clothiers who put forthe their woolle to spinne doe much complaine of the spinsters that they use great deceit by reason they doe wynde their yarne into knottes upon shorter reeles and fewer threedes by a fifth part than hath beene accustomed.

---

[1] Defoe, *Behaviour*, pp. 84-5.

[2] *Ibid*, p. 88.

[3] *Acc. of several Workhouses*, p. 59, 1725.

[4] S.P.D., civ. 97, 1618. *Petition for regulation.*

The which reeles ought to be two yardes about and
the knottes to containe fowerscore threedes apeece."[1]

On the other hand in Wiltshire the weavers, spinners
and others complained that they " are not able by
their diligent labours to gett their livinges, by reason
that the Clothiers at their will have made their workes
extreme hard, and abated wages what they please. And
some of them make such their workfolkes to doe their
houshold businesses, to trudge in their errands, spoole
their chains, twist their list, doe every command
without giving them bread, drinke or money for many
days labours."[2]

Report was made to the Council in 1631-2 that the
reele-staffe in the Eastern Counties " was enlarged by
a fift or sixt part longer than have bene accustomed and
the poores wages never the more encreased." Whereupon the magistrates in Cambridge agreed " that all
spinsters shall have for the spinning and reeling of six
duble knots on the duble reele or 12 on the single
reele, a penny, which is more by 2d. in the shilling than
they have had, and all labourers and other artificers
have the like increase. Essex and Suffolk are ready
to make the same increase provided that the same
reel and rate of increase is used in all other counties
where the trade of clothing and yarn-making is made,
otherwise one county will undersell another to the
ruin of the clothiers and the poor dependent on them.
Therefore the Council order that a proportional
increase of wages is paid according to the increase of
the reel and the officers employed for keeping a
constant reel to give their accounts to the Justices of
the Assize."[3]

Other complaints were made of clothiers who
forced their work-people to take goods instead of

---

[1] *S.P.D.*, cxxx., 65, May 13, 1662.

[2] *Hist. MSS. Com. Var. Coll.*, Vol., I., p. 94, *Wilts. Q.S. Rec.*, 1623.

[3] *Council Register*, 2nd March, 1631-2.

money in payment of wages. At Southampton in 1666 thirty-two clothiers, beginning with Joseph Delamot, Alderman, were presented for forcing their spinners " to take goods for their work whereby the poor were much wronged, being contrary to the statute, for all which they were amerced severally." The records however do not state that the fine was exacted.[1]

Low as were the spinster's wages even in seasons of prosperity, they, in common with the better paid weavers endured the seasons of depression, which were characteristic of the woollen industry. The English community was as helpless before a period of trade depression as before a season of drought or flood. Employment ceased, the masters who had no sale for their goods, gave out no material to their workers, and men and women alike, who were without land as a resource in this time of need, were faced with starvation and despair.[2] The utmost social demoralisation ensued, and family life with all its valuable traditions was in many cases destroyed.

Complaints from the clothing counties state " That the Poor's Rates are doubled, and in some Places trebbled by the Multitude of Poor Perishing and Starving Women and Children being come to the Parishes, while their Husbands and Fathers *not able to bear the cries which they could not relieve*, are fled into *France* . . . to seek their Bread."[3]

These conditions caused grave anxiety to the

---

[1] Davies (J. S.) *Southampton*, p. 272.

[2] A report to the council from the High Sheriff of Somerset says : " Yet I thincke it my duty to acquaynt your Lordshipps that there are such a multytude of poore cottages builte upon the highwaies and odd corners in every countrie parishe within this countye, and soe stufte with poore people that in many of those parishes there are three or fower hundred poore of men and women and children that did gett most of their lyvinge by spinnyng, carding and such imployments aboute wooll and cloath. And the deadness of that trade and want of money is such that they are for the most parte without worke, and knowe not how to live. This *is* a great grievance amongst us and tendeth much to mutinye."
(*S.P.D.*, cxxx., 73, May 14, 1622, High Sheriff of Somersershire to the Council.)

[3] *Second Humble Address from the poor Weavers.*

Government who attempted to force the clothiers to provide for their work-people.[1]

Locke reported to Carleton, Feb. 16th, 1622 : " In the cloathing counties there have bin lately some poore people (such chieflie as gott their living by working to Clothiers) that have gathered themselves together by Fourty or Fifty in a company and gone to the houses of those they thought fittest to relieve them for meate and money which hath bin given more of feare than charitie. And they have taken meate openly in the markett without paying for it. The Lords have written letters to ten Counties where cloathing is most used, that the Clothier, shall not put off his workemen without acquainting the Councill, signifying that order is taken for the buying off their cloathes, and that the wooll grower shall afford them his wooll better cheape but yet the cloathiers still complaine that they can not sell their cloath in Black-well Hall. . . ."[2]

The Justices of Assize for Gloucester reported March 13, 1622, that they have interviewed the Clothiers who have been forced to put down looms through the want of sale for their cloth. The Clothiers maintain that this is due to the regulations and practices of the Company of Merchant Adventurers. They say that they, the Clothiers, have been working at a loss since the deadness of trade about a year ago, " their stocks and credits are out in cloth lying upon their hands unsold, and that albeit they have bought their woolles at very moderate prices, being such as do very much impoverish the grower, yet they cannot sell

---

[1] The Council ordered the Justices of the Peace for the counties of Wilts, Somerset Dorset, Devon, Glocester, Worcester, Oxford, Kent and Suffolk, to summon clothiers and " deale effectually with them for the employment of such weavers, spinners anb other persons, as are now out of work. . . . . We may not indure that the cloathiers . . . should att their pleasure, and without giving knowledge thereof unto this Boarde, dismisse their workefolkes, who being many in number and most of them of the poorer sort are in such cases likely by their clamour to disturb the quiet and government of those partes wherein they live." (*C.R.*, 9th Feb., 1621-2.)

[2] *S.F.D*, cxxvii., 102, Feb. 16, 1622.

the cloth made thereof but to their intolerable losses, and are enforced to pawne theire clothes to keepe theire people in work, which they are not able to indure. . . . that there are at the least 1500 loomes within the County of Gloucester and in . . . the Citie and that xxs. in money and sixteene working persons and upwards doe but weekly mainteyne one loome, which doe require 1500li. in money, by the weeke to mainteyne in that trade 24000 working people besides all others that are releeved thereby, and so the wages of a labouring person is little above xiid. the week being much too little."[1]

In June of the same year the Justices of Gloucester wrote to the Council : " The distress of those depending on the Cloth trade grows worse and worse. Our County is thereby and through want of money and means in these late tymes growne poore, and unable to releeve the infynite nomber of poore people residinge within the same (drawne hither by meanes of clothing) . . . therefore very many of them doe wander, begg and steale and are in case to starve as their faces (to our great greefes) doe manifest. . . . The peace is in danger of being broken."[2]

The distress was not limited to the rural districts ; the records of the Borough of Reading describe efforts made there for its alleviation. " At this daye the complainte of the poore Spynners and Carders was agayne heard etc. The Overseers and Clothiers apoynted to provide and assigne them worke apeared and shewed their dilligence therein, yett the complaint for lacke of worke increaseth ; for a remedye is agreed to be thus, viz : every Clothier according to his proportion of . . .shall weekly assigne and put to spynning in the towne his ordinarye and course wooffe wooll, and shall not send it unto the country and if

---

[1] *S.P.D.*, cxxviii., 49, March 13, 1622.

[2] *S.P.D.*, cxxxi., 4., June 1, 1622.

sufficient be in the towne to doe it[1]." At another time it is recorded that " In regard of the great clamour of divers poore people lackinge worke and employment in spynninge and cardinge in this Towne, yt was this daye thought fitt to convent all the undertakers of the stocke given by Mr. Kendricke, and uppon their appearaunce it was ordered, and by themselves agreed, that every undertaker, for every 300li. shall put a woowf a weeke to spyninge within the Towne, as Mr. Mayour shall apoynt, and to such spynners as Mr. Mayour shall send to them[2] . . ."

In these times of distress and in all disputes concerning wages and the exactions of the employers, men and women stood together, supporting each other in their efforts for the improvement of their lot. Thus the Justices of the Peace of Devonshire reported that " complaints were made by the most parte of the clothiers weavers, spinsters and fullers between Plymouth and Teignmouth."[3] and the Council is informed that at the last Quarter Sessions in Wilts, many " weavers, spinners, and fullers for themselves and for manie hundreds more . . . complained of distress by increasing want of work. . . Clothiers giving up their trade, etc."[4]

Sometimes the petitions, though presented on behalf of spinners as well as weavers, were actually signed only by men. This was the case with the Weavers, Fullers and Spinners of Leonard Stanley and King Stanley in Gloucestershire, who petitioned on behalf of themselves and others, 800 at the least, young and old, of the said parishes, " Whereas your poore petitioners have heretofore bene well wrought and imployed in our sayd occupations belonging to the trade of

[1] Guilding, *Reading*, Vol. II., p. 159, 1623.

[2] *Ibid*, Vol. III., p. 7, Mar. 3, 1629-30.

[3] *S.P.D.*, xcvii., 85, May 25, 1618. J.P.s of Devonshire to Council.

[4] *Ibid*, cxv., 20, May 11, 1620. J.P.s of Wiltshire to Council.

clothing whereby we were able in some poore measure and at a very lowe rate to maintaine ourselves and families soe as hitherto they have not suffered any extreme want. But now soe it is that we are likely for the time to come never to be imployed againe in our callinges and to have our trades become noe trades, whereunto we have bene trained up and served as apprentices according to the lawe, and wherein we have always spent our whole time and are now unfitt for . . . other occupations, neither can we be received into worke by any clothiers in the whole countrey."[1]

At other times women took the lead in demanding the redress of grievances from which all were suffering. When the case of the say-makers abating the wages of the spinsters, weavers and combers of Sudbury was examined by the Justices, the Saymakers alleged that all others did the same, but that they were content to give the wages paid by them if these were extended by proclamation or otherwise throughout the kingdom. " But if the order is not general it will be their undoing . . ." Whereupon the Justices ordered the Saymakers to pay spinsters " for every seaven knottes one penny, the reel whereon the yarne is reeled to be a yard in length—no longer," and to pay weavers " 12d. a lb. for weaving thereof for white sayes under 5 lbs. weight."[2]

Shortly afterwards the Council received a petition from the Mayor asking to be heard by the Council or Commissioners to answer the complaint made against them. " by Silvia Harber widow set on worke by Richard Skinnir of Sudbury gent . . . for abridging and wronging of the spinsters and weavers of the said borough in their wages and for some other wrongs supposed to bee done to the said Silvià Harber,"

---

[1] S.P.D., ccxliv., 1. Aug. 1, 1633.

[2] S.P.D., clxxxix., 40, Ap. 27, 1631. J.P.s of Essex to Council.

followed by an an affidavit stating "Wee whose names are hereunder written doe testifye as followeth with our severell handes to our testification.

1. That one Silvia Harber of our Towne of Sudbury comonly called Luce Harbor did say that shee had never undertaken to peticion the Lordes of the Counsell in the Behalfe of the Spinsters of Sudbury aforesaid but by the inducement of Richard Skinner gentleman of the Towne aforesaid who sent for her twoe or three times before shee would goe unto him for that purpose, and when shee came to him hee sent her to London and bare her charges. Witness, Daniel Biat Clement Shelley.

2. That having conference with Richard Skinner aforesaid Gentleman, hee did confesse that hee would never have made any stir of complaint against the saymakers in behalf of weavers and spinsters, but that one Thomas Woodes of the towne abovesaid had given him Distaystfull wordes." Witness, Vincent Cocke.[1]

No organisation appears to have been formed by the wage-earners in the woollen Trade. Their demonstrations against employers were as yet local and sporadic. The very nature of their industry and the requirements of its capitalistic organisation would have rendered abortive on their part the attempt to raise wages by restricting the numbers of persons admitted into the trade; but the co-operation in trade disputes between the men and women engaged in this industry, forms a marked contrast to the conditions which were now beginning to prevail in the apprentice trades and which will be described later. Though without immediate result in the woollen trade, it may be assumed that it was this habit of standing shoulder to shoulder, regardless of sex jealousy, which ensured that when Industrialism attained a further development

---

[1] *S.P.D.*, cxcvii., 72, July, 1631. Affidavit about Saymakers in County of Suffolk.

in the closely allied cotton trade, the union which was then called into being embraced men and women on almost equal terms.

The broad outline of the position of women in the woollen trade as it was established in the seventeenth century shows them taking little, if any, part in the management of the large and profitable undertakings of Clothiers and Wool-merchants. Their industrial position was that of wage-earners, and though the demand for their labour generally exceeded the supply, yet the wages they received were barely sufficient for their individual maintenance, regardless of the fact that in most cases they were wholly or partly supporting children or other dependants.

The higher rates of pay for spinning appear to have been secured by the women who did not depend wholly upon it for their living, but could buy wool, spin it at their leisure, and sell the yarn in the dearest market; while those who worked all the year round for clothiers or middlemen, were often beaten down in their wages and were subject to exactions and oppression.

C. *Linen.*

While the woollen trade had for centuries been developing under the direction of capitalism, it was only in the seventeenth century that this influence begins to show itself in the production of linen. Following the example of the clothiers, attempts were then made to manufacture linen on a large scale. For example, Celia Fiennes describes Malton as a " pretty large town built of Stone but poor; . . . there was one Mr. Paumes that marry'd a relation of mine, Lord Ewers' Coeheiress who is landlady of almost all ye town. She has a pretty house in the place. There is the ruins of a very great house wh^ch belonged to ye family but they not agreeing about it Caused ye defaceing of it. She now makes use of ye roomes off ye out-buildings and gate house for weaving and Linning

Cloth, haveing set up a manuffactory for Linnen wh^{ch} does Employ many poor people."[1]

In spite of such innovations the production of linen retained for the most part its character as one of the crafts " yet left of that innocent old world." The housewife, assisted by servants and children span flax and hemp for household linen, underclothes, children's frocks and other purposes, and then took her thread to the local weaver who wove it to her order. Thus Richard Stapley, Gent., enters in his Diary : " A weaver fetched 11 pounds of flaxen yarn to make a bedticke ; and he brought me ten yds of ticking for ye bed, 3 yds and ¾ of narrow ticking for ye bolster & for ye weaving of which I paid him 10s. and ye flax cost 8d. per pound. My mother spun it for me, and I had it made into a bed by John Dennit, a tailor, of Twineham for 8d. on Wednesday, July 18th, and it was filled on Saturday, August 4th by Jonas Humphrey of Twineham for 6d. The weaver brought it home July 6th.[2] Similarly Sarah Fell enters in her Household book : " Nov. 18th, 1675, by m°. p^d. Geo. ffell weaver fo^r workeinge 32 : ells of hempe tow cloth of Mothrs. at 1d½ ell. 000.04.00 "[3]

By the industry and foresight of its female members the ordinary household was supplied with all its necessary linen without any need for entering the market, the expenses of middlemen and salesmen being so avoided. Nevertheless, it is evident that a considerable sale for linen had always existed, for the linen drapers were an important corporation in many towns. This sale was increased through an invention made about the middle of the century : By printing patterns on linen a material was produced which

---

[1] Fiennes (Celia) p. 74. *Through England on a Side-saddle.*

[2] *Suss. Arch. Coll.*, Vol. II., p. 121. *Extracts from the Diary of Richard Stapley, Gent.*, 1682-1724,

[3] Fell (Sarah) *Household Accts.*, p. 233.

closely imitated the costly muslins, or calicoes as they were then called, imported from India; but at so reasonable a price that they were within the reach of a servant's purse. Servants were therefore able to go out in dresses scarcely distinguishable from their mistresses', and the sale of woollen and silk goods was seriously affected. The woollen trade became alarmed; riots took place; weavers assaulted women who were wearing printed linens in the streets, and finally, Parliament, always tender to the woollen trade, which furnished so large a part of the national revenue, prohibited their use altogether. The linen printers recognising that " the Reason why the *English* Manufacture of linnen is not so much taken notice of as the *Scotch* or *Irish*, is this, the *English* is mostly consumed in the Country, . . . whereas the *Scotch* and *Irish* must come by sea and make a Figure at our custom's house,"[1] urged in their defence that " the linens printed are chiefly the Growth and Manufacture of *North Britain* pay 3d. per Yard to the Crown, . . . and Employ so many Thousands of *British* poor, as will undoubtedly entitle them to the Care of a British Parliament."[2]

But even this argument was unavailing against the political influence of the woollen trade. The spirit of the time favouring the spread of capitalistic enterprise from the woollen trade into other fields of action, an attempt was now made to form a Linen Company. Pamphlets written for and against this project furnish many details of the conditions then prevailing in the manufacture of linen. " How," it was said, will the establishment of a Linnen Company " affect the Kingdom in the two Pillars that support it, that of the Rents of Land and the imploying our Ships and Men at Sea, which are thought the Walls of the

---

[1] *Case of British and Irish Manufacture of Linnen.*

[2] *Case of the Linen Drapers.*

Nation. For the Rents of Land they must certainly fall, for that one Acre of Flax will imploy as many Hands the year round, as the Wooll of Sheep that graze twenty Acres of Ground. The Linnen Manufactory imploys few men, the Woollen most, Weaving, Combing, Dressing, Shearing, Dying, etc. These Eat and Drink more than Women and Children; and so as the Land that the Sheep graze on raiseth the Rent, so will the Arable and Pasture that bears Corn, and breeds Cattle for their Subsistence. Then for the Employment of our Shipping, it will never be pretendedthat we can arrive to Exportation of Linnen; there are others and too many before us in that. . . . That Projectors and Courtiers should be inspired with New Lights, and out of love to the Nation, create new Methods in Trades, that none before found out; and by inclosing Commons the Liberty of Trade into Shares, in the first place for themselves, and then for such others as will pay for both, is, I must confess, to me, a Mystery I desire to be a Stranger unto . . . The very Name of a Company and Joint-Stock in Trade, is a spell to drive away, and keep out of that place where they reside, all men of Industry. . . . The great motive to Labour and Incouragement of Trade, is an equal Freedom, and that none may be secluded from the delightful Walks of Liberty . . . a Subjection in Manufactories where a People are obliged to one Master, tho' they have the full Value of their Labour, is not pleasing, they think themselves in perpetual Servitude, and so it is observed in *Ireland*, where the *Irish* made a Trade of Linnen Yarn, no Man could ingage them, but they would go to the Market and be better satisfied with a less price, than to be obliged to one master. . . . There was much more Reason for a Company and Joint-stock to set up the Woollen Manufactory, in that ignorant Age, than there is for this of the Linnen Manufactory; that of the Woollen was a new Art not known in this

Kingdom, it required a great Stock to manage, there was required Foreign as well as Native Commodities to carry it on. . . . and when the Manufactory was made, there must be Skill and Interest abroad to introduce the Commodity where others had the Trade before them ; but there is nothing of all this in the Linnen Manufactory ; Nature seems to design it for the weaker Sex. The best of Linnen for Service is called House Wife's Cloth, here then is no need of the Broad Seal, or Joint-Stock to establish the Methods for the good Wife's weeding her Flax-garden, or how soon her Maid shall sit to her Wheel after washing her Dishes ; the good Woman is Lady of the Soil, and holds a Court within herself, throws the Seed into the Ground, and works it till she brings it there again, I mean her Web to the bleaching Ground. . . . To appropriate this which the poorest Family may by Labour arrive unto, that is, finish and bring to Market a Piece of Cloth, to me seems an infallible Expedient to discourage universal Industry. . . . . The Linnen Manufactory above any Trade I know, if (which I must confess I doubt) it be for the Good of the Nation, requires more Charity than Grandeur to carry it on, the poor Spinner comes as often to her Master for Charity to a sick Child, or a Plaister for a Sore, as for Wages ; and this she cannot have of a Company, but rather less for her labour, when they have beat all private Undertakers out. These poor Spinners can now come to their Master's Doors at a good time, and eat of their good tho' poor master's Chear ; they can reason with him, if any mistake, or hardship be put upon them, and this poor People love to do, and not be at the Dispose of Servants, as they must be where their Access can only be by Doorkeepers, Clerks, etc., to the Governors of the Company."*

---

* Linnen and Woollen Manufactory, p. 4-8, 1691.

On the other side it was urged that " All the Arguments that can be offer'd for Encouraging the woollen manufacture in *England* conclude as strongly in proportion for Encouraging the linnen manufacture in *Scotland*. 'Tis the ancient Staple Commodity there, as the Woollen is here."[1]

The part taken by women in the production of linen resembled their share in woollen manufactures. Some were weavers ; thus Oliver Heywood says that his brother-in-law, who afterwards traded in fustians, was brought up in Halifax with Elizabeth Roberts, a linen weaver.[2] Entries in the Foulis Account Book show that they were sometimes employed in bleaching but spinning was the only process which depended exclusively on their labour.

The rates of pay for spinning flax and hemp were even lower than those for spinning wool. Fitzherbert expressly says that in his time no woman could get her living by spinning linen.[3] The market price was of little moment to well-to-do women who span thread for their family's use and who valued the product of their labour by its utility and not by its return in money value ; but the women who depended on spinning for their living were virtually paupers, as is shown by the terms in which reference is made to them :—" shee beeinge very poore, gettinge her livinge by spinninge and in the nature of a widowe, her husband beeinge in the service of His Majesty."[4]

Yet the demand for yarn and thread was so great that if spinners had been paid a living wage there would have been scarcely any need for poor relief.

The relation between low wages and pauperism was hardly even suspected at this time, and though the

---

[1] *True case of the Scots Linen Manufacture.*

[2] Heywood (Rev. Oliver) *Autobiography*, Vol. I., p. 36.

[3] *Ante*, p. 48.

[4] *S.P.D.*, cccclvii., 3. June 13, 1640.

spinsters' maximum wages were settled at Quarter
Sessions, no effort was made to raise them to a subsistence level   Instead of attempting to do so Parish
Authorities accepted pauperism as "the act of God,"and
concentrated their attention on the task of reducing
rates as far as possible by forcing the pauper women
and children, who had become impotent or vicious
through neglect and underfeeding, to spin the thread
needed by the community. Schemes for this
purpose were started all over the country; a few
examples will show their general scope. At Nottingham
it was arranged for Robert Hassard to "Receave pore
children to the number of viij. or more, . .   and to
haue the benefitt of theire workes and labours for
the first Moneth, and the towne to allowe him towards
their dyett, for everie one xijd. a Weeke, and theire
parents to fynde them lodginge ; and Robert Hassard
to be carefull to teache and instructe them speedyly
in the spyninge and workinge heare, to be fitt to make
heare-cloth, and allsoe in cardinge and spyninge of
hards to make candle weeke, and hee to geue them
correccion, when need ys, and the greate wheeles
to be called in, and to be delivered for the vse of
these ymployments.[1]

A few years later in the scheme " for setting the
poore on worke " the following rates of pay were
established :—

6d. per pound for cardinge and spinning finest wool.
5d. „   -„   for ye second sort.
4d.ob. (= *oholus*,½d.) for ye third sorte.
1d. per Ley [skein] for ye onely spininge all sortes
     of linen, the reele beeing 4 yards.
ob per pound for cardinge candleweake.
1d. „   „   for pulling midling [coarser part] out
     of it.
1d. „   „   for spininge candleweake.[2]

---

[1] *Nottingham Records*, Vol. V., pp. 174-5, 1636.
[2] *Ibid*, pp. 259-60, 1649.

Orders for the Workhouse at Westminster in 1560, read that " old Women or middle-Aged that might work, and went a Gooding, should be Hatchilers of the Flax; and one Matron over them. That common Hedges, and such-like lusty naughty Packs, should be set to spinning ; and one according to be set over them. Children that were above Six and not twelve Years of Age should be sent to winde Quills to the Weavers."[1]

At a later date in London " Besides the relieving and educating of poor friendless harborless children in Learning and in Arts, many hundreds of poor Families are imployed and relieved by the said Corporation in the Manufactory of Spinning and Weaving : and whosoever doth repair either to the Wardrobe near Black-friars, or to Heiden-house in the Minories, may have materials of Flax, Hemp, or Towe to spin at their own houses. . . . leaving so much money as the said materials cost, until it be brought again in Yarn ; at which time they shall receive money for their work. . . . every one is paid according to the fineness or coarseness of the Yarn they spin. . . so that none are necessitated to live idly that are desirous or willing to work. And it is to be wished and desired, that the Magistrates of this city would assist this Corporation. . . . in supressing of Vagrants and common Beggars . . . that so abound to the hindrance of the Charity of many pious people towards this good work."[2]

The Cowden overseers carried out a scheme of work for the poor from 1600 to 1627, buying flax and having it spun and woven into canvas. The work generally paid for itself ; only one year is a loss of 7s. 8d. entered, and during the first seventeen years the amount expended yearly in cash and relief did

---

[1] Stow, *London*, Book VI., p. 60.

[2] *Poor Out-cast Children's Song and Cry.*

not exceed £6 11s. rising then in 1620 to £28 5s. 10d., after which it fell again. The scheme was finally abandoned in 1627, the relief immediately rising to £43 7s. 6d.[1]

Richard Dunning describes how in Devon " for Employing Women, . . . We agreed with one Person, who usually Employed several *Spinsters*, . . . he was to employ in *Spinning*, *Carding*, etc., all such Women as by direction of the Overseers should apply to him for Work, to pay them such Wages as they should deserve."[2]

" Mary Harrison, daughter of Henry Harrison, was comited to the hospitall at Reading to be taught to spyn and earne her livinge."[3] Similarly at Dorchester " Sarah Handcock of this Borough having this day been complayned of for her disorderly carriage and scolding in the work house . . . . among the spinsters, is now ordered to come no more to the work house to work there, but is to work elsewhere and follow her work, or to be further delt withall according to the lawe."[4]

At Dorchester a school was maintained for some years in which poor children were taught spinning : " This day John Tarrenton . . . . is agreed withall to vndertake charge and to be master of the Hospitall to employ halfe the children at present at burlinge,[5] and afterwards the others as they are willing and able, To have the howse and Tenne per annum : wages for the presente, and yf all the Children come into burlinge, and ther be no need of the women that doe now teach them to spinne, then the Towne

---

[1] *Suss. Arch. Coll.*, Vol. xx., pp. 99-100, *Acct. Book of Cowdon.*

[2] Dunning, *Plain and Easie Method*, p. 8, 1686.

[3] Guilding, *Reading*, Vol. II., p. 294.

[4] Mayo (C.H) *Municipal Records of Dorchester*, p. 667, 1635.

[5] To burl, " to dress cloth as fullers do."

to consyder of Tarrington to giue him either part or all, that is ix pownd, the women now hath.[1] . . .

Another entry, February 3rd, 1644-5, records that " Mr. Speering doth agree to provide spinning work for such poore persons that shall spin with those turnes as are now there [in the hospital house] . . . and to pay the poore for their spinning after the vsual rates for the worke they doe.[2]

In 1649 it is entered " This day Thos. Clench was here, and demanded 10 *li.* per ann. more than the stocke of the Hospital, which is 150 *li.* lent him for the furnishing of the house with worke for spinners, and for the overlooking to the children . . . the spinners shall have all the yeare 3½d. a *li.* for yearne . . . . and that there be as many children kept aworke as the roomes will hold . . . wee shall take into consideracion the setting of the poore on worke in spinning of worsted, and knitting of stockins, and also of setting vp a trade of making sackcloth.[3]

Schemes for teaching spinning were welcomed with enthusiasm by the economists of the period, because in many districts the poor rates had risen to an alarming height. They believed that if only the poor would work all would be well. One writer urged " That if the Poor of the Place do not know how to spin, or to do the Manufacture of that Place, that then there be Dames hired at the Parish-Charge to teach them ; and Men may learn to spin as well as Women, and Earn as much money at it as they can at many other employments."[4] Another writer calculated that if so employed " ixcl children wh^ch daielie was ydle may earne one w^t another vjd. a weke wh^ch

---

[1] Mayo (C. H.), *Municipal Records of Dorchester*, p. 515, 1638.

[2] *Ibid*, p. 521.

[3] *Ibid*, pp. 517-8.

[4] *Trade of England*, p. 10, 1681.

a mownte in the yere t o jMiijcxxxv[li]. Also that jciiijxx women . . ar hable to earne at lest some xijd., some xxd., and some ijs. vjd. a weeke.''[1]

This zest for teaching spinning was partly due to the fact that the clothiers were represented on the local authorities, and often the extending of their business was hampered by the shortage of spinsters. But the flaw in all these arrangements was the fact that spinning remained in most cases a grant in aid, and could not, owing to the low wages paid, maintain a family, scarcely even an individual, on the level of independence.

Children could not live on 6d. a week, or grown women on 1s. or 1s. 8d. a week. And so the women, when they depended wholly upon spinning flax for their living, became paupers, suffering the degradation and loss of power by malnutrition which that condition implies.

In a few cases this unsatisfactory aspect of spinning was perceived by those who were charged with relieving the poor. Thus, when a workhouse was opened in Bristol in 1654, the spinning scheme was soon abandoned as unprofitable.[2] Later, when girls were again taught spinning, the managers of the school " soon found that the great cause of begging did proceed from the low wages for Labour ; for after about eight months time our children could not get half so much as we expended in their provisions. The manufacturers . . . . were always complaining the Yarn was spun couarse, but would not advance above eightpence per pound for spinning, and we must either take this or have no work.'' Finally the Governor took pains therefore to teach them to produce a finer yarn at 2s. to 3s. 6d. per pound. This paid better, and would have been more profitable still if

---

[1] Tingey, *Norwich*, Vol. II, p. 355.

[2] Latimer, *Annals of Bristol*, p. 249.

the girls as they grew older had not been sent to service or put into the kitchen.[1]

Thomas Firmin, after a prolonged effort to help the poor in London, came to a similar conclusion. He explains that " the Poor of this Parish, tho' many, are yet not so many as in some others ; yet, even here there are many poor people, who receive Flax to spin, tho' thev are not all Pensioners to the Parish, nor, I hope, ever will be, it being my design to prevent that as much as may be ; . . . . there are above 500 more out of other Parishes in and about the City of *London ;* some of which do constantly follow this Employment, and others only when they have no better ; As, suppose a poor Woman that goes three dayes a Week to Wash or Scoure abroad, or one that is employed in Nurse-keeping three or four Months in a Year, or a poor Market-woman, who attends three or four Mornings in a Week with her Basket, and all the rest of the time these folks have little or nothing to do ; but by means of this spinning are not only kept within doors . . . . but made much more happy and chearful."[2]

Firmin began his benevolent work in an optimistic spirit, " had you seen, as I have done many a time, with what joy and satisfaction, many Poor People have brought home their Work, and received their money for it, you would think no Charity in the World like unto it. Do not imagine that all the Poor People in *England,* are like unto those Vagrants you find up and down in the Streets. No, there are many Thousands whose necessities are very great, and yet do what they can by their Honest Labour to help themselves ; and many times they would do more than they do but for want of Employment. Several that I have now working to me do spin, some fifteen, some sixteen,

---

[1] Cary,(John) *Proceedings of Corporation of Bristol*, p. 13, 1700.

[2] Firmin, *Some Proposals*, p. 19, 1678.

hours in four and twenty, and had much rather do it than be idle.[1]

The work developed until " He employed in this manufacture some times 1600, some times 1700 Spinners, besides Dressers of flax, Weavers and others. Because he found that his Poor must work sixteen hours in the day to earn sixpence, and thought their necessities and labour were not sufficiently supplied or recompensed by these earnings ; therefore he was wont to distribute Charity among them . . . without which Charity some of them had perished for want, when either they or their children fell ill . . . . Whoever of the Spinners brought in two pound of Yarn might take away with 'em a Peck of Coals. Because they soiled themselves by carrying away Coals in their Aprons or Skirts . . . . he gave 'em canvass bags. By the assistance and order of his Friends he gave to Men, Women and Children 3,000 Shirts and Shifts in two years."[2]

" In above £4000, laid out the last Year, reckning House-rent, Servants wages, Loss by Learners, with the interest of the Money, there was not above £200 lost, one chief reason of which was the kindness of several Persons, who took off good quantities . . at the price they cost me to spin and weave . . . . and . . . . the East India Co., gave encouragement to make their bags." But the loss increased as time went on . . . . " In 1690 his design of employing the poor to spin flax was taken up by the Patentees of the Linen Manufacture, who made the Poor and others, whom they employed, to work cheaper ; yet that was not sufficient to encourage them to continue the manufacture . . . The poor spinners, being thus deserted, Mr. *Firmin* returned to 'em again ; and managed that trade as

---

[1] Firmin, Thomas, *Life*, pp. 31-32, 1698.

[2] *Ibid*, pp 31-2, 1698.

he was wont ; But so, that he made it bear almost
its own Charges. But that their smaller Wages
might be comfortable to them he was more Charitable
to 'em, and begged for 'em of almost all Persons of
Rank with whom he had intimacy, or so much as
Friendship. He would also carry his Cloth to divers,
with whom he scarce had any acquaintance, telling
'em *it was the Poor's cloth, which in conscience they
ought to buy at the Price it could be afforded.*"[1] . . .
Finally, " he was persuaded by some, to make trial
of the *Woollen Manufacture ;* because at this, the Poor
might make better wages, than at Linen-work.
But the price of wool advancing very much, and the
London-Spinsters being almost wholly unskilful at
Drawing a Woollen-Thread, after a considerable
loss . . . . and 29 months trial he gave off
the project."[2]

Firmin's experiment, corroborating as it does the
results of other efforts at poor relief, shows that at
this time women could not maintain themselves by
the wages of flax spinning ; still less could they,
when widows, provide for their children by this
means.

But though the spinster, when working for wages
received so small a return for her labour, it must not
be forgotten that flax spinning was chiefly a domestic
art, in which the whole value of the woman's labour
was secured to her family, unaffected by the rate
of wages. Therefore the value of women's labour
in spinning flax must not be judged only according
to the wages which they received, but was more truly
represented by the quantity of linen which they
produced for household use.

---

[1] Firmin (Thomas) *Life*, pp. 33-6.

[2] *Ibid*, pp. 39-40.

D.   *Silk, and Gold and Silver.*

THE history of the Silk Trade differs widely from
that of either the Woollen or Linen Trades.   The conditions of its manufacture during the fifteenth century
are described with great clearness in a petition presented
to Henry Vl. by the silk weavers in 1455, which
" Sheweth unto youre grete wisdoms, and also prayen
and besechen the Silkewymmen and Throwestres of
the Craftes and occupation of Silkewerk within the
Citee of London, which be and have been Craftes
of wymmen within the same Citee of tyme that noo
mynde renneth unto the contrarie.   That where
it is pleasyng to God that all his Creatures be set in
vertueux occupation and labour accordyng to their
degrees, and convenient for thoo places where their
abode is, to the nourishing of virtue and eschewyng
of vices and ydelness.   And where upon the same Craftes,
before this tyme, many a wurshipfull woman within
the seid Citee have lyved full hounourably, and therwith
many good Housholdes kept, and many Gentilwymmen
and other in grete noumbre like as there nowe be
moo than a M., have been drawen under theym in
lernyng the same Craftes and occupation full vertueusly,
unto the plesaunce of God, whereby afterward they
have growe to grete wurship, and never any thing
of Silke brought into yis lande concerning the same
Craftes and occupation in eny wise wrought, but in
rawe Silk allone unwrought"; but now wrought goods
are introduced and it is impossible any longer to obtain
rawe material except of the worst quality .   .   .   .
" the sufferaunce whereof, hath caused and is like to
cause, grete ydelness amongs yonge Gentilwymmen
and oyer apprentices of the same Craftes within ye
said Citee, and also leying doun of many good and not-
able Housholdes of them that have occupied the same
Craftes, which be convenient, worshipfull and accordyng
for Gentilwymmen, and oyer wymmen of wurship, aswele

within ye same Citee as all oyer places within this Reaume." The petitioners assumed that " Every wele disposed persone of this land, by reason and naturall favour, wold rather that wymmen of their nation born and owen blode hadde the occupation thereof, than strange people of oyer landes."[1]

The petition received due attention, Statute 33, Henry VI enacting that " Whereas it is shewed to our Sovereign Lord the King in his said parliament, by the grevous complaint of the silk women and spinners of the mystery and occupation of silk-working, within the city of London, how that divers Lombards and other strangers, imagining to destroy the said mystery, and all such virtuous occupations of women in the said Realm, to enrich themselves . . . . have brought . . . . such silk so made, wrought, twined, ribbands, and chains falsely and deceitfully wrought, all manner girdels and other things concerning the said mystery and occupation, in no manner wise bringing any good silk unwrought, as they were wont." Therefore the importation of " any merchandise . . . . . . touching or concerning the mystery of silk women, (girdels which come from Genoa only excepted,)" is forbidden.[2]

This statute was re-enacted in succeeding reigns with the further explanation that " as well men as women " gained their living by this trade.

Few incidents reveal more clearly than do these petitions the gulf separating the conception of women's sphere in life which prevailed in mediæval London, from that which governed society in the first decade of the twentieth century. The contrast is so great that it becomes difficult to adjust one's vision to the implications which the former contains. Other incidents

---

[1] *Rolls of Parliament*, V., 325. *A Petition of Silk Weavers*, 34 Henry VI., c. 55.

[2] *Statutes*, II., p. 374, 33 Henry VI., c. 5.

can be quoted of the independence, enterprise, and capacity manifested by the prosperous women of the merchant class in London during the Middle Ages. Thus Rose de Burford, the wife of a wealthy London merchant, engaged in trading transactions on a large scale both before and after her husband's death. She lent money to the Bishop in 1318, and received 100 Marks for a cope embroidered with coral. She petitioned for the repayment of a loan made by her husband for the Scottish wars, finally proposing that this should be allowed her off the customs which she would be liable to pay on account of wool about to be shipped from the Port of London.[1]

It is, however, a long cry from the days of Rose de Burford to the seventeenth century, when "gentilwymmen and other wymmen of worship" no longer made an honourable living by the silk trade; which trade, in spite of protecting statutes, had become the refuge of paupers. To obviate the difficulties of an exclusive reliance on foreign supplies for the raw material of the silk trade, James I. ordered the planting of 10,000 mulberry trees so that " multitudes of persons of both sexes and all ages, such as in regard of impotence are unfitted for other labour, may bee set on worke, comforted and releved."[2]

The unsatisfactory state of the trade is shown in a petition from the merchants, silk men, and others trading for silk, asking for a charter of incorporation because "the trade of silke is now become great whereby . . . . customes are increased and many thousands of poore men, women and children sett on worke and mayntayned. And forasmuch as the first beginning of this trade did take its being from women then called silkwomen who brought

---

[1] By kind permission of Miss Eileen Power.

[2] *S.P.D.*, xxvi., 6. Jan. 1607.

upp men servants, that since have become free of all or moste of the severall guilds and corporacions of London, whose ordinances beeing for other particular trades, meet not with, nor have power to reprove such abuses and deceipts as either have or are likely still to growe upon the silk trade."[1]

A petition from the Master, Wardens and Assistants of the Company of Silk Throwers, shows that by this " Trade between Forty and Fifty thousand poor Men, Women and Children, are constantly Imployed and Relieved, in and about the City of *London* . . . . divers unskilful Persons, who never were bred as Apprentices to the said Trade of *Silk-throwing*, have of *Late years* intruded into the said Trade, and have Set up the same ; and dwelling in Places beyond the Bounds and Circuit of the Petitioners Search by their Charter, do use Divers Deceits in the *Throwing* and *Working* of the Manufacture of Silk, to the great Wrong and Injury of the Commonwealth, and the great Discouragement of the Artists of the said Trade."[2]

An act of Charles II. provided that men, women and children, if native subjects, though not apprentices, might be employed to turn the mill, tie threads, and double and wind silk, " as formerly."[3]

" There are here and there," it was said " a Silk Weaver or two (of late years) crept into some cities and Market Towns in *England*, who do employ such people that were never bound to the Trade . . . . in all other Trades that do employ the poor, they cannot effect their business without employing such as were never apprentice to the Trade . . . the Clothier must employ the Spinner and Stockcarder, that peradventure were never apprentices to any trade, else they could never accomplish their

---

[1] *S.P.D.*, clxxv., 102, Nov. 25, 1630.

[2] *Humble Petition of the Master, Wardens and Assistants of the Company of Silk Throwers.*

[3] Statutes 13 and 14, Charles II., c. 15.

end. And it is the same in making of Buttons and
Bone lace, and the like. But it is not so in this Trade ;
for they that have been apprentices to the Silk-weaving
Trade, are able to make more commodities than can
be easily disposed of . . . . because there hath
not been for a long time any other but this, to place
forth poor men's Children, and Parish Boyes unto ;
by which means the poor of this Trade have been
very numerous."[1]

During this period all the references to silk-
spinning confirm the impression that it had become
a pauper trade. A pamphlet calling for the imposition of a duty on the importation of wrought silks
explains that " The Throwsters, by reason of this
extraordinary Importation of raw Silk, will employ
several hundred persons more than they did before,
as Winders, Doublers, and others belonging to the
throwing Trade, who for the greatest part are
poor Seamen and Soldier's wives, which by this
Increase of Work will find a comfortable Subsistence
for themselves and Families, and thereby take off a
Burthen that now lies upon several Parishes, which
are at a great charge for their Support."[2]   The
" comfortable subsistence " of these poor seamen's
wives amounted to no more than 1s. 6d. or 1s. 8d.
per week.[3]

There seems here no clue to explain the transition
from a monopoly of gentlewomen conducting a
profitable business on the lines of Family Industry
to a disorganised Capitalistic Trade, resting on the
basis of women's sweated labour. The earlier monopoly was, however, probably favoured by the ex-
pensive nature of the materials used, and the necessity

---

[1] *Trade of England*, p. 18.

[2] *Answer to a Paper of Reflections, on the Project for laying a Dnty on English Wrought Silks.*

[3] *Case of the Manufacturers of Gilt and Silver Wire*, 1714.

for keeping in touch with the merchants who imported them, while social customs secured an equitable distribution of the profits. With the destruction of these social customs and traditions, competition asserted its sway unchecked, till it appeared as though there might even be a relation between the costliness of the material and the wretchedness of the women employed in its manufacture ; for the women who span gold and silver thread were in the same stage of misery.

Formerly women had been mistresses in this class of business as well as in the Silk Trade, but a Proclamation of June 11th, 1622, forbade the exercise of the craft by all except members of the Company of Gold Wire Drawers.

Under this proclamation the Silver thread of one Anne Twiseltor was confiscated by Thomas Stockwood, a constable, who entered her house and found her and others spinning gold and silver thread. " The said Anne being since married to one John Bagshawe hath arrested Stockwood for the said silver upon an action of £10, on the Saboth day going from Church, and still prosecuteth the suite against him in Guild Hall with much clamor."[1] Bagshawe and his wife maintained that the silver was sterling, and therefore not contrary to the Proclamation. Stockwood refused to return it unless he might have some of it. Therefore they commenced the suit against him.

Probably few, if any, women became members of the Company of Gold Wire Drawers, and henceforward they were employed only as spinners. Their poverty is shown by the frequency with which they are mentioned as inmates of tenement houses, which through overcrowding became dangerous to the public health. It was reported to the Council for example, that Katherine Barnaby " entertayns in her house in Great

---

[1] *C.R.*, June 16, 1624.

Wood Streate, divers women kinde silver spinners."[1]

These poor women worked in the spinning sheds of their masters, and thus the factory system prevailed already in this branch of the textile industry; the costliness of the fabrics produced forbade any great expansion of the trade, and therefore the Masters were not obliged to seek for labour outside the pauper class.

The Curate, Churchwardens, Overseers and Vestrymen of the parish of St. Giles, Cripplegate, drew up the following statement: "There are in the said Parish, eighty five sheds for the spinning Gilt and Silver Thread, in which are 255 pair of wheels.

The Masters with their Families amount unto	581
These imploy poor Parish-Boys and Girls to the number of	1275
There are 118 master Wire-Drawers, who with their wives, Children and Apprentices, make	826
Master weavers of Gold and Silver Lace and Fringes 106 Their Wives, Children, Apprentices and Journey Men amount unto	2120
Silver and Gold Bone-Lace makers, and Silver and Gold Button makers with their Families	1000
Windsters, Flatters of Gold and Silver and Engine Spinners with their Families	300
Total	6208

They continue: "The Poor's Rate of the Parish amounts to near Four Thousand Pounds per annum. . . . The Parish . . . . at this present are indebted One Thousand Six Hundred and Fifty Pounds. Persons are daily removing out of the Parish, by Reason of this heavy Burthen, empty Houses increasing. If a Duty be laid on the manufacture of Gold and Silver wyres the Poor must necessarily be increased."[2]

---

[1] *S.P.D.*, ccclix., Returns to Council . . . of houses, etc, 1637.

[2] *Case of the Parish of St. Giles, Cripplegate.*

Such a statement is in itself proof that Gold and Silver Thread making ranked among the pauper trades in which the wages paid must needs be suplemented out of the poor rates.

E. CONCLUSION.

IT has been shown that in textile industries all spinning was done exclusively by women and children, while they were also engaged to some extent in other processes, such as weaving, burling, bleaching, fulling, etc. The fact that the nation depended entirely upon women for the thread from which its clothing and household linen was made must be remembered in estimating their economic position. Even if no other work had fallen to their share, they can hardly have been regarded as mere dependants on their husbands when the clothing for the whole family was spun by their hands ; but it has been explained in the previous chapter that in many cases the mother, in addition to spinning, provided a large proportion of the food consumed by her family. If the father earned enough money to pay the rent and a few other necessary expenses, the mother could and did, feed and clothe herself and her children by her own labours when she possessed enough capital to confine herself wholly to domestic industry. The value of a woman's productive capacity to her family was, however, greatly reduced when, through poverty, she was obliged to work for wages, because then, far from being able to feed and clothe her family, her wages were barely adequate to feed herself.

This fact indicates the weakness of women's position in the labour market, into which they were being forced in increasing numbers by the capitalistic organisation of industry. In consequence of this weakness, a large proportion of the produce of a woman's labour was diverted from her family to the profit of the capitalist or the consumer ; except in the most skilled branches of the woollen industry, spinning was a pauper trade, a " sweated industry," which did not provide its workers with the means for keeping themselves and their families in a state of efficiency, but left them to some extent dependent on other sources for their maintenance.

Comparing the various branches of textile industry together, an interesting light is thrown upon the reactions between capitalistic organisation of labour and women's economic position.

Upper class women had lost their unique position in the silk trade, and the wives of wealthy clothiers and wool merchants appear to have seldom taken an active interest in business matters. Thus it was only as wage-earners that women were extensively employed in the textile trades.

Their wages were lowest in the luxury trades i.e., silk, silver and gold, and in the linen trade. The former were now wholly capitalistic, but the demand for luxuries being limited and capable of little expansion, the labour available in the pauper classes was sufficient to satisfy it. The situation was different in the linen and allied trades, where the demand for thread, either of flax or hemp, appears generally to have been in excess of the supply. Although the larger part of the linen manufactured in England was still produced under the conditions of domestic industry, the demand for thread for trade purposes was steady enough to suggest to Parish Authorities the value of spinning as a means of reducing the poor rates. It did not occur to them, however, that if the wages paid for spinning were higher the poor would have been as eager to learn spinning as to gain apprenticeship in the skilled trades, and thus the problem of an adequate supply of yarn might have been solved at one stroke with the problem of poverty itself ; no attempt was made to raise the wages, and the production of thread for trade purposes continued to be subsidised out of the poor rates. The consequent pauperisation of large numbers of women was a greater disaster than even the burthen of the poor rates. Instead of the independence and self-reliance which might have been secured through adequate wages, mothers were not only humiliated and degraded, but their physical efficiency and that of their children was lowered owing to the inadequacy of the grudging assistance given by the Churchwardens and Overseers.

The woollen trade, in which capitalistic organisation had attained its largest development, presents a more favourable aspect as regards women's wages. Already in the seventeenth century a spinster could earn sufficient money to maintain her individual self. In spite of periodic seasons of depression, the woollen trade was rapidly expanding ; often the scope of the clothiers was limited by the quantity of yarn available, and so perforce they must seek for labour outside the pauper class. Possibly a rise was already taking place in the spinsters' wages at the close of the century, and it is interesting to note that during this period the highest wages were earned, not by the women whose need for them was greatest, that is to say the women who had children depending exclusively on their wages, but rather by the well-to-do women who could afford to buy the wool for their spinning, and hold the yarn over till an advantageous opportunity arose for selling it.

Spinning did not present itself to such women as a means of filling up vacant hours which they would otherwise have spent in idleness, but as an alternative to some other profitable occupation, so numerous were the opportunities offered to women for productive industry within the precincts of the home. Therefore to induce women of independent position to work for him, the Clothier was obliged to offer higher wages than would have been accepted by those whose children were suffering from hunger.

Somewhat apart from economics and the rate of wages, is the influence which the developments of the woollen trade exercised on women's social position, through the disintegration of the social organisation known as the village community. The English village had formed a social unit almost self-contained, embracing considerable varieties of wealth, culture and occupation, and finding self-expression in a public opinion which provided adequate sanction for its customs, and determined all the details of manners and morals. In the formation of this public opinion women took an active part.

The seasons of depression in the Woollen Trade brought to such communities in the " Clothing Counties " a desolation which could only be rivalled by Pestilence or Famine. Work came to a standstill, and wholesale migrations followed. Many fathers left their starving families, in search of work elsewhere and were never heard of again. The traditions of family life and the customs which ruled the affairs of the village were lost, never to be again restored, and with them disappeared, to a great extent, the recognised importance of women in the life of the community.

The social problems introduced by the wages system in its early days are described in a contemporary pamphlet. It must be remembered that the term " the poor " as used at this time signified the pauper class, hard-working, industrious families who were independent of charity or assistance from the poor rates being all included among the " common people." " I cannot acknowledge," the writer says, " that a Manufacture maketh fewer poor, but rather the contrary. For tho' it sets the poor on work where it finds them, yet it draws still more to the place; and their Masters allow wages so mean, that they are only preserved from starving whilst they can work; when Age, Sickness, or Death comes, themselves, their wives or their children are most commonly left upon the Parish; which is the reason why those Towns (as in the *Weald of Kent*) whence the clothing is departed, have fewer poor than they had before."[1]

---

[1] *Reasons for a Limited Exportation of Wooll*, 1677.

CHAPTER V.

CRAFTS AND TRADES.

(A) *Crafts.* Influence of Gilds—Inclusion of women—Position of craftsman's wife—Purposes of Gilds—The share of women in religious, social and trading privileges—Admission chiefly by marriage—Stationer's Company—Carpenter's Company—Rules of other Gilds and Companies—Apprenticeship to women—Exclusion of women did not originate in sex jealousy—Position of women in open trades—Women's trades.

(B) *Retail Trades.* Want of technical training inclined women towards retailing—Impediments in their way—Apprenticeship of girls to shopkeepers—Prosecution of unauthorised traders—Street and market trading—Pedlars, Regraters, Badgers—Opposition of shopkeepers.

(C) *Provision Trades.*

    1. *Bakers.* Never specially a woman's trade—Widows—Share of married women.

    2. *Millers.* Occasionally followed by women.

    3. *Butchers.* Carried on by women as widows and by married women—also independently—Regrating.

    4. *Fishwives.* Generally very poor.

    5. *Brewers.* Originally a special women's trade—Use of feminine form Brewster—Creation of monopoly—Exclusion of women by the trade when capitalised—retailing still largely in hands of women.

    6. *Vintners.*

AGRICULTURE and the textile industries having been considered separately, owing to their importance and the very special conditions obtaining in both, the other forms of industry in which women were employed may be roughly divided into three classes, according to certain influences which made them more or less suitable for women's employment.—(*a*) Skilled Trades. (*b*) Retail Trades. (*c*) Provision Trades.

(*a*) *The Skilled Trades.* Most characteristic of the skilled trades are those crafts which became more or less highly organised and specialised by means of Gilds ; though girls were seldom apprenticed to the gild trades, yet her marriage to a member of the Gild conferred upon a woman her husband's rights and privileges ; and as she retained these after his death, she could, as a widow, continue to control and direct the business which she inherited from her husband. In many trades the gild organisation broke down, and though the form of apprenticeship was retained its observance secured few, if any, privileges. Some skilled trades were chiefly if not wholly, in the hands of women, and these appear never to have been organised, though long apprenticeships were served by the girls who entered them.

(b) *The Retail Trades.* The classification of retail trades as a group distinct from the Skilled Trades and the Provision Trades is somewhat arbitrary, because under the system of Family Industry, the maker of the goods was often his own salesman, or the middlemen who sold the goods to the consumers were themselves organised into gilds. Nevertheless, from the woman's point of view retailing deserves separate consideration, because, whether as a branch of Family Industry or as a trade in itself, the employment of selling was so singularly adapted to the circumstances of women, that among their resources it may almost take rank with agriculture and spinning.

(c) *The Provision Trades* also, whether concerned with the production or only with the sale of Provisions, occupy a special position, because the provisioning of their households has been regarded from time immemorial as one of the elementary duties falling to the share of women, and it is interesting to note how far skill acquired by women in such domestic work was useful to them in trade.

In all three classes of industry women were employed as their husbands' assistants or partners, but in the middle ages married women also engaged in business frequently on their own account. This was so usual that almost all the early Customs of the Boroughs enable a woman, when so trading, to go to law as though though she were a femme sole, and provide that her husband shall not be responsible for her debts. For example, the Customs of the City of London declare that: " Where a woman coverte de baron follows any craft within the said city by herself apart, with which the husband in no way intermeddles, such woman shall be bound as a single woman in all that concerns her said craft. And if the wife shall plead as a single woman in a Court of Record, she shall have her law and other advantages by way of plea just as a single woman. And if she is condemned she shall be committed to prison until she shall have made satisfaction ; and neither the husband nor his goods shall in such case be charged or interfered with. If a wife, as though a single woman, rents any house or shop within the said city, she shall be bound to pay the rent of the said house or shop, and shall be impleaded and sued as a single woman, by way of debt if necessary, notwithstanding that she was coverte de baron, at the time of such letting, supposing that the lessor did not know thereof. . . . Where plaint of debt is made against the husband, and the plaintiff declares that the husband made the contract with the plaintiff by the hand of the wife of such defendant, in such case the said defendant shall have the aid of his wife, and shall have a day until the next Court, for taking counsel with his wife."[1]

The Customal of the Town and Port of Sandwich provides that " if a woman who deals publickly in fish, fruit, cloth or the like, be sued to the amount of goods delivered to her, she ought to answer either with or without her husband, as the plaintiff pleases. But in every personal plea of trespass, she can neither recover nor plead against any body, without her husband. If she be not a public dealer, she cannot answer, being a covert baron."[2] Similarly at Rye,

---

[1] *Liber Albus*, pp. 181-2. 1419.

[2] Lyon. *Dover*, Vol. II., p. 295.

" if any woman that is covert baron be impleaded in plea of debt, covenant broken, or chattels withheld, and she be known for sole merchant, she ought to answer without the presence of her baron."[1]

In Carlisle it was said that " where a wife that haith a husband use any craft wi[th]in this citie or the liberties of the same besides her husband crafte or occupation and that he mel not w[th] her sayd craft this wife shalbe charged as woman sole. And if the husband and the wife be impledit in such case the wife shall plead as woman sole. And if she be condempned she shall goe to ward unto she haue mayd agrement. And the husband nor his guds shal not in this case be charged. And if the woman refuse to appeare and answere the husband or servand to bryng her in to answer."[2]

Though examples of the separate trading of women occur frequently in the seventeenth century, no doubt the more usual course was for her to assist her husband in his business. When this was transacted at home her knowledge of it was so intimate that she could successfully carry on the management during her husband's absence. How complete was the reliance which men placed upon their wives under these circumstances is illustrated by the story of John Adams, a Quaker from Yorkshire, who took a long journey " in the service of Truth " to Holland and Germany. He describes how a fearful being visited him by night in a vision, telling him that he had been deceived, and not for the first time, in undertaking this service, and that all was in confusion at home. " The main reason why things are so is, thy wife, that used to be at the helm in thy business, is dead." Thoroughly alarmed, he was preparing to hurry home when a letter arrived, saying that all was well,

---

[1] Lyon, *Dover*, Vol. II., p. 359.

[3] Ferguson, *Carlisle* p. 79 ; from *Dormont Book*.

" whereby I was relieved in mind, and confirmed I was in my place, and that it was Satan, by his transformation, who had deceived and disturbed me."[1]

The understanding and good sense which enabled women to assume control during the temporary absence of their husbands, fitted them also to bear the burden alone when widowed. Her capacity was so much taken for granted that public opinion regarded the wife as being virtually her husband's partner, leases or indentures were made out in their joint names, and on the husband's death the wife was left in undisturbed possession of the stock, apprentices and goodwill of the business.

A. *Skilled Trades or Crafts.*

The origin of the Craft Gilds is obscure. They were preceded by Religious Gilds in which men and women who were associated in certain trades united for religious and social purposes. Whether these Religious Gilds developed naturally into organisations concerned with the purpose of trade, or whether they were superseded by new associations whose first object was the regulation and improvement of the craft and with whom the religious and social ceremonies were of secondary importance is a disputed point, which, if elucidated, might throw some light on the industrial history of women. In the obscurity which envelopes this subject one certain fact emerges; the earlier Gilds included sisters as well as brothers, the two sexes being equally concerned with the religious and social observances which constituted their chief functions.

As the Gilds become more definitely trade organisations the importance of the sisters diminishes, and in some, the Carpenters for example, they appear to be virtually excluded from membership though

---

[1] *Irish Friend,* Vol. IV., p. 150.

this exclusion is only tacitly arrived at by custom, and is not enforced by rules. In other Gilds, such as the Girdlers and Pewterers, it is evident that though women's names do not occur in lists of wardens or assistants, yet they were actively engaged in these crafts and, like men, were subject to and protected by the regulations of their Gild or Company.

Very little is yet known of the industrial position of Englishwomen in the middle ages. Poll-tax returns show, however, that they were engaged in many miscellaneous occupations. Thus the return for Oxford in 1380 mentions six trades followed by women, viz.—37 spinsters, 11 shapesters (tailors), 9 tapsters (inn keepers), 3 sutrices (shoemakers,) 3 hucksters, 5 washerwomen, while in six others both men and women were employed, namely butchers, brewers, chandlers, ironmongers, netmakers and kempsters (wool combers). 148 women were enrolled as ancillæ or servants, and 81 trades were followed by only men.

A similar return for the West Riding of Yorks in 1379 declares the women employed in different trades to be as follows :—6 chapmen, 11 inn keepers, 1 farrier, 1 shoemaker, 2 nurses, 39 brewsters, 2 farmers, 1 smith, 1 merchant, 114 domestic servants and farm labourers, 66 websters, (30 with that surname), 2 listers or dyers, 2 fullers or walkers, and 22 seamstresses.[1] In every case these would be women who were carrying on their trade separately from their husbands, or as widows. During the following centuries women's names are given in the returns made of the tradesmen working in different Boroughs, occurring sometimes in trades which would seem to modern ideas most unlikely for them. Thus 5 widows and 35 men's names are given in a list of the smiths at Chester for the year 1574.[2]

---

[1] By kind permission of Miss Eileen Power.

[2] Harl, MSS., 2054. fo. 22., *The Smiths Book of Accts.* Chester, 1574.

It must be remembered that, except those who are classed as servants, all grown-up women were either married or widows. It was quite usual for a married woman to carry on a separate business from her husband as sole merchant, but it was still more customary for her to share in his enterprise, and only after his death for the whole burden to fall upon her shoulders. How natural it was for a woman to regard herself as her husband's partner will be seen when the conditions of family industry are considered. Before the encroachments of capitalism the members of the Craft Gilds were masters, not of other men, but of their craft. The workshop was part of the home, and in it, the master, who in the course of a long apprenticeship had acquired the technical mastery of his trade, worked with his apprentices, one or two journeymen and his wife and children. The number of journeymen and apprentices was strictly limited by the Gild rules ; the men did not expect to remain permanently in the position of wage-earners, but hoped in course of time to marry and establish themselves as masters in their craft. Apart from the apprentices and journeymen no labour might be employed, except that of the master's wife and children; but there are in every trade processes which do not require a long technical training for their performance, and thus the assistance of the mistress became important to her husband, whether she was skilled in the trade or not, for the work if not done by her must fall upon him. Sometimes her part was manual, but more often she appears to have taken charge of the financial side of the business, and is seen in the role of salesman, receiving payments for which her receipt was always accepted as valid, or even acting as buyer. In either case her services were so essential to the business that she usually engaged a servant for household matters, and was thus freed from the routine of domestic drudgery. Defoe, writing in

the first decades of the eighteenth century, notes that
" women servants are now so scarce that from thirty
and forty shillings a Year, their Wages are increased
of late to six, seven and eight pounds *per Annum*,
and upwards. . . . an ordinary Tradesman cannot
well keep one ; but his Wife, who might be useful
in his Shop, or Business, must do the Drudgery of
Household Affairs ; And all this, because our
Servant Wenches are so puff'd up with Pride
now-a-Days that they never think they go fine
enough."[1]

The position of a married woman in the tradesman
class was far removed from that of her husband's
domestic servant. She was in very truth mistress of
the household in that which related to trade as well as
in domestic matters, and the more menial domestic
duties were performed by young unmarried persons
of either sex. To quote Defoe again, " it is but
few Years ago, and in the Memory of many now living,
that all the Apprentices of the Shop-keepers and Ware-
house-keepers. . . . submitted to the most servile
Employments of the Families in which they serv'd ;
such as the *young Gentry*, their Successors in the
same Station, scorn so much as the Name of now ;
such as *cleaning* their Masters' Shoes, bringing *Water*
into the Houses from *the Conduits* in the Street,
which they carried on their Shoulders in long Vessels
call'd Tankards ; also waiting at Table, ... but
their Masters are oblig'd to keep Porters or Footmen
to wait upon the apprentices."[2]

The rules of the early Gilds furnish abundant
evidence that women then took an active part in
their husbands's trades ; thus in 1297 the Craft of
Fullers at Lincoln ordered that " none [of the craft]
shall work at the wooden bar with a woman, unless

---

[1] Defoe, *Everybody's Business is No-Body's Business*, p. 6, 1725.

[2] Defoe, *Behavionr of Servants*, p. 12, . 1724.

with the wife of a master or her handmaid,"[1] and
in 1372, when articles were drawn up for the Leather-
sellers and Pouch-makers of London, and for Dyers
serving those trades, the wives of the dyers of
leather were sworn together with their husbands
" to do their calling, and, to the best of their power,
faithfully to observe the things in the said petition
contained ; namely John Blakthorne, and Agnes,
his wife ; John Whitynge, and Lucy, his wife ; and
Richard Westone, dier, and Katherine, his wife."[2]

The craft Gilds had either disappeared before the
seventeenth century or had developed into Companies,
wealthy corporations differing widely from the earlier
associations of craftsmen. But though the Companies
were capitalistic in their tendencies, they retained
many traditions and customs which were characteristic of the Gilds. The master's place of business
was still in many instances within the precincts of
his home, and when this was the case his wife retained
her position as mistress. Incidental references often
show the wife by her husband's side in his shop
Thus Thomas Symonds, Stationer, when called as a
witness to an inquest in 1514 describes how " within
a quarter of an hower after VII. a clock in the morning,
Charles Joseph came before him at his stall and said
' good morow, goship Simondes,' and the said Simonds
said ' good morow ' to hym againe, and the wife of
the said Simons was by him, and because of the
deadly countenance and hasty goinge of Charles,
the said Thomas bad his wife looke whether Charles
goeth, and as she could perceue, Charles went into
an ale house."[3]

Decker describes a craftsman's household in " A
Shoemaker's Holiday." The mistress goes in and out

---

[1] Smith (Toulmin), *English Gilds*, p. 180.

[2] Riley (H. T.), *Memorials of London*, p. 365.

[3] Arber, *Stationers*, Vol. III., Intro, p. 19.

of the workshop, giving advice, whether it is wanted or not.

Firk : " Mum, here comes my dame and my master. She'll scold, on my life, for loitering this Monday ; . . . . "

Hodge : " Master, I hope you will not suffer my dame to take down your journeyman. . . "

Eyre : " Peace, Firk ; not I, Hodge ; . . . she shall not meddle with you . . . away, queen of clubs ; quarrel not with me and my men, with me and my fine Firk ; I'll firk you, if you do."[1]

But the meddling continues to the end of the play.

The same sort of scene is again described in " The Honest Whore," where Viola, the Linen Draper's wife, comes into his shop, and says to the two Prentices and George the servant, who are at work,

" Come, you put up your wares in good order, here, do you not, think you ? One piece cast this way, another that way ! You had need have a patient master indeed."

George replies (aside) " Ay, I'll be sworn, for we have a curst mistress."[2]

Comedy is concerned with the foibles of humanity, and so here the faults of the mistress are reflected, but in real life she is often alluded to as her husband's invaluable lieutenant. There can be no doubt that admission to the world of business and the responsibilities which rested on their shoulders, often developed qualities in seventeenth century women which the narrower opportunities afforded them in modern society have left dormant. The wide knowledge of life acquired by close association with their husbands' affairs, qualified mothers for the task of training their children ; but it was not only the mother who benefited by the

---

[1] Decker (Thos.), *Best Plays*, p. 29.

[2] *Ibid*, p. 108.

incorporation of business with domestic affairs, for while she shared her husband's experiences he became acquainted with family life in a way which is impossible for men under modern conditions. The father was not separated from his children, but they played around him while he worked, and his spare moments could be devoted to their education. Thus the association of husband and wife brought to each a wider, deeper understanding of human life.

Returning to the position of women in the Craft Gilds and the later Companies, it must be remembered that originally these associations had a three-fold purpose, (a) the performance of religious ceremonies, (b) social functions, (c) the protection of trade interests and the maintenance of a high standard of technical efficiency.

Women are not excluded from membership by any of the earlier charters, which, in most cases expressly mention sisters as well as brothers, but references to them are more frequent in the provisions relating to the social and religious functions of the Gild than in those concerning technical matters. Though after the Reformation the performance of religious ceremonies fell into abeyance, social functions continued to be an important feature of the Companies.

Entrance was obtained by apprenticeship, patrimony, redemption or, in the case of women, by marriage. The three former methods though open to women, were seldom used by them, and the vast majority of the sisters obtained their freedom through marriage. During the husband's life time their position is not very evident, but on his death they were possessed of all his trade privileges. The extent to which widows availed themselves of these privileges varied in different trades, but custom appears always to have secured to the widow, rather than to the son the possession of her husband's business.

Hitherto few records of the Gilds and Companies have been printed *in extenso* ; possibly when others are published more light may be shed on the position which they accorded to women. The Stationers and the Carpenters are selected here, not because they are typical in their dealings with women, but merely because their records are available in a more complete form than the others.

The Stationers' Company included Stationers, Booksellers, Binders and Printers ; apprenticeship to either of these trades conferred the right of freedom in the company, but the position of printer was a prize which could not be attained purely by apprenticeship ; before the Long Parliament this privilege was confined to twenty-two Printing Houses only besides the Royal Printers, vacancies being filled up by the Court of Assistants, with the approval of the Archbishop of Canterbury. Any stationer who had been made free of his Company might publish books, but printing was strictly limited to these twenty-two houses. A vacancy seldom occurred, because, according to the old English custom, on the printer's death his rights were retained by his widow, and in this Company they were not even alienated when she married again, but were shared by her second husband ; thus a printer's widow, whatever her age might be, was regarded as a most desirable " partie." The widow Francis Simson married in succession Richard Read and George Elde, the business following her, and Anne Barton married a second, third and fourth time,[1] none of the later husbands being printers.

Though amongst the printers the line of descent appears to have been more often from husband to wife and wife to husband than from father to son, a list, giving the names of the master printers as they

---

[1] Arber, *Stationers*, Vol. V., Intro. xxix-xxx.

succeeded each other from 1575 to 1635 shows that
the business was acquired by marrying the printer's
widow, by purchase from her, and also by descent.
Four women are mentioned :—William Ellis bound
to Mrs. East, a printer's widow who, having left the
trade many years was brought up in the art of printing
by Mr. Fletcher upon composition. Mrs. Griffyn
had two apprentices, Mrs. Dawson had three apprentices and Mrs. Purslow two apprentices.[1]   Another
list made in 1630 of the names of the Master Printers
of London gives twenty-one men and three women,
namely—Widdow Alde, Widdow Griffin, and " Widdow
Sherleaker lives by printing of pictures."[2]   In 1634
the names of twenty-two printers are given, among
whom are the following women—" Mr. William
Jones succeeded Rafe Blore and paies a stipend to
his wife . . . . neuer admitted.

Mistris [ ] Alde, widdowe of Edward Alde
[who] deceased about 10 yeeres since, (but she
keepes her trade by her sonne who was Ra[lph]
joyners sonne) neuer Admitted, neither capable of
Admittance.

Mistris [ ] Dawson widow of John Dawson
deceased about a yeere since [he] succeeded his vnkle
Thomas Dawson about 26 yeers since   . . .   never
admitted neither capeable, (she hath a sonne about
19 yeares old, bredd to ye trade).

Mistris [ ] Pursloe widdow of George Pursloe
who succeeded Simon Stafford about 5 yeeres since
[she was] never admitted neither capeable. (haviland,
Yo[u]ng and fletcher haue this.)

Mistris [ ] Griffin widdow of Edward Griffin
[who] succeeded Master [Melchisedeck] Bradwood
about 18 yeeres since [she was] never admitted neither

---

[1] *S.P.D.*, cccxiv., 127., Feb. 1636.

[2] *Ibid*, clxxv., 45., Nov. 12, 1630.

capable. (she hath a sonne.) (haviland, Yo[u]ng and fletcher have this yet).[1]

Men as well as women in the list are noted as " never admitted neither capable of admittance."

Whether these women took an active part in the management of the business which they thus acquired or whether they merely drew the profits, leaving the management to others, is not clear. From the notes to the above list it would appear that they often followed the latter course, but elsewhere women are mentioned who are evidently taking an active part in the printing business. For example, an entry in the Stationers Register states at a time when Marsh and Vautrollier had the sole printing of school books " It is agreed that Thomas Vautrollier his wife shall finish this present impression which shee is in hand withall in her husband's absence, of Tullie's Epistles with Lambini's annotations."[2]

After his death Vautrollier's widow printed one book but immediately after, on March 4th, 1587–8, the Court of Assistants ordered that " Mrs. Vautrollier, late wife of Thomas Vautrollier deceased, shall not hereafter print any manner of book or books whatsoever, as well by reason that her husband was noe printer at the time of his decease, as alsoe by the decrees sette downe in the Starre Chamber she is debarred from the same." This order is inexplicable, as other printers' widows exercised their husbands' business, and Thomas Vautrollier's name is duly given in the order of succession from Master Printers. Possibly the business had been transferred to her daughter, who married Field, their apprentice. Field died in 1625, his widow continuing the business.[3]

---

[1] Arber, *Transcript*, Vol. III, add, 701.

[2] Stopes (Mrs. C. C.) *Shakespeare's Warwickshire Contemporaries*, p. 7.

[3] *Ibid*, p. 8. (Some authorities state that Field married the widow, others the daughter of Vautrollier.)

Among thirty-nine printing patents issued by James I. and Charles II. is one to " Hester Ogden, als ffulke Henr. Sibbald *et* Tho. Kenithorpe for printing a book called The Sincire and True Translation of the Holy Scripture into the Englishe tounge." It appears as though Hester Ogden was no mere figure head, for His Majesty's Printers appealed against this licence on the grounds that it infringed their rights, protesting that " Mistris Ogden a maried woman one of Dr. Fulkes daughters did lately [sue] his Majesie to haue ye printing of her fathers workes, which his [Majestie] not knowing ye premises granted, and ye same being first referred [to the] Archbishop of Canterbury . . . their lordships . . . . deliuered their opinion against her, since which she hath gotten a new reference to the Lord Chancellor and Master Secretary Nanton, who not examining yᵉ title vpon oath and the Stationers being not then able to produce those materiall proofes which now they can their honors certified for her, wherevpon her friends hath his Majestie's grant for ye printing and selling of the sayed book for xxi. years to her vse . . . . Mistris Ogden hath gotten by begging from ye clergy and others diuers great somes of money towards ye printing of her fathers workes. Master Norton and myself haue for many £1000 bought ye office of his Majesties printer to which ye printing of ye translacons of the Bible or any parts thereof sett furth by the State belongs. Now the greatest parte of Dr. Fulkes worke is the new testament in English sett forth by authoritie."[1]

Another patent was granted to Helen Mason for " printing and selling the abridgment of the book of martyres,"[1] while Jane, wife of Sir Thomas Bludder, petitions Archbishop

---

[1] Arber, *Transcript*, Vol. III., p. 39.

Laud, showing that " She with John Bill an infant
have by grant from the King the moiety of the office
of King's Printer and amongst other things the printing
of Bibles. This is infringed by a printer in Scotland,
who printed many Bibles there and imported them
into England . . . . she prays the Archbishop
to hear the case himself."[2]

Many of the books printed at this time bear the
names of women printers,[3] but though women might
own and direct the printing houses, there is no indication that they were ever engaged in the manual
processes of printing. The printers' trade does in
fact furnish rather a good example of the effect upon
women's economic position of the transition from
family industry to capitalistic organisation. It is true
that many links in the evolution must be supplied
by the imagination. We can imagine the master
printer with his press, working at home with the
help of his apprentice, his wife and children ; then
as his trade prospered he employed journeymen
printers who were the real craftsmen, and it became
possible for the owner of the business to be a man or
woman who had never been bred up to the
trade.

Apprenticeship was still exacted for the journeymen. A Star Chamber decree in 1637 provides
that no " master printer shall imploy either to worke
at the Case, or the Presse, or otherwise about his
printing, any other person or persons, then such
only as are Free-men, or Apprentices to the Trade
or mystery of Printing."[1] While in 1676 the Stationers'
Company ordained that " no master-printer, or

---

[1] Arber, *Transcript*, Vol. V., lviii.

[2] *S.P.D.*, cccxxxix., p. 89.

[3] e.g. *An Essay of Drapery* . . . by William Scott, printed by Eliz. Alde
for S. Pennell, London, 1635. Calvin, *Institution of Christian Religion*. Printed
by the widowe of R. Wolfe, London, 1574. The fourthe edition of *Porta Linguarum*
is printed by E. Griffin for M. Sparke. London, 1639.

other printer or workman . . . . shall teach, direct or instruct any person or persons whatsoever, other than his or their own legitimate son or sons, in this Art or Mystery of Printing, who is not actually bound as an Apprentice to some lawful authorised Printer."[2]

From the omission here of any mention of daughters it is clear that the Master Printers' women folk did not concern themselves with the technical side of his trade; but some attempt was evidently made to use other girls in the unskilled processes, for on a petition being presented in 1635 by the younger printers, concerning abuses which they wished removed, the Stationers' Company adopted the following recommendation, " That no Master Printer shall hereafter permit or suffer by themselves or their journeyman any Girles, Boyes, or others to take off anie sheets from the tinpin of the presse, but hee that pulleth at the presse shall take off every sheete himself."[3]

The young printers were successful in their efforts to preserve the monopoly value of their position, and formed an organisation amongst themselves to protect their interests against the masters; but in this association the wives of the young printers found no place. They could no longer help their husbands who were working, not at home, but on the master's premises; and as girls were not usually apprenticed to the printing trade women were now virtually excluded from it.

Some imagination is needed to realise the social results of the change thus effected by capitalistic organisation on the economic position of married women, for no details have been discovered of the

---

[1] Arber, *Transcript*, Vol. IV., p. 534.

[2] *Ibid*, Vol. I, p. 16.

[3] *S.P.D.*, ccci., 105, Nov. 16, 1635.

printers' domestic circumstances; but as the wife was clearly unable to occupy herself with her husband's trade, neither she nor her daughters could share the economic privileges which he won for himself and his fellows by his organising ability. If his wages were sufficiently high for her to devote herself to household affairs, she became his unpaid domestic servant, depending entirely on his goodwill for the living of herself and her children; otherwise she must have conducted a business on her own account, or obtained work as a wage earner, in neither case receiving any protection from her husband in the competition of the labour market.

The wives and widows of the Masters were meanwhile actively engaged in other branches of the Stationers' Company. In a list of Publishers covering the years 1553–1640, nearly ten per cent. of the names given are those of women, probably all of whom were widows.[1] One of these, the widow of Francis Coldock, married in 1603 Isaac Binge, the Master of the Company. " She had three husbands, all Bachelors and Stationers, and died 1616, and is buried in St. Andrew Undershaft in a vault with Symon Burton her father.[2] The names of these women can be found also in the books they published. For example " The True Watch and Rule of Life " by John Brinsley the elder, printed by H. Lownes for Joyce Macham, *7th ed.* 1615, the eighth edition being printed for her by T. Beale in 1619, and " an Epistle . . . . upon the present pestilence " by Henoch Clapham, was printed by T.C. for the Widow Newbery, London, 1603. A woman who was a Binder is referred to in an order made by the Bishop of London in 1685 " to damask . . . . counterfeit Primmirs' seized at Mrs. Harris's Binder, "[1] and Women are

---

[1] Arber, *Transcript*, Vol. V., p. lxxxi-cxi.

[2] *Ibid*, Vol. V., p. lxiii.

also met with as booksellers. Anne Bowler
sold the book "Catoes Morall Distichs" . . . .
printed by Annes Griffin. The Quakers at Horsley
Down paid to Eliz. ffoulkes 3s. for their minute book,[2]
while Pepys' bookseller was a certain Mrs. Nicholls.[3]
The death of Edward Croft, Bookseller, is recorded
in Smyth's *Obituary*, " his relict, remarried since
to Mr. Blagrave, an honest bookseller, who live
hapily in her house in Little Britain."[4]

The trade of a bookseller was followed by women
in the provinces as well as in London, the Howards
paying " For books bought of Eliz. Sturton iijs.[5]
and Sir John Foulis enters in his account book
" To Ard. Hissops relict and hir husband for 3 paper
bookes at 10 gr. p. peice and binding other 4 bookes,
18. 14. 0 [Scots money], to them for a gramer and
a salust to the bairns, 1.2.0. She owes me 6/8. of
change."[6]

Presumably all the women who were engaged
in either of these allied trades in London were free
of the Stationers' Company, and in most cases they
were widows. Many apprentices were made free
on the testimony of a woman,[7] and though these

---

[1] Arber, *Transcript*, Vol. V., p. lv.

[2] Monthly Meeting Minutes. Horsleydown, 13 1mo 167$\frac{7}{8}$.

[3] Pepys, *Diary*, Vol. I., p. 26.

[4] Smyth's *Obituary*, p. 77.

[5] Howard, *Household Books*, p. 161, 1622.

[6] Foulis, Sir John, *Acct. Book*, p. 22, 1680.

[7] " Mistres Gosson. Stephan Coxe, Sworne and Admytted a Freeman of this
Companie iijs, iiijd. Note that master Warden White Dothe Reporte, for mistres
Gosson's Consent to the makinge of this prentice free. (Arbers, *Transcript*, Vol. II.,
p. 727, 1600.) Alice Gosson Late wyfe of Thomas Gosson. Henry Gosson sworne and
admitted A ffreeman of this company per patrimonium iijs. iiijd, (*Ibid*, p. 730, 1601.)
Mistries Woolff. John Barnes sworne and admitted A freeman (*Ibid*, p. 730,
1601. Jane proctor, Wydowe of William proctor. Humfrey Lympenny sworne
and admitted A ffreeman of this Companye iijs. iiijd. (*Ibid*, p. 730,
1601.) Mystris Conneway Nicholas Davyes sworn and admitted A freeman of,
this company per patrimonium iijs. iiijd, (*Ibid*, p. 7·2, 1602.)

in some cases may have almost completed their servitude before the death of their master, " Mistris Woolff " gives testimony for one apprentice in 1601, and for another in 1603, showing that she at least continued the management of her husband's business for some years, and as she received a new apprentice during this time,[1] it is evident that she had no intention of relinquishing it.

When on her husband's death the widow transferred an apprentice to some other master we may infer that she felt unable to take the charge of business upon her. This happened not infrequently, " Robert Jackson late apprentise with Raffe Jackson is putt ouer by consent of his mystres vnto master Burby to serve out the Residue of his terms of apprentishood with him, the Last yere excepted. . . . Anthony Tomson . . . . hath putt him self an apprentice to master Gregorie Seton . . . . for 8 yeres . . . . . Eliz. Hawes shall haue the services and benefit of this Apprentise during her wydohed or marrying one of the Company capable of him."[2] " John leonard apprentise to Edmond Bolifant deceased is putt ouer by the consent of the said mary Bolyfant vnto Richard Bradocke . . . . to serue out the residue of his apprentiship."[3] But whether the widow wished to continue the business as a " going concern " or not, she, and she only, was in possession of the privileges connected therewith, for she was virtually her husband's partner, and his death did not disturb her possession. The old rule of copyright recognised her position, providing " that copies

---

[1] Johne Adams of London (stationer's son) apprenticed to Alice Woolff of citie of London widowe for 8 years 2s. 6d. (Arber, *Transcript*, Vol. II, p. 253, 1601.) Other instances of apprentices being bound to women occur as for example " Wm. Walle apprenticed to Elizabeth Hawes Widow for 8 years (*Ibid*, Vol. II., p. 287, 1604.) " Thomas Richardson of York apprenticed to Alice Gosson, of citie of London wydowe for 7 years, 2s. 6d. (*Ibid*, Vol. II., p. 249, 1600).

[2] *Ibid*, p. 260, 1602.)

[3] *Ibid*, p. 262, 1602.

peculiar for life to any person should not be granted to any other but the Widow of the deceased, she certifying the title of the book to the Master and Wardens, and entering the book in the " bookes of thys Company."[1]

The history of the Carpenters' Company resembles that of the Staticners' in some respects, though the character of a carpenter's employment, which was so often concerned with building operations, carried on away from his shop, did not favour the continuance of his wife in the business after his death. The " Boke " of the ordinances of the Brotherhood of the Carpenters of London, dated 1333, shows the Society to have been at that time a Brotherhood formed " of good men carpenters of men and women" for common religious observances and mutual help in poverty and sickness, partaking of the nature of a Benefit Society rather than a Trade Union. The Brotherhood was at the same time a Sisterhood, and Brethren and Sisters are mentioned together in all but two of its articles. In the later code of ordinances, of which a copy has been preserved dated 1487, sisters are but twice mentioned, when tapers are prescribed at the burying of their bodies and prayers for the resting of their souls.[2] Women's names seldom occur in the Records, apart from entries connected with those who were tenants, or charitable grants to widows fallen into poverty, or with payments to the Bedell's wife for washing tablecloths and napkins.[3] In one instance considerable trouble was experienced because the Bedell's wife would not turn out of their house after

---

[1] Arber *Transcript*, Vol. V., p. 11, 1560.

[2] *Records of the Worshipful Company of Carpenters*, Vol. II., Intro., p. ix.

[3] For example " Itm payd to the bedells wyffe for kepyng of the gardyn vijs. *Ibid*, Vol. IV., p. 2. *Warden's Acct. Book*, 1546. She had besides iiijs. " for her hole yeres wasschyng the clothes " (p. 11) and iiijd. " for skoryng of the vessell," (p. 13) this payment was later increased to xijd. and she had " for bromes for Or Hall every quarter a jd. (p. 33) in Reward for her attendance ijs, (p. 114). Burdons wyffe for dressing your dinner xiiijd. (p. 129).

the Bedell's death. In September, 1567, "it is agreed and fullie determyned by the M^r wardeins & assystaunce of this company that Syslie burdon wydowe late wife of Richard burdon dwelling w^thin this house at the will & pleasure of the foresaid M^r & wardeins shall quyetlye & peaceablye dept out of & from her now dwellinge at Xpistmas next or before & at her departure to have the some of Twentie six shillinges & eight pence of Lawfull money of England in reward."[1] Syslie Burdon however did not wish to move, and in the following February another entry occurs " at this courte it is agreed further that Cysley burdon wydowe at the feast daye of thannunciacon of o^r Ladie S^t marye the virgin next ensueng the date abovesayd shall dept. & goe from her nowe dwellinge house wherein she now dwelleth wth in this hall & at the same tyme shall have at her deptur if she doethe of her owne voyd w^thout anye further troublynge of the M^r and wardeins of this house at that p'sent tyme the some of Twentie six shillinges eight-pense in reward."[2] Cyslie Burdon may have believed that as a widow she had a just claim to the house, for leases granted by the Company at this time were usually for the life of the tenant and his wife.[3]

Women accompanied their husbands to the Company dinners as a matter of course. In 1556 " the clothyng" are ordered to pay for " ther dynner at

---

[1] *Records of the Worshipful Company of Carpenters*, Vol. III., *Court Book*, p. 97.

[2] *Ibid*, p. 103.

[3] *Ibid*, Vol. III., pp. 10-11, March 15, 1544-5. " agreyed and codyssendyd thatt frances pope and hys wyffe schall have and hold a gardyn plott lyeng be oure hall in the prysche of alhallouns at london Wall for the tyme of the longer lever of them bothe payeing viijs. be the yere . . . the sayd [ ]pope nor hys wyffe schall not take dowene no palles nor pale postes nor Raylles In the garden nor no tres nor bussches schall nott plucke upe be the Rootes nor cutte theme downe nor no maner of erbys . . . w^towt the lycens of the Master and Wardyns of the mystery of Carpenters Aug. 10, 1564, " agreed and condissendid that Robart masckall and Elyzabeth his wiffe shall have and hold the Howse which He now occupieth duryng his lyffe and after the deseese of the said Robart to Remayne to Elizabeth his wyffe duryng her wyddohed paying yerlye x^ls of lawfull mony of England " etc, *Ibid*, Vol. III., p. 78.

the Dynner day ijs. vjd. a man whether ther wyffes
or they themselves come or no."[1] But the entries
do not suggest that the position of equal sisters which
they held in the days of the old " Boke " was maintained. Women made presents to the Company.
" Mistrys ellis," the wife of one of the masters of
the Company, presented " a sylv̄ pott psell gylt
the q̄ter daye at candylmas wayeing viij ozes &
a qter."[2] This apparently was in memory of her
deceased husband, for in the same year she "turned over"
an apprentice, and in 1564 a fine was paid by Richard
Smarte " for not comyng at yᵉ owre appoynted to
mistris Ellis beriall—xijd."[3] Neither the existence
of these two instances, which show a lively interest
in the Company, nor the absence of other references
can be taken as conclusive evidence one way or another
concerning the social position of the sisters in the
Company. Among the many judgments passed
on brothers for reviling each other, using " ondecent
words," etc., etc., only once is a woman fined for this
offence, when in 1556 the warden enters in his account
book " Resd of frances stelecrag a fyne for yll wordes
that his wyffe gave to John Dorrant ijˢ—Resd of John
Dorrant for yll wordes that he gave to Mystris frances
xvjᵈ—Resd of Wyllam Mortym̄ a fyne for callyng
of Mystris frances best ijˢ ."[4]

It is certain that the wives of carpenters, like the
wives of other tradesmen, shared the business
anxieties of their husbands, the help they rendered
being most often in buying and selling. This
activity is reflected in some rules drawn up to regulate

[1] *Records of Worshipful Company of Carpenters*, Vol. III., p. 58.

[2] *Ibid*, Vol. IV., p. 99, *Wardens Acct. Book*, 1558.

[3] In 1563 xxs. was " Resd of Wyllym barnewell at yᵉ buryall of his wiffe yᵗ she
dyd wyll to be gyven to yᵉ Company. (*Ibid*, Vol. IV., p. 147) Payd at the buryall of
barnewell's wyffe at yᵉ kyges hedd. xiiijs. iiijd. Paid to the bedle for Redyng of yᵉ
wyll viijd. (*Ibid*, Vol. IV., p. 149.)

[4] *Ibid*, Vol. IV., p. 84.

the purchase of timber. In 1554 " y^t was agreyd be the Master & wardyns and the moste parte of the assestens that no woman shall come to the waters to by tymber bourde lath q̄ters ponchons gystes & Raffters ther husbandes beyng in the town uppon payne to forfyt at ëvry tyme so fownd."[1] The Company's decision was not readily obeyed, for on March 8th, 1547, " the Master and the Wardyns w^t partt of the Assestens went to the gyldehall to have had a Redresse for the women that came to the watersyde to by stuffe,"[2] and on March 10th " was called in John Armestrong, Wyllyam boner, Wyllyam Watson, John Gryffyn and Henry Wrest there having amonyssion to warne ther wyffes that they schulde not by no stuffe at the waters syd upone payne of a fyne."[3]

On her husband's death the carpenter's wife generally retired from business, transferring her apprentices for a consideration to another master. That this practice was not universal is shown in the case of a boy who had been apprenticed to Joseph Hutchinson and was " turned over to Anne Hayward, widow, relict of Richard Hayward Carpentar."[4] Mrs. Hayward must clearly have been actively prosecuting her late husband's business. The women who " make free " apprentices seem generally to have done so within a few months of their husband's deaths. That the Company recognised the right of women to retain apprentices if they chose is shown by the following provision in Statutes dated November 10th, 1607. " If any Apprentice or Apprentices Marry or Absent themselves from their Master or Mistress During their Apprenticehood, then within

---

[1] *Records of Worshipful Company of Carpenters*, Vol. III., p. 15, *Court Book.*

[2] *Ibid*, Vol. III., p. 30.

[3] *Ibid*, Vol. III., p. 31.

[4] *Ibid*, Vol. I., p. 136.

one month the Master or Mistress is to Bring their
Indentures to the hall to be Registered and Entered,
etc" "None to Receive or take into their service
or house any Man or Woman's Apprentice Covenant
Servant or Journeyman within the limits aforesaid,
etc."[1]

When a carpenter's widow could keep her husband's
business together, no one disputed her right to
receive apprentices. Several instances of their doing
so are recorded towards the end of the century.[2] The
right to succeed her husband in his position as carpenter
and member of the worshipful company was immediately allowed when claimed by a widow ; thus the
court " agreed . . . that Johan burton wydowe
late wife of [   ] burton citezein and Carpenter of
London for that warninge hathe not ben goven unto
her from tyme to tyme at the Quarterdaies heretofore
From henseforthe shall have due warninge goven unto
her everye Quarterdaye and at the next Quarterdaie

---

[1] *Records of the Worshipful Company of Carpenters*, Vol. 1., Intro. vii-viii.

[2] *Ibid*, p. 137, May 2, 1671. Richardus Read filius Thome Read de Chart
Magna in Com. Kanc. Shoemaker po : se appren Josepho Hutchinson Bedello Hujus
Societat pro Septem Ann a die dat Indre Dat die et ann ult pred (Assign immediate
Susanne Catlin vid nuper uxor. Johannis Catlin nuper Civis et Carpenter London
defunct uten etc).
    Ibid, p. 153.   Dec. 5, 1676. Johannes Keyes filius Willi. Keyes nuper de
Hampsted in Com. Middx. Milwright ed Elizabetham Davis vid. willi Davis nuper
Civi & Carpentar de London a die date pred etc (sic)
    Ibid, p. 158. July 1, 1679. Samuell Goodfellow filius Johanni of Rowell in
Com. Northton Corwayner pon se Martha Wildey relict of Robert pro septem annis
a dat etc.
    Ibid, p. 161. Ap. 5, 1681. Georg Thomas filius Thome nuper de Carlyon in Com
Monmouth gent pon se Apprenticum Elizabeth Whitehorne of Aldermanbury
vid. Johis. pro septem Annis a dat.
    Ibid, p. 164.   Oct. 4, 1681. Richard Lynn sonn of William Lynn decd. pon se
Apprenticum Marie Lynn widdow Relict of the said William C : C: pro septem
annis a dat.
    Ibid, p. 165.   March 7, 1681-2. John Whitehorne son of John Whitehorne C : C :
Ld, pon se apprenticum Elizabethe Relict. ejusdem Joh's Whitehorne pro septem
annis a dat.
    Ibid, p. 171.   Apr. 5. 1686. Richard S'evenson sonne of Robt Stevenson late of
Dublin in the Kingedome of Ireland Pavier bound to Anne Nicholson Widowe the
Relict of Anthony Nicholson, for eight yeares.
    Ibid, p. 189. June 7, 1692. Robert Harper sonne of William Harper of
Notchford in the county of Chesheire, bound to Abigail Taylor for Seaven Yeares.

she shall paye in discharge of tharrerages behind Twelve
pence & so shall paye her Quateridge (p^d xijd.) "[1] ;
a year later " burtons widow " makes free an
apprentice Mighell Pattinson.[2]

Curiously enough, during the period 1654 to 1670,
twenty-one girls were bound apprentice at Carpenters'
Hall. Probably none of these expected to learn the
trade of a carpenter.[3] Nine were apprenticed to
Richard Hill and his wife, who lived first near St.
Michael's, Cornehill,[4] and afterwards against Trinity
Minories.[5] They were apprenticed for seven years
to learn the trade of a sempstress, and probably in
each case a heavy premium was paid, a note being
made against the name of Prudentia Cooper, who was
bound in 1664 "(obligatur Pater in 50^l pro ventute
apprenticij)."[6]

Richard Hill's wife's name is included in the Indentures three times, and in 1672 a boy was apprenticed
to " Ric. Hill Civi *et* Carpenter London necnon de
little Minories Silk Winder."[7] We may infer that
Mrs. Hill had founded the business before or after
her marriage with the carpenter, and that hers proving
profitable the husband had been satisfied with working
for wages, while retaining the freedom of the Company,
or had transferred his services to his wife's business,
adding that of a Silk winder to it. One girl originally
apprenticed to Henry Joyse was " turned over to
Anne Joyse sempstress & sole merchant without
Thomas Joyse her husband,"[8] five were apprenticed

---

[1] *Records of Worshipful Company of Carpenters*, Vol. III., p. 102, *Court Book*, 1567.

[2] *Ibid*, Vol. III., p. 200.

[3] *Ibid*, Vol. I., Intro. p. x-xi. Apprentice Entry Book.

[4] *Ibid*, Vol. I., p. 62.

[5] *Ibid*, Vol. I., p. 125.

[6] *Ibid*, Vol. I., p. 78.

[7] *Ibid*, Vol. I., p. 145.

[8] *Ibid*, Vol. I., p. 136

to Henry Joyce to learn the trade of a milliner. No mention is made of his wife, but as he received boy apprentices also,[1] it may be supposed that in fact the two trades of a carpenter and a milliner were carried on in this case simultaneously by him and his wife. The blending of these two trades is noted again in the case of Samuel Joyce ;[2] the trade the other girls were to learn is not generally specified, but Rebecca Perry was definitely apprenticed to William Addington " to learne the Art of a Sempstress of his wife."[3] Two girls were apprenticed to " Thome Clarke . . . . London Civi et Carpenter ad discend artem de Child's Coate seller existen. art. uxoris sue pro septem annis."[4]

Elizabeth Lambert, the daughter of Thomas Lambert, formerly of London, silkeman, was apprenticed in 1678 to Rebecca Cooper, widow of Thomas Cooper, " Civis Carpenter London," for seven years.[5] Another girl who had been apprenticed to this same woman in 1668 applied for her freedom in 1679, which was granted, though apparently her request was an unusual one, the records stating that " Certaine Indentures of Apprentiship were made whereby Rebecca Gyles, daughter of James Gyles of Staines, ... was bound Apprentice to Rebecca Cooper of the parish of St. Buttolph without Aldgate widdow for seaven yeares . . . . this day att a Court of assistants then holden for this Company came Rebecca Gylles Spinster sometime servant to Rebecca Cooper a free servant of this Company, and complained that

---

[1] *Records of the Worshipful Company of Carpenters*, Vol. I., p. 65, e.g. Brewin Radford (obligatur Maria Radford de Perpole in Com Dorsett vid. in 100¹ pro ventut apprentice).

[2] *Ibid*, Vol. I., p. 149, 1674. " Edmundus Wilstead filius Henrici Wilstead de Thetford in Com Norfolcie yeoman po : se appren. Samueli Joyse Civi et Carpenter London necnon de Exambia Regali London miliner pro septem annis " etc.

[3] *Ibid*, Vol. I., p. 162.

[4] *Ibid*, Vol. I., p. 148.

[5] *Ibid*, Vol. I., p. 156.

haveing served her said Mistres faithfully a Terme of seaven years wh^ch expired the twenty-fourth day of June, 1675, and often desired of her said Mistris Testimony of her service to the end shee might bee made free, her said Mistres had hitherto denyed the same ; & then presented credible persons within this Citty to testifie the truth of her said service, desireing to bee admitted to the freedome of this Company, which this Table thought reasonable, vnlesse the said Rebecca Cooper, her said Mistres on notice hereof to bee given, shall shew reasonable cause to the contrary, etc."[1] Encouraged by the success of this application, two other girls followed Rebecca Gyles' example, one being presented for her freedom at Carpenters' Hall by Thomas Clarke in 1683 and another by Henry Curtis in 1684.[2]

Thus it may be presumed that apprenticeship to a brother or sister of the Carpenters' Company conferred the right of freedom upon any girls who chose to avail themselves of the privilege, even when the trade actually learnt was not that of carpentry. Amongst the girl apprentices only one other was directly bound to a woman, namely " Elizabetha filia Hester Eitchus ux. Geo. Eitchus nuper Civi et Carpentar. pon se dict Hester matri pro septem ann a dat etc."[3] Although Hester Eitchus is here called " uxor " she must really have been a widow, for her name would not have appeared alone on the indenture during her husband's lifetime ; boy apprentices had previously been bound to him, and no doubt as in the other cases husband and wife had been prosecuting their several trades simultaneously, the wife retaining her membership in the Carpenters' Company when left a widow. An independent

[1] Jupp. *Carpenters*, p. 161, 1679.

[2] *Records of Worshipful Company of Carpenters*, Vol. I., p. 198.

[3] *Ibid*, Vol. I., *App. Entry Book*, p. 159, Feb. 3, 1679.

business must have been very necessary for the wife in cases where the husband worked for wages, and not on his own account, for in 1563 carpenter's wages were fixed " be my lorde mayors commandement . . . yf they dyd fynde themselves meat and drynke at xiiij^d the day and their servants xij^d. Itm otherwises the sayd carpynters to have viij^d the day wayges meat & drynke & their servants vj^d meat & drynke."[1] These wages would have been inadequate for the maintenance of a family in London, and therefore unless the carpenter was in a position to employ apprentices and enter into contracts, in which case he could find employment also for his wife, she must have traded in some way on her own account.

It is difficult to say how far the position of women in the Stationers' and Carpenters' Companies was typical of their position in the other great London Companies and in the Gilds and Companies which flourished or decayed in the provinces. All these organisations resembled each other in certain broad outlines, but varied considerably in details. All seem to have agreed in the early association of brothers and sisters on equal terms for social and religious purposes. Thus the Carpenters' was " established one perpetual brotherhood, or guild . . . . to consist of one master, three wardens, and commonalty of freemen, of the Mystery of Carpentry . . . . and of the brethren and sisters of freemen of the said mystery."[2] The charter granted by Henry VI. to the Armourers and Braziers provided " that the brethren and sisters of that ffraternity or guild, . . . should be of itself one perpetual community . . . . and have perpetual sucession. And that the brothers and sisters of the same ffraternity or guild, ... might choose and make one Master and two Wardens

---

[1] *Records of the Worshipful Company of Carpenters*, Vol. III., p. 75, *Court Book.*

[2] Jupp. *Carpenters*, p. 12.

from among themselves; and also elect and make another Master and other Wardens into the office aforesaid, according to the ordinances of the better and worthier part of the same brethren and sisters . . . . ."[1] In this case the sisters were regarded as active and responsible members but of the Merchant Taylors Clode says " It is clear that women were originally admitted as members and took apprentices; that it was customary in later years for women to dine or be present at the quarterly meetings is evidenced by a notice of their absence in 1603, ' the upper table near to the garden, commonly called the *Mistris Table*, was furnished with sword bearer and gentlemen strangers, there being no gentlewomen at this Quarter Day.' In many of the wills of early benefactors, sisters as well as brethren are named as ' devisees.' Thus in Sibsay's (1404) the devise is ' to the Master and Wardens and brethren and sisters ' . . . . . When an Almsman of the Livery married with the Company's consent his widow remained during her life an almswoman, and was buried by the Company. In that sense she was treated as a sister of the fraternity, but she probably exercised no rights as a member of it."[2]

The sisters are often referred to in the rules relating to the dinners, which were such an important feature of gild life. The " Grocers " provided that " Every one of the Fraternity from thenceforward, that has a wife or companion, shall come to the feast, and bring with him a lady if he pleases; [et ameyne avec luy une demoiselle si luy plest] if they cannot come, for the reasons hereafter named, that is to say, sick, big with child, and near deliverance, without any other exception; and that every man shall pay for his wife 20d.; also, that each shall pay 5s., that is

---

[1] *Armourers and Braziers. Charter and By-laws of the Company*, p. 4.

[2] Clode. *History of the Merchant Taylors*, London, Vol. I., p. 42.

to say, 20d. for himself, 20d. for his companion, and 20d. for the priest. And that all women who are not of the Fraternity, and afterwards should be married to any of the Fraternity, shall be entered and looked upon as of the Fraternity for ever, and shall be assisted and made as one of us ; and after the death of her husband, the widow shall come to the dinner, and pay 40d. if she is able. And if the said widow marries any one not of the Fraternity, she shall not be admitted to the said feast, nor have any assistance given her, as long as she remains so married, be whom she will ; nor none of us ought to meddle or interfere in anything with her on account of the Fraternity, as long as she remains unmarried."[1]

The Wardens of the Merchant Gild at Beverley were directed to make in turn yearly " one dinner for all his bretherne and theire wieves."[2] The Pewterers decided that " every man and wif that comyth to the yemandries dynner sholde paye xvjd. And every Jorneyman that hath a wif . . . . xvj[d]. And every lone man beinge a howsholder that comyth to dynner shall paye xij[d]. and every Jorneyman having no wif and comyth to dynner shall paye viij[d]. . . . . every man that hath bynne maryed w[th]in the same ij years shall geve his cocke or elfe paye xij[d] . . . . Provided always that none bringe his gest w[th] him w[th]owt he paye for his dynner as moch as he paith for hymself and that they bring no childerne w[th] them passing one & no more."[3] In 1605 it was agreed that " ther shalbe called all the whole clothyng and ther wyves and the wydowes whose husbandes have byne of the clothynge and that shalbe payed ijs. man & wyffe and the wydowes xijd. a peece."[4] In 1672, the expense

[1] Heath, *Acct. of the Worshipful Company of Grocers*, p. 53, memo. 1348.

[2] Leach, *Beverley Town Documents*, p. 95, 1582.

[3] Welch, *History of Pewterers Company*, Vol. I., p. 201, 1559.

[4] *Ibid*, Vol. II., p. 47.

of entertaining becoming irksome, " an order of Co^{rt} for ye abateing extrao^{r}dinary Feasting " was made, requiring the " Master & Wardens . . . . to deposit each 12li & spend ye one half thereof upon the Masters & Wardens ffeast this day held, and the Other moyety to be and remain to ye Comp^a use. Now this day the s^d Feast was kept but by reason of the women being invited ye Charge of ye Feast was soe extream that nothing could be cleered to ye house according to ye s^d order. There being Spent near 90li."[1]

Sisters are also remembered in the provisions made for religious observances and assistance in times of sickness. The ordinances of the Craft of the Glovers at Kingston-upon-Hull required that " every brother and syster of ye same craff^{tt} be at every offeryng within the sayd town with every brother or syster of the same crafftt as well at weddynges as at beryalles." Brethren and sisters were to have lights at their decease, and if in poverty to have them freely.[2] The " yoman taillours " made application " that they and others of their fraternity of yomen yearly may assemble . . . . near to Smithfield and make offerings for the souls of brethren and sister etc."[3] In the city of Chester, when a charter wa given to joiners, carvers and turners to become a separate Company, not part of the Carpenters' as formerly, to be called the Company of the Joiners, it is said " Every brother of the said occupacions shall bee ready att all times . . . . to come unto . . . . the burial of every brother and sister of the said occupacions."[4]

Sisters must have played an important part in the

---

[1] Welch, *Hist. of Pewterers'Company*, Vol. II., p. 145.

[2] Lambert, *Two Thousand Years of Gild Life*, p. 217, 1499.

[3] *Ibid*, p. 229, 1415.

[4] Harl. MSS., 2054, fo.5. *Charter of the Joiner's Co.*

functions of the Merchant Taylors of Bristol, for an order was made in 1401 that " the said maister and iiii wardeyns schall ordeyne every yere good and convenient cloth of oon suyt for all brothers and sisters of the said fraternity . . . ."[1] The Charter of this Company provided that " ne man ne woman be underfange into the fraternite abovesaid withoute assent of the Keper and maister etc. . . . . and also that hit be a man or woman y knowe of good conversation and honeste . . . . Also y^t eny brother other soster of thys fraternite above sayde that have trewly y payed hys deutes yat longeth to ye fraternite falle into poverte other into myschef and maie note travalle for to he be releved, he schal have of ye comune goodes every weke xxi^d of monei . . . . and yf he be a man yat hath wyfe and chylde he schal trewly departe alle hys goodes bytwyne heir and hys wyfe and children; and ye partie that falleth to hym he schal trewly yeld up to ye mayster and to ye wardynes of the fraternite obove sayde, in ye maner to fore seide. . . . . " The brothers and sisters shall share in the funeral ceremonies, etc., " also gif eny soster chyde with other openly in the strete, yat eyther schalle paye a pounde wex to ye lighte of the fraternite; and gif they feygte eyther schall paie twenty pounde wex to ye same lyte upon perryle of hir oth gif thei be in power. And gif eny soster by y proved a commune chider among her neygbourys after ones warnyng other tweies at the (delit) ye thridde tyme ye maister and ye wardeynes of ye fraternite schulle pute her out of ye compaynye for ever more."[2]

Chiding and reviling were failings common to all gilds, and were by no means confined to the sisters. The punishments appointed by the Merchant

---

[1] Fox (F. F.) *Merchant Taylors, Bristol*, p. 31.

[2] *Ibid*, p. 26-9.

Gild at Beverley for those " who set up detractions, or rehearse past disputes, or unduly abuse "[1] are for brothers only. And though it was " Agreed by the M[r] Wardens and Assystaunce " of the Pewterers that " Robert west sholde bringe in his wif vpon ffrydaye next to reconsile her self to M[r] Cacher and others of the Company for her naughty mysdemeano[r] of her tonge towarde them, "[2] the quarrelling among the Carpenters seems to have been almost confined to the men.

There can be no doubt that the sisters shared fully in the social and religious life of the Gilds ; it is also perfectly clear that the wife was regarded by the Gild or Company as her husband's partner, and that, after his death she was confirmed in the possession of his business with his leases and apprentices at least during the term of her widowhood.

But the extent to which she really worked with him in his trade and was qualified to carry it on as a going concern after his death is much more difficult to determine, varying as it did from trade to trade and depending so largely in each case upon the natural capacity of the individual woman concerned. The extent to which a married woman could work with her husband depended partly upon whether his trade was carried on at home or abroad. It has been suggested that the carpenters who often were engaged in building operations could not profit much by their wives' assistance, but many trades which in later times have become entirely closed to women were then so dependent on their labour that sisters are mentioned specifically in rules concerning the conditions of manufacture. Thus the charter of the Armourers and Brasiers was granted in the seventeenth year of James I. " to the Master and

---

[1] Leaeh, *Beverley Town Documents*, p. 78, 1494.

[2] Welch, Charles, *Hist. of Pewterers Company*, Vol. I., p. 200, 1558.

Wardens and Brothers and Sisters of the ffraternity
. . . . that from thenceforth All & all manner
of brass and copper works . . . . edged tools
. . . . small guns . . . . wrought by any
person or persons being of the same ffraternity . . .
should be searched and approved . . . . by
skilful Artificers of the said ffraternity."[1] Rules
which were drawn up at Salisbury in 1612 provide that
no free brother or sister shall " rack, set, or cause
to be racked or set, any cloth upon any tenter, on the
Sabbath day, under the forfeiture of 2s." The Wardens
of the Company of Merchants, Mercers, Grocers,
Apothecaries, Goldsmiths, Drapers, Upholsterers, and
Embroiderers were ordered to search the wares,
merchandise, weights and measures of sisters as well
as brothers.[2] " No free brother or sister is at any time
to put any horse leather into boots or shoes or any
liquored calves leather into boots or shoes, to be
sold between the feast of St. Bartholomew the Apostle
and the Annunciation of the Virgin Mary . . . .
No free brother or sister is to keep or set up any standing in the market place, except in fair times. No
brother or sister is to set open his or her shop, or to
do any work, in making or mending of boots and
shoes on the Sabbath day, on pain of twelve pence
forfeit."[3]

Rules which specifically permit the employment
of the master's wife or daughter in his trade while
excluding other unapprenticed persons, are in themselves evidence that they were often so employed.

---

[1] *Armourers and Brasiers, Charter and Bye laws of Company of.* p. 5. See also
Johnson, *Ordinances of the Drapers of London,* Vol. I., p. 280, 1524).

"(it shall not be lawful unto any brother or sister freed in this fellyship
to take mo. apprentices than may stand in good order for their degree) . . .
every brother being in the master's livery shall pay 6s. 8d. and every sister whose
husband has been of the aforesaid livery shall pay for every apprentice 6s. 8d. and
every other brother or sister not being of the master's livery shall pay for every
apprentice 3s. 4d.

[2] Hoare, Sir R. C., *Hist. of Modern Wilts,* Vol. VI., p. 34c.

[3] *Ibid,* Vol. VI., p. 343.

Thus the Glovers allowed " noe brother of this
ffraternity " to " take an apprentice vnder the full
end and tearme of seaven years ffuly to be compleat
. . . . excepting brothers son or daughter . ."[1]
No leatherseller might " put man, child or woman to
work in the same mistery, if they be not bound
apprentice, and inrolled in the same mistery ; excepting their wives and children."[2] Similarly the Girdlers
in 1344 ordered that " no one of the trade shall get
any woman to work other than his wedded wife or
daughter "[3] while by a rule of the Merchant Taylors,
Bristol " no person . . . shall cutt make or sell
any kynde of garment, garments, hose or breeches
within ye saide cittie . . . unles he be franchised
and made free of the saide crafte (widdowes whose
husbandes were free of ye saide crafte duringe
the tyme of their wyddowhedd vsinge ye same
with one Jorneyman and one apprentice only
excepted) "[4]

The association of women with their husbands in
business matters is often suggested by the presence
of both their names on indentures. Walter Beemer,
for example, was apprenticed to John Castle of Marke
and Johane his wife to be instructed and brought
up in the trade of a tanner.[5] Sometimes it is
shown by the indifference with which money
transactions are conducted either with husband or
with wife. When the Corporation at Dorchester
purchased a new mace in 1660, Mr. Sam White's
wife appears to have acted throughout in the matter.
An entry in the records for 1660 states that " the silver

[1] Ferguson, *Carlisle*, p. 212, *Glover's Gild*, 1665.

[2] Black, W. H., *Articles of the Leathersellers*, p. 21, 1398.

[3] Smythe, W. D., *Hist. of Worshipful Co. of Girdlers*, London, p. 63.

[4] Fox, F. F., *Merchant Taylors, Bristol*, pp. 64-65.

[5] *Somerset Quarter Sessions Records*, Vol. III., p. 165, 1652.

upon the old maces . . . . comes unto iij^{li}. xviij^s. iij^d, which was intended to bee delivered to Mr. Sam: White's wife towards payment for the new Maces . . . . Mr. White hath it the 18th of January, 1660. (Inserted later).

> July 3rd, 1661.—pd. Mrs. White as appeareth forward   5 0 0
>
> October 4th, 1661.—pd. Mrs. White more as appeareth forward   4 10 0
>
> About Michaelmas, Mr. Sauage pd Mrs. White in dollers   7 7 0
>
> April 26th, 1661.—It is ordered and agreed that twenty shillings a man, which shall be lent and advanced to Mr. Samuel White's wife by any of this Company towards payment for the Maces shall be repayed back to them."[1]

An equal indifference is shown by the Carpenters' Company in making payments for their ale. Sometimes these are entered to William Whytte, but quite as often to " his wyffe." For example in 1556 " Itm payd for Yest to Whytte's wyffe iiij^d"[2] " Resd of Whytte's wyffe her hole yere's Rent in ale xxix^s iiij^d "[3] " Itm payd to whytte's wyffe for ale above the rent of hyr howsse iij^s.vj^d." " Itm payd to whytte's wyff for hopyng of tobbis xvj^d."[4] Finally, in 1559, when perhaps William Whytte had departed this life, it is entered " Resd of Mother whytte hole yeres rent xxix^s.vij^d."[5]

The Pewterers, in order to check stealing, ordered that " none of the sayde Crafte shall bye anye Leade of Tylers, Laborers, Masons, boyes, nor of women Nor of none such as shall seme to be a Suspect pson," adding

---

[1] Mayo, G. H., *Municipal Records, Dorchester*, p. 466.

[2] *Rec. of Worshipful Co. of Carpenters*, Vol. IV., p. 56, *Warden's Acct. Book*, 1556.

[3] *Ibid*, Vol. IV., p. 86.

[4] *Ibid*, Vol. IV., p. 88.

[5] *Ibid*, Vol. IV., p. 101.

"that none of the sayde companye shalbe excusyd by his wif or servannte nor none other suche lyk excuse."[1]

Gild rules recognise the authority of the mistress over apprentices, the Clockmakers ordaining that "no servant or apprentice that . . . . hath without just and reasonable cause, departed from his master, mistress or dame, ... shall be admitted to work for himself,"[2] while the charter of the Glass-sellers provides suitable punishment " if any apprentice . . . . shall misbehave himself towards his master or mistress . . . . or shall lie out of his master or mistress's house without his or her privity."[3]

When a man who belonged to Gild or Company died, his wife was free to continue his business under her own management, retaining her position as a free sister, or she might withdraw from trade and transfer her apprentices to another brother. In the Carpenters' and some other trades the latter was the more usual course to follow; thus Thomas Mycock, a cutler, on taking over an apprentice who had served John Kay, deceased, six years, covenanted to pay Kay's widow 20s. a year for the three remaining years,[4] but on the other hand the widow Poynton was paid 15s. 7d. " for glass worke " by the Burgery of Sheffield;[5] showing that she had not withdrawn from business on her husband's death. It is clear that widows often lost their rights as sisters, if they took, as a second husband, a man who was not and did not become a brother of the same Gild. Thus there is an entry in the " Pewterers' Records," 1678, concerning " Mrs. Sicily Moore, formerly the wife of

---

[1] Welch, *Hist. of Pewterers' Company*, Vol. I., pp. 180-181.

[2] Overall, *Company of Clockmakers*, London, p. 43, 1632.

[3] Ramsay, Wm., *Hist. of the Glass-Sellers*, p. 125.

[4] Leader, *Hist. of Company of Cutlers*, Vol. I., p. 47, 1696.

[5] Leader, *Records of the Burgery of Sheffield*, p. 227, 1685.

Edward Fish, late member of this Comp^a dec₫, and since marryed to one Moore, a fforeignir, now also dec₫, desired to be admitted into the ffreedome of this Comp^a.   After some debate the Court agreed and soe Ordered that she shall be received into the ffreedom of the Comp^a Gratis, onely paying usuall ffees and this Condition that she shall not bind any app'ntice by virtue of the s^d Freedom."[1]

Instances occur in which an apprentice was discharged because " the wife, after the death of her Husband, taught him not."[2]   The apprentice naturally brought forward this claim if by so doing there was a chance of shortening the term of his service, but he was not always successful.   The Justices dismissed a case brought by Edward Steel, ordering him to serve Elizabeth Apprice, widow, the remainder of his term.   He was apprenticed in 1684 to John Apprice Painter-Stainer for nine years ; he had served seven years when his master died, and he now declares that Elizabeth, the widow, refuses to instruct him.   She insists that since her husband's death she has provided able workmen to instruct this apprentice, and that he was now capable of doing her good service.[3] When the " widowe Holton prayed that she [being executor to her husband] maye have the benefitt of the service of Roger Jakes, her husband's apprentice by Indenture, for the residue of the years to come, which he denyeth to performe, it was ordered that th'apprentice shall dwell and serve his dame duringe the residue of his terme, she providing for him as well work as other things fitt for him."[4]   The Girdlers having accused Richard Northy of having more than the just number of apprentices, he stated

---

[1] Welch, *Hist. of Pewterers' Company*, Vol. II., p. 153.

[2] Stow, *London*, Book V., p. 335.

[3] *Middlesex Sessions Book*, p. 47, 1691.

[4] Guilding, *Reading Records*, Vol. II., p. 362.

in his defence that the apprentice " was not any that was taken or bound by him, but was left unto him by express words in the will of his deceased mother-in-law wh^ch will, wth the probate thereof, he now produced in court."[1]

The occurrence of widows' names among the cases which came before the Courts for infringements of the Company's rules is further evidence that they were actively engaged in business. " Two bundles of unmade girdles were taken from widows Maybury and Bliss, young widows " they were ordered to pay 5s. each by way of fine for making and selling unlawful wares."[2] Richard Hewatt, of Northover in Glastonbury, fuller, when summoned to appear before the Somerset Quarter Sessions as a witness, refers to his dame Ursula Lance who had " lost 2 larrows worth five shillings and that Robert Marsh, one of the constables of Somerton Hundred, found in the house of William Wilmat the Larrows cloven in pieces and put in the oven, and the Rack-hookes that were in the larrows were found in the fire in the said house."[3]

Widows were very dependent upon the assistance of journeymen, and often chose a relation for this responsible position. At Reading " All the freman Blacksmiths in this Towne complayne that one Edward Nitingale, a smith, beinge a forreynour, useth the trade of a blacksmith in this Corporacion to the great dammage of the freemen : it was answered that he is a journey-man to the Widowe Parker, late wife to Humfrey Parker, a blacksmith, deceased, and worketh as her servant at 5s. a weeke, she being his aunt, and was advised to worke in noe other manner but as a journey-man."[4] The connection often ended in

---

[1] Smythe, *Company of Girdlers*, p. 133, 1635.

[2] *Ibid*, p. 87, 1627.

[3] *Somerset Q.S. Rec.*, Vol. III., pp. 365-6, 1659.

[4] Guilding, *Reading Records*, Vol. III., p. 502, 1640.

marriage; it was brought to the notice of one of the Quaker's Meetings in London that one of their Members, "Will Townsend . . . card maker proposes to take to wife Elizabeth Doshell of ye same place to be his wife, and ye same Elizabeth doth propose to take ye said Will to be her husband, the yonge man liveing with her as a journey-man had thought and a beliefe that she would come to owne ye truth and did propose to her his Intentions towards her as to marige before she did come to owne the truth which thinge being minded to him by ffriends. . . . he has acknowledged it soe and sayes it had been beter that he had waited till he had had his hope in some measure answered."[1]

Such marriages, though obviously offering many advantages, were not always satisfactory. A lamentable picture of an unfortunate one is given in the petition of Sarah Westwood, wife of Robert Westwood, Feltmaker, presented to Laud in 1639, showing that "your petitioner was (formerly) the wife of one John Davys, alsoe a Feltmaker, who dying left her a howse furnished with goodes sufficient for her use therein and charged with one childe, as yet but an infant, and two apprentices, who, for the residue of their termes . . . could well have atchieved sufficient for the maynetenance of themselves and alsoe of your petitioner and her child. That being thus left in good estate for livelyhood, her nowe husband became a suitor unto her in the way of marriage, being then a journeyman feltmaker. . . ."

Soon after their marriage, "Westwood following lewde courses, often beate and abused your petitioner, sold and consumed what her former husband left her, threatened to kill her and her child, turned them out of dores, refusing to afford them any means of subsistance, but on the contrary seekes the utter ruin of them both and most scandelously has traduced

---

[1] *Horsleydown Monthly Meeting Minute Book*, 19 11mo., 1675.

your petitioner giving out in speeches that she would have poysoned him thereby to bring a generall disgrace upon her, . . . and forbiddes all people where she resortes to afford her entertaignment, and will not suffer her to worke for the livelyhood of her and her child, but will have accompt of the same. . . . Albeit he can get by his labour 20/- a weeke, yet he consumes the same in idle company . . . having lewdlie spent all he had with your petitioner."[1]

Though their entrance to the Gilds and Companies was most often obtained by women through marriage, it has already been shown that their admission by apprenticeship was not unknown, and they also occasionally acquired freedom by patrimony ; thus " Katherine Wetwood, daughter of Humphrey Wetwood, of London, Pewterer, was sworn and made free by the Testimony of the Master and Wardens of the Merchant Taylors' Co., and of two Silk Weavers, that she was a virgin and twenty-one years of age. She paid the usual patrimony fine of 9s.2d."[2] More than one hundred years later Mary Temple was made free of the Girdlers' Company by patrimony.[3] No jealousy is expressed of the women who were members of the Companies, but all others were rigorously excluded from employment. Complaints were brought before the Girdlers' that certain Girdlers in London " set on worke such as had not served 7 years at the art, and also for setting forreigners and maids on worke."[4] Rules were made in Bristol in 1606, forbidding women to work at the trades of the whitawers (white leather dressers), Point makers and Glovers.[5]

---

[1] *S.P.D.*, ccccxxxv. 42, Dec. 6, 1639.

[2] Welch, *Pewterers*, Vol. II., p. 92, 1633-4.

[3] Smythe, *Company of Girdlers*, p. 128, 1747.

[4] *Ibid*, p. 88, 1628.

[5] Latimer, *Annals of Bristol*, p. 26, 1606.

In the unprotected trades where the Gild organisation had broken down, and the profits of the small
tradesmen had been reduced to a minimum by unlimited competition, the family depended upon the
labour of mother and children as well as the father for
its support.   Petitions presented to the King concerning grievances under which they suffer, generally
include wives and children in the number of those
engaged in the trade in question.   On a proposal
to tax tobacco pipes, the makers show " that all
the poorer sort of the Trade must be compelled to
lay it down, for want of Stock or Credit to carry it
on ; and so their Wives and Children, who help to
get their Bread, must of necessity perish, or become
a Charge to their respective Parishes.   That when
a Gross of Pipes are made, they sell them for 1s. 6d.
and 1s. 10d., out of which 2d. or 3d. is their greatest
Profit.   And they not already having Stock, or can
make Pipes fast enough to maintain their Families,
how much less can they be capable, when half the
Stock they have, must be paid down to pay the
King his Duty ? "[1]

The Glovers prepared a memorandum showing
the great grievances there would be if a Duty be laid
on Sheep and Lamb Skins, Drest in Oyl etc.   " The
Glovers," they say, " are many Thousands in Number,
in the Counties of England, City of London and
Liberties thereof, and generally so Poor (the said
Trade being so bad and Gloves so plenty) that mear
Necessity doth compel them to Sell their Goods daily
to the Glove-sellers, and to take what Prises they will
give them, to keep them and their Children and Families at Work to maintain them, or else they must
perrish for want of Bred."[2]

---

[1] *Humble Petition and Case of the Tobacco Pipe Makers of the Citys of London and Westminster*, 1695.

[2] *Reasons humbly offered by the Leather-Dressers and Glovers, &c.*

The Pin-makers say that their company "consists for the most part of poor and indigent People, who have neither Credit nor Money to purchase Wyre of the Merchant at the best hand, but are forced for want thereof, to buy only small Parcels of the second or third Buyer, as they have occasion to use it, and to sell off the Pins they make of the same from Week to Week, as soon as they are made, for ready money, to feed themselves, their Wives, and Children, whom they are constrained to imploy to go up and down every Saturday Night from Shop to Shop to offer their Pins for Sale, otherwise cannot have mony to buy bread."[2]

A similar picture is given in the " Mournfull Cryes of many thousand Poore tradesmen, who are ready to famish through decay of Trade." " Oh that the cravings of our Stomacks could bee heard by the Parliament and City! Oh that the Teares of our poore famishing Babes were botled! Oh that their tender Mothers Cryes for bread to feed them were ingraven in brasse . . . . O you Members of Parliament and rich men in the City, that are at ease, and drink Wine in Bowles . . . . you that grind our faces and Flay off our skins . . . . is there none to Pity . . . . Its your Taxes Customes and Excize, that compels the Country to raise the price of Food and to buy nothing from us but meere absolute necessaries; and then you of the City that buy our Worke, must have your Tables furnished . . . . and therefore will give us little or nothing for our Worke, even what you please, because you know wee must sell for Monyes to set our Families on worke, or else wee famish . . . . and since the late Lord Mayor Adams, you have put into execution an illegall, wicked Decree of the Common Counsell; whereby you have

---

[2] *Case or Petition of the Corporation of Pin-makers.*

taken our goods from us, if we have gone to the Innes to sell them to the Countrimen; and you have mur-dered some of our poor wives, that have gone to Innes to find countrimen to buie them."[1]

In each case it will be noticed that the wife's activity is specially mentioned in connection with the sale of the goods. Women were so closely connec-ted with industrial life in London that when the Queen proposed to leave London in 1641 it was the women who petitioned Parliament, declaring, " that your Petitioners, their Husbands, their Children and their Families, amounting to many thousand soules; have lived in plentifull and good fashion, by the exercise of severall Trades and venting of divers workes . . . All depending wholly for the sale of their commodities, (which is the maintenance and very existence and beeing of themselves, their husbands, and families) upon the splendour and glory of the English Court, and principally upon that of the Queenes Majesty."[2]

In addition to these Trades, skilled and semi-skilled, in which men and women worked together, certain skilled women's trades existed in London which were sufficiently profitable for considerable premiums to be paid with the girls who were apprenticed to them.[3] These girls probably continued to exercise their own trade after marriage, their skill serving them instead of dowry, the Customs of London providing that " married women who practise certain crafts in the city alone and without their husbands, may take girls as apprentices to serve them and learn their trade, and these apprentices shall be bound by their indentures of apprenticeship to both husband and wife, to learn the wife's trade as is aforesaid, and such

---

[1] *Mournfull Cryes of many Thousand Poore Tradesmen*, 1647.

[2] *Humble Petition of many thousands of Courtiers, Citizens, Gentlemens and Tradesmens Wives, &c.*

[3] Ante. p. 175.

indentures shall be enrolled as well for women as for men."[1] The girls who were apprenticed to Carpenters were evidently on this footing.

References in contemporary documents to women who were following skilled or semi-skilled trades in London are very frequent. Thus Thomas Swan is reported to have committed thefts " on his mistress Alice Fox, Wax-chandler of Old Bailey."[2] Mrs. Cellier speaks of " one Mrs. Phillips, an upholsterer,"[3] while the Rev. Giles Moore notes in his diary " payed Mistress Cooke, in Shoe Lane, for a new trusse, and for mending the old one and altering the plate thereof, £1 5 0 ; should shee dye, I am in future to inquire for her daughter Barbara, who may do the like for mee."[4] Isaac Derston was "put an app. to Anthony Watts for the term of seven years, but turned over to the widow—dwelling near : palls : who bottoms cane chaires, £2 10 0."[5] That the bottoming of cane chairs was a poor trade is witnessed by the meagreness of the premium paid in this case.

No traces can be found of any organisation existing in the skilled women's trades, such as upholstery, millinery, mantua-making, but a Gild existed among the women who sorted and packed wool at Southampton. A Sisterhood consisting of twelve women of good and honest demeanour was formed there as a company to serve the merchants in the occupation of covering pokes or baloes [bales]. Two of the sisters acted as wardens. In 1554 a court was held to adjudicate on the irregular attendance of some of the sisters. The names of two wardens

---

[1] Eileen Power, by kind permission, 1419.

[2] *C.S.P.D.* cv. 53, Jan. 19, 1619.

[3] Cellier (Mrs.) *Malice Defeated.* p. 25.

[4] *Suss. Arch. Coll.*, Vol. I., p. 123, *Journal Rev.*, 1676.

[5] *Monthly Meeting Minute Book, Peele,* Nov. 24, 1687.

and eleven sisters are given ; no one who was absent
from her duties for more than three months was permitted to return to the Sisterhood without the
Mayor's licence. " Item, y^t is ordered by the sayde
Maior and his bretherne that all suche as shall be
nomynated and appoynted to be of the systeryd
shall make a brekefaste at their entrye for a knowlege
and shal bestowe at the least xx^d or ij^s, or more as
they lyste."[1]

Possibly when more records of the Gilds and Companies have been published in a complete form, some
of the gaps which are left in this account of the position
of women in the skilled and semi-skilled trades may
be filled in ; but the extent to which married women
were engaged in them must always remain largely
a matter of conjecture, and unfortunately it is precisely
this point which is most interesting to the sociologist.
Practically all adult women were married, and
the character of the productive work which an
economic organisation allots to married women and
the conditions of their labour decide very largely
the position of the mother in society, and therefore,
ultimately, the fate of her children.   The fragmentary
evidence which has been examined shows that, while
the system of family industry lasted, it was so usual
in the skilled and semi-skilled trades for women to
share in the business life of their husbands that they
were regarded as partners.   Though the wife had
rarely, if ever, served an apprenticeship to his trade,
there were many branches in which her assistance
was of great value, and husband and wife naturally
divided the industry between them in the way which
was most advantageous to the family, while unmarried
servants, either men or women, performed the domestic
drudgery.   As capitalistic organisation developed,
many avenues of industry were, however, gradually
closed to married women.   The masters no longer

---

[1] Davies. (J., S.) *Hist of Southampton*, p. 279.

depended upon the assistance of their wives, while the journeyman's position became very similar to that of the modern artisan ; he was employed on the premises of his master, and thus, though his association with his fellows gave him opportunity for combination, his wife and daughters, who remained at home, did not share in the improvements which he effected in his own economic position. The alternatives before the women of this class were either to withdraw altogether from productive activity, and so become entirely dependent upon their husband's goodwill, or else to enter the labour market independently and fight their battles alone, in competition not only with other women, but with men.

Probably the latter alternative was still most often followed by married women, although at this time the idea that men " keep " their wives begins to prevail : but the force of the old tradition maintained amongst women a desire for the feeling of independence which can only be gained through productive activity, and thus married women, even when unable to work with their husbands, generally occupied themselves with some industry, however badly it might be paid.

B. *Retail Trades.*

The want of technical skill and knowledge which so often hampered the position of women in the Skilled Trades, was a smaller handicap in Retail Trades, where manual dexterity and technical knowledge are less important than general intelligence and a lively understanding of human nature. Quick perception and social tact, which are generally supposed to be feminine characteristics, often proved useful even to the craftsman, when his wife assumed the charge of the financial side of his business ; it is therefore not surprising to find women taking a prominent part in every branch of Retail Trade. In fact the woman who was left without other resources turned naturally to keeping a shop, or to the sale of goods in the street, as the most likely means for maintaining her children, and thus the woman shopkeeper is no infrequent figure in contemporary writings. For example, in one of the many pamphlets describing the incidents of the Civil War, we read that " Mistresse Phillips was sent for, who was found playing the good housewife at home (a thing much out of fashion) . . . . and committed close prisoner to castle." Her husband having been driven before from town, " She was to care for ten children, the most of them being small, one whereof she at the same time suckled, her shop (which enabled her to keep all those) was ransacked," £14 was taken, and the house plundered, horse and men billetted with her when she could scarce get bread enough for herself and her family without charity. She was tried, and condemned to death, when, the account continues, " Mistress Phillips not knowing but her turne was next, standing all the while with a halter about her neck over against the Gallowes, a Souldier would have put the halter under her Handkerchiefe, but she would not suffer him, speaking with a very audible voice, ' I am not ashamed to suffer reproach and shame in this cause,' a brave resolution, beseeming a nobler sex, and not unfit to be registered in the Book of Martyrs."

The woman shop-keeper is found also among the stock characters of the drama. In " The Old Batchelor " Belinda relates that " a Country Squire, with the Equipage of a Wife and two Daughters, came to Mrs. Snipwel's Shop while I was there . . . . the Father bought a Powder-Horn, and an Almanack, and a Comb-Case ; the Mother, a great Fruz-Towr, and a fat Amber-Necklace ; the Daughters only tore two Pair of Kid-leather Gloves, with trying 'em on."[1]

Amongst the Quakers, shop-keeping was a usual employment for women. Thomas Chalkley, soon

---

[1] Congreve (Wm.). *The Old Batchelor*, Act iv., Sc., viii.

after his marriage " had a Concern to visit Friends in the counties of Surrey, Sussex and Kent, which I performed in about two Weeks Time, and came home and followed my calling, and was industrious therein ; and when I had gotten something to bear my expenses, and settled my Wife in some little Business I found an Exercise on my Spirit to go over to *Ireland*."[1] Another Quaker describes how he applied himself " to assist my Wife in her Business as well as I could, attending General, Monthly and other Meetings on public Occasions for three Years."[2] The provision of the little stock needed for a shop was a favourite method of assisting widows.

The frequency with which payments to women are entered in account books[3] is further evidence of the extent to which they were engaged in Retail Trades, but this occupation was not freely open to all and any who needed it. It was, on the contrary, hedged about with almost as many restrictions as the gild trades. The craftsman was generally free to dispose of his own goods, but many restrictions hampered the Retailer, that is to say the person who bought to sell again. The community regarded this class with some jealousy, and limited their numbers. Hence, the poor woman who sought to improve her position by opening

---

[1] Chalkley, *Journal*, pp. 30–31, 1690.

[2] Bownas, Samuel, *Life of*, p. 135.

[3] The Churchwardens of St. Margaret's, Westminster, paid 6d. to " Goodwyfe Wells for salt to destroy the fleas in the Churchwarden's pew." (Cox. Churchwardens Accts., p. 321, 1610.). Among the Cromwell family receipts is one in 1624 " from ye Right wor^e ye Lady Carr by the hands of Henry Hanby, the somme of twenty and one pounds in full payment of all Reckonings from the beginninge of the world . . . . . by me ellen Sadler X (*Cromwell Family Bills and Receipts*, p. 15.) " A bill for Mrs. Willie of Ramsie the 14 of April 1636 for material and making your daughter petecoate

,,	,,	your silk grogram coate
,,	,,	your daughter's gasson shute
,,	,,	your daughter's silke moheare wascote
,,	,,	your damask coate

Total 7. 17. 9. (*Ibid*, p. 265).

a little shop, did not always find her course clear. In fact there were many towns in which the barriers between her and an honest independence were insurmountable. Girls were, however, apprenticed to shop-keepers oftener than to the gild trades, and licences to sell were granted to freewomen as well as to freemen. At Dorchester, girls who had served an apprenticeship to shopkeepers were duly admitted to the freedom of the Borough; we find entered in the Minute Book the names of Celina Hilson, apprenticed to Mat. Hilson, Governor, haberdasher, and Mary Goodredge, spinster, haberdasher of small wares; also of James Bun (who had married Elizabeth Williams a freewoman) haberdasher of small wares; Elizabeth Williams, apprenticed seven years to her Mother, Mary W., tallow chaundler, and of William Weare, apprenticed to Grace Lacy, widow, woolen draper.[1]   An order was granted by the Middlesex Quarter Sessions to discharge Mary Jemmett from apprenticeship to Jane Tyllard, widow, from whom she was to learn " the trade of keeping a linen shop,"[2] and an account is given of a difference between Susanna Shippey, of Mile End, Stepney, widow, and Ann Taylor, her apprentice, touching the discharge of the said apprentice.   It appears that Ann has

---

The Rev. Giles Moore bought " of Widdow Langley 2 more fine sheets, of Goodwyfe Seamer 9 ells. and a halfe of hempen cloath. (*Suss. Arch Coll.* Vol., I. p. 68 1656. Rev. Giles Moore's Journal).

Foulis paid, in Scots money, Jan. 22, 1692 " to Mrs. Pouries lad for aniseed, carthamums &c. 11s." (p. 144), and on Aug. 3, 1696 he " received from Eliz. Ludgate last Whits mail¹ for yᵉ shop at fosters Wyndhead 25 ᶫⁱᵇ." (p. 195). Jan. 14, 1704 " to my douchter Jean be Mrs. Cuthbertsons paymᵗ for 4 ell & ¾ flowered calico to lyne my nightgowne 7. 13. o. (p. 339)   May 23, 1704 " receaved from Agnes philp Whitsun. maill for the shop at fosters wyndhead and yᵉ key therof, and given it to the Candlemakers wife who has taken thᵉ shop 25 ᶫⁱᵇ (p. 346). (Foulis *Acct Book*). Similar entries are in the *Howard Household Book*, 1619.   To Mrs. Smith for lining [linen] for my Lord, had in Easter tearm, 5ˡⁱ xˢ.   Mrs. Smith for napry had in May vjˡⁱ iiˢ (*Howard Household Book*, pp. 105 and 161.).

[1] Mayo, *Municipal Records of Dorchester*, p. 428 -9.

[2] *Middlesex County Records*, p. 180, 1698.

often defrauded her mistress of her goods and sold them for less than cost price.[1]

Little mercy was shown to either man or woman who engaged in the Retail Trade without having served an apprenticeship. A warrant was only issued to release " Elizabeth Beaseley from the Hospital of Bridewell on her brother John Beaseley's having entered into bond that she shall leave off selling tobacco in the town of Wigan."[2]   Mary Keeling was presented at Nottingham " for falowing ye Treaid of a Grocer and Mercer and kepping open shope for on month last past, *contra Statum*, not being *aprentice*."[3]   At Carlisle it was ordered that " Isaack Tully shall submit himself to pay a fine to this trade if they shall think it fitting for taking his sister to keep & sell waires for him contrary to our order,"[4] and when it was reported that " Mrs. Studholme hath employed James Moorehead Scotsman to vend and sell goods in her shop contrary to an order of this company wee doe order that the wardens of our company shall fourthwith acquaint Mrs. Studholme yt. she must not be admitted to entertain him any long[r] in her employmt but that before our next quarter day she take some other course for keeping her shop and yt. he be noe longer employed therein till yt. time."[5] At a later date Mrs. Sybil Hetherington, Mrs. Mary Nixon, Mrs. Jane Jackson, widow, and four men, were dealt with for having shops or retailery of goods contrary to the statute.[6]

---

[1] *Middlesex County Records*, p. 2, 1690.

[2] *C. R.*   18th, August, 1640.

[3] *Nottingham Records*, Vol. V., p. 331, 1686.

[4] Ferguson, *Municipal Records, Carlisle*, p. 110, 1651.

[5] *Ibid*, p. 112,   1668.

[6] *Ibid*, p. 115, 1719.

There were fewer restrictions on retailing in London than in the provinces, and trading was virtually free in the streets of London. An act of the Common Council, passed in 1631, deals with abuses rising from this freedom, declaring " that of late it is come to passe that divers unruly people, as Butchers, Bakers, Poulters, Chandlers, Fruiterers, Sempsters, sellers of Grocery wares, Oyster wives, Herbe wives, Tripe wives, and the like ; who not contented to enjoy the benefit and common right of Citizens, by holding their market and continual Trades in their several Shops & houses where they dwell, doe . . . . by themselves, wives, children and seruants enter into, and take up their standings in the said streets and places appointed for the common Markets, unto which the country people only have in former times used to resort to vend and utter their victuall and other commodities ; in which Markets the said Free-men doe abide for the most part of the day and that not only upon Market dayes, but all the weeke long with multitudes of Baskets, Tubs, Chaires, Boards & Stooles, ... the common Market places by these disordered people be so taken up, that country people when they come with victual and provision have no roome left them to set down their . . . . baskets."[1]

In provincial towns, stalls in the market place were leased to tradesmen by the Corporation, the rents forming a valuable revenue for the town ; infringements of the monopoly were summarily dealt with and often the privilege was reserved for " free " men and women. Thus at St. Albans Richard Morton's wife was presented because she " doth ordinarilie sell shirt bands and cuffes, hankerchers, coifes, and other small lynenn wares openlie in the markett,"[2] not being free. It was as a special favour

---

[1] *Act of Common Council for reformation, etc.*

[2] Gibbs, *Corporation Records of St. Albans*, p. 62, 1613.

that leave was given to a poor woman to sell shoes in Carlisle market. The conditions are explained as follows :—" Whereas Ann Barrow the wife of Richard Barrow formerly one that by virtue of the Coldstream Act brought shoes and exposed them to sell in Carlisle market he being long abroad and his said wife poor the trade is willing to permit the said Ann to bring and sell shoes provided always they be the work of one former servant and noe more and for this permission she owns the trades favour and is thankful for it . . . . agreed and ordered that every yeare she shall pay 2s."[1]

The Corporation at Reading was occupied for a whole year with the case of the " Aperne woman." The first entry in the records states that " Steven Foord of Newbery the aperne woman's husband, exhibited a lettre from the Lord of Wallingford for his sellerman to shewe and sell aperninge [2] in towne, in Mr. Mayor's handes, etc. And thereupon tollerated to doe as formerly she had done, payeing yerely 10s. to the Hall."[3] Next year there is another entry to the effect that " it was agreed that Steven Foorde's wief shall contynue sellinge of aperninge, as heretofore, and that the other woman usinge to sell suche stuffes at William Bagley's dore shalbe forbidden, and shall not hencefourth be permitted to sell in the boroughe etc., and William Bagley shall be warned."[4] The other woman proving recalcitrant, " at Steven Foorde's wive's request and complaynte it was grannted that William Bagley's stranger, selling aperninge in con-tempt of the government, shalbe questioned."[5] Finally

---

[1] Ferguson, *Carlisle*, p. 187, 1669.

[2] Stuff for Aprons.

[3] Guilding. *Reading Records*, Vol. II., p. 171, 1624.

[4] *Ibid*, Vol. II., p. 240, 1625.

[5] *Ibid*, Vol. II., p. 252.

it was " agreed that Steven Foorde's wife shall hence-
forth keepe Markett and sell onely linsey woolsey
of their own making in this markett, according to
the Lord Wallingforde's lettre, she payeing xs. per
annum, and that noe other stranger shall hence-
forth keepe markett or sell lynsey and woolsey in this
markett."[1]

At this time, when most roads were mere bridle
tracks, and few conveniences for travel existed, when
even in towns the streets were so ill-paved that in
bad weather the goodwife hesitated before going to
the market, the dwellers in villages and hamlets were
often fain to buy from pedlars who brought goods
to their door and to sell butter and eggs to anyone who
would undertake the trouble of collection. Their
need was recognised by the authorities, who granted
a certain number of licences to Badgers, Pedlars and
Regraters, and probably many others succeeded in
trading unlicensed. This class of Dealers was
naturally regarded with suspicion by shopkeepers. A
pamphlet demanding their suppression, points out that
" the poor decaying Shopkeeper has a large Rent to
pay, and Family to Support; he maintains not
his own Children only, but all the poor Orphans and
Widows in his Parish; nay, sometimes the Widows
and Orphans of the very Pedlar or Hawker, who has
thus fatally laboured to starve him." As for the
Hawkers, " we know they pretend they are shut out
of the great Trading Cities, Towns and Corporations
by the respective Charters and all other settled Privileges of those Places, but we answer that tho' for
want of legal Introduction they may not be able to set
up in Cities, Corporations, etc., yet there are very many
Places of very great Trade, where no Corporation
Privileges would obstruct them . . . . if any
of them should be reduc'd and . . . . be brought
to the Parish to keep; that is to say, their Wives and

---

[1] *Guilding, Reading Records*, Vol. II., p. 267.

Children, the Manufacturers, the Shopkeepers who con-
fessedly make up the principal Numbers of those corporations, and are the chief Supporters of the Parishes,
will be much more willing to maintain them, than
to be ruin'd by them."[1]

The terms Badging, Peddling, Hawking and Regrating are not very clearly defined, and were used in
senses which somewhat overlap each other ; but the
Badger seems to have been a person who " dealt '
in a wholesale way. A licence was granted in 1630
to " Edith Doddington of Hilbishopps, widdowe,
to be a badger of butter and cheese and to carry the
same into the Counties of Wiltes, Hamsher, Dors^tt
and Devon, and to retourne againe with corne and
to sell it againe in any faire or markett within this
County during one whole yeare now next ensueing ;
and she is not to travell with above three horses,
mares or geldings at the most part."[2] The authorities, fearing lest corners and profiteering should
result from interference with the supply of necessaries, made " ingrossing " or anything resembling an
attempt to buy up the supply of wheat, salt, etc., an
offence. Amongst the prosecutions which were made
on this account are presentments of " John Whaydon
and John Preist of Watchett, partners, for ingross
of salt, Julia Stone, Richard Miles, Joane Miles als.
Stone of Bridgwater for ingross of salte." [3] of " Johann
Stedie of Fifehead, widdow, ... for ingrossinge of corne contrary etc,"[4] of " Edith Bruer
and Katherine Bruer, Spinsters, of Halse . . . .
for ingrossinge of corne,"[5] and of " Johann Thorne

---

[1] *Brief State of the Inland and Home Trade.*   pp. 59 and 63, 1730.

[2] *Somerset Q. S. Records*, Vol. II., p. 119, 1630.

[3] *Ibid*, Vol. II., p. 153, 1631.

[4] *Ibid*, Vol. II., p. 161.

[5] *Ibid*, Vol. II., p. 165.

. . . . widow . . . . for ingrossinge of wheate, Barley, Butter and Cheese."[1]

Pedlars and hawkers carried on an extensive trade all over the country. At first sight this would seem a business ill suited to women, for it involved carrying a heavy pack of goods on the back over long distances ; and yet it appears as though in some districts the trade was almost their monopoly. The success that attended Joan Dant's efforts as a pedlar has been told elsewhere.[2] How complete was the ascendency which women had established in certain districts over this class of trade is shown by the following definition of the term " Hawkers " :—" those that profer their Wares by Wholesale which are called Hawkers, and which are not only the Manufacturers themselves, but others besides them, viz. the Women in *London*, in *Exceter* and in *Manchester*, who do not only Profer Commodities at the Shops and Ware houses, but also at Inns to Countrey-Chapmen. Likewise the *Manchester*-men, the *Sherborn* —men, and many others, that do Travel from one Market-Town to another ; and there at some Inn do profer their Wares to sell to the Shopkeepers of the place."[3]

Though peddling might in some cases be developed into a large and profitable concern, more often it afforded a bare subsistence. The character of a woman engaged in it is given in a certificate brought before the Hertford Quarter Sessions in 1683 by the inhabitants of Epping, which states that " Sarah, wife of Richard Young, of Epping, cooper, who was accused of pocket-picking when she was about her lawfull and honest imploy of buying small wares and wallnuts " at Sabridgworth fair, is " a very honest and well-behaved woman, not given to pilfer or

---

[1] *Somerset Q. S. Records*, Vol. II., p. 223.

[2] *Ante*, p. 33.

[3] *Trade of England.* p. 21, 1681.

steale," and that they believe her to be falsely accused.[1]

While the Pedlar dealt chiefly in small wares and haberdashery, Regraters were concerned with the more perishable articles of food. In this they were seriously hampered by bye-laws forbidding the buying and selling of such articles in one day. The laws had been framed with the object of preventing a few persons buying up all the supplies in the market and selling them at exorbitant prices, but their application seems to have been chiefly directed in the interests of the shopkeepers, to whom the competition of women who hawked provisions from door to door was a serious matter, the women being contented with very small profits, and the housewives finding it so convenient to have goods brought to their very doorstep. The injustice of the persecution of these poor women is protested against by the writer of a pamphlet, who points out that "We provide Men shall not be cheated in buying a pennyworth of Eggs, but make no provision to secure them from the same Abuse in a hundred pounds laid out in Cloaths. The poor Artizan shall not be oppressed in laying out his penny to one poorer than himself, but is without Remedy, shortened by a Company in his Penny as it comes in. I have heard Complaints of this Nature in greater matters of the publik Sales of the *East India Company*, perhaps if due consideration were had of these great Ingrossers, there would be found more Reason to restrain them, than a poor Woman that travels in the Country to buy up and sell in a Market a few Hens and Chickens."[2]

Even in the Middle Ages the trade of Regrating was almost regarded as the prerogative of women. Gower wrote " But to say the truth in this instance, the trade of regratery belongeth by right rather to women.

---

[1] *Hertfordshire County Records*, Vol. I., pp. 347-8.

[2] *Linnen and Woollen Manufactury*, p. 7, 168ᵛ.

But if a woman be at it she in stinginess useth much
more machination and deceit than a man ; for she
never alloweth the profit on a single crumb to escape
her, nor faileth to hold her neighbour to paying his
price ; all who beseech her do but lose their time, for
nothing doth she by courtesy, as anyone who drinketh
in her house knoweth well."[1]

In later times the feminine form of the word is
used in the ordinances of the City of London, clearly
showing that the persons who were then carrying on
the trade were women ; thus it was said " Let no
Regrateress pass *London Bridge* towards *Suthwerk*,
nor elsewhere, to buy Bread, to carry it into the
City of *London* to sell ; because the Bakers of *Suthwerk*,
nor of any other Place, are not subject to the Justice
of the City." And again " Whereas it is common for
merchants to give Credit, and especially for Bakers
commonly to do the same with Regrateresses . . . .
. . . . we forbid, that no Baker make the benefit
of any Credit to a Regrateress, as long as he shall
know her to be involved in her Neighbour's Debt."[2]
Moreover a very large proportion of the prosecutions
for this offence were against women. " We Amerce
Thomas Bardsley for his wife buyinge Butter Contrary
to the orders of the towne in xijd."[3] " Katherine
Birch for buyinge and selling pullen [chicken] both of
one day 3s. Thos. Ravald wife of Assheton of Mercy
bancke for sellinge butter short of waight."[4] " Thomas
Massey wife for buyinge a load of pease and sellinge
them the same day. Amerced in 1s."[5] " Katharine
Hall for buyinge and sellinge Cheese both of one day

---

[1] Gower. *Le mirour de l'omme* (trans. from French verse by Eileen Power).

[2] Stow, *London*, Book V., p. 343. Assize of Bread.

Manchester Court Leet Records, Vol. IV., p. 110, 1653.

[4] *Ibid*, p. 212, 1657

[5] *Ibid*. p. 244, 1658.

6d. Anne Rishton for buyinge and sellinge butter the same day Amercd in 3. o.''[1]

As the Regrater dealt chiefly in food, her business is closely connected with the provision trades, but enough has been said here to indicate that of all retailing this was the form which most appealed to poor women, who were excluded from skilled trades and whose only other resource was spinning. The number of women in this unfortunate position was large, including as it did not only widows, whose families depended entirely upon their exertions, but also the wives of most of the men who were in receipt of day wages and had no garden or grazing rights. It has already been shown that wages, except perhaps in some skilled trades, were insufficient for the maintenance of a family. Therefore, when the mother of a young family could neither work in her husband's trade nor provide her children with food by cultivating her garden or tending cows and poultry, she must find some other means to earn a little money. By wages she could seldom earn more than a penny or twopence a day and her food. Selling perishable articles of food from door to door presented greater chances of profit, and to this expedient poor women most often turned. In proportion as the trade was a convenience to the busy housewife, it became an unwelcome form of competition to the established shopkeepers, who, being influential in the Boroughs, could persecute and suppress the helpless, disorganised women who undersold them.

(C) *Provision Trades*.

Under this head are grouped the Bakers, Millers, Butchers and Fishwives, together with the Brewers, Innkeepers and Vintners, the category embracing both those who produced and those who retailed the provisions in question.

---

[1] *Manchester Court Test Records*, p. 243, 1658.

A large proportion both of the bread and beer consumed at this time was produced by women in domestic industry. The wages assessments show that on the larger farms the chief woman servant was expected both to brew and to bake, but the cottage folk in many cases cannot have possessed the necessary capital for brewing, and perhaps were wanting ovens in which to bake. Certainly in the towns both brewing and baking existed as trades from the earliest times. Though in many countries the grinding of corn has been one of the domestic occupations performed by women and slaves, in England women were saved this drudgery, for the toll of corn ground at the mill was an important item in the feudal lord's revenue, and severe punishments were inflicted on those who ground corn elsewhere. The common bakehouse was also a monopoly of the feudal lord's,[1] but his rights in this case were not carried so far as to penalize baking for domestic purposes.

It might be supposed that industries such as brewing and baking, which were so closely connected with the domestic arts pertaining to women, would be more extensively occupied by women than trades such as those of blacksmith or pewterer or butcher; but it will be shown that skill acquired domestically was not sufficient to establish a woman's position in the world of trade, and that actually in the seventeenth century it was as difficult for her to become a baker as a butcher.

Baking.—After the decay of feudal privileges the trade of baking was controlled on lines similar to those governing other trades, but subject to an even closer supervision by the local authorities, owing to the

---

[1] Petronilla, Countess of Leicester, granted to Petronilla, daughter of Richard Roger's son of Leicester and her heirs "all the suit of the men outside the Southgate aforesaid to bake at her bakehouse with all the liberties and free customs, saving my customary tenants who are bound to my bakehouses within the town of Leicester." Bateson, (M.) *Records, Leicester*, Vol. I., p. 10.

fact that bread is a prime necessity of life. On this account its price was fixed by " the assize of bread." The position of women in regard to the trade was also somewhat different, because while in other trades they possessed fewer facilities than men for acquiring technical experience, in this they learnt the art of baking as part of their domestic duties. Nevertheless, in the returns which give the names of authorised bakers, those of women do not greatly exceed in number the names which are given for other trades ; of lists for the City of Chester, one gives thirty names of bakers, six being women, all widows, while another gives thirty-nine men and no women,[1] and a third twenty-six men and three women. The assistance which the Baker's wife gave to her husband, however, was taken for granted. At Carlisle, the bye-laws provide that " noe Persons . . . . shall brew or bayk to sell but only freemen and thare wifes."[2] and a rule at Beverley laid down that " no common baker or other baker called boule baker, their wives, servants, or apprentices, shall enter the cornmarket any Saturday for the future before 1 p.m. to buy any grain, nor buy wheat coming on Saturdays to market beyond 2 bushels for stock for their own house after the hour aforesaid."[3]

A writer, who was appealing for an increase in the assize of bread, includes the wife's work among the necessary costs of making a loaf ; " Two shillings was allowed by the assize for all maner of charges in baking a quarter of wheate over and above the second price of wheate in the market," but the writer declares that in Henry VII.'s time " the bakers . . . . . might farre better cheape and with lesse charge of seruantes haue baked a quarter of Wheate, then now

---

[1] *Harl. MSS.*, 2054, fo. 44 and 45, 2105, fo. 301.

[2] Ferguson, *Carlisle, Dormont Book*, p. 69, 1561.

[3] *Beverley Town Documents*, pp. 39-40.

they can." It was then allowed for " everie quarter of wheate baking, for furnace and wood vid. the Miller foure pence, for two journymen and two pages five-pence, for salt, yest, candle & sandbandes two pence, for himselfe, his house, his wife, his dog & his catte seven pence, and the branne to his advantage."[1]

The baker's wife figures also in account books, as transacting business for her husband. Thus the Carpenters' Company " Resd of Lewes davys wyffe the baker a fyne for a license for John Pasmore the forren to sette upe a lytyll shed on his backsyde."[2]

Although conforming in general to the regulations for other trades, certain Boroughs retained the rights over baking which had been enjoyed by the Feudal Lord, the Portmote at Salford ordering that " Samell Mort shall surcease from beakinge sale bread by the first of May next upon the forfeit of 5ls except hee beake at the Comon beakehouse in Salford."[3] In other towns the bakers were sufficiently powerful to enforce their own terms on the Borough. In York, for instance, the Corporation of Bakers, which became very rich, succeeded in excluding the country, or " boule bakers, " from the market, undertaking to sell bread at the same rates ; but the monopoly once secured they declared it was impossible to produce bread at this price, and the magistrates allowed an advance.[4] In some cases bakers were required to take out licences, these being granted only to freemen and freewomen ; in others they were formed into Companies, with rules of apprenticeship. " They shall receive no man into their saide company of bakeres, nor woman unles her husband have bene a free burges, and compound with Mr. Maior and

---

[1] Powell. *Assize of Bread.* 1600.

[2] *Records of Worshipful Company of Carpenters*, Vol. IV., p. 69, 1554.

[3] *Salford Portmote Records*, Vol. II., p. 188.

[4] *S.P.D.* cxxxiv., 36. November 27, 1622.

the warden of the company."[1]   At Reading in 1624,
" the bakers, vizt., William Hill, Abram Paise, Alexander Pether, complayne against bakers not freemen,
vizt., Izaak Wracke useth the trade his wief did use
when he marryed. Michaell Ebson saith he was
an apprentice in towne ard having noe worke doth a
little to gett bread. James Arnold will surceasse
. . . . Wydowe Bradbury alwayes hath used
to bake."[2]

That women were members of the Bakers' Companies
is shown by rules which refer to sisters as well as
brothers. In 1622 the Corporation at Salisbury
ordained that " no free brother or free sister shall at
any time hereafter make, utter, or sell bread, made
with butter, or milk, spice cakes, etc . . . . except it be before spoken for funerals, or upon the
Friday before Easter, or at Christmas . . . No
free brother or free sister shall sell any bread in the
market. No free brother or free sister shall hereafter
lend any money to an innholder or victualler, to the
intent or purpose of getting his or their custom"[3]
It is not likely that many women served an apprenticeship, but the frequency with which they are
charged with offences against the Bye-Laws is some
clue to the numbers engaged in the trade.   For
instance, in Manchester, Martha Wrigley and nine
men were presented in 1648 " for makeinge bread
above & vnder the size & spice bread."[4]   In 1650,
twenty-five men and no women were charged with
a similar offence,[5] in 1651 eleven men and no women[6]

---

[1] Lambert, *Two Thousand Years of Gild Life*, p. 307.   *Composicion of Bakers*, *Hull*., 1598.

[2] Guilding, *Reading Records*, Vol. II., p. 181.

[3] Hoare, (Sir. R. C.).   *Hist. of Wiltshire*, Vol. VI., p. 342.

[4] *Manchester Court Leet Records*, Vol. IV., p. 31.

[5] *Ibid*, p. 47.

[6] *Ibid*, p. 51.

and in 1652 are entered the names of five men and ten women[1],

The constant complaints brought against people who were using the trade " unlawfully " show how difficult it was to enforce rules of apprenticeship in a trade which was so habitually used by women for domestic purposes. Information was brought that " divers of the inhab[ts] of Thirsk do use the trade of baking, not having been apprentices thereof, but their wives being brought up and exercised therein many yeares have therefore used it . . . . and the matter referred to the Justices in Q[r] Sessions to limitt a certain number to use that trade without future trouble of any informers and that such as are allowed by the said Justices, to have a tolleration to take apprentices . . . . the eight persons, viz., Ja[s]. Pibus, Anth. Gamble. John Harrison, Widow Watson, Jane Skales, Jane Rutter, Tho. Carter and John Bell, shall onlie use and occupie the said trade of baking, and the rest to be restrayned."[2] The insistence upon apprenticeship must have been singularly exasperating to women who had learnt to bake excellent bread from their mothers, or mistresses, and it was natural for them to evade, when possible, a rule which seemed so arbitrary ; but they could not do so with impunity. Thus the Hertfordshire Quarter Session was informed " One Andrew Tomson's wife doth bake, and William Everite's wife doth bake bread to sell being not apprenticed nor licensed."[3] How heavily prosecutions of this character weighed upon the poor, is shown by a certificate brought to the same Quarter Sessions nearly a hundred years later, stating that " William Pepper, of Sabridgworth, is of honest and industrious behaviour, but

---

[1] *Manchester Court Leet Records*, p. 70.

[2] Atkinson, (J. C.), *Yorks. N. R. Q. S. Records*, Vol. I., p. 81. July 8, 1607.

[3] *Hertford Co. Records*, Vol. I, p, 32, 1600.

in a poor and low condition, and so not able to support the charge of defending an indictment against him for baking for hire (he having once taken a halfpenny for baking a neighbour's loaf) and has a great charge of children whom he has hitherto brought up to hard work and industrious labour, who otherwise might have been a charge to the parish, and will be forced to crave the relief of the parish, to defray the charge that may ensue upon this trouble given him by a presentment."[1]

The line taken by the authorities was evidently intended to keep the trade of baking in a few hands. The object may have been partly to facilitate inspection and thereby check short measure and adulteration; whatever the motive the effect must certainly have tended to discourage women from developing the domestic art of baking into a trade. Consequently in this, as in other trades, the woman's contribution to the industry generally took the form of a wife helping her husband, or a widow carrying on her late husband's business.

Millers :—It was probably only as the wife or widow of a miller that women took part in the business of milling. An entry in the Carlisle Records states " we amercye Archilles Armstronge for keeping his wief to play the Milner, contrary the orders of this cyttie."[2] But it is not unusual to come across references to corn mills which were in the hands of women; a place in Yorkshire is described as being " near to Mistress Lovell's Milne."[3] " Margaret Page, of Hertingfordbury, widow," was indicted for " erecting a mill house in the common way there,"[4] and at Stockton " One water corne milne . . . .

---

[1] *Hertford County Records*, Vol. I., p. 365, 1686.

[2] Ferguson, *Carlisle.* p. 278. April 21, 1619.

[3] J. C. Atkinson, *Yorks. N. R. O. S. Records*, Vol. II., p. 8, 1612.

Hertford County Records, Vol. II., p. 25, 1698.

is lett by lease unto Alice Armstrong for 3 lives."[1]

Such instances are merely a further proof of the activity shown by married women in the family business whenever this was carried on within their reach.

Butchers :—The position which women took in the Butchers' trade resembled very closely their position as bakers, for, as has been shown, the special advantages which women, by virtue of their domestic training, might have enjoyed when trading as bakers, were cancelled by the statutes and bye-laws limiting the numbers of those engaged in this trade. As wife or widow women were able to enter either trade equally. Both trades were subject to minute supervision in the interests of the public, and as a matter of fact, from the references which happen to have been preserved, it might even appear that the wives of butchers were more often interested in the family business than the wives of bakers. An Act of Henry VIII. " lycensyng all bochers for a tyme to sell vytell in grosse at theyr pleasure " makes it lawful for any person " to whom any complaynt shuld be made upon any Boucher his wyff servaunte or other his mynysters refusing to sell the said vitayles by true and lawfull weight . . . . to comytt evry such Boucher to warde,"[2] shows an expectation that the wife would act as her husband's agent. But the wife's position was that of partner, not servant. During the first half of the century, certainly, leases were generally made conjointly to husband and wife ; for example, " Phillip Smith and Elizabeth, his wife" appeared before the Corporation at Reading " desiringe a new lease of the Butcher's Shambles, which was granted."[3]

---

[1] Brewster, *Stockton-on-Tees*, p. 42.

[2] Statutes 27 Henry VIII. c. 9.

[3] Guilding, *Reading Records*, Vol. IV., p. 122.

Customs at Nottingham secured the widow's possession
of her husband's business premises even without a
lease, providing that " when anie Butcher shall dye
thatt holds a stall or shopp from the towne, thatt
then his wyefe or sonne shall hould the same stall
or shopp, they vsinge the same trade, otherwaies
the towne to dispose thereof to him or them thatt
will give moste for the stall or shopp : this order to
bee lykewise to them thatt houlds a stall in the Spice-
chambers."[1]

The names of women appear in lists of butchers
in very similar proportions to the lists of bakers.
Thus one for Chester gives the names of twenty men
followed by three women,[2] and in a return of sixteen
butchers licensed to sell meat in London during Lent,
there is one woman, Mary Wright, and her partner,
William Woodfield.[3]　Bye-laws which control the
sale of meat use the feminine as well as the masculine
pronouns, showing that the trade was habitually
used by both sexes. The " Act for the Settlement
and well ordering of the several Public Markets within
the City of London " provides that " all and every
Country butcher . . . . Poulterer . . . .
Country Farmers, Victuallers Laders or Kidders
. . . . may there sell, utter and put to open
shew or sale his, her or their Beef, Mutton, etc., etc.[4]
It may be supposed that these provisions relate only
to the sale of meat, and that women would not often
be associated with the businesses which included
slaughtering the beasts, but this is not the case.
Elizabeth Clarke is mentioned in the Dorchester
Records as " apprenticed 7 years to her father a

---

[1] *Nottingham Records*, Vol. V., p. 284, 1654.

[2] *Harl. MSS.*, 2105 fo., 300 b.,1565.

[3] *S. P. D.* cxix. 107. February 24. 1621.

[4] *Act for the Settlement and well Ordering of the Several Publick Markets within the City of London*, 1674.

butcher,"[1] and other references occur to women who were clearly engaged in the genuine butcher's trade. For example, a licence was granted " to Jane Fouches of the Parish of St. Clement Danes, Butcher to kill and sell flesh during Lent,"[2] and among eighteen persons who were presented at the Court Leet, Manchester, " for Cuttinge & gnashing of Rawhides for their seuerall Gnashinge of evry Hyde," two were women, " Ellen Jaques of Ratchdale, one hyde, Widdow namely Stott of Ratchdale, two hydes."[3]

Beside these women, who by marriage or apprentice-ship had acquired the full rights of butchers and were acknowledged as such by the Corporation under whose governance they lived, a multitude of poor women tried to keep their families from starvation by hawking meat from door to door. They are often mentioned in the Council Records, because the very nature of their business rendered them con-tinually liable to a prosecution for regrating. Thus at the Court Leet, Manchester, Anne Costerdyne was fined 1s. " for buyinge 4 quarters of Mutton of W^m. Walmersley & 1 Lamb of Thomas Hulme both wch shee shold the one & same day."[4] Their position was the more difficult, because if they did not sell the meat the same day sometimes it went bad, and they were then prosecuted on another score. Elizabeth Chorlton, a butcher's widow, was presented in 1648 " for buieing and sellinge both on one day " and was fined 3s. 4d.[5] She was again fined with Mary Shalcross and various men in 1650 for selling unlawful meat and buying and selling on one day.[6]

---

[1] Mayo, *Municipal Records of Dorchester*, p. 428, 1698.

[2] *S P. D.* 1. clxxxviii. James I., undated.

[3] *Manchester Court Leet Records*, Vol. V., p. 236, 1674.

[4] *Ibid*, p. 221, 1674.

[5] *Manchester Court Leet Records*, Vol. IV., p. 31.

[6] *Ibid*, p. 40.

She was presented yet again in 1653 for selling "stinking meate," and fined 5s.[1] Evidently Elizabeth Chorlton was an undesirable character, for she had previously been convicted of selling by false weights;[2] nevertheless it seems hard that when it was illegal to sell stinking meat women should also be fined for selling it on the same day they bought it, and though this particular woman was dishonest no fault is imputed to the character of many of the others who were similarly presented for regrating.

There remains yet another class of women who were connected with the Butchers' trade, namely the wives of men who were either employed by the master butchers, or who perhaps earned a precarious living by slaughtering pigs and other beasts destined for domestic consumption. In such work there was no place for the wife's assistance, and, like other wage-earners, in spite of any efforts she might make in other directions, the family remained below the poverty line. An instance may be quoted from the Norwich Records where, in a census of the poor (i.e. persons needing Parish Relief) taken in 1570, are given the names of " John Hubbard of the age of 38 yeres, butcher, that occupie slaughterie, and Margarit his wyfe of the age of 30 yeres that sell souce, and 2 young children, and have dwelt here ever."[3]

Fishwives.—There is no reason to suppose that women were often engaged in the larger transactions of fishmongers. Indeed an English writer, describing the Dutchwomen who were merchants of fish, expressly says that they were a very different class from the women who sold fish in England, and who were commonly known as fisherwives.[4] Nevertheless that

---

[1] *Manchester Court Leet Records*, Vol. IV., p. 68.

[2] *Ibid*, p. 15, 1648.

[3] Tingey, J. C., *Records of the City of Norwich*, Vol. II., p. 337.

Ante., p. 36.

in this, as in other trades, they shared to some extent in their husband's enterprises, is shown by the presentment of " John Frank of New Malton, and Alice his wife, for forestalling the markett of divers paniers of fishe, buying the same of the fishermen of Runswick or Whitbye. . . . before it came into the markett."[1]

The position of the sisters of the Fishmongers' Company, London, was recognised to the extent of providing them with a livery, an ordinance of 1426 ordaining that every year, on the festival of St. Peter, " alle the brethren and sustern of the same frat'nite " should go in their new livery to St. Peters' Church, Cornhill.[2] An ordinance dated 1499 however, requires that no fishmonger of the craft shall suffer his wife, or servant, to stand in the market to sell fish, unless in his absence.[3] An entry in the Middlesex Quarter Sessions Records notes the " discharge of Sarah, daughter of Frances Hall. Apprenticed to Rebecca Osmond of the Parish of St. Giles' Without, Cripplegate, ' fishwoman ' "[4] A member of the important Fishmongers' Company would hardly be designated in this way, and Rebecca Osmond must be classed among the " Fishwives " who are so often alluded to in accounts of London. Their business was often too precarious to admit of taking apprentices, and their credit so low that a writer in the reign of Charles I., who advocated the establishment of " Mounts of Piety " speaks of the high rate of interest taken by brokers and pawnbrokers " above 400 in the hundred " from " fishwives, oysterwomen and others that do crye thinges up and downe the streets."[5] It was in this humble class of

[1] Atkinson, J. C. *Yorks. N. R. Q. S. Records*, Vol. I., p. 121, 1608.

[2] Herbert, *Livery Companies of London*, Vol. II., p. 44.

[3] *Ibid*, Vol. II., p. 35.

[4] *Middlesex County Records*, p. 160, 1696.

[5] *A Project for Mounts of Piety*. *Lansdowne MSS.*, 351 fo., 18b.

trade rather than in the larger transactions of fish-mongers, that women were chiefly engaged. In London no impediments seem to have been placed in the way of their business, but in the provinces they, like the women who hawked meat, were per-secuted under the bye-laws against regrating. At Manchester, the wife of John Wilshawe was amerced " for buyinge Sparlings [smelts] and sellinge them the same day in 6d."[1] while at the same court others were fined for selling unmarketable fish.

Brewers :—It has been shown that the position which women occupied among butchers and bakers did not differ materially from their position in other trades ; that is to say, the wife generally helped her husband in his business, and carried it on after his death ; but the history of brewing possesses a peculiar interest, for apparently the art of brewing was at one time chiefly, if not entirely, in the hands of women. This is indicated by the use of the feminine term brewster. Possibly the use of the masculine or feminine forms may never have strictly denoted the sex of the person indicated in words such as brewer, brewster, spinner, spinster, sempster, sempstress, webber, webster, and the gradual disuse of the feminine forms may have been due to the grammatical tendencies in the English language rather than to the changes which were driving women from their place in productive in-dustry ; but the feminine forms would never have arisen in the first place unless women had been engaged to some extent in the trades to which they refer, and it often happens that the use of the feminine pronoun in relation to the term " brewster " and even " brewer " shows decisively that female persons are indicated. At Beverley a bye-law was made in 1364 ordaining that " if any of the community abuse the affeerers of Brewster-gild for their affeering,

---

[1] *Manchester Court Leet Records*, Vol. IV., p. 112, 1654.

in words or otherwise, he shall pay . . . . to the commuunity 6s. 8d."[1] In this case Brewster might no more imply a woman's trade than it does in the modern term " Brewster-Sessions," but in 1371 a gallon of beer was ordered to " be sold for 1½d. . . . . and if any one offer 1½d. for a gallon of beer anywhere in Beverley and the ale-wife will not take it, that the purchaser come to the Gild Hall and complain of the brewster, and a remedy shall be found,"[2] while a rule made in 1405 orders that " no brewster or female seller called tipeler " shall " permit strangers to remain after 9 p.m."[3] Similar references occur in the Records of other Boroughs. At Bury the Customs provided in 1327 that " if a woman Brewer (Braceresse) can acquit herself with her sole hand that she has not sold contrary to the assize [of ale] she shall be quit "[4]; at Torksey " when women are asked whether they brew and sell beer outside their houses contrary to the assize or no, if they say no, they shall have a day at the next court to make their law with the third hand, with women who live next door on either side or with others."[5]

It was ordered at Leicester in 1335 that " no brew-eress, sworn inn-keeper or other shall be so bold as to brew except (at the rate of) a gallon of the best for 1d,"[6] and though the feminine form of the noun has been dropped, the feminine pronoun is still used in 1532 when "hytt is enacteyd y^at no brwar y^at brwys to sell, sell aboffe iid the gallan & sche schall typill

[1] *Beverley Town Documents.* p. 41.

[2] *Ibid*, p. 41.

[3] *Ibid*, p. lv.

[4] Bateson, (M.), *Borough Customs*, Vol. I., p. 185

[5] *Ibid*, Vol. I., p. 185, 1345.

[6] Bateson, (M.), *Records of Leicester*, Vol. II., p. 21

be no mesure butt to sell be ye dossyn & ye halfe dossyn."[1]

The exclusive use of the feminine in these bye-laws differs from the expressions used in regard to other trades when both the masculine and feminine pronouns are habitually employed, suggesting that the trade of brewing was on a different basis.

It must be remembered that before the introduction of cheap sugar, beer was considered almost equally essential for human existence as bread. Beer was drunk at every meal, and formed part of the ordinary diet of even small children. Large households brewed for their own use, but as many families could not afford the necessary apparatus, brewing was not only practised as a domestic art, but became the trade of certain women who brewed for their neighbours. It is interesting to note the steps which led to their ultimate exclusion from the trade, though many links in the chain of evidence are unfortunately missing. In 1532 brewers in Leicester are referred to as " sche," but an Act published in 1574 shows that the trade had already emerged from petticoat government. It declares that " No inhabitantes what soeuer that nowe doe or hereafter shall in theire howsses vse tiplinge and sellinge of ale or beare, shall not brewe the same of theare owne, but shall tunne in the same of the common brewars therfore appoynted ; and none to be common brewars but such as nowe doe vse the same, ... and non of the said common brewars to sell, or . . . . to tipple ale or beare by retayle . . . . the Brewars shall togeyther become a felloweship. etc."[2] This separation of brewing from the sale of beer was a policy pursued by the government with the object of simplifying the collection of excise, but it was

---

[1] Bateson, (M.), *Records of Leicester*, Vol. III., p. 33.

[2] *Ibid*, Vol. III., p. 153.

also defended as a means for maintaining the quality of the beer brewed. It was ordayned in the Assize for Brewers, Anno 23, H. 8, that " Forasmuch as the misterie of brewing as a thing very needfull and necessarie for the common wealth, hath been alwaies by auncient custom & good orders practised & maintained within Citties, Corporate Boroughs and market Townes of this Realm, by such expert and skilfull persons, as eyther were traded and brought up therein, by the space of seuen yeares, and as prentizes therin accepted : accordingly as in all other Trades and occupations, or else well knowne to be such men of skill and honestie, in that misterie, as could and would alwaie yeeld unto her Maiesties subiects in the commonwealth, such good and holsome Ale and Beere, as both in the qualitie & for the quantitie thereof, did euer agree with the good lawes of the Realme. And especiallie to the comfort of the poorer sort of subiectes, who most need it, untill of late yeares, sondrie persons . . . . rather seeking their owne private gaine, then the publike profite of their countrie, haue not onelie erected and set uppe small brewhouses at their pleasures : but also brew and utter such Ales and Beere, for want of skill in that misterie as both in the prices & holesomnes thereof, doth utterlie disagree with the good lawes and orders of this Realm ; thereby also ouerthrowing the greater and more auncient brewhouses." It is therefore recommended that these modern brewhouses should be suppressed in the interest of the old and better ones.[1]

The argument reads curiously when one reflects how universal had been the small brewhouses in former days. The advantages from the excise point of view which would be gained by the concentration of the trade in a few hands is discussed in a pamphlet which remarks that " there is much Mault made in

---

Powell, John. *The Assize of Bread.*

private Families, in some Counties half, if not two thirds of the Maults spent, are privately made, and undoubtedly as soon as an Imposition is laid upon it, much more will, for the advantage they shall gain by saving the Excise . . . . if Mault could be forbidden upon a great penalty to be made by any persons, but by certain publick Maulsters, this might be of availe to increase the Excise."[1] The actual conditions prevailing in the brewing industry at this time are described as follows in another pamphlet. Brewers are divided into two classes, " The Brewer who brews to sell by great measures, and wholly serves other Families by the same ; which sort of Brewers are only in some few great Cities and Towns, not above twenty through the land . . . . The Brewers who brews to sell by retail . . . . this sort of Brewers charges almost only such as drink the same in those houses where the same is brewed and sold . . . . and therefore supplies but a small proportion of the rest of the land, being that in almost all Market Towns, Villages, Hamlets, and private houses in the Countrey throughout the land, all the Inhabitants brew for themselves, at least by much the greatest proportion of what they use."[2]

In order to extend and strengthen their monopoly the " Common Brewers " brought forward a scheme in 1620, asking for a certain number of common brewers to be licensed throughout the kingdom, to brew according to assize. All other inn-keepers, alehouse keepers and victuallers to be forbidden to brew, " these brew irregularly without control," and " offering to pay the King 4d. on every quart of malt brewed." The scheme was referred to the Council who recommended " that a proclamation be issued forbidding ' taverners, innkeepers, etc. to sell any beer

---

[1] *Considerations Touching the Excise*, p. 7.

[2] Rockley, Francis.

but such as they buy from the brewers.'" To the objections " that brewers who were free by service or otherwise to use the trade of brewing would refuse to take a licence, and when apprentices had served their time there would be many who might do so," it was replied that it was " not usual for Brewers to take any apprentices but hired servants and the stock necessary for the trade is such as few apprentices can furnish."[1] Thus the rise of the " common brewer" signalises the complete victory of capitalistic organisation in the brewing trade. In 1636 Commissioners were appointed to " compound with persons who wished to follow the trade of common Brewers throughout the Kingdom."[2] The next year returns were received by the Council, giving the names and other particulars of those concerned in various districts. The list for the " Fellowshipp of Brewers now living in Newcastle-upon-Tyne with the breath and depth of their severall mash tunns " gives the names of fifty-three men and three women, widows.[3] A list of such brewers in the County of Essex " as have paid their fines and are bound to pay their rent accordingly "[4] (i.e. were licensed by the King's Commissioners for brewing) includes sixty-three men and four women, while the names of one hundred and twenty-four men and eight women are given in other tables containing the amounts due from brewers and maultsters in certain other counties,[5] showing that the predominance of women in the brewing trade had then disappeared, the few names appearing in the lists being no doubt those of brewers' widows.

---

[1] *S. P. D.*, cxii., 75. February 9, 1620.

[2] *C. R.* November 9, 1636.

[3] *S. P. D.* ccclxxvii., 62, 1637.

[4] *S. P. D.* ccclxxvii., 64, 1637.

[5] *S. P. D.* ccclxxxvii., 66.

The creation of the common brewers' monopoly was very unpopular. At Bury St. Edmunds a petition was presented by " a great no. of poor people " to the Justices of Assize, saying that for many years they had been relieved " by those inn-keepers which had the liberty to brew their beer in their own houses, not only with money and food, but also at the several times of their brewing (being moved with pity and compassion, knowing our great extremities and necessities) with such quantities of their small beer as has been a continual help and comfort to us with our poor wives and children : yet of late the common brewers, whose number is small and their benefits to us the poor as little notwithstanding in their estate they are wealthy and occupy great offices of malting, under pretence of doing good to the commonwealth, have for their own lucre and gain privately combined themselves, and procured orders from the Privy Council that none shall brew in this town but they and their adherents."[1] At Tiverton the Council was obliged to make a concession to popular feeling and agreed that " every person being a freeman of the town and not prohibited by law might use the trade of Common Brewer as well as the four persons formerly licensed by the Commissioners, " but the petition that the ale-house keepers and innkeepers might brew as formerly they used was refused, " they might brew for their own and families use; otherwise to buy from the Common Brewers."[2]

The monopoly involved the closing of many small businesses. Sarah Kemp a widow, petitioned the Council because she had " been forced to give up brewing in Whitefriars, and had been at g^t loss both in removing her implements and in her rents," asking " that in consideration of her loss she might

---

[1] *Hist. MSS. Com.*, 14 Rep. App., VIII., p. 142.

[2] *C. R.* June 12, 1640. Order concerning the Brewers of Tiverton.

have license to erect brick houses on her messuage in Whitefriars." This was granted on conditions.[1] A married woman, Mary Arnold, was committed to the Fleet on March 31st, 1639, " for continuing to brew in a house on the Millbank in Westminster, contrary to an order against the brewers in Westminster and especially against Michael Arnold." The Council ordered her to be discharged, on her humble admission to brew no more in the said house, but to remove within ten days ; and on bond from her husband that neither he nor she nor any other shall brew in the said house, and that he will remove his brewing vessels within ten days.[2]

The closing of the trade of brewing to women must have seriously reduced their opportunities for earning an independance; that they had hitherto been extensively engaged in it is shown by frequent references to women who were brewsters ; for example, Mrs. Putland was rated 5s. on her brew-house ;[3] Jennet Firbank, wife of Steph. Firbank, of Awdbroughe, a recusant, was presented at Richmond for brewing, a side note adding " she to be put down from brueing."[4] Margaret, the wife of Ambrose Carleton and Marye Barton were presented at Carlisle for " brewing (being foryners) and therefore we doe emercye either of them vi^s 8d."[5] At Thirske, Widow Harrington, of Hewton, Chr. Whitecake, of Bransbie, Rob. Goodricke, of the same (for his wife's offence) were presented, all for brewing.[6] And at Malton, a few years later, " Rob. Driffeld,

---

[1] *C. R.* 22nd March, 1638-9.

[2] *C. R.* May 8, 1639.

[3] *Strood Churchwardens' Accounts*, Add. MSS., 36937, p. 263., 1683.

[4] Atkinson, (J. C.), *Yorks. N. R. Q. S. Records*, Vol. I., p. 95., 1607.

[5] Ferguson, *Carlisle*, p. 280, *Court Leet Rolls*. October 21, 1625.

Atkinson, (J. C.), *Yorks. N. R. Q. S. Records*, Vol. I., p. 159, 1609.

a brewster of Easingwold, was presented for suffering unlawful games att cardes to be used at unlawful times in the night in his house. . . . . and the wife of the said Driffeld for that she will not sell anie of her ale forth of doores except it be to those whom she likes on and makes her ale of 2 or thre sortes, nor will let anie of her poore neighbours have anie of her drincke called small ale, but she saith she will rather give it to her Swyne then play it for them "[1] Isabell Bagley and Janyt Lynsley " both of Cowburne bruesters " were fined 10s. each " for suffering play at cardes in their houses, &c,"[2] and at Norwich, Judith Bowde, brewer, was fined 2s. 9d.[3]

Although women had lost their position in the brewing trade by the end of the seventeenth century, they were still often employed in brewing for domestic purposes. Sometimes one of the women—servants on a large farm, brewed for the whole family, including all the farm servants.[4] In other cases a woman made her living by brewing for different families in their own houses. Thus in the account of a fire on the premises of a certain Mr. Reading it is described how his " Family were Brewing within this Place . . . . The Servants who were in the House perceiving a great smoak rose out of Bed, and the Maid running out cried Fire and said *Wo worth this Bookers wife* (who was the Person whom Mr. *Reading* imployed to be his Brewer) *she hath undone us.*"[5] Lady Grizell Baillie enters in her Household Account Book, " For Brewing 7 bolls Malt by Mrs. Ainsly 10s. For a ston hopes to the said Malt out of which I had a puntion very

---

[1] Atkinson, (J. C.), *Yorks N. R. Q. S. Records*, Vol. II., pp. 53-54, 1614.

[2] *Ibid*, Vol. I., p. 93, 1607.

[3] Tingey, (J. C.), *Records of City of Norwich*, Vol. I., p. 388, 1676.

[4] Ante., p. 50.

[5] *True Account how Mr. Reading's House.*

strong Ale 10 gallons good 2nd ale and four puntions of Beer.   14s."[1]

Naturally the women who brewed for domestic purposes sometimes wished to turn an honest penny by selling beer to thirsty neighbours at Fairs and on Holidays, but attempts to do so were severely punished.   Annes Nashe of Welling, was presented " for selling beer by small jugs at Woolmer Grene and for laying her donng in the highway leading from Stevenage to London."[2]   A letter to a Somerset Magistrate pleads for another offender :—" Good Mr. Browne, all happiness attend you.   This poor woman is arrested with Peace proces for selling ale without lycense and will assure you shee hath reformed it and that upon the first warning of our officers ever since Easter last, which is our fayre tyme, when   most   commonly   our   poore   people   doe offend in that kinde ; I pray you doe her what lawful kindness you may, and hope she will recompense you for your paynes, and I shall be ready to requite it in what I may, for if she be committed she is absolutely undone.   Thus hoping of your favour I leave you to God and to this charitable work towards this poor woman.   Your unfeined friend, Hum. Newman."[3]

Though with the growth of capitalism and the establishment of a monopoly for " Common Brewers " women were virtually excluded from their old trade of brewing, they still maintained their position in the retail trade, their hold upon which was favoured by the same circumstances which turned their energies to the retail side of other businesses.

A tendency was shown by public opinion to regard licences as suitable provision for invalids and widows who might otherwise require assistance from the rates.

---

[1] Baillie, Lady Grizell, *Household Book.* p. 91.   1714.

[2] *Hertford County Records*, Vol. I., p. 68.   1641.

[3] *Somerset Q. S. Records*, Vol. II., pp. 40-1, 1627.

Thus an attempt made at Lincoln in 1628 to reduce the numbers of licences was modified, " for that it appeareth that divers poor men and widows, not freemen, have no other means of livelihood but by keeping of alehouses, it is agreed that such as shall be approved by the justices may be re-admitted, but that none hereafter be newly admitted untill they be first sworn freemen."[1] According to a pamphlet published early in the next century, " Ale-houses were originally Accounted Neusances in the *Parish's* where they were, as tending to Debauch the Subject, and make the People idle, and therefore Licences to sell Beer and Ale, where allow'd to none, but Ancient People past their Labours, and Invalides to keep them from Starving, there being then no *Act* of *Parliament* that *Parishes* should Maintain their own Poor. But the Primitive Intention in granting Licences being now perverted, and all sorts of People Admitted to this priviledge, it is but reason the Publick should have some Advantage by the Priviledges it grants. . ."[2] Many examples of this attitude of mind can be observed in the Quarter Sessions Records. For instance, Mary Briggs when a widow was licensed by the Hertfordshire Quarter Sessions to sell drink, and by the good order she kept in her house and the goodness of the drink she uttered and sold she got a good livelihood, and brought up three children she had by a former husband. She married John Briggs, woodard and servant to Lord Ashton, she continuing her business and he his. Her husband was returned as a papist recusant, and on his refusing to take oaths the court suppressed their alehouse. Mrs. Briggs appealed on the ground that her business was carried on separately and by it she maintained her children by her former husband. Her claim was supported by a petition

---

[1] *Hist. MSS. Com.*, 14 Rep., app. viii., p. 99, 1629.

[2] Phipps, (Thomas), *Proposal for raising £1,000,000 Sterling yearly.*

from her fellow parishioners, declaring that John
Briggs was employed by Lord Ashton and " meddles
not with his wife's trade of victualling and selling
drink."[1]　Other examples may be found in an order
for the suppression of Wm. Brightfoot's licence who
had " by surprize " obtained one for selling beer　. .
showing that he was a young man, and capable to
maintain his family without keeping an alehouse,[2]
and the petition of John Phips, of Stondon, labourer,
lately fallen into great need for want of work.　He
can get very little to do among his neighbours, " because
they have little for him to do, having so many poore
laborious men besides within the said parish."　He
asks for a licence to sell beer " for his better livelihood
and living hereafter, towards the mayntenance of
himself, his poor wife and children."[3]　Licences were
refused at Bristol to " John Keemis, Cooper, not
fit to sell ale, having no child ; he keeps a tapster
which is no treeman that have a wife and child," and
also to " Richard Rooke, shipwright, not fit to sell
ale, having no child, and brews themselves." A Barber
Surgeon was disqualified, having no child, " and also
for entertaining a strange maid which is sick."[4]

Very rarely were doubts suggested as to the propriety
of the trade for women, though a bye-law was passed
at Chester ordaining that " no woman between the
age of xiii & xl yeares shall kepe any taverne or ale-
howse."[5]　At times complaints were made of the conduct of alewives, as in a request to the Justices of
Nottingham " that your Worshipps wyll take some
order wythe all the alewyfes in this towne, for we thinke
that never an alewyfe dothe as hir husband is bownd

[1] *Hertford County Records*, Vol. I., p. 289, 1678.

[2] *Middlesex Sessions Book*, p. 23, 1690.

[3] *Hertford County Records*, Vol. I., p. 174, 1665.

[4] Latimer, *Bristol*, p. 359.　1670.　*Court Leet for St. Stephen's Parish.*

[5] *Harl. MSS.*, 2054 (4), fo., 6.

to,"[1] but there is no evidence of any marked difference in the character of the alehouses kept by men and those kept by women. The trade included women of the most diverse characters. One, who received stolen goods at the sign of the " Leabord's Head " in Ware, had there a " priviye place " for hiding stolen goods and suspicious persons " at the press for soldiers she hid five men from the constables, and can convey any man from chamber to chamber into the backside. There is not such a house for the purpose within a hundred miles."[2] In contrast to her may be quoted the landlady of the Inn at Truro, of whom Celia Fiennes wrote, " My Greatest pleasure was the good Landlady I had, she was but an ordinary plaine woman but she was understanding in the best things as most—ye Experience of reall religion and her quiet submission and self-Resignation to ye will of God in all things, and especially in ye placeing her in a remoteness to ye best advantages of hearing, and being in such a publick Employment wch she desired and aimed at ye discharging so as to adorn ye Gospel of her Lord and Saviour, and the Care of her children."[3]

Vintners :—The trade of the Vintner had no connection with that of the Brewer. Wine was sold in Taverns. In London the Vintners' Company, like the other London Companies, possessed privileges which were continued to the wife upon her husband's death, but women were probably not concerned in the trade on their own account. A survey of all the Taverns in London made in 1633 gives a total of 211, whereof six are licensed by His Majesty, 203 by the Vintners' Company and two are licensed by neither, one is unlicensed, " inhabited by An Tither, whoe lately made a tavern of the Starr on

---

[1] *Nottingham Records*, Vol. IV., p. 325, 1614.

[2] *Hertford County Records*, Vol. I., p. 59, 1626.

[3] Fiennes, (Celia), p. 226 *Through England on a Side-Saddle*.

Tower Hill where shee also keepes a victualling house unlicensed." One licensed by the Earl of Middlesex. Amongst those duly licensed are the names of a few widows. In Cordwainer Street Ward, there was only one Tavern, "kept by a widdowe whose deceased husband was bound prentice to a Vintener and so kept his taverne by vertue of his freedome of that companye after his termes of apprentizhood expired."[1]

Conclusion.

The foregoing examination of the relation of women to the different crafts and trades has shown them occupying an assured position wherever the system of family industry prevailed. While this lasted the detachment of married women from business is nowhere assumed, but they are expected to assist their husband, and during his absence or after his death to take his place as head of the family and manager of the business.

The economic position held by women depended upon whether the business was carried on at home or elsewhere, and upon the possession of a small amount of capital. The wives of men who worked as journeymen on their masters' premises could not share their husbands' trade, and their choice of independent occupations was very limited. The skilled women's trades, such as millinery and mantua-making, were open, and in these, though apprenticeship was usual, there is no reason to suppose that women who worked in them without having served an apprenticeship, were prosecuted; but as has been shown the apprenticeship laws were strictly enforced in other directions, and in some cases prevented women from using their domestic skill to earn their living.

While women could share their husbands' trades they suffered little from these restrictions,

---

[1] S.P.D. ccl., 22, November 6, 1633. Lord Mayor and others to the Council.

but with the development of capitalistic organisation the numbers of women who could find no outlet for their productive activity in partnership with their husbands were increasing and their opportunities for establishing an independent industry did not keep pace ; on the contrary, such industry became ever more difficult. The immediate result is obscure, but it seems probable that the wife of the prosperous capitalist tended to become idle, the wife of the skilled journeyman lost her economic independence and became his unpaid domestic servant, while the wives of other wage earners were driven into the sweated industries of that period. What were the respective numbers in each class cannot be determined, but it is probable that throughout the seventeenth century they were still outnumbered by the women who could find scope for productive activity in their husbands' business.

Chapter VI

PROFESSIONS

Introductory—Tendencies similar to those in Industry.—Army—Church—Law closed to women. Teaching—Nursing—Medicine chiefly practised by women as domestic arts. Midwifery.

(A). *Nursing.* The sick poor nursed in lay institutions—London Hospitals—Dublin—Supplied by low class women—Women searchers for the plague—Nurses for small-pox or plague—Hired nurses in private families.

(B) *Medicine.* Women's skill in Middle ages—Medicine practised extensively by women in seventeenth century in their families, among their friends and for the poor—Also by the village wise woman for pay—Exclusiveness of associations of physicians, surgeons and apothecaries.

(C) *Midwifery.* A woman's profession—Earlier history unknown—Raynold's translation of "the byrthe of mankynd."—Relative dangers of child-birth in seventeenth and twentieth centuries—Importance of midwives—Character of their training—Jane Sharp—Nicholas Culpepper—Peter Chamberlain—Mrs. Cellier's scheme for training—Superiority of French training—Licences of Midwives—Attitude of the Church to them—Fees—Growing tendency to displace midwives by Doctors.

Conclusion. Women's position in the arts of teaching and healing lost as these arts became professional.

Introductory.

SIMILAR tendencies to those which affected the industrial position of women can be traced in the professions also, showing that, important as was the influence of capitalistic organisation in the history of women's evolution, other powerful factors were working in the same direction.

Three professions were closed to women in the seventeenth century, Arms, the Church and the Law.

The Law.—It must be remembered that the mass of the "common people" were little affected by "the law" before the seventeenth century. "Common law" was the law of the nobles,[1] while farming people and

---

[1] *Holdsworth*, Vol. III., p. 408.

artizans alike were chiefly regulated in their dealings with each other by customs depending for interpretation and sanction upon a public opinion which represented women as well as men. Therefore the changes which during the seventeenth century were abrogating customs in favour of common law, did in effect eliminate women from what was equivalent to a share in the custody and interpretation of law, which henceforward remained exclusively in the hands of men. The result of the elimination of the feminine influence is plainly shown in a succession of laws, which, in order to secure complete liberty to individual men, destroyed the collective idea of the family, and deprived married women and children of the property rights which customs had hitherto secured to them. From this time also the administration of the law becomes increasingly perfunctory in enforcing the fulfilment of men's responsibilities to their wives and children.

Church.—According to modern ideas, religion pertains more to women than to men, but this conception is new, dating from the scientific era.

Science has solved so many of the problems which in former days threatened the existence of mankind, that the " man in the street " instinctively relegates religion to the region in which visible beauty, poetry and music are still permitted to linger ; to the ornamental sphere in short, whither the Victorian gentleman also banished his wife and daughters. This attitude forms a singular contrast to the ideas which prevailed in the Middle Ages, when men believed that supernatural assistance was their sole protection against the " pestilence that walketh in darkness " or from " the arrow that flieth by day." Religion was then held to be such an awful power that there were men who even questioned whether women could, properly speaking, be considered religious at all. Even in the seventeenth century the practice of religion and the holding of correct ideas concerning it were deemed to be essential for the maintenance of human existence, and no suggestion was then made that religious observances could be adequately performed by women alone.

Ideas as to the respective appropriateness of religious power to men and women have differed widely ; some races have reserved the priesthood for men, while others have recognised a special power enduing women ; in the history of others again no uniform tendency is shown, but the two influences can be traced acting and reacting upon each other.

This has been the case with the Christian religion, which has combined the wide-spread worship of the Mother and Child with a passionate splitting of hairs by celibate priests in dogmatic controversies concerning intellectual abstractions. The worship of the Mother and Child had been extirpated in England before the beginning of the seventeenth century ; pictures of this subject were denounced because they showed the Divine Son under the domination of a woman. One writer accuses the Jesuits of representing Christ always " as a sucking child in his mothers armes "—" nay, that is nothing they make him an underling to a woman," alleging that " the Jesuits assert (1) no man, but a woman did helpe God in the work of our Redemption, (2) that God made Mary partaker and fellow with him of his divine Majesty and power, (3) that God hath divided his Kingdom with Mary, keeping Justice to himselfe, and yielding mercy to her." He complains that " She is always set forth as a woman and a mother, and he as a child and infant, either in her armes, or in her hand, that so the common people might have occasion to imagine that looke, what power of overruling and commanding the mother hath over her little child, the same hath she over her son Jesus . . . . the mother is compared to the son, not

as being a child or a man, but as the saviour and
mediator, and the paps of a woman equalled with
the wounds of our Lord, and her milke with his
blood . . . . But for her the holy scriptures
speake no more of her, but as of a creature, a woman
. . . . saved by Faith in her Saviour Jesus
Christ . . . . and yet now after 1600 yeares
she must still be a commanding mother and must
show her authority over him . . . . she must be
saluted as a lady, a Queen, a goddesse and he as a child."[1]

The ridicule with which Peter Heylin treated the
worship of the Virgin Mary in France seems to have
been pointed more at the notion of honouring
motherhood, rather than at the distinction given
to her as a woman, for he wrote " if they will worship
her as a Nurse with her Child in her arms, or at her
breast, let them array her in such apparel as might
beseem a Carpenter's Wife, such as she might be
supposed to have worn before the world had taken
notice that she was the Mother of her Saviour.
If they must needs have her in her state of glory
as at Amiens; or of honour (being now publikely
acknowledged to be the blessednesse among Women)
as at Paris : let them disburden her of her Child.
To clap them thus both together, is a folly equally
worthy of scorn & laughter."[2]

The reform which had swept away the worship
of divine motherhood had also abolished the enforced
celibacy of the priesthood ; but the priest's wife
was given no position in the Church, and a tendency
may be noted towards the secularisation of all women's
functions. Convents and nunneries were abolished,
and no institutions which might specially assist
women in the performance of their spiritual, educational or charitable duties were established in

---

[1] *C. W.* 1641. *The Bespotted Jesuite.*

[2] Heylin (Peter), *The Voyage of France*, p. 29, 1673.

their place. There was, in fact, a deep jealousy of any influence which might disturb the authority and control which the individual husband exercised over his wife, and probably the seventeenth century Englishman was beginning to realise that nothing would be so subversive to this authority as the association of women together for religious purposes. If a recognised position was given to women in the Church, their lives must inevitably receive an orientation which would not necessarily be identical with their husband's, thus creating a danger of conflicting loyalties. Naturally, therefore, women were excluded from any office, but it would be a mistake to suppose that their subordination to their husbands in religious matters was rigidly enforced throughout this period. Certainly in the first half of the century their freedom of thought in religion was usually taken for granted, and possibly amongst the Baptists, certainly amongst the Quakers, full spiritual equality was accorded to them. Women were universally admitted to the sacraments, and therefore recognised as being, in some sort, members of the Church, but this was consistent with the view of their position to which Milton's well known lines in " Paradise Lost " give perfect expression, the ideal which, in all subsequent social and political changes, was destined to determine women's position in Church and State :—

> " Whence true authoritie in men, though both
> Not equal, as their sex not equal seem'd,
> For contemplation hee and valour form'd
> For softness shee, and sweet attractive Grace,
> Hee for God only, shee for God in him :
>
> .   .   .   .   .
>
> To whom thus Eve with perfect beauty adornd
> My Author and Disposer, what thou bidst
> Unargu'd I obey ; so God ordains,
> God is thy Law, thou mine ; to know no more
> woman's happiest knowledge and her praise."

Nevertheless, though excluded from any position in the hierarchy of recognised servants of the Church, it must not be supposed that the Church was independent of women's service. To their hands necessity rather than the will of man had entrusted a duty, which when unfulfilled makes all the complicated organisation of the Church impotent ; namely, the bending of the infant mind and soul towards religious ideals and emotions. The lives of the reformers of the seventeenth century bear witness to the faithfulness with which women accomplished this task. In many cases their religious labours were extended beyond the care of their children, embracing the whole household for their field of service. The life of Lettice, Viscountess Falkland, gives an example of the sense of responsibility under which many religious women lived. Lady Falkland passed about an hour with her maids, early every morning " in praying, and catechizing and instructing them ; to these secret and private prayers, the publick morning and evening prayers of the Church, before dinner and supper ; and another form (together with reading Scriptures and singing Psalms) before bedtime, were daily and constantly added . . . . neither were these holy offices appropriate to her menial servants, others came freely to joyn with them, and her Oratory was as open to her neighbours as her Hall was . . . . her Servants were all moved to accompany her to the Sacrament, and they who were prevailed with gave up their names to her, two or three dayes before, and from thence, she applied herself to the instructing of them . . . and after the Holy Sacrament she called them together again and gave them such exhortations as were proper for them."[1]

The quarrel between Church and State over the teaching profession is an old story which does not

---

[1] *Falkland, Lady Letice, Vi-countess, Life and Death of.*

concern this investigation. It is sufficient to note that in England neither Church nor State considered that the work of women in training the young entitled them to a recognised position in the general social organisation, or required any provision apart from the casual arrangements of family life.

Teaching.—The question of the standard and character of the education given to girls is too large a subject to be entered into here; it can only be remarked that the number of professional paid women teachers was small. The natural aptitude of the average woman for training the young, however, enabled mothers to provide their children, both boys and girls, with a very useful foundation of elementary education.

The professions of medicine, midwifery and nursing are very closely allied to each other; for neither was there any system of instruction on a scientific basis available for women, whose practice was thus empirical; but as yet science had done little to improve the skill even of the male practitioner.

Nursing.—Nursing was almost wholly a domestic art.

Medicine.—Though we find many references to women who practised medicine and surgery as professions, in the majority of cases their skill was used only for the assistance of their family and neighbours.

Midwifery.—Midwifery was upon a different footing, standing out as the most important public function exercised by women, and being regarded as their inviolable mystery till near the beginning of the seventeenth century. The steady process through which in this profession women were then supplanted by men, furnishes an example of the way in which women have lost their hold upon all branches of skilled responsible work, through being deprived of opportunities for specialised training.

The relative deterioration of woman's capacity in comparison with the standard of men's efficiency cannot be more clearly shown than in the history of midwifery. Even though the actual skill of midwives may not have declined during the seventeenth century men were rapidly surpassing them in scientific knowledge, for the general standard of women's education was declining, and they were debarred from access to the higher branches of learning. As the absence of technical training kept women out of the skilled trades, so did the lack of scientific education drive them from the more profitable practice of midwifery, which in former times tradition and prejudice had reserved as their monopoly.

A—*Nursing.*

Whatever arrangements had been made by the religious orders in England for the care of the sick poor were swept away by the Reformation. The provision which existed in the seventeenth century for this purpose rested on a lay basis, quite unconnected with the Church. Amongst the most famous charitable institutions were the four London Hospitals ; Christ's Hospital for children under the age of sixteen, St. Bartholomew's and St. Thomas's for the sick and impotent poor, and Bethlehem for the insane.

There is no evidence that the women of the upper classes took any part in the management of these hospitals. The squalor and the ugly and disgusting details which are associated with nursing the diseased and often degraded poor, was unredeemed by the radiance with which a mystic realisation of the Divine Presence had upheld the Catholic Saints, or by the passionate desire for the service of humanity which inspired Florence Nightingale. Thus it was only the necessity for earning their daily bread which induced any women to enter the profession of nursing during this period, and as the salaries offered were considerably lower than the wages earned by a competent servant in London, it may be supposed that the class attracted did not represent the most efficient type of women.

The rules appointed for the governance of nurses show that the renunciations of a nun's life were required of them, but social opinion in Protestant England set no seal of excellence upon their work, however faithfully performed, and the sacrifices demanded from the nurses were unrewarded by the crown of victory.

During the reign of Edward VI. there were a matron and twelve sisters at St. Bartholomew's who received in wages £26 6s. 8d. In addition the matron received 1s. 6d. per week for board wages and the sisters 1s. 4d. per week, and between them £6 per year for livery, while the matron received 13s. 4d. for this purpose.[1] The rules for the governance of the sisters were as follows :—" Your charge is, in all Things to declare and shew yourselves gentle, diligent, and obedient to the Matron of this House, who is appointed and authorised to be your chief Governess and Ruler. Ye shall also faithfully and charitably serve and help the Poor in all their Griefs and Diseases, as well by keeping them sweet and clean, as in giving them their Meats and Drinks, after the most honest and comfortable Manner. Also ye shall use unto them good and honest Talk, such as may comfort and amend them ; and utterly to avoid all light, wanton, and foolish Words, Gestures, and Manners, using yourselves unto them with all Sobriety and Discretion, and above all Things, see that ye avoid, abhor, and detest Scolding and Drunkenness as most pestilent and filthy Vices. Ye shall not haunt or resort to any manner of Person out of this House, except ye be licensed by the Matron ; neither shall ye suffer any light Person to haunt or use unto you, neither any dishonest Person, Man or Woman ; and so much as in you shall lie, ye shall avoid and shun the Conversation and Company of all Men.

---

[1] Stow, *London*, I., pp., 185-186.

Ye shall not be out of the Woman's Ward after the Hour of seven of the Clock in the Night, in the Winter, Time, nor after Nine of the Clock in the Night in the Summer : except ye shall be appointed and commanded by the Matron so to be, for some great and special cause that shall concern the Poor, (as the present Danger of Death or extreme Sickness), and yet so being commanded, ye shall remain no longer with such diseased Person than just Cause shall require. Also, if any just Cause of Grief shall fortune unto any of you, or that ye shall see Lewdness in any Officer, of other Person of this House, which may sound or grow to the Hurt or Slander thereof, ye shall declare the same to the Matron, or unto one or two of the Govenours of this House, that speedy Remedy therein may be had; and to no other Person neither shall ye talk or meddle therein any farther. This is your Charge, and with any other Thing you are not charged."[1]

The Matron was instructed to " receive of the Hospitaler of this House all such sick and diseased Persons as he . . . . shall present unto you," and to " have also Charge, Governance & Order of all the Sisters of this House. . . .that every of them. . . . do their Duty unto the Poor, as well in making of their Beds, and keeping their Wards, as also in washing and purging their unclean Cloaths, and other Things. And that the same Sisters every night after the Hour of seven of the Clock in the Winter, and nine of the Clock in the Summer, come not out of the Woman's Ward, except some great and special Cause (as the present Danger of Death, or needful Succour of some poor Person). And yet at such a special time it shall not be lawful for every Sister to go forth to any Person or Persons (no tho' it be in her Ward) but only for such as you shall think virtuous, godly, and discreet. And the

---

[1] Stow, *London*, app., p. 58.

same Sister to remain no longer with the same sick Person then needful Cause shall require. Also at such times as the Sisters shall not be occupied about the Poor, ye shall set them to spinning or doing some other Manner of Work, that may avoid Idleness, and be profitable to the Poor of this House. Also ye shall receive the Flax . . . . the same being spun by the Sisters, ye shall commit to the said Governors . . . . You shall also . . . . have special Regard to the good ordering & keeping of all the Sheets, Coverlets, Blankets, Beds, and other Implements committed to your Charge, ... Also ye shall suffer no poor Person of this House to sit and drink within your House at no Time, neither shall ye so send them drink into their Wards, that thereby Drunkenness might be used and continued among them."[1]

In Christ's Hospital there were two Matrons with salaries of £2 13s. 4d. per annum and forty-two women keepers with salaries of 40s. per annum. Board wages were allowed at the rate of 1s. 4d. per week for the " keepers " and 1s. 6d. for the Matrons. There was one keeper for fifteen persons.[2] The Matron was advised " Your office is an office of great charge and credite. For to yow is committed the Governance and oversight of all the women and children within this Hospital. And also to yow is given Authoritie to commaunde, reprove, and rebuke them or any of them . . . . Your charge is also to searche and enquire whether the women do their Dutie, in washing of the children's sheets and shirts, and in kepeing clean and sweet those that are committed to their Charge ; and also in the Beddes, Sheets, Coverlets, and Apparails (with kepeing clean Wards and Chambers) mending of such as shall be

---

[1] Stow, *London*, App. pp. 57-58.

[2] *Ibid*, I. pp. 175. 6.

broken from Time to Time. And specially yow shall give diligent Hede, that the said Washers and Nurses of this Howse be alwaies well occupied and not idle ; . . . . you shal also once every Quarter of the Year examine the Inventorie."[1]

The nurses were instructed that they must " carefully and diligently oversee, kepe, and governe all those tender Babes & yonglings that shal be committed to your Charge, and the same holesomely, cleanely and swetely nourishe and bring up . . . . kepe your Wardes and every Part thereof swete and cleane . . . . avoid all Idleness when your Charge and Care of keping the Children is past, occupie yourselves in Spinning, Sewing, mending of Sheets and Shirts, or some other vertuous Exercise, such as you shal be appointed unto. Ye shal not resort or suffer any Man to resort to you, before ye have declared the same to the almoners or Matron of this Howse and obtained their Lycense and Favour, so to do . . . . see that all your children, before they be brought to Bed, be washed and cleane, and immediately after, every one of yow quietly shal go to your Bed, and not to sit up any longer ; and once every night arise, and see that the Children be covered, for taking of Colde."[2]

Some idea of the class of women who actually undertook the important duties of Matron for the London Hospitals may be gathered from a petition presented by Joane Darvole, Matron of St. Thomas's Hospital, Southwark, to Laud. She alleged " that she was dragged out of the Chapel of the Hospital at service and dragged along the streets to prison for debt, to the hazard of her life, " she being a " very weak sickly and aged woman," clothes torn from her back and cast into a swoon. She petitions against the

---

[1] Stow, *London*, app., p. 42.

[2] Stow *London*, app., p. 43.

profanation of God's house and the scandal to the congregation.[1]

Sick and wounded soldiers were tended at the Savoy, where there were thirteen Sisters, whose joint salaries amounted to £52 16s. 8d. per annum.[2] Among the orders for the patients, nurses and widows in the Savoy and other hospitals in and about London occur the following regulations :—4[thly] " That every soldier or nurse .... that shall profanely sweare " to pay 12d. for the first offence, 12d. for the second, and be expelled for the third. 8[thly] " That if any souldier shall marye any of the nurses of the said houses whilst hee is there for care or (recov)ery they both shall be turned forth of the House. 11[thly] No soldier under cure to have their (wiv)es lodge with them there except by the approbation of the Phisicion. 12[thly] No nurse to be dismissed without the approval of 2 of the Treasurers for the relief of maimed soldiers at least. Nurses to be chosen from among the widows of soldiers if there are among them those that be fit, and those to have 5s. per weeke as others usually have had for the service. 14[thly] soldiers, wounded and sick, outside the hospitals not to have more than 4s. per week. Those in St. Thomas's and Bartholomew's hospital 2s. a week, those in their parents', masters' or friends' houses, according to their necessities, but not more than 4s. per week. 15[thly] Soldiers' widows to receive according to their necessities, but not more than 4s. a week. 19[thly] If any of the nurses . . . . . shalbee negligent in their duties or in giving due attendance to the . . . . sicke souldiers by daye or night or shall by scoulding, brawlinge or chidinge make any disturbance in the said hospitall, she shall forfeite 12d. for 1st offence, week's pay for second,

---

[1] S.P.D., cccclv., 87. May 30th, 1640.

[2] Stow, London I., p. 211.

be dismissed for the third. 20^{thly} If any widow after marriage shall come and receive weekly pensions as a soldier's widow contrary to the ordinance of parl^t he which hath married her to repay it, & if he is unable she shall be complained of to the nearest J.P. and be punished as a de(ceiver)."[1]

There was one nurse for every ten patients in the Dublin hospitals, and the salary was £10 per annum, out of which she had to find her board.[2]

The opportunity which the hospitals afforded for training in the art of nursing was entirely wasted. The idea that the personal tending of the sick and forlorn poor would be a religious service of special value in the sight of God had vanished, and their care, no longer transformed by the devotion of religious enthusiasm, appeared a sordid duty, only fit for the lowest class in the community. Well-to-do men relieved their consciences by bequeathing money for the endowment of hospitals, but the sense of social responsibility was not fostered in girls, and the expression of charitable instincts was almost confined in the case of women to their personal relations.

Outside the hospitals employment was given to a considerable number of women in the tending of persons stricken with small-pox or the plague, and in searching corpses for signs of the plague. London constables and churchwardens were ordered in 1570 " to provide to have in readiness Women to be Provyders & Deliverers of necessaries to infected Howses, and to attend the infected Persons, and they to bear reed Wandes, so that the sick maie be kept from the whole, as nere as maie be, needful attendance weyed."[3]

In the town records of Reading it is noted " at this daye Marye Jerome Wydowe was sworn to be

---

S. P. D., dxxxix, 231. November 15, 1644.

[2] S. P. D., Interreg : I. 62, p. 633. 17 Aug., 1649.

Stow, London, V., p. 433.

a viewer and searcher of all the bodyes that shall
dye within this boroughe, and truly to report and
certifye to her knowledge of what disease they dyed,
etc. ; and Anne Lovejoy widowe, jurata, 4ˢ a weeke
a peice, allowing iiijs. a moneth after."[1] " Mary
Holte was sworne to be a searcher of the dead bodyes
hencefovrth dyeinge within the boroughe (being
thereunto required) having iiijs. a weeke for her
wages, and iiid a corps carryeing to buryall, and iiijs
a weeke a moneth after the ceassinge of the plague."[2]
In 1637 it was " agreed . . . . with old
Frewyn and his wief, that she shall presentlye goe
into the house of Henry Merrifeild and be aidinge
& helpinge to the said Merrifeild and his wief, during
the time of their visitacion [plague] . . . . She
shall have dyett with them, and six weekes after their
visitacion ended. And old Frewin to have 2s. a week
duringe all that tyme paid him, and 2s. in hand.
And she shall have 2ˢ a weeke kept for her & paid
her in th'end of the sixe weekes after."[3] Later " it
was thought fitt the Woman keeper and Merifielde's
wenche in the Pest-house, it beinge above vj weekes
past since any one dyed there, should be at libertie
and goe hence to her husbande's house, she havinge
done her best endevour to ayre and cleanse all the
beddes & beddinge & other things in both the houses.
. . . for her mayntenance vj weekes after the
ceassinge of the sicknes, she keepinge the wenche
with her, they shalbe paid 3s. a weeke for and towardes
their mayntenance duringe the vj weekes."[4] In
1639 the Council " Agree to geve the Widowe Lovejoye
in full satisfaccion for all her paynes taken in and
about the visited people in this Towne in this last

---

[1] Guilding, *Reading Records*, Vol. II., p. 241, 1625.

[2] *Ibid*, Vol. II., p. 244, 1625.

[3] *Ibid*, Vol. III., p. 371.

[4] *Ibid*, Vol. III., p. 384, 1637.

visitacion xls. in money, and cloth to make her a kirtle and a wascote, and their favour towards her two sonnes-in-lawe (beinge forreynours) about their fredome."[1] On a petition in 1641 from Widow Lovejoy " for better allowance & satisfaction for her paines aboute the visited people ; . . . . it was agreed that she shall have xxxs. soe soone as the taxe for the visited people is made uppe."[2]

In rural districts where hospitals were seldom within reach, entries are not infrequently found in the parish account books of payments made to women for nursing the poor. " Item. To Mother Middleton for twoe nights watchinge with Widow Coxe's child being sick."[3] " To Goody Halliday, for nursing him & his family 5 weeks £1 5 ; to Goody Nye, for assisting in nursing, 2s. 6d.[4] . . . . to Goody Peckham for nursing a beggar, 5s. For nursing Wickham's boy with the small pocks 12s."[5] A Hertfordshire parish paid a woman 15s. for her attendance during three weeks on a woman and her illegitimate child.[6] A Morton man was ordered to pay out of his next half-year's rent for the grounds he farmed of Isabelle Squire " 20s to Margt. Squire, who attended and looked to her half a year during the time of her distraction."[7]

Sometimes nurses were provided for the poor by religious and charitable ladies, who, like Lettice, Viscountess Falkland, " hired nurses to serve them."[8] Sick nurses were also engaged by well-to-do people to attend upon themselves or their servants. Thus the Rev.

---

[1] Guilding, *Reading Records*, Vol. III., p. 459.

[2] *Ibid*, Vol. IV., p. 8.

[3] *Sussex Arch. Coll.*, Vol. XXIII., p. 90. Hastings Documents. 1601.

[4] *Sussex Arch. Coll.*, Vol. XX., p. 117. *Acc. Book of Cowden.* 1704.

[5] *Ibid*, p. 118.

[6] *Hertford County Records*, Vol. I., p. 435, 1698.

[7] Atkinson, J. C., *Yorks. N. R. Q. S. Records*, Vol. VII., p. 91. 1688.

[8] *Falkland, Lady Letice, Vi-countess, Life and Death of.*

Giles Moore enters in his journal " My mayde being
sicke I payd for opening her veine 4d. to the Widdow
Rugglesford, for looking to her, I gave 1s. and to old
Bess for tending her 3 days and 2 nights I gave 1ˢ; in
all 2ˢ 4ᵈ."[1] A little later, when the writer himself
was " in an ague. Paid Goodwyfe Ward for being
necessary to me 1s."[2] Though his daughter was
with him, a nurse watched in the chamber when
Colonel Hutchinson died in the prison at Dover.[3]

A few extracts from account books will supply
further details as to the usual scale of remuneration
for nurses ; no doubt in each case the money given
was in addition to meat and drink. Sarah Fell enters
" by mᵒ given Ann Daniell for her paines about
Rachell Yeamans when she died 05.00."[4] Timothy
Burrell " pd. Gosmark for tending Mary 3 weeks
6s."[5] Lady Grisell Baillie engaged a special nurse
for her daughter Rachy at a fee of 5s.[6] At Herstmonceux Castle they " pd Hawkin's wife for tending
the sick maiden 10 days 3s. Pd. Widdow Weeks
for tending sick seruants a fortnight 4s."[7] Sir John
Foulis in Scotland paid " to Ketherin in pᵗ paymᵗ
& till account for her attendance on me the time of
my sickness 12. 0. 0 " [scots].[8] " To Katherine tueddie
in compleat paymᵗ for her attendance on me wⁿ I
was sick 20. 0. 0." [scots].[9] " To my good douchter
jennie to give tibbie tomsone for her attendance
on my wife the time of her sickness 5. 16. 0. [scots]."[10]

---

[1] *Sussex Arch. Coll.*, Vol. I., p. 72. *Rev. Giles Moore's Journal.*

[2] *Ibid*, Vol. 1., p. 100. 1667.

[3] *Memoirs of Col. Hutchinson*, p. 377.

[4] Fell (Sarah), *Household Accounts*, p. 285. June 20, 1676.

[5] *Sussex Arch. Coll.*, Vol. III., p. 123. *Journal of Timothy Burrell.* 1688.

[6] *Baillie, Lady Grisell, Household Book.* Intro. lxvii.

[7] *Sussex Arch. Coll.*, Vol. XLVIII., p. 121. 1643-1649.

[8] Foulis, Sir John, *Account Book*, p. 346. May 23, 1704.

[9] *Ibid*, p. 396. August 22, 1705.

[10] *Ibid*, p. 314. January 28, 1703.

All the above instances refer to professional nursing ; that is to say to the tending of the sick for wages, but nursing was more often of an unprofessional character. Sickness was rife in all classes, and for the most part the sick were tended by the women of their household or family. The claim for such assistance was felt beyond the limits of kinship, and in the village community each woman would render it to her neighbour without thought of reward. The solidarity of the community was a vital tradition to the village matron of the early seventeenth century, and it was only in cases of exceptional isolation or difficulty, or where the sick person was a stranger or an outcast that the services of a paid nurse were called in. Probably the standard of efficiency was higher in domestic than in professional nursing, because professional nurses received no systematic training. Their rate of remuneration was low, the essential painfulness of their calling was not concealed by the glamour of a religious vocation, still less was it rewarded by any social distinction. Therefore the women who took up nursing for their livelihood did so from necessity, and were drawn from the lower classes.

Illness was so frequent in the seventeenth century that few girls can have reached maturity without the opportunity of practising the art of nursing at home ; but amongst the " common people," that is to say all the class of independent farmers and tradesmen, the housewife can hardly have found time to perfect her skill in nursing to a fine art. Probably the highest level was reached in the households of the gentry, where idleness was not yet the accepted hall-mark of a lady, and the mistress felt herself to be responsible for the training of her children and servants in every branch of the domestic arts, amongst which were reckoned both medicine and nursing.

(B). *Surgery and Medicine.*

The position held by mediæval women in the arts

of healing is shown in such books as Mallory's " Morte d'Arthur." When wounds proved intractable to the treatment of the rough and ready surgeons who attended in the vicinity of tourneys, knights sought help from some high-born lady renowned for her skill in medicine. It is true that popular belief assigned her success to witchcraft rather than to the knowledge and understanding acquired by diligent study and experience, but a tendency to faith in the occult was universal, and the reputation of the ladies probably bore some relation to their success in the cures attempted, for, according to the author of " The Golden Bough," science is the lineal descendant of witchcraft. The position of pre-eminence as consultants was no longer retained by women in the seventeenth century. Schools and Universities had been founded, where men could study medicine and anatomy, and thus secure for themselves a higher standard of knowledge and efficiency ; but, though women were excluded from these privileges they were not yet completely ousted from the medical profession, and as a domestic art medicine was still extensively practised by them.

Every housewife was expected to understand the treatment of the minor ailments at least of her household, and to prepare her own drugs. Commonplace books of this period contain recipes for making mulberry syrup, preserving fruit and preparing meats, mingled with, for example, prescriptions for plague water, which is " very good against the plague, the smallpox, the measles, surfeitts . . . . and is of a sovereign nature to be given in any sickness " " An oyle good for any ach—and ointments for sore eyes or breasts, or stone in the kidney or bladder." And in addition, " my brother Jones his way of making inks."[1] " The Ladies Dispensatory " contains " the Natures, Vertues and Qualities of all Herbs, and Simples

---

[1] *Add. MSS.* 36308.

usefull in Physick. Reduced into a Methodical Order,"
the diseases to be treated including those of men,
as well as women and children.[1]

As was the case in other domestic arts, girls depended for
their training in medicine chiefly on the tradition they
received from their mothers, but this was reinforced
from other sources as occasion offered. " The Ladies
Dispensatory " was not the only handbook published
for their use ; sometimes, though schools were closed
to women, an opportunity occurred for private coach-
ing. Thus Sarah Fell entered in her account book,
" July ^{ye} 5° 1674 by m° to Bro : Lowe^r y^t hee gave
Thomas Lawson fo^r comeinge over hithe^r to Instruct
him & sist^{rs}, in the knowledge of herbs. 10.00,"[2]
and when Mrs. Hutchinson's husband was Governor
of the Tower she allowed Sir Walter Raleigh and Mr.
Ruthin during their imprisonment to make experiments
in chemistry " at her cost, partly to comfort and divert
the poor prisoners, and partly to gain the knowledge
of their experiments, and the medicines to help such
poor people as were not able to seek physicians.
By these means she acquired a great deal of skill,
which was very profitable to many all her life."[3]

Neither did ladies confine their services to their
own household, but extended their benefits to all
their suffering neighbours. The care of the sick poor
was considered to be one of the duties of a " Person of
Quality," whose housekeepers were expected " to have
a competent knowledge in Physick and Chyrurgery,
that they may be able to help their maimed, sick and
indigent Neighbours ; for Commonly, all good and
charitable Ladies make this a part of their House-
keepers business."[4] The " Good Woman " is des-

---

[1] Sowerby (Leonard) *The Ladies' Dispensatory.* 1651.

[2] Fell, (Sarah). *Household Accounts*, p. 95. July 5, 1674.

[3] *Memoirs of Col. Hutchinson*, p. 12.

[4] *Compleat Servant-maid*, p. 40.

cribed as one who " distributes among the Indigent, Money and Books, and Cloaths, and Physick, as their severall Circumstances may require," to relieve " her poorer Neighbours in sudden Distress, when a Doctor is not at Hand, or when they have no Money to buy what may be necessary for them; and the charitableness of her Physick is often attended by some cure or other that is remarkable. God gives a *peculiar Blessing* to the Practice of those Women who have no other design in this Matter, but the doing Good : that neither prescribe where they may have the Advice of the Learned, nor at any time give or recommend any thing to try Experiments, but what they are assured from former Tryals is safe and innocent ; and if it do not help cannot hurt."[1]

The provision made by Lady Falkland of " antidotes against infection and of Cordials, and other several sorts of Physick for such of her Neighbours as should need them, amounted yearly to very considerable summes . . . her skil indeed was more than ordinary, and her wariness too . . . . Bookes of spiritual exhortations, she carried in her hand to these sick persons."[2] Mrs. Elizabeth Bedell " was very famous and expert in Chirurgery, which she continually practised upon multitudes that flock'd to her, and still *gratis*, without respect of persons, poor or rich. It hapned occasionally that some would return like the heald Samaritan, with some token of thankfulness ; though this was seldom. But God did not fail to reward them with (that which in Scripture is most properly call'd his reward) children, and the fruit of the womb. 3 sons and 4 daughters."[3]

Expressions of gratitude to women for these medical services occur in letters and diaries of the time.   The

---

[1] Rogers, Timothy. *Character of a Good Woman*, p. 42-43.

[2] *Falkland, Lady Lettice, Vi-countess, The Life and Death of.*

[3] *Bedell, (Wm.), Life and Death of*, p. 2.

Rev. R. Josselin enters January 27th, 1672, " My
L. Honeywood sent her coach for me : y^r I stayd
to March 10, in wch time my Lady was my nurse &
Phisitian & I hope for much good : . . . . they
considered ye scurvy. I tooke purge & other things
for it ; "[1] Marmaduke Rawdon met with a carriage
accident, in which he strained his " arme, but comminge
to Hodsden his good cossen Mrs. Williams, with hir
arte and care, quickly cured itt, and in ten dayes
was well againe."[2]

Nor was the practice of medicine confined to Gentlewomen ; many a humble woman in the country,
the wife of farmer or husbandman, used her skill for
the benefit of her neighbours. In their case, though
many were prompted purely by motives of kindness
and goodwill, others received payment for their
services. How much the dependence of the common
people on the skill of these " wise women " was taken
for granted is suggested by some lines in " The
Alchemist," where Mammon assures Dol Common

> " This nook, here, of the Friers is no Climate
> For her to live obscurely in, to learne
> Physick, and Surgery, for the Constable's wife
> Of some odde Hundred in Essex."[3]

Though their work was entirely unscientific, experience and common sense, or perhaps mere luck,
often gave to their treatment an appearance of success
which was denied to their more learned rivals. Thus
Adam Martindale describing his illness says that
it was " a vehement fermentation in my body
. . . ugly dry scurfe, eating deep and spreading broad. Some skilfull men, or so esteemed, being
consulted and differing much in their opinions, we were
left to these three bad choices . . . . in this greate

---

[1] Josselin, (R.), *Diary*, pp. 163-4.

[2] *Rawdon*, (*Marmaduke*), *Life of*, p. 85.

[3] Jonson, (Ben.) *The Alchemist*, Act IV., Sc. I.

straite God sent us in much mercie a poore woman,
who by a salve made of nothing but Celandine and
a little of the Mosse of an ashe root, shred and boyled
in May-butter, tooke it cleare away in a short time,
and though after a space there was some new breakings
out, yet these being annointed with the same salve
. . . . . were absolutely cleared away."[1]

The general standard of efficiency among the
men who professed medicine and surgery was very
low, the chief work of the ordinary country practitioner being the letting of blood, and the wise woman
of the village may easily have been his superior in
other forms of treatment. Sir Ralph Verney, writing
to his wife advises her to " give the child no phisick but
such as midwives and old women, with the doctors
approbation, doe prescribe ; for assure yourselfe
they by experience know better than any phisition
how to treate such infants."[2] Of Hobbes it was said
that he took little physick and preferred " an experienced old woman " to the " most learned and
inexperienced physician."[3]

Dr. Turbeville, a noted oculist in the West
Country, was sent for to cure the Princess of
Denmark, who had a dangerous inflammation
of the eyes. On his return he is reported to have
said that " he expected to learn something of these
Court doctors, but, to his amazement he found them
only spies upon his practice, and wholly ignorant
as to the lady's case ; nay, farther, he knew several
midwives and old women, whose advice he would
rather follow than theirs."[4] He died at Sarum
in 1696, and his sister, Mrs. Mary Turbeville,
practised afterwards in London " with good

---

[1] *Martindale (Adam), Life of*, p. 21. 1632.

[2] *Verney Family*, Vol. 2, p. 270. 1647.

[3] *Dictionary of National Biography*.

[4] Hoare, Sir R. C., *History of Modern Wilts*. Vol. VI., p. 465

reputation and success. She has all her brother's receipts, and having seen his practice, during many years, knows how to use them. For my part, I have so good an opinion of her skill that should I again be afflicted with sore eyes, which God forbid! I would rely upon her advice rather than upon any pretenders or professors in London or elsewhere."[1]

Events, however, were taking place which would soon curtail the practice of women whose training was confined to personal experience, tradition and casual study. The established associations of physicians, surgeons and apothecaries, although of recent growth, demanded and obtained, like other companies, exclusive privileges. Their policy fell in with the Government's desire to control the practice of medicine, in order to check witchcraft. Statute 3, Henry VIII., enacted that " none should exercise the Faculty of Physick or Surgery within the City of *London* or within Seven Miles of the same, unless first he were examined, approved and admitted by the Bishop of *London*, or the Dean of *St. Paul's*, calling to him or them Four Doctors of Physick, and for Surgery other expert Persons in that Faculty, upon pain of Forfeiture of £5 for every Month they should occupy Physick or Surgery, not thus admitted " because " that common Artificers, as Smiths, Weavers, and Women, boldly and accustomably took upon them great Cures, and Things of great Difficulty, in the which they partly used Sorceries and Witchcraft, and partly applied such Medicines unto the Diseased, as were very noyous, and nothing meet therefore."[2]

The restrictions were extended to the provinces. A Charter given to the Company of Barber-Surgeons at Salisbury in 1614 declared that " No surgeon or barber is to practise any surgery or barbery, unless

---

[1] Hoare, Sir R. C., *History of Modern Wilts*, Vol. VI., p. 467.

[2] Stow, *London* I., p. 132.

first made a free citizen, and then a free brother of
the company. Whereas, also, there are divers women
and others within this city, altogether unskilled in
the art of chirurgery, who do oftentimes take cures
on them, to the great danger of the patient, it is
therefore ordered, that no such woman, or any other,
shall take or meddle with any cure of chirurgery,
wherefore they, or any of them shall have or take
any money, benefit or other reward for the same,
upon pain that every delinquent shall for every cure
to be taken in hand, or meddled with, contrary to
this order, unless she or they shall be first allowed by
this Company, forfeit and lose to the use of this
Company the sum of ten shillings."[1]

The Apothecaries were separated from the Grocers
in 1617, the charter of their company providing that
" No person or persons whatsoever may have, hold,
or keep an Apothecaries Shop or Warehouse, or that
may exercise or use the Art or Mystery of Apothecaries, or make, mingle, work, compound, prepare,
give, apply, or administer, any Medicines, or that may
sell, set on sale, utter, set forth, or lend any Compound
or Composition to any person or persons whatsoever
within the City of London, and the Liberties thereof,
or within Seven Miles of the said city, unless such
person or persons as have been brought up, instructed,
and taught by the space of Seven Years at the least,
as Apprentice or Apprentices, with some Apothecary
or Apothecaries exercising the same Art, and being a
Freeman of the said Mystery." Any persons wishing
to become an Apothecary must be examined and
approved after his apprenticeship.[2]

It will be observed that there is little in their
charters to distinguish the medical from other
city Companies, and while the examination required

---

[1] Hoare, Sir R. C., *History of Modern Wilts*, Vol. VI., p. 341.

[2] Barrett, *History of Apothecaries*, Intro., p. xxvii.

by the Faculties of Medicine and Surgery in the City
of London excluded women altogether, the Apothecaries still admitted them by marriage or apprenticeship. " M^{ris} Lammeere Godfrey Villebranke her son
both Dutch Pothecarys " are included in a certificate made by the Justices of the Peace to the Privy
Council, of the foreigners residing in the Liberty of
Westminster.[1] A journeyman who applied for the
freedom of the company, stated that he was serving
the widow of an apothecary. His application was
refused time after time through difficulties owing to
a clause in the Charter. Counsel's opinion was
taken, and finally he was admitted provided he kept
a journeyman and entered into a bond of £100 to
perform the same, that he gave £10 and a spoon to
the Company, took the oaths and paid Counsel's
fees.[2] He subsequently married the widow. Similar
rules obtained in the provinces, as is shown by the
admittance of Thomas Serne in 1698–9 to the freedom
of the City of Dorchester on payment of 40s. because
he had " married a wife who had lived as apprentice
for 20 years to an apothecary."[3]

The jurisdiction of companies was local, and where
no company existed boys were apprenticed to surgery
for the sake of training, though such an apprenticeship conferred no monopoly privilege. Surgery
was sometimes combined with another trade. John
Croker describes in his memoir how he was bound
apprentice in 1686 to one John Shilson " by trade
a serge-maker, but who also professed surgery ; with
whom I went to be instructed in the art of surgery."[4]
The operation of these various Statutes and Charters
being local and their enforcement depending upon

---

[1] *S. P. D.*, ccc., 75. October 1635.

[2] Barrett, *History of Apothecaries*, pp., 28–9.

Mayo, C. H., *Municipal Records of Dorchester*, p. 428.

Croker, (John), *Brief Memoirs*, p. 5.

the energy of the parties interested, it is difficult to determine what was their actual and immediate effect on the medical practice of women. Statute 3, Henry VIII., must have been enforced with some severity, for a later one declares " Sithence the making of which said Act the companie & felowship of surgeons of London, minding oonly their own lucres, and nothing the profit or ease of the diseased or patient, have sued, troubled and vexed divers honest persons as well men as women, whom God hath endued with the knowledge of the nature, kind, and operation of certain herbes, roots and waters, and the using & ministering of them to such as been pained with customable diseases, as women's breasts being sore, a pin and the web in the eye, &c., &c., and yet the said persons have not taken any thing for their pains or cunning."[1]

Not only the Surgeons but the Apothecaries also, enforced observance of the privileges which the King had granted to them, and in consequence a Petition of many thousands of citizens and inhabitants in and about London was presented on behalf of Mr. William Trigg, Practitioner of Physick, saying that he " did abundance of good to all sorts of people in and about this City: when most of the Colledge Doctors deserted us, since which time your Petitioners have for above twenty yeares, in their severall times of Sicknesses, and infirmities taken Physick from him . . . . in which time, we doe verily believe in our consciences, that he hath done good to above thirty thousand Persons; and that he maketh all his Compositions himselfe, not taking anything for his Physick from poor people ; but rather releiving their necessities, nor any money from any of us for his advice ; and but moderately for his Physick : his custome being to take from the middle sort of Patients 12d., 18d., 2s., 2s. 6d. as they please to give, very seldom five shillngs unlesse from such as take

---

Statutes at Large. 34 Henry VIII. C.8.

much Physick with them together into the Countrey.
. . . . there is a good and wholesome law made
in the 34th year of King Henry 8 C. 8. Permitting
every man that hath knowledge and experience in
the nature of Herbs, Roots and waters, to improve
his Talent for the common good and health of the
people," and concluding that unless Dr. Trigg is
allowed to continue his practice " many poore
people must of necessity perish to death . . . . .
for they are not able to pay great fees to Doctors
and Apothecaries bills which cost more then his
advice and Physick; nor can we have accesse unto
them when we desire, which we familiarly have to
Dr. *Trigg* to our great ease and comfort."[1]

Prudence Ludford, wife of William Ludford of
Little Barkhampton, was presented in 1683 " for
practising the profession of a chyrurgeon contrary
to law,"[2] but many women at this time continued
their practice as doctors undisturbed ; for example,
Mrs. Lucy Hutchinson casually mentions that one
of her maids went to Colson, to have a sore eye cured
by a woman of the town.[3] While Mrs. D'ewes was
travelling from Axminster to London by coach, her
baby boy cried so violently all the way, on account
of the roughness of the road that he ruptured himself, and was left behind at Dorchester under the care
of Mrs. Margaret Waltham, " a female practitioner."[4]

The account books of Boroughs and Parishes show
that the poor received medical treatment from men
and women indiscriminately. A whole series of such
payments occur in the minute book of the Dorchester
Corporation. " It is ordered that the V[li] to
be paid to Peter Salanova for cutting of Giles

---

[1] *Humble Petition of many thousands of Citizens, and Inhabitants in and about London*

[2] *Hertford Co. Records*, Vol. I. p. 328.

[3] *Memoirs of Col. Hutchinson*, p. 427.

[4] Yonge, Walter, *Diary*, Intro., xxii.

Garrett's leg shall be paid out of the X^{li} yearly paiable out of the Hospitall for pious vses . . . . to have the one halfe having cutt of his leg already, and the other halfe when he is thoroughly cured.[1] . . . . Unto the Widdow Foote xs. for the curing of the Widow Huchins' lame leg at present ; and xs. more when the cure is finished[2]. . . . Mr. Losse should be payed by the Steward of the Hospital the somme of viij li for his paynes and fee as Phisitian in taking care of the poore of the Towne for the last yeare . . . . as it hath bin formerly accustomed . . . . Vnto Mr. Mullens the somme of thirty shillings for curing Hugh Rogers of a dangerous fistula."[3] Three pounds more (three having already been paid) was ordered to be given to " Cassander Haggard for finishing the great cure on John Drayton otherwise Keuse."[4] In another case the Council tendered to Mr. Mullens, " the chirurgeon, the some of xxx^s for curing of Thomas Hobbs, but he answered hee would consider of it next weeke [He declined]."[5]

At Cowden the overseers paid to Dr. Willett for " reducing the arm of Elizth Skinner, and for ointment, cerecloths and journeys, £2 ; three years later a further sum of 10s. was given " to Goodwife Wells for curing Eliz Skinner's hand."[6] " Mary Olyve was paid 6s. 8d. " for curing a boye that was lame " at Mayfield,[7] and 15s. was given to " Widow Thurston for healing of Stannard's son," by the churchwardens at Cratfield.[8] In Somerset £5 was

[1] Mayo, C. H., *Municipal Records of Dorchester*, p. 516, 1640.

[2] *Ibid*, p. 518. 1651

[3] *Ibid*, p. 518, 1649-50.

[4] *Ibid*, pp. 518–9. 1652-1654.

[5] *Ibid*, p. 519.

[6] *Sussex Arch. Coll.*, Vol. XX., p. 114. *Account Book of Cowden*, 1690.

[7] *Ibid*, Vol. XVIII., p. 196. *Accounts of Parish of Mayfield*.

[8] *Cratfield Parish Papers*, p. 179. 1640.

paid to " Johane Shorley towards the cure of Thomas Dudderidge.   Further satisfaction when cure is don."[1]

Such entries show that though women may have practised surgery and medicine chiefly as domestic arts, nevertheless their skill was also used professionally, their natural aptitude in this direction enabling them to maintain their position throughout the seventeenth century even when deprived of all opportunities for systematic study and scientific experiments, and in spite of the determined attacks by the Corporations of physicians and surgeons ; but their success was owing to the fact that Science had as yet achieved small results in the standard of medical efficiency.

(C). *Midwifery*.

It has been shown that the employment of women in the arts of medicine, nursing and teaching was chiefly, though not entirely, confined to the domestic sphere ; midwifery, on the other hand, though occasionally practised by amateurs, was, in the majority of cases, carried on by women who, whether skilled or unskilled, regarded it as the chief business of their lives, and depended upon it for their maintenance. Not only did midwifery exist on a professional basis from immemorial days, but it was formerly regarded as a mystery inviolably reserved for women ; and though by the seventeenth century the barrier which excluded men had broken down, the extent to which the profession had in the past been a woman's monopoly is shown by the fact that the men who now began to practise the art were known as men-midwives.

The midwife held a recognised position in Society and was sometimes well-educated and well-paid. Nothing is known as to the mediæval history of midwifery in England ; and possibly nothing ever will be

---

[1] *Somerset Q. S. Records*, Vol. III., p. 212. 1653.

known concerning it, for the Englishwoman of that period had no impulse to commit her experience and ideas to writing. All the wisdom which touched her special sphere in life was transmitted orally from mother to daughter, and thus at any change, like the Industrial Revolution, which silently undermined the foundations of society, the traditional womanly wisdom could vanish, leaving no trace behind it. Even in the Elizabethan period and during the seventeenth century, when most women could read and many could write, they show little tendency to record information concerning their own affairs. But the profession of midwifery was then no longer reserved exclusively for women. The first treatise on the subject published in England was a translation by Raynold of " The Byrth of Mankynd." He says in his preface that the book had already been translated into " Dutche Frenche, Spanyshe and dyvers other languages. In the which Countries there be fewe women that can reade, but they wyll haue one of these bookes alwayes in readinesse . . . . it beinge lykewyse sette foorth in our Englyshe speeche . . . . it may supply the roome and place of a good Mydwyfe, ... and truly . . . . there be syth the fyrst settynge forth of this booke, right many honourable Ladyes, & other Worshypfull Gentlewomen, which have not disdayned the oftener by the occasion of this booke to frequent and haunt women in theyr labours, caryinge with them this booke in theyr handes, and causyng such part of it as doth chiefely concerne the same pourpose, to be read before the mydwyfe, and the rest of the women then beyng present ; whereby ofttymes, then all haue been put in remembraunce of that, wherewith the laboryng woman hath bene greatly comforted, and alleuiated of her thronges and travayle . . . . But here now let not the good Mydwyves be offended with that, that is spoken of the badde. For verily there is no science, but that it hath his Apes, Owles, Beares and Asses . . . . at the fyrst commyng abroade of this present booke, many of this sorte of mydwyves, meuyd eyther of envie, or els of mallice, or both, diligented . . . . to fynde the meanes to suppresse . . . . the same ; makyng all wemen of theyr acquayntaunce . . . . to beleeue, that it was nothyng woorth : and that it shoulde be a slaunder to women, forso muche as therein was descried and set foorth the secretes and priuities of women, and that euery boy and knaue hadd of these bookes, readyng them as openly as the tales of Robinhood &c."[1]

It is sometimes supposed that childbirth was an easier process in former generations than it has become since the developments of modern civilisation. The question has a direct bearing on the profession of midwifery, but it cannot be answered here, nor could it receive a simple answer of yes or no, for it embraces two problems for the midwife, the ease and safety of a normal delivery and her resources in face of the abnormal.

No one can read the domestic records of the seventeenth century without realising that the dangers of childbed were much greater then than now; nevertheless the travail of the average woman at that time may have been easier. There was clearly a great difference in this respect between the country woman, inured to hard muscular labour, and the high born lady or city dame. The difference is pointed out by contemporary writers. McMath dedicated " the *Expert Midwife* " to the Lady Marquies of Douglas because " as it concerns all Bearing Women . . . . so chiefly the more Noble and Honourable, as being more Excellent, more Tender, and Delicate, and readily more opprest with the symptoms." Jane Sharp confirms this, saying that " the poor Country people,

---

[1] Raynold, *The Byrth of Mankynd*, Prologue.

where there are none but women to assist (unless it
be those that are exceeding poor and in a starving
condition, and then they have more need of meat
than Midwives) . . . . are as fruitful and as
safe and well delivered, if not much more fruitful,
and better commonly in Childbed than the greatest
Ladies of the Land."[1]

Rich and poor alike depended upon the midwife to
bring them safely through the perils of childbirth,
and it is certain that women of a high level of intelligence and possessing considerable skill belonged to the
profession. The fees charged by successful midwives
were very high, and during the first half of the century
they were considered in no way inferior to doctors
in skill. It was natural that Queen Henrietta Maria
should send for one of her own country women to
attend her, French midwives enjoying an extraordinarily high reputation for their skill at this time.
The payment in 1630 of £100 to Frances Monnhadice,
Nurse to the Queen, " for the diet & entertainment
of Madame Peron, midwife to the Queen," and further
of a "Warrant to pay Madame Peron £300 of the
King's gift "[2] shows the high value attached to her
services.

That English midwives were often possessed of
ample means is shown by a deposition made by
" Abraham Perrot, of Barking parish, Gentleman,"
who " maketh oath that a month before the fire
. . . . he . . . . paid unto Hester Shaw
Widow, ... the summe of £953. 6. 8."[3] the said
Mrs. Shaw being described as a midwife; but
relations who were members of this profession
are never alluded to in letters, diaries or memoirs.
From this absence of any social reference it is difficult

---

[1] Sharp (Jane), *The Midwives Book*, p. 3.

[2] *S. P. D.* 1630. Sign Manual Car. I., Vol. VII. No. 11.

[3] *Mrs. Shaw's Innocency Restored.* 1653.

to determine from what class of the community they were drawn, or what were the circumstances which led women to take up this responsible and arduous profession. No doubt necessity led many ignorant women to drift into the work when they were too old to receive new ideas and too wanting in ambition to make any serious effort to improve their skill, but the writings of Mrs. Cellier and Mrs. Jane Sharp prove that there were others who regarded their profession with enthusiasm, and who possessed an intelligence acute enough to profit by all the experience and instruction which was within their reach.

The only training available for women who wished to acquire a sound knowledge of midwifery was by apprenticeship ; this, if the mistress was skilled in her art, was valuable up to a certain point, but as no organisation existed among midwives it was not possible to insist upon any general standard of efficiency, and many midwives were ignorant of the most elementary circumstances connected with their profession. In any case such an apprenticeship could not supply the place of the more speculative side of training, which can only be given in connection with schools of anatomy where research work is possible, and from these all women were excluded.

As has been said, many women who entered the profession did not even go through a form of apprenticeship, but acquired their experience solely, to use Raynold's words, " by haunting women in their labours." In rural England it was customary when travail began, to send for all the neighbours who were responsible women, partly with the object of securing enough witnesses to the child's birth, partly because it was important to spread the understanding of midwifery as widely as possible, because any woman might be called upon to render assistance in an emergency.

Several handbooks on Midwifery were written in response to the demand for opportunities for scientific training by the more intelligent members of the profession. One of the most popular of these books, which passed through many editions, was published in 1671 by Jane Sharp " Practitioner in the art of Midwifery above 30 years." The preface to the fourth edition says that " the constant and unwearied Industry of this ingenious and well-skill'd midwife, Mrs. Jane Sharp, together with her great Experience of Anatomy & Physick, by the many years of her Practice in the art of Midwifery hath . . . . . made them . . . . much desired by all that either knew her Person . . . . or ever read this book, which of late, by its Scarceness hath been so much enquired after . . . . as to have many after impressions." The author says that she has " often sate down sad in the Consideration of the many Miseries Women endure in the Hands of un-skilful Midwives ; many professing the Art (without any skill in anatomy, which is the Principal part effectually necessary for a Midwife) meerly for Lucres sake. I have been at Great Cost in Translations for all Books, either French, Dutch or Italian of this kind. All which I offer with my own Experience."[1]

Jane Sharp points out that midwives must be both speculative and practical, for " she that wants the knowledge of Speculation, is like one that is blind or wants her sight : she that wants the Practice, is like one that is lame & wants her legs, ... Some perhaps may think, that then it is not proper for women to be of this profession, because they cannot attain so rarely to the knowledge of things as men may, who are bred up in Universities, Schools of Learning, or serve their Apprenticeship for that end and purpose, where anatomy Lectures being frequently read the

---

[1] Sharp, Mrs. Jane, *The Midwives Book, or the whole Art of Midwifery discovered.*

situation of the parts both of men and women . . . are often made plain to them. But that objection is easily answered, by the former example of the Midwives amongst the Israelites, for, though we women cannot deny that men in some things may come to a greater perfection of knowledge than women ordinarily can, by reason of the former helps that women want ; yet the Holy Scriptures hath recorded Midwives to the perpetual honour of the female Sex. There not being so much as one word concerning men midwives mentioned there . . . . it being the natural propriety of women to be much seeing into that art ; and though nature be not alone sufficient to the perfection of it, yet further knowledge may be gain'd by a long and diligent practice, and be communicated to others of our own sex. I cannot deny the honour due to able Physicians and Chyrurgions, when occasion is, Yet . . . . where there is no Men of Learning, the women are sufficient to perform this duty . . . . It is not hard words that perform the work, as if none understood the Art that cannot understand Greek. Words are but the shell, that we oftimes break our Teeth with them to come at the kernel, I mean our brains to know what is the meaning of them ; but to have the same in our mother tongue would save us a great deal of needless labour. It is commendable for men to employ their spare time in some things of deeper Speculation than is required of the female sex ; but the art of Midwifery chiefly concerns us."[1]

Though the schools of Medicine and Anatomy were closed to women, individual doctors were willing to teach the more progressive midwives some of the science necessary for their art ; thus Culpeper dedicated his " Directory " to the midwives of England in the following words :—" Worthy Matrons, You are of

---

[1] Sharp, Mrs. Jane ,The Midwives Book, pp. 2–4.

the number of those whom my soul loveth, and of whom I make daily mention in my Prayers : . . . . If you please to make experience of my Rules, they are very plain, and easie enough ; . . . . If you make use of them, you wil find your work easie, you need not call for the help of a Man-Midwife, which is a disparagement, not only to yourselves, but also to your Profession : . . . . All the Perfections that can be in a Woman, ought to be in a Midwife ; the first step to which is, To know your ignorance in that part of Physick which is the Basis of your Act . . . . If *any want Wisdom, let him ask it of God* (not of the *Colledg of Physitians*, for if they do, they may hap to go without their Errand, unless they bring Money with them)."[1]

Efforts made by Peter Chamberlain to secure some systematic training for midwives drew upon himself the abuse, if not persecution, of his jealous contemporaries. In justifying the course he had taken he pleads " Because I am pretended to be Ignorant or Covetous, or both, therefore some ignorant Women, whom either extream Povertie hath necessitated, or Hard-heartedness presumed, or the Game of Venus intruded into the calling of Midwifry (to have the issues of Life & Death of two or three at one time in their hands, beside the consequence of Health and Strength of the Whole Nation) should neither be sufficiently instructed in doing Good, nor restrained from doing Evil ? . . . . . The objection infers thus much. Because there was never any Order for instructing and governing of Midwives, therefore there never must be . . . . It may be when Bishops are restored again, their Ordinaries will come in to plead their care. Of what ? Truly that none shall do good without their leave. That none shall have leave, but such as will take their Oath and pay Money. That

---

[1] Culpeper, Nich., Gent., Student in Physick and Astrologie, *Directory for Midwives.*

taking this Oath and paying their Money with the
testimonie of two or three Gossips, any may have leave
to be as ignorant, if not as cruel as themselves, ...
but of Instruction or Order amongst the Midwives,
not one word."[1]

The danger which threatened midwives by the
exclusion of women from the scientific training
available for men, did not pass unnoticed by the leading
members of the Profession. They realised that the
question at stake did not concern only the honour
of their Profession, but involved the suffering, and in
many cases even the death, of vast numbers of women
and babies who must always depend on the skill of midwives and urged that steps should be taken to raise the
standard of their efficiency. Mrs. Cellier[2] pointed out

---

[1] Chamberlain (Peter), *A Voice in Rhama, or the Crie of Women and Children.* 1646.

[2] Cellier (Mrs.). *A scheme for the foundation of a Royal Hospital, Harleian Miscellany, Vol. IV. pp.* 142-147.
The scheme was well thought out, and some details from it may be given here as showing the aspirations of an able woman for the development of her profession. Mrs. Cellier proposed that the number of midwives admitted to the first rank should be limited to 1000, and that these should pay a fee of £5 on admittance and the like sum annually. All the midwives entering this first rank should be eligible for the position of Matron, or assistant to the Govenment.
Other midwives may be admitted to the second thousand on payment of half the above fees.
The money raised by these fees is to be used for the purpose of erecting " one good, large and convenient House, or Hospital," . . . . for the Receiving and Taking in of exposed Children, to be subject to the Care, Conduct and Management of one Governess, one female Secretary, and twelve Matron Assistants, subject to the visitation of such Persons, as to your Majesty's Wisdom shall be thought necessary . . . . the children to be afterwards educated in proper Learning, Arts and Mysteries according to their several capacities. As a further endowment for this institution, Mrs. Cellier asks for one fifth part of the voluntary charity collected in the Parishes comprised within the Limits of the weekly Bills of Mortality, and that in addition collecting Boxes may be placed in every Church, Chapel, or publick Place of Divine Service of any Religion whatsoever within their limits. The scheme further provides " that such Hospital may be allowed to establish twelve lesser convenient houses, in twelve of the greatest parishes, each to be governed by one of the twelve Matrons, Assistants to the Corporation of the Midwives, which Houses may be for the taking in, delivery and month's Maintenance, at a price certain of any woman, that any of the parishes within the limits aforesaid, shall by the overseers of the poor place in them ; such women being to be subject, with the Children born of them, to the future care of that parish, whose overseers place them there to be delivered, notwithstanding such House shall not happen to stand in the proper Parish." . . . .

" That, within the Space of twenty years last past, above six thousand women have died in child-bed, more than thirteen thousand children have been born abortive, and above five thousand chrysome infants have been buried, within the weekly bills of mortality ; above two-thirds of which, amounting to sixteen thousand souls, have in all probability perished, for want of due skill and care, in those women who practise the art of midwifery . . . . To remedy which, it is humbly proposed, that your Majesty will be graciously pleased to unite the whole number of skilful midwives, now practising within the limits of the weekly bills of mortality, into a corporation, under the government of a certain number of the most able and matron-like women among them, subject to the visitation of such person or persons, as your Majesty shall appoint ; and such Rules for their good government, instruction, direction, and administration as are hereunto annexed."

Then follow proposals for the care of the children, requiring that they may be privileged to take to themselves Sirnames and to be made capable, by such names, of any honour or employment, without being liable to reproach, for their innocent misfortune, and that the children so educated may be free members of every city and corporation.

After the first settlement, no married woman shall " be admitted to be either governess, secretary, or any of the twelve principal assistants to the Government and that no married person of either sex shall be suffered to inhabit within the said Hospital, to avoid such inconveniences as may arise, as the children grow to maturity ; . . . . if any of these Persons do marry afterwards, then to clear their accounts and depart the house, by being expelled the society."

Among many interesting rules for governing the Hospital, Mrs. Cellier appoints " That a woman, sufficiently skilled in writing and accounts, be appointed secretary to the governess and company of midwives, to be present at all controversies about the art of midwifery, to register all the extraordinary accidents happening in the practise, which all licensed midwives are, from time to time, to report to the society ; that the female secretary be reckoned an assistant to the government, next to the governess and capable of succeeding in her stead."

" That the principal physician or man-midwife, examine all extraordinary accidents and, once a month at least, read a publick Lecture to the whole society of licensed midwives, who are all to be obliged to be present at it, if not employed in their practise." The lectures to be kept for future reference by the midwives.

" That no men shall be present at such public lectures, on any pretence whatsoever, except such able doctors and surgeons, as shall enter themselves students in the said art, and pay, for such their admittance, ten pounds, and ten pounds a year." The physicians and surgeons so admitted were to be " of Council with the principle man-midwife and be capable of succeeding him, by election of the governess, her secretary, twelve assistants, and the twenty-four lower assistants,"

Mrs. Cellier succeeded with her proposal, in so far
that His Majesty agreed to unite the midwives into
a Corporation by Royal Charter, but there the matter
rested."[1]

In France women were more fortunate, for a noted
school of midwifery had already been established
at the Hotel Dieu in Paris, at which every six weeks
dissections and anatomies were especially made for the
apprentices of the institution, both past and present.[2]
Before entering on their profession the French midwives were required to pass an examination before the
chirurgeons.   Their professional reputation stood so
high that Pechey alludes to one of them as " that
most Famous Woman of the World, *Madam Louise
Burgeois*, late Midwife to the Queen of *France*.   The
praises that we read of all those that ever heard of her
are not so much a flourish as truth ; for her reasons are
solid experiences, and her witnesses have been all
of the most eminent Persons of *France* : and not only
of her, but as we have already exprest, of the most
excellent known Men and Women of this Art of
other Countries."[3]

According to Mrs. Cellier, English midwives were
for a time examined by the College of Surgeons, but
as their records for the years in question are missing
there is no means of ascertaining the numbers of those
who presented themselves for examination.   She
says that Bishops did not " pretend to License Midwives till Bp. *Bonner's* time, who drew up the
Form of the first License, which continued in full
force till 1642, and then the Physicians and Chirurgeons contending about it, it was adjudged a Chy-
rurgical operation, and the Midwives were Licensed
at *Chirurgions-Hall*, *but not till they had passed three*

---

[1] Cellier, (Eliz.). *To Dr. ———, an answer to his Queries concerning the Colledg of Midwives*, p. 7.

[2] Carrier (Henriette.) *Origine de la Maternité de Paris.*

[3] Pechey, *Compleat Midwife*, Preface.

examinations, before six skilful Midwives, and as many Chirurgions expert in the Art of Midwifery. Thus it continued until the Act of Uniformity passed, which sent the Midwives back to *Doctors Commons,* where they pay their money (*take an oath which it is impossible for them to keep*) and return home as skilful as they went thither. I make no reflections on those learned Gentlemen, the Licensers, but refer the curious for their further satisfaction to the Yearly Bills of Mortality, from 42 to 62 ; Collections of which they may find at *Clerkshall.* Which if they please to compare with these of late Years, they will find there did not then happen the eight part of the Casualities either to Women or Children, as do now."[1]

In granting licences to midwives the Bishops were supposed to make some enquiry as to their professional attainments. Among the " articles to be enquired of " during Diocesan visits was one " whether any man or woman within your Parish, hath professed or practised Physick or Chyrurgery ; by what name or names are they called, and whether are they licensed by the Bishop of the Diocesse, or his Vicar Generall, and upon whom have they practised, and what good or harm have they done ? "[2] And again, " whether any in your Parish do practise Physicke or chirurgery, or that there be any mid-wife there, or by what authority any of them do practise, or exercise that profession."[3] But the interest of the Bishops was concerned more with the orthodoxy of the midwife than with her professional skill.

A midwife's licence was drawn up as follows : beginning :—" Thomas Exton, knight, doctor of laws, commisary general, lawfully constituted of the right worshipful the dean & chapter of St.

---

[1] Cellier (Eliz.). *to Dr. —— an answer to his Queries concerning the Colledg of Midwives,* p. 6.

[2] *Exeter, Articles to be enquired of by the Churchwardens.* 1646.

[3] *Canterbury, Articles to be enquired.* 1636.

Paul's in London; to our beloved in Christ, Anne Voule, the wife of Jacob Voule, of the parish of St Gile's Cripplegat, sendeth greeting in our Lord God everlasting : Whereas, by due examination of diverse, honest, and discreet women, we have found you apt and able, cunning and experte, to occupy & exercise the office, business & occupation of midwife," and continuing after many wise and humane rules for her guidance with an exhortation " to be diligent, faithful and ready to help every woman travelling of child, as well the poor as the rich, and you shall not forsake the poor woman and leave her to go to the rich ; you shall in no wise exercise any manner of witchcraft, charms, sorcery, invocation, or other prayers, than such as may stand with God's laws, and the king's," concluding thus :—" Item, you shall not be privy to or consent that any priest or other party shall in your absence, or your company, or of your knowledge or sufferance, baptize any child by any mass, Latin service, or prayers than such as are appointed by the laws of the Church of England ; neither shall you consent that any child borne by any woman, who shall be delivered by you, shall be carried away without being baptized in the parish by the ordinary minister where the said child is born."[1]

The Bishops' interest in midwives may have been caused partly by a praiseworthy desire to secure an adequate supply for the assistance of women in each parish. But from the Church's point of view, the midwife's chief importance was not due to the fact that the life of mother and child might depend on her skill, but to her capacity for performing the rites of baptism. The reasons for granting her this authority are explained as follows :—" in hard Labours the Head of the Infant was sometimes baptized before the whole delivery. This Office of Baptizing

---

[1] *Sussex Arch. Coll.*, Vol. IV., pp., 249-50. Extracts from Parish Registers.

in such Cases of Necessity was commonly performed by the Midwife; and 'tis very probable, this gave first Occasion to Midwives being licensed by the Bishop, because they were to be first examined by the Bishop or his delegated Officer, whether they could repeat the Form of Baptism, which they were in Haste to administer in such extraordinary Occasion. But we thank God our times are reformed in Sense, and in Religion."[1] Though the midwife was only expected to baptize in urgent cases she might strain her privilege, and baptize even a healthy infant into the Roman Church. Her power in this respect was regarded with suspicion and jealousy by English Protestants, not only because she might inadvertently admit the infant to the wrong fold, but because it resembled the conferring of office in the Church upon women; however, as no man was usually present at the birth of a child, and it was fully believed that delay might involve the perpetual damnation of the dying infant's soul, no alternative remained. Peter Heylyn, in writing of Baptism, comments on the difficulty, saying that " the first Reformers did not only allow the administration of this Sacrament [Baptism] in *private* houses, but permitted it to private persons, even to women also." He continues that when King James, in the Conference at Hampton Court, seemed offended because of this liberty to women and laicks, Dr. Whitgift, Archbishop of Canterbury, denied that the words gave this liberty, and Dr. Babington alledged " that the words were purposely made ambiguous as otherwise the Book might not have passed Parliament. To whom it was replied by the Bishop of London that there was no intent to deceive any, but the words did indeed " intend a permission of private persons to Baptize in case of *necessity*."[2]

The fear of secret baptisms into the Catholic

[1] Watson, *Clergyman's Law*, p. 318.
[2] *Heylyn (Peter), Cyprianus Anglicus, p. 27.*

Church is shown in a letter which states that " the wief of Frances Lovell esq^r of West Derh^m is noted for a recusant. And the said Frances had a childe about three yeares past christianed by a midwief sent thither by the La. Lovell, and the midwief's name cannot be learned."[1]

It was this danger which led to the prosecution of women who practised without licences. The Church-wardens at Lee presented " the Widow Goney and the wife of Thomas Gronge being midwives & not sworne." In Hadingham they report " We have two poore women exercising the office of midwives, one Avice Rax and the wife of one John Sallerie,"[2] and elsewhere " Dorothye Holding wief of Jo. Holding & Dorothye Parkins wief of Wm Parkins " were presented " for exercising the office of midwives without License."[3]

The fees charged by midwives varied from £300 in the case of the French Midwife who attended the Queen, to the sum of 1s. 6d. paid by the Parish of Aspenden to the midwife who delivered a woman " received by virtue of a warrant from the justices."[4] In most cases the amount paid by the parents was supplemented by gifts from the friends and relations who attended the christening.[5] Thus the baby's

---

[1] Bacon, (Sir Nat.). *Official Papers*, p. 176. 1591.

[2] *S. P. D.*, ccxcvi., 17. August 21, 1635. *Visitation presentments by the Churchwardens.*

[3] *S. P. D.*, ccxcv., 6. August 19, 1636.

[4] *Hertford County Records*, Vol. I., p. 435. 1698.

[5] The Rev. Giles Moore " gave Mat [his adopted daughter] then answering for Edwd. Cripps young daughter 5s. whereof shee gave to the mydwyfe 2s & 1s. to the Nurse. Myself gave to the mydwyfe in the drinking bowle 1s. (*Sussex Arch. Coll.*, Vol. I., p. 113. *Rev. Giles Moore, Journal.*)

Later is entered in the Journal, he being god-father " 1674. Mat was brought to bed of a daughter. Gave the mydwyfe, goodwyfe & Nurse 5s. each." (*Ibid*, p. 119.)

After Lady Darce's confinement at Herstmonceux Castle, is entered in the accounts " paid my Lord's benevolence to Widdow Craddock the midwife of Battle £5. o. o. (*Sussex Arch. Coll.*, Vol. xlviii. 1643-1649.)

Entries in a similar book of the Howard family give " To my young ladye's mid-wyfe xx^s (p. 22^{-}-8) To Mrs. Fairfax her Midwife by my Lord xx^s . . . . by my Ladie xx^s. More to Mrs. Fairefax her midwife by my Ladie's commaund iij^{li} " (*Howard Household Book*, p. 263. 1629.)

death meant a considerable pecuniary loss to the midwife. An example of her payment in such a case is given in Nicholas Assheton's diary; he enters on Feb. 16, 1617. " My wife in labour of childbirth. Her delivery was with such violence as the child dyed within half an hour, and, but for God's wonderful mercie, more than human reason could expect, shee had dyed, ... divers mett and went with us to Downham; and ther the child was buried . . . my mother wth me laid the child in the grave . . . Feb. 24, the midwyfe went from my wyffe to Cooz Braddyll's wyffe. She had given by my wyffe xxs and by me vs."[1]

The Churchwardens at Cowden entered in their account book 1627 " Item, paide for a poore woman's lying in 3. o." 1638. " to John Weller's wife for her attendance on the widow Smithe when she lay in 2.o."[2]

The account book of Sir John Foulis of Ravelstone gives many details of the expenses incurred at confinements in Scotland. His wife appears to have been attended by a doctor, as well as a midwife, and the latter's fee was the higher of the two. The payments are in Scots money.[3] " Mar. 26 1680, to the doctor Steinsone for waiting on my wife in her labour 2 guines at 33 P. sterl. p.piece, 27. 16. o, to Elspie dicksone, midwife, 40. 12. o, to her woman 2. 18. o." On November 26, 1692 there is another payment

---

Sarah Fell records the presents given to her sister's midwife —Jan ye 1st 1675 by m^o Lent Bro. Lowe^r to give Jane Chorley his wifes midwife   1. 00.00
by m^o Mothe^r gave to s^d midwife   5. 00
by m^o Sist^r Sus : sist^r Rach : & I gave he^r   5. 00
(Dec. 6. 1676. By M^o Given ffran. Laite Sister Lowers middwife by ffathe^r & Mothe^r 5s. by sist^r Sus : 2s. by sist^r Rach : 2s. myselfe 4s.   Dec. 10, 1677 by m^o Mothe^r gave ffrances Layte when she was middwife to Sist^r Lower of litle Love-day Lowe^r 02.06, by m^o sist^r Susannah gave he^r then 01.00 by m^o sister Rachell gave her then 01.00 (Fell, Sarah, *Household Accounts*).

[1] Assheton (Nicholas), *Journal*, p. 81.

[2] *Sussex Arch. Coll.*, Vol. XX., p. 101 and p. 104. *Account Book of Cowden.*

[3] One pound Scots—2od. sterling.

" to my wife to give doctor Sibbald for his attendance
on her in childbed and since to this day 5 guineas
66. o. o." Jan. 31, 1704 " to my son W^m to give the
midwife when his wife was brought to bed of her
sone Jo^n 3 guineas 42. 12. o. to my douchter
Crichtoune to give the midwife for me halfe a
guinie.7. 2. o.

The size of the gratuities given to the midwife by
the friends and acquaintances who gathered at a
society christening in London may be judged from
Pepys, who enters in his diary when he was Godfather
with Sir W. Pen to Mrs. Browne's child " I did give
the midwife 10s."[1] His gratuities to people of lower
rank were smaller, and of course the gifts made by
the " common people " and those of the gentry in the
provinces were much more modest.

In the latter part of the century there are indications
of a growing tendency among the upper classes to
replace the midwife by the doctor. The doctors
encouraged the tendency. Their treatises on midwifery, of which several were published during this
time, deprecate any attempt on the midwife's part
to cope with difficult cases. Dr. Hugh Chamberlain points out " nor can it be so great a discredit
to a Midwife . . . . to have a Woman or Child
saved by a Man's assistance, as to suffer either to die
under her own hand."[2] In making this translation
of Maurice's work on Midwifery, Chamberlain omitted
the anatomical drawings, " there being already severall
in English ; as also here and there a passage that
might offend a chast English eye ; and being not
absolutely necessary to the purpose ; the rest I have,
as carefully as I could, rendered into English for the
benefit of our midwives."[3] This line of thought is

---

[1] Pepy's *Diary*, Vol. I., p. 308. 1661.

[2] Chamberlain (Dr. Hugh). *Accomplisht Midwife* : *Epistle to the Reader*.

[3] *Ibid.*

carried yet further by McMath, who says in the preface to " The Expert Midwife " that he has " of purpose omitted a Description of the parts in a woman destined to Generation, not being absolutely necessary to this purpose, and lest it might seem execrable to the more chast and shamfaced through Baudiness and Impurity of words ; and have also endeavoured to keep all Modesty, and a due Reverence to Nature : nor am I of the mind with some, as to think there is no Debauchery in the thing, except it may be in the abuse."[1]

The notion that it was indecent for a woman to understand the structure and functions of her own body fitted in with the doctors' policy of circumscribing the midwife's sphere ; McMath continues " Natural Labour, where all goes right and naturally, is the proper work of the Midwife, and which she alone most easily performs aright, being only to sit and attend Nature's pace and progress . . . . and perform some other things of smaller moment, which Physicians gave Midwifes to do, as unnecessary & indicent for them, and for the Matronal chastity (tho some of Old absurdly assigned them more, and made it also their office to help the Delivery, and not by Medicaments only and others, but Inchantments also.)."[2]

Clearly in a profession which often holds in its hands the balance between life and death, those members who are debarred from systematic study and training must inevitably give way sooner or later to those who have access to all the sources of learning, but the influences which were prejudicing women's position in midwifery during the seventeenth century were not wholly founded on such reasonable grounds ; they were also affected by much more

---

[1] McMath (Mr. James, M.D.). *The Expert Mid-wife.*

[2] *Ibid.*

general, undefined and subtle causes. It may even be doubted whether the superior knowledge of the seventeenth century doctor actually secured a larger measure of safety to the mother who entrusted herself to his management than was attained by those who confided in the skill of an experienced and intelligent midwife. Chamberlain admits that the practice of doctors " not onely in England but thoughout Europe ; . . . . hath very much caused the report, that where a man comes, one or both [mother or child] must necessarily dye ; and makes many for that reason forbear sending, untill either be dead or dying."* He continues " my Father, Brothers and myself (though none else in Europe that I know) have by God's blessing, and our industry, attained to, and long practised a way to deliver a woman in this case without any prejudice to her or her Infant."

The discovery to which Chamberlain refers was the use of forceps, which he and his family retained as a profound secret. Therefore this invention did not rank among the advantages which other doctors possessed over midwives at this period. Even when, a century later, the use of forceps became generally understood, the death rate in childbed was not materially reduced, for it was only with the discovery of the value of asepsis that this heavy sacrifice was diminished. We must therefore look for the explanation of the growing ascendancy of male practitioners to other causes beside the hypothetical standard of their greater efficiency. Their prestige rested partly on an ability to use long words which convinced patients of their superior wisdom ; it was defended by what was fast becoming a powerful corporation ; and more potent in its effect was the general deterioration in the position of women which took place during the century. A lessening

---

of confidence in womanly resourcefulness and capacity in other walks of life, could not fail to affect popular estimation of their value here too ; and added to this were the morbid tendencies of the increasing numbers of oversexed society women who were devoted to a life of pleasure. The fact that similar tendencies were visible in France, where an excellent scientific training was open to women, shows that the capture of the profession by men was not only due to superior skill.

The famous French Midwife, Madame Bourgeois, told her daughter " There is a great deal of artifice to be used in the pleasing of our Women, especially the young ones, who many times do make election of Men to bring them to bed. I blush to speak of them, for I take it to be a great peice of impudence to have any recourse unto them, unless it be a case of very great danger. I do approve, I have approved of it, and know that it ought to be done, so that it be concealed from the Woman all her life long ; nor that she see the surgeon any more."[1]

Whatever may have been the explanation, midwifery had ceased to be a monopoly for women when the " man-midwife " made his appearance in the sixteenth century, but it is only in the latter half of the seventeenth century that the profession passes definitely under the control of men. The doctors who then secured all the more profitable class of work, were united in a corporation which was often directed by men possessed of a disinterested enthusiasm for truth, and considerable proficiency in their art, even though many in their ranks might regard their profession merely as a means for acquiring personal fame or wealth. But the interest of the corporations of physicians and surgeons was centred more upon their profession than upon the general well-being of the community,

---

[1] Pechey, *Compleat Midwife*, p. 349. Secrets of Madame Louyse Bourgeois, midwife to the Queen of France, which she left to her Daughter as a guide for her.

and they did not regard it as part of their duty to secure competent assistance in childbirth for every woman in the community. They took a keen professional interest in the problems of midwifery, but the benefits of their research were only available for the wives or mistresses of rich men who could afford to pay high fees. Far from making any effort to provide the same assistance for the poor, the policy of the doctors, with some exceptions, was to withold instruction from the midwives on whom the poor depended, lest their skill should enable them to compete with themselves in practice among the wealthy.

Conclusion.

The foregoing examination of the character and extent of women's professional services has brought several interesting points to light. It has been shown that when social organisation rested upon the basis of the family, as it chiefly did up to the close of the Middle Ages, many of the services which are now ranked as professional were thought to be specially suited to the genius of women, and were accordingly allotted to them in the natural division of labour within the family. The suggestions as to the character and conditions of these services during the Middle Ages, rest upon conjectures drawn from the comparison of a few generally accepted statements concerning the past, with what appears at the opening of the seventeenth century to be a traditional attitude to women, an attitude which was then undergoing rapid modifications. A more thorough and detailed examination of their position in the preceding centuries may show that it was far less stable than is generally supposed, but such a discovery need not disturb the explanation which is here given of the tendencies deciding the scope of women's professional activity within in the seventeenth century.

First among these was the gradual emergence of the arts of teaching and healing, from the domestic or family sphere to a professional organisation. Within the domestic sphere, as women and men are equally members of the family, no artificial impediment could hinder women from rendering the services which nature had fitted them to perform ; moreover, the experience and training which family life provided for boys, were to a large extent available for girls also. Coincident with a gradual curtailment of domestic activities may be observed a marked tendency towards the exclusion of women from all interests external to the family. The political theories of the seventeenth century regarded the State as an organisation of individual men only or groups of men, not as a commonwealth of families ; in harmony with this idea we find that none of the associations which were formed during this period for public purposes, either educational, economic, scientific or political, include women in their membership. The orientation of ideas in the seventeenth century was drawing a rigid line between the State, in which the individual man had his being, and family matters. The third tendency was towards the deterioration of women's intellectual and moral capacity, owing to the narrowing of family life and the consequent impoverishment of women's education. The fourth tendency was towards an increasing belief in the essential inferiority of women to men.

It will be seen that these tendencies were interdependent. Their united effect was revolutionary, gradually excluding women from work for which in former days, nature, it was supposed, had specially designed them. Thus the teaching of young children, both girls and boys, had been generally entrusted to women, many men acknowledging in later life the excellence of the training which they had received from their mothers, and it cannot be doubted that women were upon the whole successful in transmitting to their children the benefit of the education and experience which they had themselves received. But no amount of didactic skill can enable persons to teach what they do not themselves possess, and so the scope of the training given by women depended upon the development of their own personalities. When family traditions and family organisation were disturbed, as perhaps they would have been in any case sooner or later, but as they were to a more marked extent during the Civil War, the sources from which women derived their mental and spiritual nourishment were dried up, and without access to external supplies their personality gradually became stunted.

Women were virtually refused access to sources of knowledge which were external to th family, and hence, with a few exceptions they were confined in the teaching profession to the most elementary subjects. Women were employed in the " dames schools " attended by the common people, or, when they could read and write themselves, mothers often instructed their children in these arts ; but the governesses employed by gentlefolks, or the schoolmistresses to whom they sent their daughters for the acquisition of the accomplishments appropriate to young ladies, were seldom competent to undertake the actual teaching themselves ; for this masters were generally engaged, because few women had gone through the training necessary to give them a sound understanding of the arts in question. Women were not incapable of teaching, but as knowledge became more specialized and technical, the opportunities which home life provided for acquiring such knowledge proved inadequate ; and consequently women were soon excluded from the higher ranks of the teaching profession.

The history of their relation to the arts of Healing is very similar. Other things being equal, as to some extent they were when the greater part of human life was included within the family circle, the psychic and emotional female development appears to make women more fitted than men to deal with preventive and remedial medicine. The explanation of this fact offers a fascinating field for speculation, but involves too wide a digression for discussion here, and in its support we will only point out the fact that in the old days, when no professional services were available, it was to the women of the family, rather than to the men, that the sick and wounded turned for medicine and healing. Yet in spite of this natural affinity for the care of suffering humanity, women were excluded from the sources of learning which were being slowly organised outside the family circle, and were thus unable to remain in professions for which they were so eminently suited.

The suspicion that the inferior position which women occupied in the teaching profession and their exclusion from the medical profession, was caused rather by the absence of educational opportunities than by a physiological incapacity for the practice of these arts, is strengthened by the remarkable history of Midwifery; which from being reserved exclusively for women and practised by them on a professional basis from time immemorial, passed in its more lucrative branches into the hands of men, when sources of instruction were opened to them which were closed to women. Just as the amateur woman teacher was less competent than the man who had made art or the learned languages his profession, so did the woman who treated her family and neighbours by rule of thumb, appear less skilful than the professional doctor, and the uneducated midwives brought their profession into disrepute. The exclusion of women from all the sources of specialised training was bound to re-act unfavourably upon their characters, because as family life depended more and more upon professional services for education and medical assistance, fewer opportunities were offered to women for exerting their faculties within the domestic sphere and the general incompetence of upper class women did in fact become more pronounced.

Chapter VII

CONCLUSION

Great productive capacity of women under conditions of Family and Domestic Industry—no difference between efficiency of labour when applied for domestic purposes or for trade.

Rate of wages no guide to real value of goods produced—married women unlikely to work for wages when possessing capital for domestic industry—Women's productiveness in textile industries—Agriculture—Other industries—Professional services.

Capitalism effected economic revolution in women's position—By (a) substitution of individual for family wages—(b) employment of wage-earners on master's premises—(c) rapid increase of master's wealth.

Exclusion of women from skilled trades not originally due to sex jealousy—Women's lack of specialised training due, (a) to its being unnecessary; (b) the desire to keep wife in subjection to husband—Reduction in the value to her family of woman's productive capacity by substitution of wage-earning for domestic industry—Effect of her productive energy on her maternal functions and her social influence.

THE preceding chapters have demonstrated the great productive capacity which women possessed when society was organised on the basis of Family and Domestic Industry. There was then no hard and fast line dividing domestic occupations from other branches of industry, and thus it has not been possible to discover how much of women's labour was given to purposes of trade and how much was confined to the service of their families; but as labour was at this time equally productive, whether it was employed for domestic purposes or in Trade, it is not necessary to discriminate between these two classes of production in estimating the extent to which the community depended upon women's services. The goods produced and the services rendered to their families by wives and daughters, must if they had been idle have employed labour otherwise available for Trade; or to put the position in another way, if the labour of women had been withdrawn from the domestic industries and applied to Trade, more goods would have been produced for the market, which goods the said women's families would then have obtained by purchase; but while by this means the trade of the country would be greatly increased, unless the efficiency of women's labour had been raised by its transference from domestic to other forms of industry, the wealth of the community would remain precisely the same.

Nevertheless, in estimating a country's prosperity domestic production is generally overlooked, because, as the labour devoted to it receives no wages and its results do not enter the market, there is no mechanical standard for estimating its value. For similar reasons Home Trade is commonly considered to be of less importance than Foreign Trade, because, as the latter passes through the Customs, its money value can be much more readily computed, and because the man in the street, like King Midas, has imagined that gold is wealth. But we are here considering the production of goods and services, not of gold, and from this point of view, the woman who spins thread to clothe her family, and she who furnishes by her industry milk and cheese, eggs and pork, fruit and vegetables for the consumption of her family, has produced exactly the same goods, no more and no less, than if she had produced them for the market, and whether these goods are consumed by her own family or by strangers makes absolutely no difference to their real value.

Neither can the value of a woman's productive activity be judged by the wages she receives, because the value of a pair of sheets is the same, whether the flax has been spun by a well-to-do farmers' wife who meanwhile lives in affluence, or by a poor woman earning wages which are insufficient to keep body and soul together. The labour required for spinning the flax was the same in either case, for there was no difference in the type of spinning wheel she used, or in her other facilities for work ; it was only later, when organisations for trading purposes had enormously increased productive capacity by the introduction of power and the sub-division of labour, that the same productive capacity, devoted to domestic purposes, became relatively inferior in results. This change between the relative efficiency of domestic and industrial labour could not fail, when it took place, to exert a marked influence on the economic position of married women, because while their husbands earned sufficient money to pay rent and a few outgoing expenses, they had no inducement to work for wages, their labour being more productive at home. Women who fed and clothed themselves and their children by means of domestic industry gratified in this way their sense of independence as effectively as if they had earned the equivalent money by trade or wages. Considering the low rates paid to women, it may be supposed that few worked for wages when possessed of sufficient stock to employ themselves fully in domestic industries ; on the other hand there were a considerable number who were in a position to hire servants, and who, having learnt a skilled trade, devoted themselves to business, either on their own account or jointly with their husbands.

If the general position of women in the whole field of industry is reviewed, it will be seen that, beyond question, all the textile fabrics used at this time, with the exception of a few luxuries, were made from the thread which was spun by women and children, the export trade in cloth also depending entirely on their labour for spinning and to some extent for the other processes. In agriculture the entire management of the milch cows, the dairy, poultry, pigs, orchard and garden, was undertaken by the women, and though the mistress employed in her department men as well as women servants, the balance was redressed by the fact that women and girls were largely employed in field work. The woman's contribution to farming is also shown by the fact that twice as much land was allowed to the colonists who were married as to those who were single. The expectation that the women and children in the husbandman class would produce the greater part of their own food is proved by the very low rate of wages which Quarter Sessions fixed for agricultural labour, and by the fact that when no land was available it was recognised that the wage earner's family must be dependent on the poor rate.

Though the part which women played in agriculture and the textile industries is fairly clear, a great obscurity still shrouds their position in other directions. One fact however emerges with some distinctness; women of the tradesman class were sufficiently capable in business, and were as a rule so well acquainted with the details of their husband's concerns, that a man generally appointed his wife as his executrix, while custom universally secured to her the possession of his stock, apprentices and goodwill in the event of his death. That she was often able to carry on his business with success, is shown by incidental references, and also by the frequency with which widow's names occur in the lists of persons occupying various trades.

How much time the wives of these tradesmen actually spent over their husband's business is a point on which practically no evidence is forthcoming, but it seems probable that in the skilled trades they were seldom employed in manual processes for which they had received no training, but were occupied in general supervision, buying and selling. It is not therefore surprising to find women specially active in all branches of the Retail Trade, and girls were apprenticed as often to shop-keepers as to the recognised women's trades such as millinery and mantua-making.

The assistance of the wife was often so important in her husband's business, that she engaged servants to free her from household drudgery, her own productive capacity being greater than the cost of a servant's wages. Apart from exceptional cases of illness or incompetence, the share which the wife took in her husband's business, was determined rather by the question whether he carried it on at home or abroad than by any special appropriateness of the said business to the feminine disposition. Thus, though women were seldom carpenters or masons, they figure as pewterers and smiths. In every business there are certain operations which can conveniently be performed by women, and when carried on at home within the compass of the family life, the work of a trade was as naturally sorted out between husband and wife, as the work on a farm. No question arose as to the relative value of their work, because the proceeds became the joint property of the family, instead of being divided between individuals.

With regard to the services which are now classed as professional, those of healing and teaching were included among the domestic duties of women. Illness was rife in the seventeenth century, for the country was devastated by recurrent epidemics of small-pox and the plague, besides a constant liability to ague and the other ordinary ailments of mankind; thus the need for nursing must have been very great. The sick depended for their tending chiefly upon the women of their own households, and probably the majority of English people at this time, received medical advice and drugs from the same source. Women's skill in such matters was acquired by experience and tradition, seldom resting upon a scientific basis, for they were excluded from schools and universities. Acquired primarily with a view to domestic use, such skill was extended beyond the family circle, and women who were wise in these matters sometimes received payment for their services. Midwifery alone was really conducted on professional lines, and though practised in former days exclusively by women, it was now passing from their hands owing to their exclusion from the sources of advanced instruction.

It is difficult to estimate the respective shares taken by men and women in the art of teaching, for while the young were dependent on home training, they received attention from both father and mother, and when the age for apprenticeship arrived the task was transferred to the joint care of master and mistress. With regard to learning of a scholastic character, reading was usually taught by women to both boys and girls, who learnt it at home from their mothers, or at a dame's school; but the teaching of more advanced subjects was almost exclusively in the hands of men, although a few highly educated women were engaged as governesses in certain noble families where the Tudor tradition still lingered. Generally speaking, however, when a girl's curriculum included such subjects as Latin and Arithmetic her instruction, like her brothers, was received from masters, and this was equally true in the case of accomplishments which were considered more appropriate to the understanding of young ladies. Women rarely, if ever, undertook the teaching of music, painting or dancing. From these branches of the teaching profession they were debarred by lack of specialised training.

Thus it will be seen that the history of women's position in the professions, follows a very similar course to that of the developments in the world of Industry; work, for which they appeared peculiarly fitted by disposition or natural gifts, while it was included within the domestic sphere, gradually passed out of their hands when the scene of their labour was transferred to the wider domains of human life.

Capitalism was the means by which the revolution

in women's economic position was effected in the industrial world. The three developments which were most instrumental to this end being:—

(*a*) the substitution of an individual for a family wage, enabling men to organise themselves in the competition which ruled the labour market, without sharing with the women of their families all the benefits derived through their combination.

(*b*) the withdrawal of wage-earners from home-life to work upon the premises of the masters, which prevented the employment of the wage-earner's wife in her husband's occupation.

(*c*) the rapid increase of wealth, which permitted the women of the upper classes to withdraw from all connection with business.

Once the strong hand of necessity is relaxed there has been a marked tendency in English life for the withdrawal of married women from all productive activity, and their consequent devotion to the cultivation of idle graces; the parasitic life of its women has been in fact one of the chief characteristics of the parvenu class. The limitations which surrounded the lives of the women belonging to this class are most vividly described in Pepys' Journal, where they form a curious contrast to the vigour and independence of the women who were actively engaged in industry. The whole Diary should be read to gain a complete idea of the relations of married life under these new circumstances, but a few extracts will illustrate the poverty of Mrs. Pepys' interests and her abject dependence on her husband. Most curious of all is Pepys' naïve admission that he was trying to " make " work for his wife, which furnishes an illustration of the saying " coming events cast their shadows before them."

" Nov. 12, 1662. much talke and difference between us about my wife's having a woman, which I seemed much angry at that she should go so far in it without . . . . my being consulted. 13th. Our discontent again and sorely angered my wife, who indeed do live very lonely, but I do perceive that it is want of worke that do make her and all other people think of ways of spending their time worse. June 8. 1664. Her spirit is lately come to be other than it used to be, and now depends upon her having Ashwell by her, before whom she thinks I shall not say nor do anything of force to her, which vexes me, and makes me wish that I had better considered all that I have done concerning my bringing my wife to this condition of heat. Aug. 20. I see that she is confirmed in it that all I do is by design, and that my very keeping of the house in dirt, and the doing this and anything else in the house, is but to find her employment to keep her within, and from minding of her pleasure, which though I am sorry to see she minds it, is true enough in a great degree. Jan. 14. 1667–8. I do find she do keep very bad remembrance of my former unkindness to her and do mightily complain of her want of money and liberty, which will rather hear and bear the complaint of than grant the contrary . . . . . Feb. 18. a ring which I am to give her as a valentine. It will cost me near £5 she costing me but little in comparison with other wives, and I have not many occasions to spend money on her. Feb. 23. with this and what she had she reckons that she hath above £150 worth of jewels of one kind or another ; and I am glad of it, for it is fit the wretch should have something to content herself with."

While the capitalistic organisation of industry increased the wealth of the masters, it condemned a large proportion of the craftsmen to remain permanently in the position of journeymen or wage-earners with the incidental result that women were excluded from their ranks in the more highly skilled trades. Under the old system of Family Industry, labour and capital had been united in one person or family group of persons, but capitalism brought them into conflict ;

and the competition which had previously only existed between rival families was introduced into the labour market, where men and women struggled with each other to secure work and wages from the capitalist. The keystone of the journeymen's position in their conflict with capital, lay in their ability to restrict their own numbers by the enforcement of a long apprenticeship and the limitation of the number of apprentices. On gaining this point the journeymen in any trade secured a monopoly which enabled them to bargain advantageously with the masters. Their success raised them into the position of a privileged class in the world of labour, but did nothing to improve the position of the other wage-earners in unskilled or unorganised trades.

When their organisation was strong enough the journeymen allowed no unapprenticed person to be employed upon any process of their trade, however simple or mechanical; a policy which resulted in the complete exclusion of women, owing to the fact that girls were seldom, if ever, apprenticed to these trades. It has been shown that under the old system, craftsmen had been free to employ their wives and daughters in any way that was convenient, the widow retaining her membership in her husband's gild or company with full trading privileges, and the daughters able, if they wished, to obtain their freedom by patrimony. Journeymen however now worked on their masters' premises, their traditions dating from a time when they were all unmarried men; and though the majority of them had renounced the expectation of rising above this position of dependence, the idea that they should extend their hardly won privileges to wife or daughter never occurred to them.

Thus came about the exclusion of women from the skilled trades, for the wives of the men who became capitalists withdrew from productive activity, and the

wives of journeymen confined themselves to domestic
work, or entered the labour market as individuals,
being henceforward entirely unprotected in the conflict by their male relations. Capitalistic organisation
tended therefore to deprive women of opportunities
for sharing in the more profitable forms of production,
confining them as wage-earners to the unprotected
trades. It would be an anachronism to ascribe this
tendency to sex-jealousy in the economic world.
The idea of individual property in wages had
hardly arisen, for prevailing habits of thought still
regarded the earnings of father, mother and children
as the joint property of the family, though controlled
by the father ; and thus the notion that it could be
to men's advantage to debar women from well-paid
work would have seemed ridiculous in the seventeenth
century. Though the payment of individual wages
was actually in force, their implication was hardly
understood, and motives of sex-jealousy do not dominate
the economic world till a later period. While the
family formed the social unit the interests of husband
and wife were bound so closely together, that neither
could gain or suffer without the other immediately
sharing the loss or advantage.

The momentous influence which some phases of
Capitalism were destined to exert upon the economic
position of women, were unforeseen by the men who
played a leading part in its development, and passed
unnoticed by the speculative thinkers who wrote
long treatises on Theories of State Organisation.
The revolution did not involve a conscious demarcation of the respective spheres of men and women
in industry ; its results were accidental, due to the
fact that women were forgotten, and so no attempt
was made to adjust their training and social status
to the necessities of the new economic organisation.
The oversight is not surprising, for women's relation
to the " Home " was regarded as an immutable

law of Nature, inviolable by any upheaval in external social arrangements.

Thus the idea that the revolution in women's economic position was due to deliberate policy may be dismisssed. Capitalism is a term denoting a force rather than a system ; a force that is no more interested in human relations than is the force of gravitation; nevertheless its sphere of action lies in the social relations of men and women, and its effects are modified and directed by human passions, prejudices and ideals. The continuance of human existence and its emancipation from the trammels that hamper its progress, must depend upon the successful mastery of this as of the other forces of Nature.

If we would understand the effect of the introduction of Capitalism on the social organism, we must remember that the subjection of women to their husbands was the foundation stone of the structure of the community in which Capitalism first made its appearance. Regarded as being equally the law of Nature and the Law of God, no one questioned the necessity of the wife's obedience, lip service being rendered to the doctrine of subjection, even in those households where it was least enforced. Traditional ideas regarded the common wealth, or social organisation, as an association of families, each family being a community which was largely autonomous, and was self-contained for most of life's purposes; hence the order and health of the commonwealth depended upon the order and efficiency of the families comprised within it. Before the seventeenth century the English mind could not imagine order existing without an acknowledged head. No one therefore questioned the father's right to his position as head of the family, but in his temporary absence, or when he was removed by death, the public interest required his family's preservation, and the mother quite naturally stepped into his place, with all its attendant responsibilities and privileges. In this family organisation all that the father gained was shared by the mother and children, because his whole life, or almost his whole life, was shared by them. This is specially marked in the economic side of existence, where the father did not merely earn money and hand it to the mother to spend, but secured for her also, access to the means of production; the specialised training acquired by the man through apprenticeship did not merely enable him to earn higher wages, but conferred upon his wife the right to work, as far as she was able, in that trade.

Capitalism, however, broke away from the family system, and dealt direct with individuals, the first fruit of individualism being shown by the exclusion of women from the journeymen's associations; and yet their exclusion was caused in the first place by want of specialised training, and was not the necessary result of Capitalism, for the history of the Cotton Trade shows, in later years, that where the labour of women was essential to an industry, an effective combination of wage-earners could be formed which would include both sexes.

Two explanations may be given for women's lack of specialised training. The first, and, given the prevailing conditions of Family Industry, probably the most potent reason lay in the belief that it was unnecessary. A specialised training, whether in Science, Art or Industry, is inevitably costly in time and money; and as in every trade there is much work of a character which needs no prolonged specialised training, and as in the ordinary course of a woman's life a certain proportion of her time and energy must be devoted to bearing and rearing children, it seemed a wise economy to spend the cost of specialised training on boys, employing women over those processes which chiefly required general intelligence and common-sense.

It has been shown that this policy answered well enough in the days of Domestic and Family Industry when the husband and wife worked together, and the wife therefore reaped the advantages of the trading privileges and social position won by her husband. It was only when Capitalism re-organised industry on an individual basis, that the wife was driven to fight her economic battles single handed, and women, hampered by the want of specialised training, were beaten down into sweated trades.

The second explanation for women's lack of special-ised training is the doctrine of the subjection of women to their husbands. While the first reason was more influential during the days of Family and Domestic Industry, the second gains in force with the develop-ment of Capitalism. If women's want of specialised training had been prejudicial to their capacity for work in former times, such training would not have been withheld from them merely through fear of its weakening the husband's power, because the husband was so dependent upon his wife's assistance. There was little talk then of men " keeping " their wives ; neither husband nor wife could prosper without the other's help. But the introduction of Capitalism, organising industry on an individual basis, freed men to some extent from this economic dependence on their wives, and from henceforward the ideal of the subjection of women to their husbands could be pursued, unhampered by fear of the dangers resulting to the said husbands by a lessening of the wife's economic efficiency.

A sense of inferiority is one of the prime requisites for a continued state of subjection, and nothing contributes to this sense so much, as a marked inferiority of education and training in a society accustomed to rate everything according to its money value. The difference in earning capacity which the want of education produces, is in itself sufficient to stamp a class as inferior.

There is yet another influence which contributed to the decline in the standard of women's education and in their social and economic position, which is so noticeable in the seventeenth century. This period marks the emergence of the political idea of the "mechanical state" and its substitution for the traditional view of the nation as a commonwealth of families. Within the family, women had their position, but neither Locke, nor Hobbes, nor the obscure writers on political theory and philosophy who crowd the last half of the seventeenth century, contemplate the inclusion of women in the State of their imagination. For them the line is sharply drawn between the spheres of men and women; women are confined within the circle of their domestic responsibilities, while men should explore the ever widening regions of the State. The really significant aspect of this changed orientation of social ideas, is the separation which it introduces between the lives of women and those of men, because hitherto men as well as women lived in the Home.

The mechanical State *quâ* State did not yet exist in fact, for the functions of the Government did not extend much beyond the enforcement of Justice and the maintenance of Defence. Englishmen were struggling to a realisation of the other aspects of national life by means of voluntary associations for the pursuit of Science, of Trade, of Education, or other objects, and it is in these associations that the trend of their ideas is manifested, for one and all exclude women from their membership; to foster the charming dependence of women upon their husbands, all independent sources of information were, as far as possible, closed to them. Any association or combination of women outside the limits of their own families was discouraged, and the benefits which had been extended to them in this respect by the Catholic Religion were specially deprecated. Milton's statement sums up very fairly the ideas of this school of thought regarding the relations that should exist between husband and wife in the general scheme of things. They were to exist " He for God only, she for God in him." The general standard of education resulting from such theories was inevitably inferior ; and the exclusion of women from skilled industry and the professions, was equally certain to be the consequence sooner or later, of the absence of specialised training.

The general effect upon women of this exclusion, which ultimately limited their productive capacity to the field of household drudgery, or to the lowest paid ranks of unskilled labour, belongs to a much later period. But one point can already be discerned and must not be overlooked. This point is the alteration which took place in the value to her family of a woman's productive capacity when her labour was transferred from domestic industry to wage-earning, under the conditions prevailing in the seventeenth century. When employed in domestic industry the whole value of what she produced was retained by her family ; but when she worked for wages her family only received such a proportion of it as she was able to secure to them by her weak bargaining power in the labour market. What this difference amounted to will be seen when it is remembered that the wife of a husbandman could care for her children and feed and clothe herself and them by domestic industry, but when working for wages she could not earn enough for her own maintenance.

This depreciation of the woman's productive value to her family did not greatly influence her position in the seventeenth century, because it was then only visible in the class of wage-earners, and into this position women were forced by poverty alone. The productive efficiency of women's services in domestic industry remained as high as ever, and every family which was possessed of sufficient capital for domestic industry, could provide sufficient profitable occupation for its women without their entry into the labour market. Independent hard-working families living under the conditions provided by Family and Domestic Industry, still formed the majority of the English people. The upper classes, as far as the women were concerned, were becoming more idle, and the number of families depending wholly on wages was increasing, but farmers, husbandmen and tradesmen, still formed a class sufficiently numerous to maintain the hardy stock of the English race unimpaired. Thus, while the productive capacity of women was reduced in the seventeenth century by the idleness of the *nouveau riche* and by the inefficiency of women wage-earners which resulted from their lack of nourishment, it was maintained at the former high level among the intermediate and much larger class, known as " the common people."

Though from the economic point of view intense productive energy on the part of women is no longer necessary to the existence of the race, and has been generally abandoned, an understanding of its effect upon the maternal functions is extremely important to the sociologist. No complete vital statistics were collected in the seventeenth century, but an examination of the different evidence which is still available, leaves no doubt that the birth rate was extremely high in all classes, except perhaps that of wage-earners. It was usual for active busy women amongst the nobility and gentry, to bear from twelve to twenty children, and though the death rate was also high, the children that survived appear to have possessed abundant vitality and energy. Neither does the toil which fell to the lot of the women among the common people appear to have injured their capacity for motherhood; in fact the wives of husbandmen were the type selected by the wealthy to act as wet nurses for their children. It is only among the class of wage-earners that the capacity for reproduction appears to have been checked, and in this class it was the under-feeding, rather than the over-working of the mothers, which rendered them incapable of rearing their infants.

The effect of the economic position of women, must be considered also in relation to another special function which women exercise in society, namely the part which they play in the psychic and moral reactions between the sexes. This subject has seldom been investigated in a detached and truly scientific spirit, and therefore any generalisations that may be submitted have little value. It will only be observed here that the exercise by women of productive energy in the Elizabethan period, was not then inconsistent with the attainment by the English race of its high-water mark in vitality and creative force, and that a comparison of the social standards described by Restoration and Elizabethan Dramatists, reveals a decadence, which, if not consequent upon, was at least coincident with, the general withdrawal of upper-class women from their previous occupation with public and private affairs.

Undoubtedly the removal of business and public interests from the home, resulted in a loss of educational opportunities for girls ; a loss which was not made good to them in other ways, and which therefore produced generations of women endowed with a lower mental and moral calibre. The influence of women upon their husbands narrowed as men's lives drifted away from the home circle and centred more round clubs and external business relations. Hence it came about that in the actual social organisation prevailing in England during the last half of the seventeenth century, the influence or psychic reaction of women upon men was very different in character and much more limited in scope, than that exercised by them in the Elizabethan period. When considered in regard to the historical facts of this epoch, it will be noticed that the process by which the vital forces and energy of the people were lowered and which in common parlance is termed emasculation, accompanied an evolution which was in fact depressing the female forces of the nation, leaving to the male forces an ever greater predominance in the directing of the people's destiny. The evidence given in the preceding chapters is insufficient to determine what is cause and what is effect in such complicated issues of life, and only shows that a great expenditure of productive energy on the part of women is not, under certain circumstances, inconsistent with the successful exercise of their maternal functions, nor does it necessarily exhaust the creative vital forces of the race.

The enquiry into the effect which the appearance of Capitalism has produced upon the economic position of women has drawn attention to another isssue, which concerns a fundamental relation of human society, namely to what extent does the Community or State include women among its integral members, and provide them with security for the exercise of their functions, whether these may be of the same character or different from those of men.

It has been suggested that the earlier English Commonwealth did actually embrace both men and women in its idea of the " Whole," because it was composed of self-contained families consisting of men, women and children, all three of which are essential for the continuance of human society ; but the mechanical State which replaced it, and whose development has accompanied the extension of Capitalism, has regarded the individual, not the family, as its unit, and in England this State began with the conception that it was concerned only with male individuals. Thus it came to pass that every womanly function was considered as the private interest of husbands and fathers, bearing no relation to the life of the State, and therefore demanding from the community as a whole no special care or provision.

The implications of such an idea, together with the effect which it produced upon a society in which formerly women had been recognised as members, though perhaps not equal members, cannot be fully discussed in this essay ; the investigation would require a much wider field of evidence than can be provided from the survey of one century. But from the mere recognition that such a change took place, follow ideas of the most far-reaching significance concerning the structure of human society ; we may even ask ourselves whether the instability, superficiality and spiritual poverty of modern life, do not spring from the organisation of a State which regards the purposes of life solely from the male standpoint, and we may permit ourselves to hope that when this mechanism has been effectively replaced by the organisation of the whole, which is both male and female, humanity will receive a renewal of strength that will enable them to grapple effectively with the blind force Capitalism ;—that force which, while producing wealth beyond the dreams of avarice, has hitherto robbed us of so large a part of the joy of creation.

AUTHORITIES.

(The numbers in leaded type are the press marks in the British Museum.)

Account of Several Workhouses for Employing and Maintaining the Poor, etc.　　*London* 1725.　　**1027 i. 18 (9).**

Act of Common Council for the reformation of sundry abuses practised by divers persons upon the common markets and streets of the City of London.　　1631.　　**21 l. 5 (4).**

Act for the settlement and well ordering of the severall Publick Markets within the City of London.
　　1674.　　**21 l. 5 (58).**

Acts and Ordinances of the Interregnum II.　　1651.

Add. MSS. 36308.

Answer to a Paper of Reflections on the Project for laying a Duty on English Wrought Silks.　　**8223 e. 9 (75).**

Arber, Edward.　Transcript of the Registers of the Company of Stationers of London.　　1554-1640.　*London*, 1876.

Assheton, Nicholas, Esq.　Journal of; ed. by Rev. F. R. Raines.　　*Chetham Soc.*, 1848

Astell, Mary.　A serious proposal to the Ladies for the advancement of their true and greatest Interest, by a Lover of her sex.　　1694.　**12314 a. 22.**

Atkinson, J. C.　Quarter Sessions Records for the North Riding of Yorkshire.　　*London*, 1884.　**R. ac. 8190.**

Bacon, Francis.　Works of; ed. by Spedding.　*London*, 1858.

Bacon, Sir Nathaniel, of Stiffkey, Norfolk.　Official Papers of, 1580-1620.　*Royal Hist. Soc. Camden, 3rd Series.*
1915

Baillie, Lady Grisell.　Household Book of, ed. by R. Scott-Moncrieff.　　*Edinburgh*, 1911.　**R. ac. 8256.**

Banks, John.　A Journal of the Life of.　*London*, 1712.

Barrett, C. R. B.　History of the Society of Apothecaries of London.　　*London*, 1905.　**7680 f. 14.**

Bateson, Mary.　Borough Customs.
　　Selden Society, Vol. XVIII., 1904.　**R. ac. 2176.**

———— Records of the Borough of Leicester.
　　Cambridge, 1905.　**2367 b. 5.**

Batt, Mary.　Testimony to the Life and Death of.　1683.

Bedell, Wm. True relation of the life and death of the Right Reverend Father in God, Lord Bishop of Kilmore In Ireland. *Camden Society*, 1872. **R. ac. 8113/98.**

Best, Henry. Rural Economy in Yorkshire in 1641.
Surtees Society, 33. *Durham*, 1857.

Black, W. H. History and Antiquities of the Worshipful Company of Leathersellers of the City of London.
London 1871. **1890 c. 5.**

Bownas, Samuel. Life and Travels of. *London* 1756.

Brathwaite, Richard. Anniversaries upon his Panarete continued—with her contemplations penned in the languishing time of her sicknesse. *London* 1635. **Huth 68.**

———— The English gentleman and English gentlewoman in one volume concluded : the 3rd edition with a Ladies Love Lecture and a supplement. *London* 1641. **30 e. 6**

Brewster, John. Parochial History and Antiquities of Stockton upon Tees. *Stockton* 1796. **2368 d. 3**

Brief State of the Inland or Home Trade of England, and of the oppressions it suffers, and the Dangers which threaten it from the Invasion of Hawkers, Pedlars and Clandestine Traders of all sorts. *London* 1730. **104 h. 20.**

British Friend.

Bund, J. W. Willis. Worcestershire County Records.
Worcester 1900. **010360 i.**

Burton, John Richard. History of Kidderminster.
1890. **10368 h. 27.**

C. W. The Bespotted Jesuite. *London* 1641. **E. 166 (3).**

Calendar State Papers. Domestic Series (C. S. P. D.).

Canterbury. Articles to be enquired of by the Churchwardens, etc. **698 n. 20 (18).**

Carpenters, Records of the Worshipful Company of.
1913. **W.P. 2524.**

Cary, John. Account of the Proceedings of the Corporation of Bristol in execution of the Act of Parliament for the better Employing and Maintaining the Poor of that City. *London* 1700. **1027 i. 18 (3).**

Carrier, Henriette. Origines de la Maternité de Paris.
1888. **7687 eee. 31.**

Case of the Linen Drapers and other Dealers in Printed Callicoes and Linens. **816 m. 13 (49).**

Case of British and Irish Manufacture of Linnen, Threads, and Tapes, etc. **1887 b. 60 (6).**

Case of the Manufacturers of Gilt and Silver Wire. **1887 b. 60 (9).**

Case of the Parish of St. Giles. 8223 e. 9 (23).

Case of the Woollen Manufacturers of Great Britain, and of the Poor they imploy. 1887 b. 60 (32).

Case or Petition of the Corporation of Pin-makers. 816 m. 13.

Cellier, Elizabeth, Mrs. Scheme for the foundation of a Royal Hospital. *London* 1687. *Harl. Misc. Vol. iv.*

———— To Dr.——an answer to his Queeries concerning the Colledg of Midwives. 1687-8. 1178 h. 2 (2).

———— Malice Defeated. 1680. 515 l. 1 (10).

Chalkley, Thomas. Collection of the Works of. *London* 1751.

Chamberlain, Hugh, Dr. Trans. Treatise on Midwifery by F. Maurice. 1672.

Chamberlain, Peter. Dr. in Physick, Fellow of the Colledge of London, and one of His Majestie's Physicians Extraordinary. A voice in Rhama or the Crie of Women and Children. *London* 1646. **B.M. E. 1181.**

Charter of the Joiners' Co. Chester. *Harl. MSS.* 2054, *fo.* 5.

Charter and By-laws of the Company of Armourers and Brasiers, in the City of London. 1554-1640.
1873. 08227 b. 13.

Child, Sir Josiah. A New Discourse of Trade, etc.
2nd ed. *London* 1694. 712 c. 5.

———— Short Addition. 1668. 1029 b. 1.

Churchwardens' Accounts. Steeple Ashton. *Wilts Notes and Queries.* *London* 1911. **R. pp. 6049 m.**

———— St. Michael's in Bedwardine, Worcester.
Oxford 1896. **R. Ac. 8166/8.**

Clode, Charles M. Memorials of the Guild of Merchant Taylors, City of London. *London* 1875. **2366 d. 2.**

———— Early History of the Guild of Merchant Taylors of the Fraternity of St. John the Baptist, London.
London 1888. 8248 f. 18.

Clothiers' Complaint, or Reasons for Passing the Bill.
London 1692. 711 f. 28.

Compleat Servant-maid, or the Young Maiden's Tutor.
London 1700. 1037 a. 42.

Congreve, Wm. Works of. *London* 1710. 641 d. 3.

Considerations touching the Excise of Native and Forreign Commodities (as formerly established) as also how the present Excise settled on His Majesty may (with some additions) be improved to the sum resolved on by the Commons in Parliament. 712 m. 1 (3).

Costello, Louisa S. Memoirs of Eminent Englishwomen.
London 1844. 1023 i. 8.

Council Register.

Cox, Rev. J. C. Churchwardens' Accounts. 1913. 2260 b. 3.
———— Three Centuries of Derbyshire Annals as illus-
trated by the Records of the Quarter Sessions of the
County of Derby. London 1890. 010358 l. 28.

Cratfield. Accounts of the Parish of. Ed. by Wm. Holland
and J. J. Raven. 1895. 010358 l. 42.

Croker, John. Brief Memoirs of. London 1839.

Cromwell Family. Bills and Receipts. Vol. II. 1546-1672.
Add. Mss. 33,461.

Crosfield, Helen G. Margaret Fox of Swarthmoor Hall.
London 1913

Culpeper, Nicholas, Gent., Student in Physick and Astrologie.
Directory for Midwives. 1651. E. 1340.

Davenant (Inspector-General of Exports and Imports). An
Account of the trade between Greate Britain, France,
Holland, etc., . . . delivered in his reports made to
the Commissioners for Publick Accounts. 1715.

Davies, J. S. History of Southampton. London 1883. 2368 cc. 5.

Decker, Thomas. Best Plays. Ed. by E. Rhys.
London 1887. 11773 bb. 14.

Declaration of the Estate of Clothing now used within this
Realme of England. 712 G. 16 (1).

Defoe, Daniel. The Behaviour of Servants in England.
London 1724. 1137 h. 6.
———— Every-Body's Business is No-Body's Business.
London 1725. 1137 h. 6 (2).

Dunning, Richard, Gent. A plain and easie Method shewing
how the office of overseer of the Poor may be managed,
whereby it may be £9,000 per annum Advantage to the
County of Devon, without abating the weekly Relief of
any Poor, or doing a Penny damage to any Person.
London 1686. 1027 i. 17.

Dunsford, M. Historical Memoirs of the Town and Parish of
Tiverton. Exeter 1790. 2368 d. 3.

Englands Way to win wealth and to employ Ships and
Mariners, etc., by Tobias, Gentleman, Fisherman and
Mariner. 1614. Harleian Misc., Vol. III.

Evelyn, John. Diary of. Ed. by Wm. Bray. 1906. 10854 f. 11.

Exeter. Articles to be enquired of by the Churchwardens.
1636. 698 n. 20 (19).

Eyre, Captain Adam. A Dyurnall. 1646. *Surtees Society*,
    Vol. LXV. *Durham* 1877. **R. ac.** 8045/53.

Falkland, Lady Letice Vi-countess. The Virtuous, Holy,
    Christian Life and Death of the late, by John Duncon.
                 London 1653. **701 b. 12.**

Fanshawe, Lady. Memoirs of. Wife of Sir Richard
    Fanshawe, Bart. *London* 1905. **012207 i.**

Fell, Sarah. Swarthmoor Household Accounts.

Ferguson, R. S. Municipal Records of the City of Carlisle.
               Carlisle 1887. **R. ac.** 5630/5.

Fiennes, Celia. Through England on a Side Saddle in the
    time of William and Mary. Being the Diary of C. F.
              London 1888. **10854 g. 23.**

Firmin, Thomas. The Life of. *London* 1698. **857 h. 26.**

———— Some Proposals for the imploying of the Poor,
    especially in and about the City of London.
              London 1678. **1027 i. 32.**

Fitzherbert, Sir Anthony. Book of Husbandrye. 1555. **969 a. 32 (1).**

Foulis, Sir John, of Ravelston. Account Book of. 1671-1707.
              Edinburgh 1894. **R. ac.** 8256.

Fox, F. F. Some Account of the Merchant Taylors, Bristol.
             Bristol 1880. **10352 l. 17.**

Further Considerations for encouraging the woollen Manu-
    facturers of this Kingdom. **1852 d. 1 (41).**

Gentlemen's Magazine. May, 1834. Vol. I., Letter to
    Lord Althorp on the Poor Laws by Equitas.

Gibbs, A. E. Corporation Records—St. Albans.
             St. Albans 1890. **10351 cc. 56.**

Grasier's Complaint. *London* 1726. **712 G. 16.**

Guilding, J. M. Reading Records. 1892. **2366 d. 4.**

Hale, Sir Matthew. Method Concerning Relief and
    Employment of the Poor. *London* 1699. **1027 i. 18 (1).**

———— Discourse touching Provision for the Poor.

Hamilton, A. H. A. Quarter Sessions Records, Queen
    Elizabeth to Queen Anne. 1878. **6006 a. 14.**

Hardy, W. J. Hertford County Records, 1581-1698.
             Hertford 1905. **010360 K. 7.**

———— Middlesex County Records. 1905. **5805 d. f. 2.**

Harl, MSS. 2054, 2105, relating to City of Chester.

Harley, Letters of the Lady Brilliana. *Intro. and notes by*
    Thos. Taylor Lewis. *London* 1853. **R. ac.** 8113/56

Haynes, John. Great Britain's Glory, or an account of the Great Numbers of Poor employed in the woollen and silk manufactures. *London* 1715. **1029 a. 6 (3).**

———— View of the Present State of the Clothing Trade in England. *London* 1706. **1029 a. 6 (2).**

Heath, J. B. Some account of the Worshipful Company of Grocers of the City of London. *London* 1854. **1302 m. 2.**

Herbert, Wm. History of the Twelve Great Livery Companies of London. 1836.

Heylyn, Peter, D.D. The Historical and Miscellaneous Tracts of; and an account of the life of the Author. *London* 1681. **479 d. 11.**

———— Cyprianus Anglicus. 1668. **C82 f. 2.**

———— Voyage of France. 1673. **10170 aaa. 8.**

Heywood, Rev. Oliver, 1630-1702. His autobiography, diaries, anecdote and event books, *ed. by J. Horsfall Turner.* 1882. **4907 e. 4.**

Historical MSS. Commission 14 Rep. App. VIII.

———— Various Collections. Vol. I.

———— ———— Vol. IV.

Hoare, Sir R. C. History of Modern Wiltshire. Old and New Sarum or Salisbury. *London* 1843.

Holdsworth, W. S. A History of Eng. Law. 1903.

Holroyd, Joseph, cloth factor, and Sam. Hill, Clothier, Letter Books of. *Halifax* 1900. **7958 h.**

Howard, Lord William of Naworth Castle. Selections from the Household Books of. *Surtees Society, Vol. LXVIII. Durham* 1878. **R. ac. 8045/55.**

Howell, James. Familiar Letters. *London* 1754. **G. 2118.**

Humble Petition and Case of the Tobacco Pipe Makers of the City of London and Westminster. 1695. **816 m. 12.**

Humble Petition of many thousands of Courtiers', Citizens', Gentlemen's and Tradesmen's wives, etc. *Feb.* 10, 1641. **669 f. 4 (59).**

Humble Petition of the Master, Wardens and Assistants of the Company of Silk Throwers, London. **816 m. 13 (115).**

Hunter, Joseph. History and Topography of Ketteringham. *Norwich* 1851. **10351 h. 10.**

Hutchinson, Memoirs of the Life of Colonel, written by his widow, Lucy. *Ed. by C. H. Firth.* 1906. **12207 p.p.**

Irish Friend. Vol. IV. Account of remvarkable visions and passages of John Adams, of Yorkshire.

James, John. History of the Worsted Manufacture in
England. *London* 1857. **2270 bb. 16.**

Johnson, Rev. A. H. History of the Worshipful Company of
Drapers of London. 1914. **W.P. 3016.**

Jonson, Ben. Plays. 1756. **673 f. 13-19.**

Josselin, Rev. Ralph. The Diary of. 1616-1683, *ed. for the
Royal Historical Society by E. Hockcliffe.* 1908. **R. ac. 8118/17.**

Jupp, Ed. B. Historical Account of the Worshipful Company
of Carpenters of the City of London.
London 1887. **10350 dd. 17.**

King, Gregory (Rouge Dragon). Natural and Political Obser-
vations and Conclusions upon the state and condition of
England, 1696. *Ed. by G. Chalmers.*
London 1910. **1137 k. 27.**

Lambert, Rev. J. Malet. 2,000 years of Gild Life, Kingston-
upon-Hull. **2240 f. 9.**

Lamond, Eliz. Discourse of the Common Weal of this Realm
of England. First printed in 1581.
Cambridge 1893. **8009 aaa. 33.**

Lansdowne MSS. 161 fo. 127. Letter from Mayor of Southampton to Sir J. Cæsar *re* suit of Rachell Tierry.

———— 351 fo. 18 b. A Project for Mounts of Piety.

Latimer, John. Annals of Bristol. *Bristol* 1900. **2367 bb. 1.**

Leach, Arthur F. Beverley Town Documents. *Selden
Society, Vol. xiv.* *London* 1900. **R. ac. 2176.**

Leader, John Daniel. Extracts from the earliest book of
Accounts belonging to the Town Trustees of Sheffield.
1566-1707. *Sheffield* 1879. **8228 aa. 11.**

———— Records of the Burgery of Sheffield, commonly
called the Town Trust. *London* 1897. **010358 f. 63.**

Leader, Robert Eadon. History of the Company of Cutlers
in Hallamshire. *Sheffield* 1905. **1889 e. 10.**

Leland, John. The Itinerary of, 1535-1543. *Ed. by L.
Toulmin Smith.* *London* 1907. **2366 d. 6.**

Linnen and Woollen Manufactory discoursed, with the Nature
of Companies and Trade in General.
London 1691. **712 m. 1 (14).**

Lipson, E. An Introduction to the Economic History of
England. I. the Middle Ages. *London* 1915. **W.P. 2753.**

Little Red Book of Bristol. *Ed. by F. B. Bickley.* **10370 h. 22.**

Lyon, John. History of Town and Port of Dover.
Dover 1813. **191 b. 6.**

Manchester Court Leet Records. **1887.**

Martindale, Adam, The Life of, written by himself. *Ed. by Richard Parkinson. Cheetham Society, Vol. IV.* 1845. **R. ac. 8120.**

McMath, James, M.D. The Expert Midwife. 1694. **7581 de. 19.**

Mayo, C. H. Municipal Records of the Borough of Dorchester. Dorset. *Exeter* 1908. **010360 k. 11.**

Monthly Meeting Minute Books of the Society of Friends, Horselydown and Peele.

Mournfull Cryes of many thousand Poore Tradesmen, 1647.
669 f. 11 (116).

Murray, Lady Mary, of Stanhope. Memoirs of Lives and Characters of the Rt. Hon. Geo. Baillie of Jerviswood, and of Lady Grisell Baillie. *Edinburgh* 1822. **614 g. 29.**

Nash, T. History and Antiquities of Worcester. 1781.

Nicholas Papers. Correspondence of Sir Edward Nicholas, Secretary of State. *Ed. by G. F. Warner.*
Camden Society 1886. **R. ac. 8113/127.**

Nicholson, Dame Magdalen, widow of Sir Gilbert Elliot, first Baronet of Stobbs, by Alexander O. Curle. Some notes of the Account Book of. *In Proceedings of the Society of Antiquaries of Scotland.* 1904-1905. Vol. *XXXIX., pp.* 120-132. **R. ac. 5770. 2.**

Nottingham, Records of the Borough of. *London* 1889. **2366 d. 1.**

Osborne, Dorothy. Letters to Sir William Temple. *Ed. by E. A. Parry.* **10921 bbb. 34.**

Overall, W. H. Analytical Index to the Series of Records known as the Remembrancia, preserved among the Archives of the City of London. 1579-1664.
London 1878.

———— Some account of the Company of Clockmakers of the City of London. *London* 1881. **10349 gg. 11.**

Pechey, John. Fellow of the Colledge of Physicians. The Compleat Midwife's practice enlarged.
London 1698. **778 b. 44.**

Pepys, Samuel. Diary and Correspondence. *Ed. by* Rev. Mynors Bright. *London* 1875. **100854 ee. 1.**

Petty, Dorothy, the case of, in Relation to the Union Society, at the White Lyon by Temple Bar, whereof she is Director. 1710. **816 m. 10/82.**

Phipps, Thomas, Esq. His Proposal for Raising 1,000,000 of Pounds Sterling Yearly. 1712. **8223 e. 9 (60).**

Poor out-cast Children's Song and Cry. *London* 1653. **669 f. 16 (93).**

Powell, John. The Assize of Bread. *London* 1600. **C. 40 d. 54.**

The Proverb Crossed or a new Paradox maintained, etc.,
Being a Full Clear and Distinct answer to a Paper of an
English Gentleman, who endeavours to demonstrate
that it is for the Interest of England, that the Laws
against the Transportation of Wooll should be repealed.
London 1677. **712 g. 16 (16)**.

Pseudonismus, Considerations concerning Common-fields and
Inclosures.   1654. **E. 719 (9)**.

Ramsey, Wm. History of Worshipful Company of Glass-
sellers of London.   1898. **8248 g. 19**.

Rawdon, Marmaduke, of York, the Life of. *Ed. by Richard
Davies. Camden Society, Vol. LXXXV.* **R. ac. 8113/80**

Raynold, Thomas. The byrth of Mankynde, otherwyse
named the woman's booke, newly set furth, corrected
and augmented.   *London* 1545. **1177 h. 1**.

Reasons for a Limited Exportation of Wooll. 1677. **712 g. 16 (14)**.

Reasons humbly offered to the Honourable House of Commons by the Leather-dressers and Glovers.   **816 m. 13 (39)**.

Remarks upon Mr. Webber's Scheme and the Draper's
Pamphlet.   1741. **1029 d. 4 (5)**.

Report of Commission on Decay of Clothing Trade. 1622.
                                        Stowe **554 fo. 45-49**.

Report of the Commissioners on the Condition of the Hand-
loom weavers, 1841. Mr. Chapman's Report.

Riley, H. T. Chronicles of the Mayors and Sheriffs of
London, 1188-1274.   *London* 1863. **9510 h. 12**.

———— Memorials of London and London Life. 1868.

Riley, W. H. Translation of the Liber Albus, of the City
of London. Compiled 1419, by John Carpenter, clerk,
and Richard Whittington, Mayor. *London* 1861. **9510 f. 22**.

Rockley, Francis, Esq., Presenteth that the Revenue of Excise.
                                        816 m. 6 (2).

Rogers, J. E. Thorold. History of Agriculture and Prices.
                                Oxford 1866-1902.

———— Oxford City Documents.   1891. **R. ac. 8126/10**.

Rogers, Timothy, M.A. The Character of a Good Woman,
both in a Single and Marry'd State, in a Funeral Discourse on Prov. 31, 10, occasion'd by the Decease of Mrs.
Elizabeth Dunton.   *London* 1697. **1417 b. 29**.

Rolls of Parliament.

Salford, The Portmote or Court Leet Records of the Borough
or Town and Royal Manor of, 1597-1669.
Cheetham Society 1902. *Vol. xlvi. new series.*   **R. ac. 8120,**

Scheme to prevent the running of Irish Wools to France.
By a Merchant of London. *London* 1743. **1029 d. 4** (3).

Second Humble Address from the Poor Weavers and Manufacturers to the Ladies. **816 m. 14** (84).

Sharp, Jane. The Midwives Book or the whole art of Midwifery discovered, by Mrs. Jane Sharp, Practioner in the
art of Midwifery above thirty years. *London* 1671. **1177 b. 19.**

Shaw's, Mrs., Innocency restored and Mr. Clendon's
Calumny retorted, notwithstanding his late Triumphing,
by sundry Depositions, making out more than ever she
by Discourse or writing did positively charge upon him.
London 1653. **E. 730 596** (8).

Short Essay upon Trade in General, etc., by a Lover of his
Country. *London* 1741. **1029 d. 4** (2).

Smith, L. Toulmin. English Gilds. 1870. **R. ac. 9925/33.**

Smith's Book of Accounts, Chester, 1574. **Harl. MSS. 2054 fo. 22.**

Smyth, Richard, The Obituary of. Secondary of the poultry
Compter, London; being a catalogue of all such persons
as he knew in their life. *Ed. by Sir Henry Ellis.*
Camden Society, 1849. **R. ac. 8113/44.**

Smythe, W. Dumville. Historical Account of the Worshipful Company of Girdlers, London. *London* 1905. **8248 e. 44.**

Somerset Quarter Sessions Records. *Ed. by Rev. E. N.
Bates Harbin.* 1913. **R. ac. 8133/17.**

Sowerby, Leo. Ladies Dispensatory, containing the nature,
virtues and qualities of all Herbs and simples usefull in
Physick reduced into a methodical order, for their more
ready use in any sicknesse, or other accident of the Body.
London 1651. **E. 1258.**

State Papers. Domestic Series (S.P.D.).

Statutes at Large.

Stone, Jolley. Court Precedents. 1673, **Harl. MSS. 1628.**

Stopes, Mrs. C. C. Shakespeare's Warwickshire Contemporaries. 1897. **11765 d. 17.**

Stow, John. Survey of the cities of London and Westminster. Written at first MDXCVIII., brought down from the
year 1633 to the present time by John Strype.
London 1720. **1791 d. 5.**

Strood, Churchwarden's Acc. Book. 1555-1763. **Add. MSS. 36937.**

Sussex Archeological Collections.
Account Book of Cowden. Vol. XX.
Burrell, Timothy, Journal of. Vol. III.
Danny Papers. Vol. X.
East Sussex Parochial Documents. Vol. IV.

Everenden and Frewen Account Books. Vol. IV.

Hastings Documents. Vol. XXIII.

Herstmonceux Castle House Accounts. Vol. XLVIII.

Mayfield Overseer's Accounts. Vol. XVIII.

Moore, Rev. Giles, Journal of. Vol. I.

Stapley, Rich., Diary of. Vol. II.

Taylor, Randall. A Discourse of the Growth of England in Populousness and Trade since the Reformation.
1689. **712 m. 1 (13).**

Tawney, R. H. The assessment of Wages in England by the Justices of the Peace—*in the vierteljahrschrift für Sozial und Wirtschaftsgeschichte. XI. Band Drittes Heft and Viertes Heft.* 1913.

Thornton, Mrs. Alice. of East Newton, Co. York. Autobiography. *Surtees Society, Vol. LXII.* 1873 **R. ac. 8045/50**

Tingey, J. C. Assessment of Wages for Norfolk. *English Historical Review, Vol. XIII.*

——— Records of the City of Norwich.
Norwich 1906. **2368 cc. 4.**

Trade of England. Revived and the abuses thereof Rectified.
London 1681. **712 g. 16 (20).**

True Account how Mr. Reading's House at Santoft happened to be Burnt. **816 m. 10/112.**

True Case of the Scots Linen Manufacture. **816 m. 13 (55).**

Verney, F. P. Memoirs of the Verney Family during the Civil Wars. *London* 1892. **2407 f. 12.**

Vives, office and duetie of an husband. Trans. by Thos. Paynell. 1550. **G. 10325.**

Watson, Wm. The Clergyman's Law. 1747. **516 m. 10.**

Weavers True Case, or the wearing of Printed Calicoes and Linnen Destructive to the Woollen and Silk Manufacturers. 1719. **T. 1814 (8).**

Welch, Charles. History of the Worshipful Company of Pewterers of the City of London. *London* 1902. **8248 f., 15.**

Welford, Richard. History of Newcastle and Gateshead.
London 1885. **2367 bb. 7.**

Wilkinson, Robert. The Merchant Royal, or woman a ship, etc. in conjugal duty, set forth in a collection of ingenious and delightful wedding sermons. Original ed., 1607.
London 1732. **4454 b. 9.**

Wycherley, Wm. Plays. *London* 1735. **644 a. 19.**

Yonge, Walter. Diary at Colyton and Axminster, Co. Devon. 1604-1628. *Ed. by Geo. Roberts.*
Camden Society 1848. **R. ac. 8113/41.**

WAGES ASSESSMENTS.

County.		Reference.
Buckingham	..	Hamilton, A. H. A., Quarter Sessions Records from Queen Eliz. to Queen Anne.
Cardigan ..	..	Dyson, Humfrey., Proclamations of Queen Elizabeth. G6463 (331b.).
Chester	..	Harleian MSS., 2054 (3) f. 5 2b.
Derbyshire ..	..	Cox, J. C., Three Centuries of Derbyshire Annals.
Devonshire ..	..	Hamilton, A. H. A., Quarter Sessions Record.
Dorsetshire ..	..	Sussex Archeological Collections, Vol. I., p. 75.
Essex	..	Ruggles, Thomas, History of the Poor, pp. 123-5. 1027 i. 1.
Gloucestershire	..	Rogers, J. E. Thorold, History of Agriculture and Prices. Vol. VI., p. 694.
Hertfordshire	..	Hardy, W. J., Hertford County Records.
Kent	..	Rogers, J. E. T., History of Agriculture and Prices. Vol. VII., p. 623.
Kingtson-upon-Hull		Dyson, Humfrey, Proclamations. G6463 (77).
Lancashire ..	..	Rogers, J. E. T., History of Agriculture and Prices. Vol. VI., p. 689.
Lincolnshire	..	Hist. MSS. Com., Duke of Rutland, Vol. I., p. 460.
London	..	Lord Mayor's Proclamations. 21 h. 5 (61).
Middlesex ..	..	Hardy, W. J., Middlesex County Records.
Norfolk	..	English Historical Review, Vol. XIII., p. 522.
Rutland	..	Archeologia, Vol. XI., pp. 200-7.
St. Albans ..	..	Gibbs, Corporation Records.
Somerset	..	Somerset Quarter Sessions Records.
Suffolk	..	Cullum, Sir John., History of Hawstead.
Warwickshire	..	Archeologia, Vol. XI., p. 208.
Wiltshire ..	..	Hist. MSS. Com. Var. Coll., Vol. I., p. 163.
Worcestershire	..	Hist. MSS. Com. Var. Coll., Vol. I., p. 323.
Yorkshire :		
East Riding	..	Rogers, J. E. T., History of Agriculture and Prices, Vol. VI., p. 686.
North Riding	..	Atkinson, J. C., Yorkshire, North Riding Quarter Sessions Records, Vols. VI. and VII.

INDEX.

Agriculture, 9, 42-92 *passim*, 93, 150, 292 *seq.*, *see* Apprentice, Capitalism, Dairy, Farmer, Husbandman, Labourer, Pig-keeping, Poultry-keeping, Spinning, Wages, Wage-earner, Wife, Yeoman ; *conditions for rearing children*, 43, 92.

Alehouse, 91 *seq.*, 101, 225, 229, 231-233 *passim* ; *see* Brewing, Innkeeper; *livelihood for widows and infirm people*, 230-232.

Alewife, 222, 232 ; *see* Brewing.

Apothecaries, 184, 259-263 *passim*, *see* Doctor, Gild.

Apprentice, 6, 26, 112, 144, 156, 185, 195, 211, 213, 293 ; *agriculture*, 59 ; *Gild trades, boys*, 163, 165 *seq.*, 177, 185, 187, 260, *girls*, 10, 150, 166, 175 *seq.*, 185, 195, 261, 298 ; *other trades, boys*, 159, 185, 214, 226, 261, *girls*, 151, 194, 217, 220, 293 ; *retail trades*, 200 *seq.* ; *silk trade*, 138, 141 *seq.* ; *weavers*, 104 *seq*, 122 ; *duties of apprentices*, 5, 157 ; *restriction of numbers*, 10, 156, 188, 298 ; *apprentices of women*, 162, 168 *seq.*, 173, 179, 194, 220 ; *of widows*, 104, 162, 168 *seq.*, 173 *seq.*, 183, 187 *sea.*, 190, 293.

Apprenticeship, 146, 151, 156, 160 *seq.*, 165, 177, 184, 191, 194, 196, 200 *seq.*, 212-214 *passim*, 234, 261, 269 *seq.*, 298, 301.

Apprentice Trade, 106.

Aristocracy, *see* Capitalist ; *character of women*, 38-41, 253, 289, 296 *seq.*, 305 *seq.* ; *confinements*, 267 *seq.* ; *occupations*, 14-27, 35, 38, 53 *seq.*, 253, 255 *seq.*

Armourers and Brasiers, 178, 183 *seq.* See Gild.

Assheton Nicholas, 280.

Astell Mary, 38.

Assize, *of beer*, 224 ; *of bread*, 211.

Badger, 204 *seq.*

Baillie, Lady Grisell, 16, 68, 229.

Bakers, 8, 92, 202, 208-215 *passim* ; *corporations of*, 212 *seq.* ; *restrictions on*, 210, 211, 215 ; *women bake for domestic purposes*, 47, 50, 210, 214 ; *for sale*, 30, 213, 214 ; *wife assists husband*, 211 *seq.*, 215.

Baptist, 240.

Barber-surgeons, 259-263 *passim*, 265, 276, 284 ; *see* Gild.

Barrymore, Lady, 14.

Bedell, Mrs. Eliz., 256.

Best, 60-62 *passim*, 78.

Beverley, 180, 183, 211, 221 *seq.*

Binder, 161, 167.

Birth-rate, 4, 43, 86 *seq.*, 305.

Bleacher, 129, 145.

Bookseller, 161, 168.

Bourgeois, Mme. Louise, 275, 284.

Borough, 209, *see* Corporations.

Brathwaite, Richard, 29, 53.

Brewing, 8, 11, 209, 221-233 *passim* ; *see* Alehouse, Ale-wife, Apprentices, Capitalism, Domestic, Gild ; *Brewster* 11, 155, 221 *seq.*, 229 ; *Common Brewers*, 223-227 *passim*, 230 ; *Fellowship of*, 223-226 ; *for domestic purposes*, 5, 8, 47, 50, 210, 223 ; *for retail*, 210, 222-230 ; *for wages*, 229 *seq.*

Bristol, 103, 134, 182, 185, 191, 232.

Burford, Rose de, 140.

Burling, 105 *seq.*, 132, 145.

Bury, 222.

Bury St. Edmunds, 227.

Business affairs of family, 41, *see* Family ; *managed by wife*, 16, 21 *seq.*, 54 *seq.*, *superior capacity of Dutch women*, 36-38 *passim* ; *wife unequal to*, 20, 22 *seq.* ; *women's capacity for*, 20, 34, 38 *seq.*

Butcher, 155, 202, 209 *seq.*, 216-219 *passim*, 221 ; *see* Apprentices ; *selling wool*, 107 ; *wage-earners*, 219.

Buttons, 142, 144.

Butter, 8, 49, *see* Dairy.

Cane-chair bottoming, 195.

Capitalism, 6, 300, 308; *see* Capitalistic Organisation, Family Industry, Gilds, Industrialism, Linen, Silk, Textile Trades, Woollen; *definition of*, 7; demand for labour, 90 *seq.*; *effect on Domestic Industry*, 8, 11, 94; effect on Family Industry, 8, 10, 11, 94, 142, 156, 165, 196, 297; *effect on Marital Relations*, 40 *seq.*, 158, 167, 197, 235, 296, 299, 301 *seq.*; *effect on Motherhood*, 8 *seq.*, 11 *seq.*, 306; effect on Social Organisation, 8 *seq.*, 40, 148, 300, 306 *seq.*; *effect on women's economic position*, 8 *seq.*, 10, 92, 94, 96, 98, 145 *seq.*, 165, 167, 196, 235, 295-299 *passim*, 301, 302, 307; *effect on women's morale and physique*, 41; *in agriculture*, 43, 56, 92; *in brewing*, 11, 226, 230; *in Crafts and Trades*, 156, 158, 165,196.

Capitalists, *see* Aristocracy; *Definition of*, 14; *idleness of wives and daughters*, 10, 38, 41, 50, 235, 296-298 *passim*, 305; *women's activity as Capitalists*, 14-41 *passim*.

Capitalistic organisation, 13, 94, 146, 196, 236; *see* Capitalism, Industrialism.

Carding, *employment for poor*, 116, 132; *men*, 102, 116; *women*, 99, 108, 120 *seq.*, 141.

Card-maker, 190.

Carlisle, 44, 53, 153, 201, 203, 211, 215.

Carpenter, 170-178 *passim* 187, 195; *see* Companies.

Carrier of letters, 63.

Cellier, Mrs., 195, 269, 273-276 *passim*.

Chamberlain, Dr. Hugh, 281, 283.

Chamberlain, Peter, 272 *seq.*

Chandler, *wax and tallow*, 155, 195, 200, 202.

Chapmen, 109, 155, 206.

Cheese, 8, 49, 53, 208.

Chester, 155, 181, 211, 217, 232.

Child, Sir J., 36.

Child's coate seller, 176.

Children, 22, 45, 88, 147 *seq.*, 192-194 *passim*, 196, 256; *see* Agriculture, Apprentices, Capitalism, Cost of Living, Education, Family, Father, Housing, Husband, Infant Mortality Mother, Nursing, Poor, Settlement, Wages, Wage-earners, Widow, Wife; *attending gild dinners*, 180; *employment in agriculture*, 59 *seq.*, 64; *in textile manufacture*, 9, 97 *seq.*, 106, 108, 112-114 *passim*, 125, 130-134

passim, 140-144 *passim*, 292; *reduce women's wage-earning capacity*, 68 *seq.*, 92, 136, 147; *right to work in father's trade*, 156, 165, *seq.*, 185, *share in family property*, 7, 182; *share in supporting family*, 12, 72, 79, 105, 192 *seq.*, 293; *under-feeding of*, 64, 86 *seq.*, 118.

Child-birth, 46, 267, 273, 276, 283, 285; *see* Aristocracy, Common-people, Midwifery.

Church, 236-242; *supervision of midwives*, 277 *seq.*

Clockmakers, 187.

Clothiers, 98-102 *passim*, 108-112 *passim*, 117-124 *passim*, 141, 147; *see* Poor; *force workpeople to take goods for wages*, 117 *seq.*; *women*, 9, 100-102 *passim*, 124.

Cloth-workers, 184.

Coal-owner, 34.

Common-people, 3, 257, 305; *definition of*, 148, 253; *child-birth*, 267-269 *passim*; *women's position controll d by necessity*, 41.

Companies, 10, 25-27 *passim*, 189, 207, 212, 259, 260 *seq.*; *see* Corporations, Gilds, Apothecaries, Armourers and Braziers, Bakers, Barber-surgeons, Binders, Book-sellers, Brewsters, Butchers, Carpenters, Clockmakers, Clothworkers, Cutlers, Drapers, Dyers, Embroiderers, Fishmongers, Fullers, Girdlers, Glass-sellers, Glovers, Goldsmiths, Gold-wire Drawers, Grocers, Joiners, Leather-sellers, Mercers, Merchants, Merchant Taylors, Mid-wives, Painter-Stainers, Pewterers, Physicians, Point-makers, Printers, Publishers, Shoe-makers, Smiths, Stationers, Tailors, Upholsterers, Whit-awers.

Congreve, 3.

Contractors, 31.

Cooking, 11.

Corporations (Municipal), 151, 199-204 *passim*, 209, 212, 218, 224, 263; *see* Boroughs, Companies, Customs, Gilds, Beverley, Bristol, Bury, Bury St. Edmunds, Carlisle, Chester, Dorchester, Exeter, Grimsby, Hull, Kingtson-upon-Hull, Leicester, Lincoln, London, Manchester, Norwich, Nottingham, Newcastle-upon-Tyne, Reading, Rye, Salford, Salisbury, Sandwich, St. Albans, Sheffield, Southampton, Tiverton, **Torksey, York.**

Cost of living, 68-79 *passim*,134; *diet of children*, 68, 71, 223; *servants*, 68; *difference between men, women and children*, 71-73 *passim*, 127; *Family of three Children*, 68, 73.

Cotton trade, 94, 124.

Cowden, parish of, 131, 264, 280.

Cows, 45, 47, 53, 55, 57, 209, 292; *see* Dairy, Milking.

Crafts, 10, 150-197; *see* Gilds, Trades.

Craftsman, 10, 197.

Cromwell family, 18, 69.

Culpeper, Nicholas, 271 *seq*.

Custom (habit), 155, 158-161.

Customs, 160; *see* Corporations; *excise*, 140.

Cutler, 187.

Cutworks, 32.

Dairy, *see* Butter, Cheese, Cows, Milking; *produce for domestic consumption*, 5, 43; *as pin-money*, 54; *supplementing family income*, 55; *women's sphere*, 5, 50, 53, 292.

Dant, Joan, 32 *seq*., 206.

Daughters, 176 *seq*., 197 *seq*., 252, 284; *see* Burling, Education; *employed in parents' trade*,184, *seq*.,195, 200, 217, 298; *enters company by patrimony*, 191, 298; *hired out as weavers*, 103; *sustaining parents*, 115.

Decker, Thos., 158 *seq*.

Defoe, Daniel, 96, 115 *seq*., 156 *seq*.

Distaff, 13, 48, 107, 111.

Doctor, *see* Apothecaries, Barber-surgeons, Physicians, Midwifery.

Domestic Industry, 4 *seq*., 8, 40, 47-49, 151, 210, 254, 302; *see* Baking, Brewers, Capitalism, Dairy, Family Industry, Servants, Spinning, Textile Trades; *definition of*, 4-6 *passim*; *drudgery performed by servants*, 156 *seq*., 294, 304; *effect on women's economic position*, 145, 290, 292; *girls' work*, 11 *seq*.; *men's work*, 5.

Dorchester, 132 *seq*., 185, 200, 217, 261, 263 *seq*.

Drapers, 184, 200; *see* Gild.

Dunning, Richard, 132.

Dyer, 111, 155; *of leather*, 158; *in Ireland*, 18.

Education, 36, 242, 286 *seq*., 295, 302-306 *passim*; *see* Apprentice, Children, Mother, Poor Relief, Teaching; *arithmetic unnecessary for girls*, **52**; *industrial*, 71, 130-135 *passim*; *influence of domestic and family industry*, 40; *institutions*, 239; *medical*, 255, 288; *nurses*, 249; *want of specialised training for girls*, 243, 288, 301, 304.

Embroiderer, 184.

Elizabethan Period, Women of, 2, 3, 9, 38, 41.

Estate Management, 14, 15, 17.

Evelyn, John, 115.

Everenden, 62.

Executrix, 39, 188, 293.

Exeter, 206.

Eyre, Adam, 54.

Farmer, 42-56 *passim*, 108, 155; *see* Agriculture, Capitalism; *definition of*, 43; *demand for labour*, 81, 83, 90, 91; *finds sureties for married labourers*, 83 *seq*.; *preference for unmarried labourers*, 12; *wife's occupation*, 46-50 *passim*, 111, 112; *women's characteristics*, 43 *seq*.

Farrier, 155.

Father, 39, 45, 56, 79, 86, 145, 237; *deserts starving family*, 118, 148; *head of family*, 6, 300; *interest in children*, 5, 54, 160, 295; *profits of family industry vested in father*, 6, 7, 182, 294, 299.

Falkland, The Lady, 18-20 *passim*.

Falkland, The Lady Letice, 241, 251, 256.

Family, 73, 80, 100, 106, 122, 144, 204, 219, 242, 286, 291, 294, 299, 304, 307; *see* Business, Capitalism, Father, Mother, Wages, Wage-earners, Widow, Wife; *basis of social organisation*, 285, 288, 290, 299 *seq*.; *chargeable to Parish*, 80-88 *passim*, 134, 142, 146, 204; *dependence on wages*, 43, 56, 178, *see* Husbandmen, Wage-earners; *size of*, 86 *seq*.; *traditions lost*, 118, 148, 237, 287; Family Industry 6-11 *passim*, 92, 94, 96 *seq*., 102, 142, 151, 156, 165, 192 *seq*., 196, 216, 234, 290, 297, 301 *seq*., 305, *see* Capitalism; Fanshawe, Lady, 22.

Fell, Sarah, 17, 51, 255.

Felt-maker, 190.

Fiennes, Celia, 62, 73, 124, 233.

Firmin, Thomas, 135-137 *passim*.

Fishmonger, 219 *seq*.

Fishwives, 36, 209, 219-221; *oyster-wives*, 202, 220.

Fitzherbert, Sir Anthony, 46-50,129.

Flax, 64, 146, 246, 291 ; *sowing*, 40, 48, 128.

Foulis, Sir John, 32, 280 *seq.*

Foreign Women, *Dutch merchants*, 36 *seq.*, 219 ; *Flanders, workers of woollen cloths*, 103 ; *French midwives*, 268, 275, 284.

Fullers, 121, 145, 155, 157, 189.

Garden, *women's sphere*, 5, 9, 48, 50, 53, 292.

Gardiner, Lady, 15.

Gilds, 10, 141, 150, 154-156 *passim*, 192, 196 ; *see* Apprentice, Capitalism, Companies, Journeyman, Wife ; *admission to*, 160 *seq.*, 176 *seq.*, 179, 191 ; *charters*, 140, 160, 178, 181-183 *passim* ; 187, 259 ; *development into Companies*, 158 ; *functions, religious, social and for trade purposes* 154, 160, 171-181 *passim* ; *revilings*, 172, 182, 183 ; *rules*, 157 *seq.*, 179 *seq.*, 187 ; *women's position in*, 150 154-191 *passim* ; *in woman's trade*, 195 *seq.*

Girdlers, 185, 189 ; *see* Companies.

Glass-sellers, 187 ; *see* Companies.

Glovers, 181, 185, 191 *seq.* ; *see* Companies.

Gold and Silver Thread, 26, 143-145 *passim* ; *pauper trade*, 145 *seq.*

Goldsmith, 184 ; *see* Companies.

Gold-wire Drawers, *see* Gold and Silver Thread.

Grimsby, 31.

Grocers, 179, 184, 201 *seq.*, 260 ; *see* Companies.

Haberdasher, 200.

Hale, Sir Matthew, 79.

Harber, Sylvia, 122 *seq.*

Harley, Brilliana Lady, 15 *seq.*

Harley, Sir E., 16.

Harrowing, 87.

Hawkers, 204-207 *passim*.

Hay-making, 49, 62.

Hellyard, Elizabeth, 34 *seq.*

Heylyn, Peter, 54 *seq.*, 239, 278.

Heywood, Oliver, 87, 129.

Hobbes, 258, 303.

Holroyd, Joseph, 30.

Home, 4 ; *see* Industrial Revolution ; *includes workshop*, 7 *seq.*, 156-160 *passim*, 294 ; *men's sphere as well as women's*, 303 ; *opportunities for production in home*, 147 ; *wage-earners work away from home*, 296.

Howell, James, 37, 53.

Hospitals, 243-249 ; *see* Nurses.

Household, *accounts*, 17 ; *affairs*, 157 ; *of craftsmen*, 158 *seq.* ; *size of*, 15, 50, 99.

Housing, 73-81 *passim*.

Huckster, 155.

Hull, 30, 212 *seq.*

Husband, 10, 12, 15, 17, 18, 20, 22-24 *passim*, 34, 39, 46, 49, 88 *seq.*, 95, 118, 171-173 *passim*, 212, 228, 233 *seq.*, 240, 306 ; *see* Wife ; *acquires wife's rights*, 161, 213 ; *assists wife*, 199, 214, 301 ; *companionship with wife*, 160, 183, 301-303 *passim*, 306 ; *dependence on wife's assistance*, 16, 36 *seq.*, 46, 153, 165, 194, 196, 211 ; *ill-treatment of wife*, 191 ; *independence of wife*, 41 197 ; *meddles not with wife's trade*, 231 *seq.* ; *not responsible for wife's debts*, 151 *seq.*

Husbandman, 3, 56-64 *passim* ; *definition of*, 43, 57 ; *girls' environment*, 87 ; *independence*, 56 ; *rent*, 57 ; *wages, men*, 59-62 *passim*, *women*, 60-63 *passim* ; *wife's occupation*, 60-64 *passim*, 111 *seq.* ; *wife as wet-nurse*, 58 ; *women's characteristics*, 58 *seq.*

Hutchinson, Mrs. Lucy, 23 *seq.*, 255, 263.

Hutchinson, Colonel, 23 *seq.*, 252.

Keeper of tennis court, 25.

King, Gregory, 55, 80, 86.

Kingston-upon-Hull, 103, 181.

Knitting, 18, 26, 133.

Idleness, 138, 253.

Industrialism, 94, 123 ; *see* Capitalism ; *attempted introduction of factory system*, 99, 124.

Industrial Revolution, 8 *seq.*

Industry, *see* Domestic, Family, Capitalism.

Infant Mortality, 58, 86, 273, 276, 283, 305.

Inn-keeper, 155, 209, 213, 225, 227, 233.

Insurance Office, 33.

Ireland, 18, 126.

Ironmonger, 155.

Joiners, 181 ; *see* Companies.

Jonson, Ben, 28, 257.

Josselin, the Rev. R., 50, 257.

Journey-man, 156, 159, 180, 212, 297 *seq.* ; *see* Widows ; *employed by women*, 174, 185, 189, 261 *organisation of*, 10, 166; *wives and daughters excluded*, 10, 166, 197, 234, 298, 301; *wife unpaid servant*, 10.

Labourer, *see* Farmer, Husbandman, Wage-earner, Wages.
Laundry, *maid*, 50; *work*, 5, 13, 49, 135, 155.
Law, 236 *seq.*
Lace, *see* Ireland; *bone-lace*, 142, 144.
Leather-sellers, 158, 185; *see* Companies.
Leicester, 210, 222 *seq.*
Leland, 99.
Lincoln, 157.
Linen manufacture, 94, 96, 124-137 *passim*, 138; *see* Drapers, Flax, Poor, Spinning, Weaving; *appropriateness to women*, 128 *seq.*; *capitalistic*, 124, 136; *company*, 126-128 *passim*, 136; *domestic*, 5, 40, 48, 96, 125, 128, 129, 137; *family*, 128; *in Ireland*, 126 *seq.*; *printers*, 126; *in Scotland*, 126, 129; *wages for spinning*, 48, 95 *seq.*, 128-137 *passim*, 146.
London, 29, 31, 33, 131, 135, 138-141 *passim*, 152, 158-195 *passim*, 202, 206, 208, 217, 220, 233, 243-249 *passim*, 258-263 *passim*, 281.

Malt-making, 47, 49 *seq.*, 224-226 *passim*.
Manchester, 206, 213, 218, 221.
Mansell, Lady, 35.
Mantua-making, 195, 234, 293.
Marriage, 191; *see* Poor-relief, Wife, Mother; *confers woman's rights on her husband*, 261; *strengthens man's economic position*, 39.
Married Woman; *see*, Mother, Wife.
Market, 4, 119, 202, 204, 217, 291; *corn-market*, 211; *Farmer's wife attends market*, 49-51; *labour-market*, 145, 167, 298; *price of spinning*, 129; *market spinner*, 107, 109 *seq.*, 113; *town*, 224 *seq.*; *thread, yarn and wool, sold in market*, 107-109 *passim*, 112, 127 *seq.*; *woman*, 135.
Martindale, Adam, 55, 257.
McMath, James, 267, 282.
Medicine, 242, 253-265 *passim*, 286, 288, 294; *see* Poor, Servants; *domestic practice*, 242, 254-257 *passim*; *education of women*, 255, 294; *their exclusion from schools*,

254, 265, 294; *fees*, 262, 264; *Licensed by Bishop*, 276; *professional practice*, 242, 254, 257-259 *passim*, 263 *seq*; *restrictions on women*, 259 *seq.*; *women's skill extended to neighbours*, 255-257 *passim*, 294.
Mercers, 184, 201.
Merchant, 29, 36, 140, 155, 180-184 *passim*; *see* Joan Dant.
Middle-man, 110, 124; *see* Market-spinner.
Midwife, 258; *see* Midwifery; *Baptism by*, 277-279 *passim*; *Fees*, 268, 279-281 *passim*; *Licences*, 272-279 *passim*; *Man-midwife*, 265, 271 *seq.*, 284; *Prosecutions of*, 279.
Midwifery, 242 *seq.*, 265-285, 288; *see* Midwife; *chiefly professional*, 265, *doctor's assistance*, 271, 280-284 *passim*; *French*, 268. 275, 279, 284; *training of women for*, 269-275 *passim*, 288.
Milking, 47.
Mill, 47, 210, 215 *seq.*
Miller, 209, 212, 215 *seq.*; *wages of*, 66.
Milliner, 176, 195, 234, 293.
Milton, John, 240, 304.
Money-lender, 28 *seq.*, *see* Pawnbroker.
Monopolies and patents, 25-28 *passim*.
Moore, Rev. Giles, 252.
Mother, 43, 63 *seq.*, 73, 125, 196, 198, 214; *see* Capitalism, Domestic Industry, Spinning, Wages, Widow, Wife; *desertion of children*, 86; *educating children*, 21, 95, 159, 242, 286, 295; *head of family*, 7, 234, 300; *sharing father's work*, 6 *seq.*; *supporting family*, 12, 29, 55, 64, 78 *seq.*, 114, 178, 192-194 *passim*, 198; *tending children*, 47, 63, 95; *underfeeding*, 87-89 *passim*, 306; *value of productive activity*, 145, 290 *seq.*, 304; *worship of*, 238 *seq.*
Motherhood, *women's capacity for* 8 *seq.*, 58, 87, 305.
Murray, Lady, 16.

Needlework, 13.
Netmaker, 155.
Newcastle-upon-Tyne, 34, 226.
Nicholson, Dame Margaret, 60.
Norwich, 107, 116, 219, 229.
Nottingham, 130, 201, 217, 232.
Nurse, *sick*, 13, 135, 155; *salaries*, 243-246 *passim*, 248, 250 *seq.*
Nursing, 242-253; *see* Poor, Servants.

Ogden, Hester, 164.
Orphan, *see* Children, Poor Relief.
Osborne, Dorothy, 57.

Painter-Stainer, 188.
Paper-maker, 32.
Pauper, *see* Poor.
Pawnbroker, 28 *seq.*, *see* Money-lender.
Pechey, 275.
Pedlar, 32, 204-207 *passim*.
Pepys Samuel, 3, 38 *seq.*, 59, 62, 281, 296 *seq.*
Peronne, Mme., 268.
Petitions, *from women*, 23-27 *passim*, 118, 121, 138; *of married woman objected to*, 77.
Petty, Dorothy, 33 *seq.*
Pewterers, 183, 186 *seq.*, 191, 210, 294; *see* Companies.
Physicians, 259, 262, 265, 271, 275 *seq.*, 284.
Politics, *see* Petitions; *women's interest in*, 23 *seq.*
Pig-keeping, 5, 48, 52 *seq.*, 292.
Pin-maker, 193.
Point-maker, 191.
Poor, *see* Hospitals, Midwife, Silk, Spinning, Wages, Wage-earners; *census of*, 219; *clothiers' poor*, 109; *confinements*, 277, 280; *education of*, 130-134 *passim*; *increased wages*, 115; *medical attendance*, 255 *seq.*, 263-265 *passim*; *not all vagrants*, 135; *nursing*, 243, 251 *seq.*; *relief*, 69-92 *passim*, 118, 129-137 *passim*, 204; *set on work*, 110, 120, 130-137 *passim*; 140, 148; *synonymous with pauper*, 148; *widows and orphans maintained by parish*, 204; *workhouse*, 72, 131-134 *passim*.
Poultry-keeping, 5, 48, 50, 87, 209, 292.
Pregnancy, 24, 72 *seq.*, 82, 89.
Printer, 161-167; *see* Companies.
Professions, 5, 236-289 *passim*; *see* Church, Education, Law, Medicine, Midwifery, Nursing, Teaching; *services*, 4 *seq.*, 294 *seq.*; *women's position in*, 13, 304.
Projector, 28.
Provision Trades, 150, *seq.*, 209-234 *passim*; *see* Alehouse, Alewife, Apprentices, Baker, Brewing, Butcher, Fishwife, Inn-keeper, Malt Making, Miller, Retail Trade, Vintner, Wife, Widow; *women's position in*, 10 *seq.*
Publisher, 167; *see* Companies.
Pulling pease, 61 *seq.*

Quakers, 51, 168, 199, 240; *see* Fell; Adams (*wife of John*), 153; Banks; (*wife of John*), 44; Batt, Mary, 45 *seq.*; Bownas (*wife of Samuel*), 52; Townsend, Will., marriage of, 190.

Rawdon, Marmaduke, 257.
Raynold, 266 *seq.*, 269.
Reading, 85, 132, 189, 203 *seq.*, 213 216, 249 *seq.*
Regrater, 204 *seq.*, 207-209 *passim*, 218 *seq.*
Religion, *independence of married women*, 240.
Restoration Period, *women of*, 2, 9, 38, 41.
Retail Trade, 197-209 *passim*; *see* Chapmen, Badgers, Haberdashers, Hawkers, Pedlars, Regrater, Shopkeepers; *women's position in*, 10 *seq.*, 150 *seq.*, 156, 172, 197, 209, 293.
Rous, Margaret, 17.
Rye, 152 *seq.*

Salford, 52 *seq.*, 84, 212.
Salisbury, 184, 213, 258 *seq.*
Salisbury, Earl of, 25, 111.
Sandwich, 152.
Salt concerns, 17 *seq.*
Scotland, 126, 129.
Scottish, 140.
Semptsress, 155, 175 *seq.*, 202, 221.
Servants, 5 *seq.*, 26, 155 *seq.*, 176, 187, 202, 220, 241; *see* Brewing, Journeyman, Wages, Wages assessments; *diet of*, 68, 88; *dresses* 126; *employed in domestic drudgery*, 5, 157, 196, 292, 294; *employed in spinning*, 125; *farm*, 47, 50, 116, 210, 229; *married*, 81, 88; *scarcity of*, 56; *housekeepers' duties*, 255; *medical attendance on*, 252, 263; *men servants brought up by women*, 141; *of clothiers*, 101; *nursing of*, 251 *seq.*; *shoemaker*, 66, 203; *training of*, 253; *women, scarcity of*, 157.
Sex-jealousy, *an anachronism*, 299; *absence in woollen trade*, 95, 123, *exclusion of women from trades*, 103, 105, 106, 191.
Shakespeare, 3.
Sharp, Jane, 269-271 *passim*.
Shearing, *corn*, 49, 60; *sheep*, 62.
Sheffield, 187.
Shepherd, 62.
Shipping, 29-31 *passim*.

Shoemaker, 155, 158 *seq.*, 184, 202 *seq.*, see Servants

Shopkeeper, 158, 168, 198-209 *passim.*

Silk manufacture, 94, 126, 138-143 ; see Apprentices, Poor, Textiles, Weaving ; *capitalistic,* 142 ; *occupation of gentlewomen,* 10, 138-140 *passim,* 142 ; *refuge of paupers,* 140-142 *passim,* 146 ; *silk-women,* 140 ; *stockings,* 26 *seq.* ; *wages,* 142.

Smith, 155, 189, 210, 259, 294.

Social position of women, 8, 40, 249, 283, 306 *seq.*

Southampton, 101, 195 *seq.*

Spinning, 5 ; see Poor, Linen, Woollen ; *demand for,* 95, 110, 112 *seq.*, 124, 129, 146 ; *domestic industry,* 9, 40, 64, 96, 125, 129, 137, 147, 291 *seq.* ; *employment of poor,* 13, 100, 110 *seq.*, 128-137 *passim,* 146 *seq.*, 209, 291 ; *instruction in,* 13, 111, 130-137 ; *monopoly of women and children,* 93, 102, 145, 292 ; *organisation of,* 107-113, 123 *seq.* ; *resource for mothers,* 9, 13, 63, 95, 151, 209 ; *wages, see* Linen, Woollen ; *withdraws women from agriculture and service,* 112, 115.

Spinner, 18, 102, 110, 113, 117, 120, 128 *seq.*, 141, 221 ; *market spinner,* 107, 109 *seq.*, 113.

Spinster, 95 *seq.*, 107-109 *passim,* 112-136 *passim,* 147, 155, 221 ; *classes of,* 111 *seq.*

Spreading muck, 62.

St. Albans, 202.

Stapley, Richard, 125.

State, 242, 286, 299, 303, 307 *seq.*

Stationers, 158, 161-170 *passim* ; see Companies.

Stumpe, 99 ; see Clothier.

Suckle calves, 47.

Surgeons, see Barber-surgeons.

Surgery, see Medicine.

Tailor, 155, 181.

Tanner, 185.

Thatching, 61.

Taylor, Randall, 58.

Teaching, 242, 265, 286 *seq.*, 294 *seq.*

Textile Trades, 9, 93-149 *passim,* 150 ; see Bleaching, Burling, Capitalism, Carding, Clothiers, Cotton, Domestic Industry, Family Industry, Fuller, Gold and Silver, Knitting, Linen, Silk, Spinning, Spinner, Weaver, Wage-earner, Wages,

Woollen, *industrial organisation of,* 96 ; *proportion of women's labour,* 93 *seq.*, 97 *seq.*, 114, 133 *seq,* 292 ; *proportion of children's labour,* 108, 112, 114, 116, 133 *seq.* ; *women's position in,* 93 *seq.*, 95, 146.

Thierry, Rachel, 100 *seq.*

Thornton, Mrs. Alice, 16.

Tiverton, 227.

Tobacco-pipe makers, 192.

Torksey, 222.

Trades, see Crafts, Provision, Retail Textile ; *women's occupation in,* 10, 146, 293.

Turbeville, Mrs. Mary, 258 *seq.*

Upholsterer, 184, 195.

Vantrollier (wife of Thos.), 163.

Verney, Lady, 20 ; *Sir Edmund,* 15 ; *Sir Ralph,* 15, 20, 258.

Vintners, 209, 233 *seq.*

Village Community, 56, 253 ; *disintegration of,* 148 ; *vigorous stock of,* 42 ; *women's influence in,* 148.

Vives, 37.

Wage-earner, 4, 6, 64-92 *passim,* 99 ; see Agriculture, Birth-rate, Butcher, Capitalism, Children, Infant Mortality, Journeyman, Marriage, Motherhood, Spinning, Silk, Textile Manufactures, Wages, Widow, Wife, Woollen ; *definition of,* 43, 65 ; *children of,* 86 *seq.* ; *class of undesirables,* 90 ; *combination among,* 121-124 *passim,* 298, 301 ; *family income,* 65-69 *passim,* 71, 79 *seq.*, 178 ; *insolvency,* 80-92 *passim,* 129, 146-149, 209, 293 ; *numbers of,* 4, 90 *seq.*, 305 ; *wife of,* 9 *seq.*, 76-89 *passim,* 235 ; *her earning capacity,* 68 *seq.*, 89, 92, 147 *seq.*, 209, 292 ; *her virtual exclusion from skilled trades,* 298.

Wages, 35, 59, 65, 100, 301 ; see Brewing, Carpenters, Doctors, Husbandmen, Linen, Nurse (sick), Midwife, Miller, Poor, Spinning, Silk, Woollen ; *assessments,* 50, 59 *seq.*, 62, 65-67 *passim,* 72, 83, 90, 210, 293 ; *di erence between family and individual wages,* 7, 296, 299 ; *day labourers, men,* 9, 56, 60-62 *passim,* 65 *seq.*, 96 ; *day labourers, women,* 9, 60-66 *passim,* 68, 72, 89 ; *servants, men,* 50, 56, 65 *seq.* ;

servants, women, 50, 65, 157; married men, 65 seq., not expected to keep family, 12, 86, 90, 293; relation to cost of living, 10, 68 seq., 79 seq., 83, 89, 95, 130, 134-137 passim, 145, 178; women's, do not represent value of their work, 64, 137, 145, 291 seq., 304.

Weaver, 155, 259; see Apprentices, assault women, 126; complaints against clothiers, 114, 117-123 passim, domestic purposes, 40, 64, 125; linen, 18, 124 seq., 128, 136; women, 129; woollen, 18, 99, 111, 116; women, 102-106, 145; forbidden to weave cloth, 103; widow, 103 seq.; ribbons and tape; 104; silk, 138, 141; Wages, 120, 149.

Webber, 102, 221,; see Weaver.

Webster, 102, 155, 221; see Weaver.

Weeding, 62, 89.

Wet-nurse, 26, 58.

Whipping dogs out of Church, 63.

Whit-awers, 191.

Winchcombe, John, 99.

Winnowing, 49.

Widow, 29, 33, 45, 86, 100, 122, 129, 137, 156, 171, 177, 189 seq., 195, 200, 201, 204 seq., 209, 213, 216, 218, 227, 230, 249-252 passim, 264, 268; see Apprentices, Housing, Journeymen, Poor Relief, Weaver; dependence on journeymen, 185, 189, seq., 261; membership in late husband's gild, 160 seq., 168, 174, 176 seq., 179 seq., 183, 185, 187, 233 seq., 261, 298; pensions to, 69, seq. 170; of soldiers, 248 seq. succession to late husband's business, 11, 30-34 passim, 104 seq., 151, 154 seq., 160-163 passim, 167-173 passim, 188 seq., 215, 217, 221, 293.

Wife, 45, 70, 216, 237, 280; see Alehouse, Baker, Business, Capitalist, Dairy, Doctor, Domestic, Farmer, Household Management, Husbandman, Journeyman, Mother,

Pig-keeping, Poultry-keeping, Shopkeeper, Sick nursing, Spinning, Wage-earner; economic position of, 11, 292; membership in husband's gild, 150, 160, 171 seq., 179 seq., 191, 261, 301; mutual dependence of husband and wife, 12, 41, 44, 49, 54 seq., 300-302 passim; pauperisation of wife, 92, 147, 149; wife provides food and clothes for family, 12 seq., 39, 60, 63, 90, 94, seq., 106, 112, 125, 137, 145, 291, 293, 304; separate business, 17, 40, 151-156 passim, 165, 175-178 passim, 194 seq., 202 seq., 206, 208, 214, 219, 221, 228 seq., 231; settlement, 80-89 passim; soldier's wife, 142; subjection to husband, 16, 35, 41, 45, 197, 240, 302-304 passim; working in husband's business, 29, 34 seq., 40 seq., 45, 95, 100-102 passim, 144, 151, 153-159 passim, 163, 172 seq., 175, 184-187 passim, 192 seq., 196 seq., 202, seq., 212, 215 seq., 220, seq., 229, 234 seq. 293 seq., 302.

Woollen manufacture, 42, 94, 97-124 passim, 126, 129, 138; see Clothiers, Drapers, Poor, Spinning, Weaver; capitalistic, 94, 96 seq., 123 seq., 147; domestic, 49, 106; family, 97, 106; dependence on women's and children's labour, 97 seq. 112, 114; fluctuations in trade, 98 seq., 110 seq., 118-122 passim, 147 seq.; instruction in, 110 seq.; men and women wage-earners unite in trade disputes, 116-123 passim; political power, 126; wages for spinning, 49, 95-97 passim, 100, 108 seq., 113-118 passim, 120, 122 seq., 124, 134 seq., 137; women's position in, 98, 102 seq., 106, 124; wool-combers, 155.

Wycherley, 3, 37.

Yeoman, 9, 50, 76, 90.

York, 212.